SORCERY

IN THE

BLACK ATLANTIC

Sorcery

IN THE

Black Atlantic

———

EDITED BY

LUIS NICOLAU PARÉS

AND

ROGER SANSI

THE UNIVERSITY OF CHICAGO PRESS

Chicago and London

LUIS NICOLAU PARÉS is professor of anthropology at the Federal University of Bahia, Brazil.

ROGER SANSI is lecturer in anthropology at Goldsmiths, University of London.

The University of Chicago Press, Chicago 60637
The University of Chicago Press, Ltd., London
© 2011 by The University of Chicago
All rights reserved. Published 2011
Printed in the United States of America

20 19 18 17 16 15 14 13 12 11   1 2 3 4 5

ISBN-13: 978-0-226-64577-3   (cloth)
ISBN-13: 978-0-226-64578-0   (paper)

ISBN-10: 0-226-64577-0   (cloth)
ISBN-10: 0-226-64578-9   (paper)

Library of Congress Cataloging-in-Publication Data

Sorcery in the black Atlantic / edited by Luis Nicolau Parés
    and Roger Sansi.
        p. cm.
    Includes bibliographical references and index.
    ISBN-13: 978-0-226-64577-3 (cloth : alk. paper)
    ISBN-13: 978-0-226-64578-0 (pbk. : alk. paper)
    ISBN-10: 0-226-64577-0 (cloth : alk. paper)
    ISBN-10: 0-226-64578-9 (pbk. : alk. paper) 1. Witchcraft—Brazil.
2. Magic—Brazil. 3. Witchcraft—South Africa. 4. Magic—South
Africa. I. Parés, Luis Nicolau. II. Sansi, Roger.
    BF1584.B7S66 2011
    133.4'308996—dc22   2010017307

⊗ The paper used in this publication meets the minimum requirements
of the American National Standard for Information Sciences—Perma-
nence of Paper for Printed Library Materials, ANSI Z39.48-1992.

Contents

1

Introduction: Sorcery in the Black Atlantic

ROGER SANSI AND LUIS NICOLAU PARÉS

IN 2004, Scotland Yard commissioned a report examining attitudes to-ward child abuse among ethnic minorities in East London. The report made reference to the belief that children were being abused in exorcism rituals in many Pentecostal churches. One of the informants is said to have told the researchers that he had heard about African children being smuggled into Britain to be sacrificed. No evidence was offered, but then this was just research about "beliefs." This report was leaked to the BBC at the beginning of June 2005,[1] conveniently at the same time that three immigrants of Angolan origin were convicted of child cruelty, "over the torture of an eight-year-old girl they thought was a witch."[2] They all had been attending a Pentecostal church of Brazilian origin, the Universal Church of the Kingdom of God, (in)famous for its public exorcisms, which has gathered an extensive following among Lusophone and African immigrants. In the news, these cases were linked with an uncanny revelation: hundreds of African boys had "vanished" from schools.[3] Next to this report, the Web page presents a digital reproduction of "Adam," the torso of a black boy found in the Thames some years before, which is the origin of some morbid research into African ritual sacrifices of children (Ranger 2007).[4]

Girls abused in London and torsos of black boys found in the Thames; African boys disappearing from school and child traffic in Africa; child sacrifice and Brazilian Pentecostal exorcism. Unrelated events are swiftly connected in an uncanny work of prestidigitation, including hi-tech digital images of torsos and forensic drawings of abused children. *Les correspondances symboliques*, Baudelaire would say, or contiguous magic, in Frazer's more prosaic description. It all could make sense, if we believe in our fears, suspicions, gossip, and prejudices. Furthermore, this incredible work of prestidigitation was engineered by two respectable institutions, known for their enlightened search of truth: the BBC and Scotland Yard. But where was the evidence that all these things were connected? The "exorcism scandal" bewitched the media in Britain for the whole month of June, until some dissenting voices started to talk about a "racist witch hunt."[5] By then, however, a population of hundreds of thousands of Africans, in particular Pentecostal Africans, was already under suspicion. "What if some of that was true?" some people still may ask. In fact, shortly before completing this introduction, the local London newspaper *Evening Standard* published a two-page report on an African church in the United Kingdom, with the title "Miracles and claims of baby-snatching," mixing rumors of child trafficking, sorcery, syncretism, and extreme wealth.[6] That is how sorcery works: not by fully demonstrating its power, but by opening a possible doubt; one is never fully sure it is not true.

Tales of satanic abuse of children are not new in Britain—on the contrary, they have filled the news in recent years (Fontaine 1998; Comaroff 1997), but they were not explicitly linked to African immigrants. Yet these witch hunts had already occurred in other points of the Black Atlantic; for example, in Cuba, in the postemancipation era, several cases of child death and disappearance involving "black sorcerers" were denounced, and, particularly after the "race war" of 1912, black sorcery was intensely persecuted. But denunciations of the ritual murder of children were not so frequent before, in the times of slavery and the Spanish colonial rule, as Stephan Palmié's chapter in this volume explains: this sorcery emerged with the New Republic and its insecurities in regards to the former slaves.

It is uncanny how history seems to repeat itself, but with meaningful differences; otherwise history would be just sorcery, an enchantment that brings us back in a time loop. This is precisely one of the more powerful tricks of sorcery, its circularity: the ability to seem always identical to itself, always the same, in the fifteenth century and today. Anthropology and history are engaged, as Taussig (2003) would ironically say, in the arduous and perhaps helpless task of revealing sorcery's tricks: we have to demonstrate how what seems to be the same is in reality always at least a little bit different. One of the main points of this book is to discuss the historicity of sorcery and in particular how the discourses and practices of sorcery have been shaped through the historical space of the Black Atlantic.[7]

Sorcery and Modernity

Sorcery accusations and witch hunts burgeon in certain points in the history of the Atlantic, moments seen by its social agents as crucial and liminal, events of "modernity" some would say, in the wider sense of radical change and transformation. What is interesting, however, is that this can be applied not only to the believers of sorcery and the witch-hunters but also to the persecutors of these beliefs—the modernizers, who see the witch-believers and witch-hunters as the forces of tradition, conspiring against modernization. In these liminal periods, sorcery emerges in all its ambiguity as a force that can shift the balance in one direction or the other: either it looms to bring us back to an obscure past from which we can never escape or it takes us down to the precipice of an unknown, foreign darkness and away from our pristine origins.

After Evans-Pritchard (1937), anthropologists and historians described beliefs in witchcraft and sorcery both in African and modern Europe as mechanisms of social control in traditional communities (Wilson 1951; Middleton 1961; Marwick 1967) against an excessive accumulation of power and wealth, individualism, and external influences, the "evils" of modernity. But defending tradition against modernity, sorcery beliefs would be inevitably defeated by the later: sorcery, as an irrational traditional belief, should disappear in an enlightened, modern, and rational society. This idea was not fundamentally questioned by anthropologists and historians until not so long ago.

However, the paradox that many historians encountered was that modernity brought with it an efflorescence of sorcery accusations in periods of quick social change, like the witch hunts that plagued Europe at the times of religious revolution in the seventeenth century. These witch hunts were explained by historians precisely as a reaction to this quick social change. In the words of Jean Fontaine, "Nostalgia for the past, which is represented as an ideal of which present society falls short, and disenchantment with the present support the revival of the traditional idea that the good society is being undermined by a secret conspiracy of its enemies" (Fontaine 1998, 192). But inevitably, this reaction would fail, because the witch-hunters would have an irrational, "millenarian" vision of history, anchored to the past and unable to understand the dialectics of modernity.

But the question could be reframed in different terms: are these witch hunts just a reaction against modernity or an attempt to come to grips with it? Is the witch hunt simply an irrational understanding of the present and of history? Is the witch hunt antimodern, or is it perhaps fully modern? In wider terms, is modernity fully rational or does it have its own forms of magic? These are the questions that a recent anthropological literature has been asking, in the context of the explosion of accusations of sorcery in postcolonial Africa (Comaroff and Comaroff 1993; Geschiere 1997; Ciekawy and Geschiere 1998; Moore and Sanders 2001; Meyer and

Pels 2003). According to some of these authors, sorcery, rather than dis-appearing with modernity, would incorporate "the magic of modernity" and adapt to the new situation. Modernity would have its own forms of magic, as Marx explained; Taussig (1980) introduced the discussion on local appropriations of "commodity fetishism"; the Comaroffs (2001) have described the rationality of contemporary capitalism in terms of millenari-anism. The contemporary revival of sorcery in the periphery of the capital-ist world system would not be an irrational resistance to modernity but, on the contrary, an adaptation to its modern forms of magic.

This literature is now being criticized from different angles, partially because of the indeterminate use of the term "modernity" (Englund and Leach 2000; Ashforth 2005) and partially because of excessive presentism (Kapferer 2002; Ranger 2007). Reading sorcery outbursts and scares as a reaction to current events, economical, political, and social, causes one to partially forget the longer historical perspective and the everyday reality of sorcery practices and discourses before—and after—these outbursts. This criticism may be partially correct, and we will not engage here in a discus-sion on what is the magic of modernity or what is modernity in general; Peter Geschiere's chapter in this book gives a more extensive response to these arguments. In any case, the literature on the modernity of witchcraft has correctly pointed out the ambiguous relation of sorcery with the for-mation of the local and the foreigner, the present and the past. And these are points that we definitely want to discuss: the historicity and territorial-ity of sorcery. The ambiguity of sorcery, its liminal position in the bound-ary, is what makes it especially relevant in situations of quick social change in which established borders and identities are questioned. This has been shown again by recent ethnographies, which may not address directly the question of modernity but rather interrogate the historicity and territori-ality of sorcery through development, governance, or ethnography itself (Smith 2008; West 2005, 2007).

The aim of this book is to discuss these ideas in the wider historical and geographical framework of the Black Atlantic, showing how the expansion of discourses, accusations, and practices of sorcery have often been inte-gral to processes of colonization and state formation in Atlantic history. Accusations of sorcery have proliferated around and across the Atlantic shores for centuries. Witch scares and witch hunts have achieved notoriety now and again: in the early colonial period, with the first and yet unset-tled European settlements in Africa and the Americas; with the colonial wars and the expansion of the slave trade; at the times of the abolition of slavery in the Americas; and in the last decades, in a context of globaliza-tion and economic instability, migration, and fluxes of capital and culture.

And yet, so far few authors have addressed the historicity and territoriality of sorcery in the Black Atlantic.[8] This book's main purpose is to address the formations and transformations of discourses and practices of sorcery through a historical, Atlantic perspective.

In exploring discourses of sorcery in the wider context of Atlantic history, our aim is to reframe the discussion beyond contemporary Africa. We do not intend to identify the specificities of the postcolonial situation in that continent, but how the issues raised by recent discussions on sorcery are relevant well beyond that specific context. On the other hand, a wider historical and geographical perspective can help overcome the recurrent cul-de-sacs of the Africanist literature, like the repeated discussion on the particularities of "Africa" and its own forms of "modernity" (again, see Geschiere's chapter for further discussion). At this point it should be clear that we are not proposing to look at the problem of sorcery in the Black Atlantic as an extension of a certain African template or to interpret the New World forms as resulting from an African diaspora. On the contrary, we propose that discourses of sorcery, even if articulated in the language of "traditional institutions" and despite potential transatlantic continuities, acquired particular relevance and historicity in certain critical situations; and this historicity is not a specifically or exclusively African phenomenon.[9]

Nonetheless, discourses of sorcery, witchcraft, and fetishism have been used historically to separate Africa from the Atlantic and ultimately to deny the existence of the Atlantic as a space of culture. By projecting Africa as the place of sorcery and the occult, as opposed to Europe and the Enlightenment (Mudimbe 1994; Meyer and Pels 2003) since the eighteenth century, the discourse of the West has denied the possibility of intermediate spaces, which were European, African, and American at the same time. These intermediate spaces, the colonies and postcolonies of the Atlantic world, were difficult to classify in the imperialist narrative either as "wild" Africa or "civilized" Europe. Sorcery appeared (and still appears) in the nightmares of the Atlantic postcolonial elites, as the spell that tied them to Africa, primitivism, and the past, the "other" within. Only by fighting sorcery could they reach Europe, modernity, and the future. But before going deeper into the history of the Black Atlantic, maybe we should consider what we are talking about when we discuss sorcery.

Ambiguous Terms

It is interesting to note that in the anthropological literature, "witchcraft" came to be the dominant concept, in opposition to "sorcery." The distinction had been first made by Evans-Pritchard (1937), taking the two equivalent terms to translate for two different Azande words that according to him described quite different phenomena: witchcraft was an innate quality often unconsciously activated, while sorcery the conscious use of an acquired technique. The validity of these distinctions is questionable, as was endlessly discussed by anthropologists for decades (Middleton and Winter 1963; Marwick 1967).

In this introduction, we have opted to privilege the term "sorcery" rather than "witchcraft" or "magic," primarily for the sake of coherence and consistency, but we do not think that an analytical distinction between the terms is tenable.[10] In fact we think it is absolutely necessary to discuss the histories of the use of these terms more than their utility as "concepts." "Sorcery" and "witchcraft" are not devoid of history outside the borders of anthropology, they are actually overcharged with it. One of our main goals in this book is also to promote the discussion on the history of the terms and the discourses they conveyed within the context of Atlantic colonialism and postcolonialism. Even now, some anthropologists feel compelled to say that when they use any of these words they are translating a specific "native" term. Yet the natives often use foreign terms too. In West Africa, European terms like *sorcellerie* or *le féticheur* are commonly used. In other points of the Atlantic, African or African-derived terms often coexist with the European ones—like *macumba* and *mandinga* in Brazil and Portugal, *obeah* in the Caribbean, and *voodoo* a little throughout the world. Sometimes, different terms are used in different contexts: Ciekawy (1998) brilliantly argued how the Kimijikenda use the term *utsai* differently from the English "witchcraft," which is preferentially employed in a bureaucratic context.[11] According to Ciekawy, the discourse of witchcraft is dialectically related to "statecraft" in ways that the discourse of *utsai* was not. Like sorcery itself, in some cases foreign words seem to better convey the power of the occult. The use of these words is a clear evidence of the intense circulation of discourses of sorcery between the different parts of the Atlantic during several centuries. It is quite difficult to think that, in most regions of the Atlantic, the discourse of "sorcery" has not been transformed by this history of intense exchange in the last five hundred years or that European discourses about sorcery have not influenced African ones and the other way around. Not only did discourses circulate, confront, and transform each other, but new terms and discourses were created in this passage: such as the discourse of fetishism, as discussed in Roger Sansi's chapter. And yet, most of the literature up to now has ignored this Atlantic circularity, describing African and European discourses on sorcery autonomously, even in opposition to each other (Austen 1993).

The Place and Time of Sorcery

Regardless of this Atlantic geography, the discursive place of sorcery is often in the remote past; and its subversive power, when it appears without warning in the here and now, comes from this temporal distance. The idea that the occult or sorcery is an arcane body of knowledge that comes from a hidden, ancient, and distant repository is central to modern reappropriations, from Rudolf Steiner's *Anthroposophy* to Wicca. Concealment of some supposed deeper, more ancient truth is always key to the discourse of sorcery (Johnson 2002; Pels 2003; Taussig 2003). This truth has to be revealed but only in part, because it is precisely this secrecy that makes it powerful. It is interesting to look at how this rhetoric of concealment, instead of being an obstacle, constitutes a common denominator that facilitates the sorcery of the other to be appropriated and to circulate across geographical and cultural boundaries.

As Kapferer underscored, Evans-Pritchard inaugurated an anthropological approach in which "magic and witchcraft are not part of a clearly bounded and internally consistent 'system of knowledge' [. . .] They are always contextually relative, situationally adaptive, *never abstract*" (Kapferer 2002, 7). Indeed, sorcery must be practical; it has to achieve some specific ends. The "techniques of enchantment" (Gell 1988, 1992) cannot be reduced to a simple matter of dogma or blind faith, they have to prove *a kind of* effective. It is not enough to believe in the sorcerer's secret, its power has *empiricism* to be tested; it has to be partially revealed in order to achieve its goal. If a spell does not work, another has to be found to replace it. Skepticism—or the suspicious of falseness, trickery, and artifice—is also constitutive to the discourse of sorcery. This ambiguity between secrecy and skepticism (Taussig 2003) is precisely what allows sorcery to be so dynamic, to have such plasticity, because when old spells do not work, new elements, new words, new techniques can always be summoned. And very often they are presented as ancient, secret elements, which were once hidden and are now revealed. In other terms, this ambiguity results in a dynamics of circularity that allow sorcery discourse to encompass and generate new truths, by seemingly keeping old ones hidden; the circle is, after all, a spin whose dynamic energy generates a supplement.

Nonetheless, this does not mean that all forms of sorcery are interchangeable: it is important to take into account the complexities of local contexts and the historicity of their inner cultural interactions to fully grasp sorcery's multifaceted diversity. For instance, while in some contexts the ritual manipulation of material objects with the direct or indirect intervention of various kinds of spiritual entities is privileged, in another

INTRODUCTION · 7

context the occult is rather mediated by the sorcerer's body, emphasizing bodily transformations, nocturnal flights, or other embodied psychic powers. Such differences, which are reminiscent of the distinction between sorcery and witchcraft, suggest differing expressions of sorcery tending toward "objectification" or "subjectification," the predominance of one or the other varying according to context. Although the ambiguity of the discourse of sorcery will always elude any attempt of rigid classification, it is also necessary to account for the plurality of local practices.

Moreover, the best sorcery not only comes from the secrets of the past but often comes from another place, from some other people who are perceived as having deeper levels of knowledge than we do or as being more evil than we are. Kapferer has said in relationship to Sri Lanka that the most powerful spells always come from elsewhere: foreign "magic" is particularly highly prized (Kapferer 2002, 105). In the ruins of Persepolis, archeologists have found Egyptian eyes of Horus designed to protect against the evil eye. As we will see in this volume, travelers in Brazil and in the Portuguese Atlantic world wore amulets called *mandinga* bags, supposedly made by African Muslim doctors, but which not infrequently contained Catholic ritual implements and were produced outside Africa. In Sierra Leone today, according to Shaw (1997, 859), Lebanese traders are rumored to be powerful sorcerers. Is Egypt the origin of all sorcery? Is it Africa? Does it matter? What matters is that the amulet allegedly comes from somewhere else, a mysterious arcane place—the place of sorcery. The Place of Witches in Sierra Leone is said to be an invisible, hypertechnological and ultramodern city (Shaw 1997). This does not necessarily contradict our previous statement—that often the place of sorcery is in the remote past: the essential point is that the place of sorcery is not coeval (Fabian 1983) with everyday life; it is essentially other because it exists in another space and time, but at the same time, it is able to intervene in the here and now.

The overall implication is that the sorcerer is the "other" (Ciekawy 1998), in many cases the intimate "other within" but still the dangerously different. It also means that the other is seen as the source of evil, although this moral theory emerges when the other is perceived as a threat to the established order, as a competitor. In the history of the Black Atlantic this has often been the case, as when sorcery has been identified with women, other religions (Islam, Judaism, "fetishism"), or Africa. But this negative perception of the other is, paradoxically, what makes it fascinating (Geschiere, this volume): because it is mysterious, dangerous, this alterity is desirable. Again, this is another paradox of sorcery: its radical alterity and its radical negativity are what make it alluring, charming (of course the word "charm" has this double meaning, as it does in Portuguese, *feitiço*).

Because of this intrinsic negative alterity, <u>sorcery operates as a rela-</u><u>tional connection, mediating power asymmetries between the dissimilar</u>: men and women, Europe and Africa, master and slave, the strong and the weak. As explored in João José Reis's chapter, in the master-slave relation- ships <u>sorcery practices can be envisaged as an indirect form of resistance,</u> as the oblique <u>weapon of the weak.</u> In Katherine Fidler's paper, we see how sorcery is not only a discourse of adaptation to an external power but also a weapon of insurgency.

one of my
points
regarding
witchcraft
—which is not
an original
theory either

Within the subaltern spaces of the socially weak, the idiom of sorcery may extrapolate the Christian moral association with absolute evil and diabolic intervention and act as a basic cognitive orientation to deal with the unexplainable, most often misfortune. <u>Sorcery mediates and expresses</u> <u>interpersonal tensions and power struggles, whether in the kinship, reli-</u><u>gious, or political domains.</u> Rather than dichotomist values of good and evil, sorcery engages a subversive moral ambiguity where notions of order and disorder, of increase and decrease of "life force," and of dominion over or defense against the others are central.

The discourse of sorcery is ultimately a discourse on <u>agency, or its lack</u> thereof: the recurrent references to tying together, bonding, and the neces- sity of "armoring" or "sealing" the body make explicit the fundamental processes of objectification and bondage that lay at its core. Its fundamen- tal ambiguity is that, although it provides tools to understand and relate to new realities like the Comaroffs and Geschiere say, it is also based on the pessimistic premise of the incommensurable (because hidden, and nonco- eval) power of the sorcerer, which ties its victims in his web of sortileges. In these conditions, its victims can hardly be recognized as agents.

The <u>Foucauldian frame of this narrative of witchcraft as a discourse of</u> <u>power is clear.</u> As Ciekawy (1998), Shaw (1997), and Meyer and Pels (2003) have argued, and as Sansi also argues in his chapter in this volume, if in a different manner, the <u>discourse of witchcraft was used to construct Africa</u> <u>as an "other."</u> But it did not end up there, because many were caught "in between," creating a range of situations that resulted in the formation of ambiguous identities, like, for example, the postcolonial elites in the Black Atlantic, who participate in the discourse of the "othering," being simulta- neously this other themselves. On the one hand, many of the narratives on modern witchcraft in Africa are directed to the elites: traders, politicians, people with connections to the world system. The discourse on witchcraft in this sense is reversing the colonial attribution of witchcraft beliefs and practices to the rural, illiterate, poor, and traditional Africans. Or fur- ther than that, it is questioning the distance between one and the other, the traditional, poor, rural and the modern, urban, cosmopolitan: it is a discourse that expresses the intimate connection between both, their circularity, their bondage. On the other hand, the narratives of sorcery at the other side of the Atlantic as we will see, for example, in early twentieth-century Cuba or Brazil, expressed precisely the opposite phenomenon: the elites' fear of the sorcery of their former slaves, a fear intensified by the fact that one and the other, the sorcerer and his possible elite victims, have many things in common. And yet, even if they seem to be the opposite, we can see that in fact both Latin American and African postcolonial contexts presuppose the intimate interdependence of all the actors involved in sorcery, their circularity, their bondage.

To sum up, sorcery discourse is eminently malleable, transformable, and adaptable to many different realities because of its ambiguity and circularity. And the particular discourses of sorcery in the Atlantic are a clear example of this. What is interesting about the Black Atlantic, on the other hand, is the special relevance of the discourse of sorcery in particular points of its history. These situations, we argue, are always defined by a basic problem: the incorporation of alterity, effected either through mimesis or segregation, through absorption or rejection. Sorcery, with its plasticity and ambiguity, emerges as a master trope to deal with these many-faceted processes of incorporation. What modernizing intellectuals in postcolonial situations on both sides of the Atlantic seem to have asked is, How do we step out of the circle of sorcery? How do we step out of the Black Atlantic?

Ambiguity, Plasticity, Creativity, History

The adaptability and plasticity of sorcery are the result of its ambivalence and circularity, and it is precisely on this ambiguity that lies the creative potential of sorcery. The emphasis on the creative aspect of sorcery, as Pels has observed (2003), has a long and noble pedigree in preromantic thinking, from Herder and Diderot, and is being recovered by contemporary anthropologists like Taussig and Kapferer. Is the sorcerer really the demiurge, the natural genius these writers project? This may bring us back to Evans-Pritchard's classic, and much criticized, distinction between witchcraft and sorcery. Witchcraft is supposed to be an innate, internal characteristic of the person—a gift, or better, a curse. Sorcery on the other hand is a technique and as such it can be taught, learned, sold, bought, given away, and stolen. But if that was so, then sorcery could be simply described as a technique—an idea that some authors indeed have defended (Gell 1988). For Alfred Gell, the only difference is that magic is a symbolic technique: "From an observer's point of view, there is a distinction, in that efficacious technical strategies demonstrably exploit the causal properties of things in the sequence of purposes, whereas magic does not" (Gell 1988, 7). What we take Gell to mean by this sentence is that in magic there is always a missing link—something in between the premise and the achievement of the final objective that remains unknown, unexplainable, a mystery: transforming the handkerchief into a dove, water into wine. Of course, we could also say that, according to this definition, all technologies are symbolic to a certain extent; in these terms, authors like Shaw (1997) and Ashforth (2005) have explained the multiplication of witchcraft in Africa in relation to the expansion of new technologies. But what is important to point out is that for a technology to be seen as magical, there has to be a doubt about its procedure: the doubt, and not the belief, is what constitutes magic. How did the sorcerer do that? Where is the trick? Because either there is a trick—a rational explanation—or the sorcerer is an uncommon person—he has the gift of putting together things that naturally cannot be. If the trick is revealed, there is no sorcery—just technology, artifice. If there is no trick, then we are in the presence of something or somebody extraordinary—a god, a devil, or a witch. Again the distinction between sorcery and witchcraft is ambiguous. But mentioning this ambiguity once again is not quite enough. Perhaps it is more useful then to shift our gaze away from people and in the direction of things. From the perspective of a rationalist "methodological philistinism" all sorcerers would be, at the end of the day, impostors, but that does not mean that there is no sorcery. On the contrary, the world is always magical, since it is always, inevitably, partially unknown and impossible to explain in its totality. As anthropologists since Boas and Lévi-Strauss have known, the fact that we do not know everything in the world does not stop humans from making sense of it—or putting it in Lévi-Strauss's more elegant formulation, the world is not fully known, but it has to be fully meaningful (in particular for the anthropologist). And so, in a big part of our everyday lives, we play by "tricks": we do things and say things that we do not fully understand—jumping one or two steps "in the sequence of purposes." *Homo non intelligendo fit omnia*: man, not understanding, made everything, as Vico said.

In the face of unexplainable facts, and more acutely in the face of misfortune, we need names, we need something or somebody to take the responsibility. History is always personal for the people who live in it, despite of what structural historians may say. Sorcery and antisorcery, or witch hunts, give us quick answers for complex issues, which have an autonomous power that overcomes our agency and cannot be reduced to personal responsibilities: but we need to understand our social world in personal terms and to put the blame on somebody. The disjuncture between the world and our knowledge and power to control it is especially evident in moments of radical social change and transformation, when history knocks on the door. It is right then that sorcery may come in handy to help us get some protection from the unexpected or that we may accuse others of using occult forces against us. Sorcery becomes again a way of producing meaning, a social theory to make sense of unexpected and adverse events for which no traditional explanation exists.

And yet it would be a bit sad to conclude with a point that looks too much like the scapegoating argument that functionalist anthropologists have cherished for generations. It has to be clear that despite its limitations, discourses of sorcery are not just *mistaken* judgments of history: we shall not fall in the trap of sorcery here, the discourse of sorcery is not just an illusion, a false construction, but it produces historical changes. By transforming their nightmares—their eternal return to the past, their bondage to tradition, the insurmountable difference with the North, the denial of coevalness—into an articulated discourse, postcolonial societies are producing something else, making history in unpredicted ways. To rephrase it again, the circularity of sorcery is based on the trick of the eternal return, but in fact, this trick produces new truths. Basile Ndjio's paper in this volume is an excellent example of that, going beyond the astonishment in front of the proliferation of sorcery accusations in Cameroon and South Africa and looking at how different political actors managed to gather from this situation elaborate interpretations of current events that could eventually become hegemonic. Our research cannot stop at the identification of the problem, fascinated by its charming oddity; we have to follow its consequences and the historical transformations it operates. Otherwise we too will fall victim to the spell.

The Black Atlantic and the Lusophone World

The continued study of witchcraft and sorcery in Africa has not been paralleled in other parts of the Black Atlantic,[12] probably because of the different historical trajectory each continent followed. By the end of the nineteenth century, postcolonial countries like Brazil and Cuba were under the shock of the end of slavery. The presence of the former slaves in these societies was a major concern for the national elites, and the survival of African religions was an object of public outcry and police persecution. As Yvonne Maggie notes in her contribution to this volume, the persecution of sorcery in these countries took a very different path than in the African colonies of the British Empire: it was not the accusers but the practitioners of sorcery who were persecuted. In this sense, the belief in the "reality" or effectiveness of sorcery was not denied, but, on the contrary, it was reinforced.

This contradiction was already noted by some of the first researchers on African American religions, like Raimundo Nina Rodrigues. Professor in the Faculty of Medicine in Bahia, Rodrigues was marked by the scientific racism and lombrosianism of the period, and while he identified the "fetishist animism" of the black population as a form of social illness, he defended it against police persecution (Rodrigues 1935). As the twentieth century progressed, a continuous effort was made to distinguish between sorcery and religious practices, the latter identified as legitimate forms of African culture to be respected and even valorized by the state as constitutive of the national culture.[13] Together with practitioners, anthropologists were active agents in identifying and legitimizing the authenticity of some Afro-Brazilian cult houses. On the other hand, accusations of sorcery would target other houses identified with the loss of authenticity, mixture, syncretism, and also pathology. This theme is examined by Daniel Stone's chapter in the context of Pernambucan Xangô. As a result, ethnographies on African American religions very often have downplayed the presence of sorcery practices that could question their authenticity. Even today, it is very difficult to find academic research on Brazilian Candomblé that addresses issues of sorcery.[14]

On the other hand, in the 1980s, historians like Laura de Mello e Souza (1986) and Luiz Mott (1993, 1997), working on colonial history, grew progressively interested on sorcery (*feitiçaria*). Following an agenda imposed by anthropologists, the issue of origins was inevitably present in their research as they tried to identify in colonial times the antecedents of contemporary practices and beliefs. They also interpreted sorcery practices as forms of slave resistance. But colonial records, especially those of the Inquisition, offered a more complex picture, describing situations that obviously integrated persons, rituals, objects, beliefs, words, and spirits of different origins in a situation that the historians often could not help but qualify as "syncretistic." Looking at the anthropologists for assistance in understanding this situation proved of little help.

In recent years, the dramatic transformations in the religious field are obliging anthropologists to rectify their historical silence in regards to sorcery. The eruption of Pentecostalism as a major religious force in many of the countries of the Black Atlantic has brought with it a return of old accusations of devil worship and sorcery directed against African American religions (Birman, this volume). This phenomenon also has a counterpart in Africa, where many independent African churches emerge as counter-sorcery movements.

In the face of all this evidence, today it is impossible to avoid the topic of sorcery in the Black Atlantic. Understanding the urgency of a discussion on this theme, we organized two conferences, one in Salvador de Bahia, Brazil, in October 2006 and one in London in January 2007.[15] Most of the essays in this volume are a result of these conferences and the discussion they generated. The papers that follow bring together different historical periods, from the early colonial period to today, and places, from Brazil to Cameroon, Cuba, Angola, and South Africa. Overall, we have preferred to remain faithful to the hegemony of the Lusophone Atlantic in the conferences. The literature on these regions has been so far absolutely marginal to the discussions on these subjects in the English- and French-speaking world (and therefore the dominant academic literature), which have been centered around not just the African continent but even some specific countries (Cameroon and South Africa in particular). The fact is that the research on sorcery in Portuguese in the last decades has been vibrant and of an exceptional quality, but it has been largely unnoticed in the English- and French-speaking world (Bethencourt 1987; Souza 1986; Mott 1993; Calainho 2004; Pantoja 2004; Maggie 1975, 1992). In the conferences we understood that the confrontation between these two literatures was not only necessary to "fill a gap," but that more widely it could help recast the question of sorcery in contemporary history and anthropology and shake the spell of "Africa," as we have argued in this introduction.

Yet it is not our intention to propose that sorcery in the Lusophone Atlantic had a particular history or cultural specificity. On the contrary, our aim is to show both how the questions raised by the literature on witchcraft and modernity in Africa may be relevant for other regions in the Atlantic and how, conversely, it is necessary to rethink this literature in a more thoroughly historical and Atlantic setting. Hence, while we recognize the need to develop studies on local and historical specificities, bringing together African and Latin American perspectives in the wider Atlantic context was central to our project.

The volume starts with Roger Sansi's essay on the transformations of the discourse of sorcery in the Black Atlantic. Tracing the historicity of terms like *feitiço*, "fetish," and "fetishism" in the seventeenth- and eighteenth-century Black Atlantic, he examines how the Portuguese notions of sorcery (*feitiçaria*) became African fetishism, a key concept in the Western intellectual tradition. Laura de Mello e Souza, author of the classic account of the persecution of practitioners of sorcery (*feitiçaria*) in colonial Brazil, *The Devil and the Land of the Holy Cross* (1986), discusses in the second chapter of this volume the dialog between historians and anthropologists as regards the problem of sorcery's origins in the context of Portuguese America. She describes eighteenth-century practices not just as survivals of an African or European past but also as the result of the colonizing process in which diverse cultural traditions were combined in very particular ways.

João José Reis's chapter shows how Candomblé and its associated sorcery/ritual practices were only marginally organized as a conscious weapon of resistance against slavery. Reis claims that slavery represented one among other misfortunes against which Candomblé priests had to fight when healing slave clients. And yet he acknowledges that Candomblé still operated as resistance insofar as it challenged slavery by competing with masters for the slave's time, labor, and resources.

Katherine Fidler's essay on the insurrection in Pondoland in 1959 brings a totally different perspective on sorcery as a "weapon of the weak": the Congo Movement employed the discourse of sorcery as it openly sought to create a nation separate from that of apartheid South Africa. In this case, supposedly traditional and modern discourses, like sorcery and nationalism, are brought together in ways that show how sorcery discourse is not just a weapon of social stability but also of open subversion and violence.

The following chapters investigate the emergence of the question of sorcery in the changing legal and scientific framework of postslavery societies. Stephan Palmié looks at "black wizardry" (*brujería negra*) in Cuba as a "moral artifact." Describing its trajectory in the twentieth century, Palmié shows how this artifact has been filled with different political and moral content, initially as a key term in the construction of a "scientific" discourse on race and national identity and in the last decades as an object of cultural heritage in a context of changing visions of socialist consciousness and citizenship. Looking at the concept as it were in the *longue durée*, Palmié does not only describe the use of the discourse of sorcery at a certain point in time as a reaction against or an incorporation of "modernity" or as a comment on its historical time but describes it further as formative of its own objects—for example, Cuban "modernity" in its different incarnations.

Following the ambivalent dichotomy between sorcery and science, Daniel Stone's chapter examines the work of the *Serviço de Higiene Mental* (SHM; Mental Hygiene Service) in Recife, Brazil, during the 1930s. The SHM's psychiatric evaluations of spiritualist mediums emphasized their mental instability and the danger that they presented to society. In contrast, Xangô, the local variety of Afro-Brazilian religion, was described as the expression of a "primitive mentality," a cultural backwardness, not a pathological dysfunction, and minimized the risk represented by this religion. In this sense, the SHM actually got entangled in the power disputes between Xangô practitioners and spiritualists, taking the part of the underdog—since spiritualism was more closely associated with the white elites.

Yvonne Maggie's chapter analyzes the criminal processes against the practice of sorcery in Brazil from the declaration of the republic in 1889, one year after the abolition of slavery, until today, showing how the penal code and law practice in Brazil reflects a widespread and shared belief in the power of sorcery. As mentioned, the Brazilian repression of practices of sorcery never challenged the belief but in many ways made it legitimate. Maggie's strong hypothesis is that, in fact, sorcery is not just a language through which social issues are expressed, but it is these issues themselves; sorcery is not just a way to talk about envy, it is envy itself. In this sense, sorcery is an institution that does not exist *in spite of* the legal system; it exists precisely because of the legal system, as its necessary counterpart.

The comparison with contemporary situations in postcolonial Africa opens up interesting perspectives. Basile Ndjio brilliantly shows how the discourse of sorcery was variously and violently activated, both in Cameroon and South Africa, during the 1990s process of political democratization. While in Cameroon, the *gru* witch hunt institution was used by members of the ruling classes as both a "weapon of the strong" and a "technology of power," which allowed them to stay in power, in postapartheid South Africa, the discourse of zombification and enslavement in "occult economies" was used as a "weapon of the weak" by the subaltern blacks excluded from the "magic" wealth facilitated by the Black Economy Empowerment policies. In both cases, discourses on sorcery were not just a hopeless reaction to change but also a tool used by political actors to seize it and manage the interpretation of current events in their favor.

The next two chapters address contemporary dynamics of interaction between sorcery's beliefs and practices and Pentecostal and other churches. Luena Nunes Pereira's chapter looks at the role the state, nongovernmental organizations, and diverse churches play in relation to the accusations of sorcery regarding children and adolescents among the Bakongo in Angola. Pereira examines how these institutions have been constructing several perceptions and forms of interventions, suggesting a tension between a more legal bias of protection toward children—which tends to minimize the cultural aspects—and the social projects of family reintegration of these children, which rely more on local cultural forms of conflict resolution. Pereira also notes that while the Catholic Church is active in the resolution of the kinship conflicts that initiate the accusations, the action of Pentecostal churches is more evident in processes of spiritual healing of the children considered sorcerers.

Patricia Birman's essay on Rio de Janeiro examines the convergence and intertextuality between Pentecostal churches and the state in defining and creating stigmatized evil territories, the favelas, where marginality, crime, and sorcery are merged in such a way that drug dealers become Afro-Brazilian devils and vice versa. In her second ethnographic case on a "community of believers," Birman shows evangelical efforts to "Pentecostalize" sectors of the state, articulating a new form of political-religious action that takes as its mission the moral reconfiguration of the marginal and violent territories. Hence, with the state and the media joining in, the Pentecostal war against Afro-Brazilian practices forces favela dwellers, if not to full conversion, at least to an ambivalent partial adherence.

Peter Geschiere's final chapter, drawing on the cases discussed such as those presented by Ndjio, rethinks the argument of the relation between witchcraft and modernity, clearly stating that both terms are not fixed anthropological concepts but discourses that are in circulation in Africa and the Atlantic world today, used to make sense of (or disguise?) contemporary transformations. But he also questions very strongly interpretations of these situations in terms of an African modernity, and retraditionalization, forcefully arguing that the particular entanglements of these terms is not relevant only or specific to Africa but that they may be central to rethinking what we understand as modernity in general.

Despite the great thematic diversity of all these essays, there are recurrent issues that connect various historically localized discourses on sorcery: its relational nature in power inequalities, in terms of kinship, labor, the state, or all of those; its radical negativity and alterity; and its plasticity and creativity resulting from its essential ambiguity. The rhetoric of concealment and secretism, together with the attribution of sorcery to the other, have promoted a constant flow and circularity of ideas and practices across cultural boundaries and maybe nowhere is this so true as in the Black Atlantic.

Notes to Chapter One

1. "Exorcisms Are Part of Our Culture," *BBC News*, June 3, 2005, http://news.bbc .co.uk/1/hi/uk/4596127.stm.

2. "'Witch' Child Cruelty Trio Guilty," *BBC News*, June 3, 2005, http://news.bbc .co.uk/1/hi/england/london/4607435.stm.

3. "Hundreds of Children 'Vanishing,'" *BBC News*, May 13, 2005, http://news.bbc .co.uk/1/hi/uk/4541603.stm.

4. "New Nigerian Leads in Torso Murder," *BBC News*, March 6, 2003, http://news .bbc.co.uk/1/hi/england/2824417.stm.

5. Ian Cobain and Vikram Dodd, "How Media Whipped up a Racist Witch-Hunt. Despite the Lurid Headlines, Police Dismiss Claims of Child Sacrifice," *Guardian*, June 25, 2005, media.guardian.co.uk/site/story/0,14173,1514334,00.html.

6. "'Miracles' and Claims of Baby-Snatching—Why Is Deya Ministry Thriving in London?" *Evening Standard*, December 2, 2009.

7. In this introduction, we often use the term "discourse," many times next to "practice." Just to clarify our use, we do not use "discourse" in terms of "expression"—or a verbal representation of something else—a practice. Many years after Foucault, it is common sense in anthropology that discourses are not just expressive but also performative. Discourse *is* practice. We often just add the term "practices" after "discourses" as a sort of paraphrase that would make that point clearer.

8. An exception would be the work of Rosalind Shaw (1997, 2002), on the memories of slavery in Sierra Leone, which is certainly an inspiration for this volume, although in many respects we find her connection of witchcraft to sorcery a bit too lineal (see Sansi's paper in this volume for further discussion).

9. On the other hand, we are not advocating that sorcery be identified in every moment of radical historical change in the history of the Atlantic. Recent (May 2008) outbursts of xenophobia in Italy and South Africa may respond to narratives familiar to the discourse of sorcery (like the story of the Italian baby stolen by the gypsies in Naples that was used as an excuse for the pogrom on their camp), but that does not mean that we have to read them in terms of sorcery discourse if this discourse in fact is not used. Sometimes it is too easy to fall into the trap of calling everything "magic" or "sorcery"; we have to recognize that often anthropologists have been guilty of trying to make their material more spectacular by using flashy (or charming) terms.

10. Recent literature has privileged the terms "magic" or the "occult" because of the negative connotations of sorcery or witchcraft (Meyer and Pels 2003). But we are interested precisely in these negative connotations.

11. In interactions with administrative officials or in discussions concerned with constructing an administrative investigation concerning magical harm.

12. An exception is the prescient and influential work of Michael Taussig (1987) on shamanism that, in fact, inspired all the recent literature on magic and modernity. And yet it is difficult to categorize Taussig as a scholar of the Black Atlantic since his work by far overcomes this as well as other disciplinary boundaries.

13. In Cuba this process was greatly influenced by the work of Fernando Ortiz (1940) and Lydia Cabrera (1954), and in Brazil, by the work of writers and anthropologists like Arthur Ramos (1934), Roger Bastide (1978), and Pierre Verger (1981).

14. One exception would be Yvonne Maggie's *Guerra de orixá* (1975).

15. The first conference, entitled "Colóquio Internacional: A Feitiçaria no Atlântico Negro," was held on October 19–20, 2006, at the Center of Afro-Oriental Studies of the Federal University of Bahia, Salvador. The second one, entitled "Culture and the State in the Lusophone Black Atlantic: Sorcery and Politics in the Black Atlantic: From the Colonial World to Globalization," was held on January 17–20, 2007, at the Institute for the Study of the Americas, London. We would like to thank all the participants in these conferences and the institutions that sponsored them: the Arts and Humanities Research Council through the project "Cultures of the Lusophone Black Atlantic," at King's College London, and CAPES (Coordenação do Aperfeiçoamento do Pessoal de Nível Superior) and FAPESB (Fundação do Amparo a Pesquisa do Estado da Bahia) in Brazil.

2

Sorcery and Fetishism in the Modern Atlantic

ROGER SANSI

IN THE LAST DECADE, several authors have shown how the identification between Africa and sorcery is part of the process of construction of Africa as an "other," separated from Europe not only in space but also in history; sorcery would make Africa a prisoner of the past (Ciekawy 1998; Shaw 1997; Pels 1998; Meyer and Pels 2003). On the other hand, the relationship between witchcraft and modernity has been widely debated in the recent Africanist literature: authors like the Comaroffs (1993) or Geschiere (1997, this volume) have proposed that the rise of witchcraft accusations in Africa in the last decades is not a traditionalist and irrational reaction to the globalization process, a "return to tradition," but, on the contrary, a process of incorporation of the sorcery of modernity, which is not particularly African: the magic of capitalism, based on commodity fetishism.

But capitalism did not contact Africa for the first time with globalization: the Atlantic coast of Africa were always inside the process of construction of the modern world, the Atlantic world of capitalism. Maybe then the "magic" of capitalism arrived in Africa much before? Could it be in fact that African sorcery was deeply transformed by early contact with the West? Was it maybe even *formed* by this contact?

I will not go so far in this paper. I am primarily interested in the ambiguous contiguity between two terms: sorcery and fetishism. In some instances they seem to be identical, while at other times they appear to be radically different. The terms "fetish" and "fetishism" were first used by European travelers in West Africa in the late seventeenth and eighteenth centuries, to identify the religion and the objects of cult of the Africans they encountered. In fact these terms come from the Portuguese *feitiçaria*, which means "sorcery," and *feitiço*, which means "spell"; interestingly enough, the Portuguese origin of these terms was misrecognized by the travelers

19

who coined the term, their enemies and competitors from other European nations.

The history of the term "fetish" was researched by William Pietz in a wonderful set of papers (1985, 1987, 1988) that have been extremely influential on recent anthropological thinking (Latour 2001; Keane 2007; Graeber 2005). However, in that long history of the term most authors, including Pietz, are more interested in the last bit: fetishism. They mention that the Portuguese *feitiço* is the origin of the fetish, but they rarely consider that the meaning of these two terms is not the same. The *feitiço*, for the Portuguese in the early modern world, was not a specifically African phenomenon, but something universal and contemporary, common to all; it was not something that made Africans different, like the fetish, but something they had in common with them, that happened to all humans, regardless of their origin. Each country could have its specific traditions, but sorcery was eminently exchangeable and exportable. This is what made, precisely, foreign forms of sorcery extremely popular—for example, as we will see, the so-called *mandinga*. On the other hand, the fetish was seen by later European travelers as a specifically African religion and something that made Africans radically different, and incommensurable, with Europeans.

The discourse of the fetish became later the discourse of fetishism—the elementary form of primitive religion. Elementary, but still radically other. And it was not only used to objectify Africa but also, and in opposition to that, to think about what constituted European modernity. The supposed triumph of modernity over fetishism, the overcoming of its ambiguities between construction and truth, objects and subjects, is central to this constitution.

Later on, as we know, this same discourse was applied to the modern West, in terms of its "commodity fetishism," by Marx. The Marxist discourse on the "fetishism of modernity" replaces the radical alterity of the eighteenth century by a radical commensurability: instead of saying "they are fetishists, they are totally different from us," it says, "they are fetishists, just like us." David Graeber (2005) has recently taken this argument to its logical conclusion, by proposing that in fact, fetishism is a general theory of human creativity.

But there is more to this story than a good comparison between African sorcery and the sorcery of modernity. It is not only the case that capitalism can be compared to African fetishism; capitalism, and its forms of sorcery, are not only comparable, and therefore adaptable, to African sorcery, but they are also the outcome of a historical process that developed on the coasts of the Atlantic. The fact is that this very discourse is the result of a historical encounter that was misrecognized at its time. The Atlantic colonial world, which was formed before this process of separation of Africa and Europe in the eighteenth century, offers an unsettling counterpoint to the European model of modernity. Denying the centrality of this colonial world in the formation of the fetish, the Europeans who identified it with Africa denied the historicity and modernity of the term, as well as of the world that produced it. This Atlantic colonial world, in particular those colonies formed by weak, defeated colonial powers like Portugal, does not seem to have a place in dominant discourses of the modernity-tradition, Europe-Africa dialectic; it remains an unstable and dangerous middle term. This was true in the eighteenth century and is probably still quite true today.

In this paper, I propose to describe the historicity of the discourse of the fetish in the modern Atlantic. My argument will be based on the uses of a number of terms and their historical transformation, starting with the late medieval Portuguese discourse of *feitiçaria* and *feitiço*, which are commonly translated by "sorcery" in English. I will then move to contrast this discourse with what became its phantasmal other in the Lusophone Atlantic, the *mandinga*. After that, I will look at the transformation of *feitiço* into fetish and the formation of the discourse of fetishism. In the last sections, I will look at the application of this discourse of fetishism in Brazil and how it was used in opposition to *feitiçaria*. To conclude, I will consider the persistence of these discourses in contemporary scholarship.

The Feitiço

The terms *feitiço* and *feitiçaria* appear in written Portuguese in a legal context: King João I issued laws against sorcery in 1385 and 1403 forbidding his subjects to "work spells or bonds, or invoke devils" (*obrar feitiços ou ligamentos, ou chamar diabos*; Pietz 1987, 31). Pietz described the etymology of *feitiço* from the Latin *factitius*, "fictitious," which also originated terms like "artifice": the *feitiço* is something made (also, *coisa feita*), a false thing; further, *feitiço* in Portuguese also means "charm, something made to seduce."

From its very origin, it is quite uncertain what is being condemned: is it the deception of con artists or the work of those allied with the devil? For Taussig (2003) or Pels (2003), sorcery discourse is constituted by a fundamental ambiguity between secrecy and skepticism. The occultation of a supposed secret is often central to sorcery. That hidden truth can be revealed only in part, precisely because it is occultation that makes sorcery powerful: the spell is always potentially something false, an artifice, a trick, but there is also the doubt that it can contain a hidden true knowledge. These dialectics of secrecy and skepticism are precisely what give plasticity to the discourse of sorcery: the occultation, instead of being an obstacle, facilitates the appropriation of new elements, which are described as more secret, more hidden, more fundamental, at a deeper level of knowledge.

I would add two other forms of ambiguity: the second one, between accuser and accused, and a third, between subject and object. Sorcery is more an accusation than a self-defined practice, as the anthropological literature has always pointed out; but by acknowledging it, the accused can acquire a power over the accuser, the hidden power of the sorcerer. Third, and last, is the ambiguity between object and subject: sorcery is an art of seduction, through which people become objects to the will of others; or, on the contrary, objects act like people with their own will. Sorcery is a trap that binds together accuser and accused, truth and falsity, people and things.

The practices and objects described by the Inquisition records as *feitiçaria* and *feitiços* seem to have two main orientations: to protect against unfortunate events and to propitiate fortunate events. On the one hand, the body is seen as a place of potential danger, where devils and beasts can enter (Bethencourt 1987, 57), and therefore it is necessary to protect it, "sealing the body" (*fechar o corpo*), as it is still said nowadays in different parts of the Lusophone world. On the other hand, amulets are also supposed to influence people, or, to use the correct term, to achieve "grace"— (*Alcançar graça com quem quisesse*; Bethencourt 1987, 68), particularly in love or social affairs.

The elements that make amulets should be also in some ways exceptional: the rope of a hanged man, a broken mirror, parts of bodies of beasts, bones of dead people, or the saliva of somebody dying (Bethencourt 1987, 52–53, 85). The actual origin of and way of collecting these things are perhaps more important to understand their value than what they represent: more than the symbolism of the rope and the saliva, whatever it may be, what matters is that they were collected in the most exceptional events—like the transit between life and death—and they are indexes of this event. Any saliva or rope would not do; but these particular ones have power, they are *feitiços*. Their power is more a result of this indexicality— this causal relation with the supernatural event—than their symbolism, what they represent.

The plasticity of magical practices is a consequence of the unpredictability of the relation between humans and beings from the other world. Sorcery is not ignorant of the laws of nature. On the contrary, it is very much grounded on them: it just adds that, when an event cannot be explained in relation to these laws, when something extraordinary happens, we should look for an effective cause behind these laws—in these invisible agencies.

This is precisely the central point that Evans-Pritchard (1937) was making in his work on the Azande, as Kapferer concludes (Kapferer 2002, 7), defining sorcery as an essentially adaptive, contextual, and concrete discourse that cannot be easily confined in specific "systems of knowledge."

What was socially described as *feitiçaria* therefore was more a loose body of beliefs and practices related to fear and desire, the unexpected, the marvelous, and fate than a positive and systematized body of knowledge. That is what would make it particularly appropriate to incorporate many forms of ritual practice, objects, and people from the more disparaged origins.

Mandinga

It can be no surprise that *feitiçaria* blossomed in the early modern Portuguese colonial world, crossed by randomly dangerous events and encounters, taking new forms. In the context of the first centuries of the colonial enterprise we see the emergence of a new term, *mandinga*, which became synonymous with *feitiçaria* in the Lusophone Atlantic.[1] In the sixteenth century, various groups coming from the former empire of Mali, identified as "Mandinga" by the Portuguese, conquered parts of the coast of Guinea, where they encountered the first Portuguese settlements. The Portuguese settlers, *lançados* and *tangomagos* (Portuguese and half-African traders that explored trade routes in the interior) started to use objects for protection and amulets produced by Mandinga marabous.[2] In 1656, in Chaceu, Ambrosio Gomes, "a white man" tied some cords around the arm of Crispina Peres, a woman who was giving birth, cords he got from the Mandinga (Sweet 2003, 181).

The amulets, called *bolsas de mandinga*, became extremely popular in the Portuguese world at the beginning of the eighteenth century, well beyond Guinea (Mott 1988a; Calainho 2004; Sweet 2003). In 1700, a Capeverdean slave, Francisco, was selling a variety of *bolsas* in Lisbon, to protect from fights, win at games, and seduce people. In 1729, Luis de Lima, born in Ouidah, confessed to the Inquisition that he used *mandingas* in Porto and Pernambuco. He also named twenty-six other slaves from the Mina coast who used *mandingas*. Most of them had spent time in Brazil before coming to Portugal. One of them, a Bahian-born slave, Manuel da Piedade, sold ingredients for *bolsas de mandinga*. Other Africans, from Ouidah were accused later of manufacturing *mandingas*. It is interesting to note that none of the people I mentioned were actually Mandingo or even from Guinea. Their clients were both slaves and masters, black and white, African and Portuguese (Sweet 2003, 183; Calainho 2004, 53).

What did the Inquisition judges find in these *bolsas de mandinga*? Altar stones, pieces of paper with Christian orations, rocks, sticks, roots, bones, hair, animal skins, feathers, powders, and consecrated particles. The usual stuff of *feitiçaria*: random objects collected in the more extraordinary situations.

These pouches were also used at the remote extremes of the colonial world. By the beginning of the eighteenth century, Vicente de Morais, a freed man and soldier in the backlands of Angola, was accused by the Inquisition of being a *mandingueiro* and making pouches. It is interesting to note that in that case, the name for the pouches is not always *mandinga:* sometimes they are called "Sallamanca," "Cabo Verde," or "São Paulo." Vicente confessed that he had a pouch to protect him in combat. In it the judges found a pebble of an altar stone, and a Catholic prayer. Vicente also confessed that a white friend had given him a pouch but that he could not "test it" because he had given it to somebody else (Pantoja 2004, 129-30).

Sweet (2003) and Harding (2000) described *mandinga* pouches as objects of African resistance against the Portuguese empire and slavery. Harding sees the *bolsa de mandinga* "as part of the continuing effort to re-order a world fractured by slavery [. . .] they were also an effort in the direction of adjusting the balance of power, of moderating the caprice of the dominant order. The *bolsas* and other *feitiços* represented a counterforce" (Harding 2000, 31-2). Since Bastide (1978), it is commonly held by many authors that *feitiçaria* was an instrument of slave resistance. It is undeniable that, in a slave society, many sorcery cases revolved around master and slave relations (see Reis, this volume). But it may be a bit reductive to explain sorcery discourse just as a function of slave resistance or African cultural resistance in general. First of all, this argument does not explain why the actual material components of these pouches and the spells and rituals prayed upon it were not necessarily African. On the contrary, they were often Catholic. Second, the argument of slave resistance does not correspond with the discourses of the practitioners of *feitiçaria* as they are recorded: the objective of the *bolsas de mandinga* was to seal the body (*fechar o corpo*) against the influence not only of people but also of spirits (Souza 1986, 132) and to influence the good will of people (of course, in many cases, masters) *and* spirits. These spirits of the dead and the devil were real social agents for the people who used the *bolsas*, as real as slaves and masters. Third, it does not account for the fact that the *bolsas* were used by people of all social origins and social classes, slaves and free, blacks and whites, including slave masters. *Feitiçaria* was a part of everyone's everyday life (Souza 1986, 133).

Mandinga pouches blended European, African, and maybe even indigenous practices (Souza 1986, 131). This does not mean that it is necessary to downplay the conflicts and violence generated by slavery. Of course, the Portuguese colonial society was an extremely violent and unfair social system. But this violence was not reducible to a slave/master, black/white contradiction; it took many other forms: from religious persecution of Jews and Muslims, to class conflict between noblemen and the populace, metropolitans and colonials, and men and women, even to conflicts between slaves of different origins, slaves and freedmen, and so on. The discourse of the *mandinga* pouch, and of *feitiçaria* in general, is in many ways a discourse about everyday power and the violence of all against all.

This is clearly shown in the numbers of the Inquisition trials. The Inquisition cannot easily be reduced to an institution that repressed slaves and their African culture. Only sixty-two of the 652 cases of *feitiçaria* denounced to the Portuguese Inquisition between the seventeenth and the eighteenth centuries were blacks and mulattos, or less than 10 percent. Of these, almost 49 percent were free and 18 percent were freed (*forros*): only a third were slaves (Calainho 2004, 62–3). Apparently, the Inquisition was not persecuting slaves and Africans per se: it was persecuting heretics.

It is, however, true that more and more Africans were accused of sorcery as colonization and slavery increased in the eighteenth century, in particular in Brazil.[3] Why were Africans progressively identified with *feitiçaria*? Maybe for the popular imagination the devil often took the face of the stranger within. Bethencourt (1987) discusses cases in sixteenth century Portugal in which many of the *curandeiras* and *feitiçeiras* were Muslim and Jewish converts, *moriscas* and *cristãs novas*. By the late eighteenth century, Jews and Muslims had been clearly replaced by Africans. But their clients were the same: poor and rich, black and white, Portuguese and African.

The paradox of sorcery seems to be that the apparently powerless foreigner, the outsider, the unknown, is the most powerful sorcerer. It is interesting to note the variations as regards the origin of the pouch in the above-mentioned case of the Angolan soldier: in Angola, the pouch may not be just *mandinga*, but "Cabo Verde," "São Paulo," and "Sallamanca": the four corners of the Atlantic. The important thing, more than the origin itself, is that it is not from *here* but from somewhere else, from some strange and special place that, like the contents of the bag, is exceptional. What is objectified in the pouches is not of an African origin: the pouch contains the relics and traces of exceptional events in which the world of the living and the dead meet. Indexing these events, they help people to confront the unexpected in their lives. The symbolism of the object is not as important as the fact that they "work," that they make miracles. In the case of the Angolan soldier, he clearly stated that he did not know it was magical until it "worked." The miraculous event is necessary, and the pouch is an index of this miracle.

This is an important point. Pouches needed to be tested: they had to work in crucial situations so that people could recognize their power. Only then did they become their *bolsa*, their personal index, in an event that defines one's life in relation to this object. For Pietz, this is one of the central questions of the problem of the fetish, what he calls "personalization." Finding a fetish is an event that cannot be predicted: it is a single happening in which people find something unforeseen that they recognize as a part of themselves, something that becomes personified. Pietz explains this point wonderfully, making reference to Leiris and the surrealist notion of the *objet trouvé*, "these crisis moments of singular encounter and indefinable transaction between the life of the self and that of the world become fixed, in both places and things, as personal memories that retain a peculiar power to move one profoundly" (Pietz 1985, 12).

The *bolsas de mandinga* are the objectifications of these events, of these personal histories. They are not just symbols or tokens of one or another religion, one or another culture, one or another race or continent, but indexes of the personal lives of people in the Lusophone world, a life marked by trade, transience, and uncertainty. Their value is a recognition of the singular values generated by events, which cannot be explained by the elements that become a part of the situation before it happens: they have a particular historicity (Latour 2001, 131).

Still, if many of the questions that would be central to the problem of the fetish, as Pietz defines it, like its personalized historicity, are already contained in the *feitiço* and the *mandinga*, the formation of the notion of the *fetish* is also, in itself, deeply historical and connected to a new frame of relations between people and things, Europe and Africa, history and tradition. There is in fact a radical difference between *feitiço* and fetish: *feitiço* is an object of sorcery, while the fetish is the foundation of a religion. We will address this radical shift, from *feitiço* to fetish, further on in this paper. But now we should take a short digression on "Africa."

Africa

Before going on to the question of the fetish, I would like to go back to one of the questions we were asking at the beginning of this paper. As we have seen, the discourse of *feitiçaria* was fully formed in Portugal before this country had any direct contact with the coasts of West Africa. Could it be that African traditional forms of sorcery had been radically transformed by the colonial contact with European discourses and practices?

That is the risky but interesting hypothesis that Rosalind Shaw has developed in her work in the last few years. Shaw reached the conclusion that Atlantic history, and the slave trade in particular, marked deeply the practices of witchcraft in Sierra Leone. In fact, Shaw believes that the "consumption" or objectification of people, which characterizes sorcery, is in fact a result of the slave trade (Shaw 2002, 11). In that sense, the identification among modernity, capitalism, and sorcery would not be a new thing: sorcery always was integral to modernity, "a modernity whose very nature was, and is, witch-like" (2002, 16).

The argument is very interesting, but maybe it is a bit too perfect as a narrative of origins: sorcery would not come from primitive, dark, and traditional Africa but from slavery and capitalism. The argument manages to redeem the victim and build a culprit that is worthy of pitiless criticism. But when we analyze the historical process in depth, the argument becomes more complex, and the agencies more difficult to disentangle.

Shaw works on early colonial Portuguese chronicles to defend the idea that among the Temne of Sierra Leone, certain ritual practices radically changed with the escalation of the slave trade in the late seventeenth century. According to Shaw, the Portuguese chroniclers who visited Sierra Leone before this period do not mention sorcery (Shaw 1997, 2002). This is actually wrong: the chronicles she uses do mention sorcery, but the translation she used transformed the Portuguese *feitiçeiro* into the English "fetish-men." This ambiguity between *feitiço* and fetish is not uncommon, as we have seen, but interestingly enough it can lead to this misreading, which is not irrelevant: by talking about fetish-men, Shaw can take for granted that the Portuguese were describing priests and not sorcerers. In more general terms, it is also clear from these texts that the Temne were familiar with slavery and used ritual means to stop their slaves from escaping (Shaw 2002, 52). That is, I would say, a form of objectifying people that predates the Atlantic slave trade.

It is indeed tempting to say that African peoples had a moral economy, like E. P. Thompson's precapitalist European popular classes (Austen 1993), that was radically upset by the eighteenth century slave trade and early capitalism. That would further add up to an argument on the "Red Atlantic" (Rediker and Linebaugh 2001) that would describe the formation of an Atlantic working class, which would reframe premodern moral economies into modern revolutionary ideologies. But I think that this history is more complex, and more confusing. More than the formation of a working class in contraposition to an imperial project, we have to look at several competing colonial projects, which were not just competing for power and wealth but also around ideas; and this includes not only European colonial projects but also African ones, like the Mandinga, for example.

That is precisely something that we can find in Shaw's work: in spite of these weaknesses in her argument, Shaw has offered a very interesting picture of the situation in Sierra Leone in the early colonial period, which can open clues toward a more complex reading of these transformations. For example, Shaw illustrates how some of the key transformations in ritual practices of what the Portuguese would call "sorcery" were related to the arrival of the Mende (whom the Portuguese would call Mandinga) and the establishment of their kingdoms in the sixteenth century. According to Shaw (2002, 42), the Mandinga marabous became the more prestigious ritual specialists among the Temne, more or less at the same time that *mandinga* was becoming extremely popular in the Lusophone world. On the other hand, the Portuguese also had their own magical powers: after all, the term that was used to define the Portuguese and half-castes that ventured into the interior to trade was *tangomago*, after the Mende term *tangoma*, a priest of the Kola trade (Shaw 2002, 270 n.4). In general terms, what these exchanges show is a complex setting of competing colonial projects, in which the supremacy of one or the other, the Mende or the Portuguese, was still not totally defined, and in which sorcery played a part in objectifying the power of the enemy.

All this said, I would not dismiss altogether the idea that the escalation of the slave trade to the Americas from the late seventeenth century on would radically upset the life and culture of peoples in the West Coast of Africa. On the contrary, that process radically changed the balances of power that had been established between different European powers and between Europeans and Africans in the first centuries of colonialism. The outcome of this process, however, is not just changes in the practices of sorcery but the redefinition of the problem of sorcery into a new question: fetishism.

The Fetish

The conversion of Africans was not a priority for Portuguese discoverers. The Portuguese had no intention to occupy most of inland Africa and no intention to promote Christianity there, unless they were asked by the local powers—and the kings wanted to convert. This happened in different times and different places, but the enthusiasm of most African kings for Christianity quickly faded away, in most cases. For example, the king of

Benin in the early sixteenth century asked for missionaries but then lost interest, made them prisoners, and almost starved them to death. According to João de Barros (1553), he was only interested in the missionaries if their sorcery helped him fight his enemies. In one case, however, as it is well-known, Christianity became the religion of the state: in Congo, the king and his son converted to Christianity.[4] According to MacGaffey, in Congo, "Christianity was a new means to approach the highest *nzambi* [God] whose existing representative, the king, felt that his powers were threatened by the multiplication of lesser *nzambi* (shrines, charms) controlled by his nominal subordinates" (MacGaffey 1986, 199). The king tried to monopolize Christianity since its very beginning and restrict its cult to the higher aristocracy. This was the way of securing the power over the *nzambi* and consequently over his land and people. The hegemony of Christianity in Kongo was then troubled first by the reluctance of the aristocracy to share their knowledge of Christian higher magic and then by the reluctance of the lower classes of farmers to abandon their local *nzambi*.

In other parts of the coast of Africa, the missionization did not take place. In the upper parts of Guinea, the Portuguese relied strongly on *tangomagos* and *lançados*, as we have seen—Portuguese or descendants of Portuguese who knew the land and spoke the local languages. After some generations, the legitimacy of their claims to Portuguese ancestry was often questioned by many European travelers—probably because they were also their rivals in trade—who thought that the *tangomagos* and *lançados'* knowledge of Christianity had been reduced to wearing large crucifixes and rosaries, together with their *mandinga* pouches.[5]

But the history of the fetish was not built so much in Angola and the upper part of Guinea as in the Golf of Guinea, in ports like Elmina and Ouidah. After discovering gold, the king of Portugal decided to keep strict control on what was going to be called the Gold Coast, founding a settlement under his direct command, the Castle of São Jorge da Mina. There, in the words of one of its latter captains, never a human soul was converted.[6] The Portuguese stayed in the coast—they did not create colonies or send *tangomagos* and *lançados* to the backlands. However, it seems that populations of half-castes or "mulattos" flourished in the coast, near Portuguese settlements. On the other hand, the area was of great interest to the rivals of Portugal. From relatively early in the sixteenth century, we have accounts from Dutch, English, Danish, and French travelers who were competing for a trading space on the coast with the Portuguese and finally overcame them by the mid-seventeenth century. The travelers were the most critical of the population of half-castes, the mulattos, who were deceitful and nasty with both Africans and Europeans (Bosman 1705). They were equally surprised and annoyed at the *fetissos*. These travelers said that the Africans used the word *fetisso*; we do not know to what extent this had become a word commonly used in African languages or whether it was used only in interaction with Europeans, assuming that they understood the term. Probably the exchange between Europeans and Africans was often mediated by Portuguese speakers, maybe these mulattos that Willem Bosman mentions. Whatever the case is, the word was known and used when talking to Europeans. The paradoxical result was that for the Europeans, the *fetissos* became an African thing.

But what is more interesting is that for Protestants like De Marees and Bosman, the *fetissos* were not just magic charms, or *feitiços*; they were themselves the gods of the Africans and the *fetisseros* were their priests.[7] The Catholic distinction between sorcery and religion was superfluous: magic and ritualistic religion were the same thing. The religion of the Africans was the *fetisso*, and this placed them at an irredeemable distance from Protestant Europeans. In this way, similar to the way in which *mandinga* became synonymous with African sorcery in the Portuguese colonial world, because it was foreign and strange, the Portuguese *feitiço* became synonymous with African religion in the trading ports of West Africa.

The *fetisso*, fetish, *fetiche* started then to be associated directly with Africa, regardless of the Portuguese, who disappeared from the accounts. The new Protestant travelers refused to recognize the agency of the devil or the spirits of the dead behind the cult of fetishes. The fetishes were held to be artifices made by humans in their stupidity and greed, God being a remote creator in a disenchanted world. The story and the enchantment of the fetish would then become purely a work of the deception of a false priest who was nothing else but a charlatan.

Bosman's account of fetish worship in Guinea is illustrative. He makes no mention of the devil as the cause of the fetish: it is only the stupidity and greed of Africans. He explains that Africans say that when God created the world he made men white and black. He gave to the black man the option to choose first between two gifts: gold or "the knowledge of the arts of reading and writing" (Bosman 1705, 146). The black man chose gold. Therefore, with time he became the slave of the white man, who with his arts took the black man's gold and even his body, in slavery. But Bosman interpreted the story as a corroboration of his idea that Africans were ignorant people led simply by greed and interest and that their fetish priests misled them to worship their fetishes. In many ways, he inaugurated a discourse on Africa that still persists today and not only among Western traders: that the problem of Africa is Africans themselves, their greed, corruption, and, in particular, their backward culture and beliefs.

Bosman explains how when he asked an African how many gods they had, the African answered laughing that they had as many as they wished. They just made one when they needed one. They knew that they made artificial gods, and yet they worshiped them. For Bosman this was clear proof that their religion was only guided by interest (Bosman 1705, 367). Bosman makes reference in one of his cases to the snake cult in Ouidah. He tells of a snake that abandoned his worshipers and went speedily to the town of their enemies, "at which they were overjoyed" (Bosman 1705, 367). The former enemies became the new worshipers of the runaway snake.

For Bosman, "How their Gods are represented to them, or what Idea they form of them, I never yet could learn, because indeed they do not know themselves" (Bosman 1705, 155). What troubles Bosman is the difficulty he has in explaining the fetish in terms of representation—and indeed it cannot be understood as a representation or a symbol or something else. It is clear that they do not represent anything: they are the objects of the cult itself. The snake of Ouidah was not the symbol of anything but the object of the cult itself.

I have pointed out that the *feitiço* is essentially an index—a sign that does not stand for an object through a mental representation but that is the consequence of an act, an index of an exceptional event that becomes an entirely new being, with its living breath. Maybe this, for a man of the Enlightenment like Bosman, was impossible to accept, since the modern Enlightenment theory of agency is anthropocentric—only humans have agency: their action is guided by intentions or, better, by their will, while other events are natural, and nature is guided by laws, not intentions. Therefore, for a modern thinker, a sacred snake speeding to the enemies would not necessarily mean that it wanted to be worshiped by them, because a snake is a stupid animal that follows the laws of nature and has no will—only humans have will. In the traveler's accounts, it is commonly stated that Africans worship the first thing they find on their way; the first thing they fancy, they recognize as their fetish. This was seen by European thinkers as a demonstration of their ignorance of the natural laws, their lack of understanding that nonhuman beings in the world do not have a will but are ruled by laws. One might return again to Evans-Pritchard (and maybe even invoke Wittgenstein) and claim that magic is not ignorant of the laws of nature; it only looks for human meaning behind events when these events are uncannily exceptional. It is not any snake that becomes a god, but if that snake crosses fields in the middle of a war, it is difficult not to believe that this has a meaning—that there is a will behind it.

But is this magical thinking so far removed from the Enlightenment? Bosman compares fetish worship to Catholicism: "If it was possible to convert the Negroes to the Christian Religion, the Roman-Catholics would succeed better than we should, because they agree on several particulars, especially on their ridiculous Ceremonies" (Bosman 1705, 154). Other Protestant traders agreed. For the Huguenot Jean Barbot, "these people have fetishes [. . .] just like Roman Catholics have their saints" (Barbot 1992, 578). It should be no wonder that in the early eighteenth century, after long and bloody wars over religion and commerce throughout the world, Protestant and freethinking traders would despise and reject anything that suggested papistry. What they found in common between these religions was their externalism, the relevance they gave to rituals, displays of objects, and the hierarchic power of religious congregations and in particular their transactional character—that they were based on exchanges with the divine through made-up mediators like fetishes, spirits, saints, and priests. They made and sold the divine. In contrast, the Protestants understood their own puritan practice as a private relationship between individuals and God, through their thought and faith, not through made-up objects or rituals, or performances, in a relationship that was not based in transactions, exchanges, and making deals. On the contrary, production and exchange belonged to the economy, as Marx explained very well; in fact, the economy can be understood in terms of fetishism: it is a human institution, an artifact, that has acquired its own agency, the "hidden hand" independent from the will of humans, acquiring quasi-natural status—but not quite natural. But of course Bosman and those like him would never recognize that—it would be like recognizing the hybrid nature of modernity (Latour 1993).

In these terms, I would not be so sure that the likes of Bosman would not really understand the fetish: in fact they organized their economy around it. It was religion more than the fetish that troubled them. In *Du culte des dieux fétiches*, Charles de Brosses (1760) finally developed a full-fledged theory of the fetish and invented the term "fetishism." Arguing that fetishism, or the cult of things, is the origin of all religion, de Brosses organized the most powerful argument against religion that was ever made in a century of skepticism. By identifying the worship of objects as a first step in a process leading to more spiritual forms of religion, it was finally possible to integrate the criticism of religion to a general theory of progress that would see the Enlightenment as the last, logical end of human achievement: in modern Europe, men had finally managed to relate to objects just in terms of their true value as commodities, separating their religious beliefs from material things altogether. From then on, Africa was distant from Europe not only in space but also in time. For Hegel (1837), Africans were out of history since their relation to the world was not mediated by understanding but by pure fancy; the particular historicities of the fetish would be radically incompatible with History with a capital H. By the same token, all the colonies that were not ruled by enlightened Europe, but by backward and decadent empires, countries like Brazil and most of Latin America, started to fall into a historical limbo, a no-man's-land between the irredeemably ahistorical Africa and the dynamic modernity of Europe, a nightmare that in many ways is still at the background of a lot of what we hear about Africa and Latin America in the media, among politicians, and among many professional intellectuals. What happened to fetishism, for example, in Brazil?

Feitiçaria *and Fetishism in Brazil*

We find the first traces of the progressive distance between the Portuguese *feitiço* and the African fetish in an early eighteenth-century Portuguese dictionary. In the definition of *feitiço*, the author mentions that one possible origin of the word is the African term *fetiche*, "name that the people of Guinea, in Africa, give to the idols they worship" (*nome que os povos de Guinè, na Africa dão a os idolos que eles adorão*; Bluteau 1713, 66).[8] Curiously enough, he has inverted the facts. He does not recognize that *fetiche* comes from *feitiço*; he thinks that it is the other way around!

European travelers in Brazil did use the term "fetish" in reference to some objects used by Africans.[9] On the other hand, Lusophone intellectuals, at least since Bluteau, knew the term *fetiche*, but it does not seem to have been commonly used prior to the mid-nineteenth century, when the influence of Comte and positivism makes them more popular (Corrêa 1998). For example, Tobias Barreto, in the 1870 article *Moisés e Laplace*, discusses the fetishist cult at the origins of humanity, but he thinks that fetishism is at "a great distance from us" (*a grande distancia de nos*), faraway in time. He does not seem to contemplate the possibility of living with actual fetishists in his own time, but he criticizes Catholicism as a modern kind of fetishism, worse than the primitive one, which enslaves the ignorant masses.[10] This is an important point I think, to understand the uses of the term "fetishism" in Brazil. Contained in any theory of fetishism is an implicit criticism of religion as an institution of social control—essentially of Catholicism. This is particularly important at this point in time in Brazil, with respect to what was called the religious question: the Catholic

Church's opposition to Freemasonry had ended with an open confrontation with the Empire—which had many masons among its highest ranks. The Brazilian church is seen by freethinking intellectuals like Barreto as an archaic, medieval, obscurantist institution. Popular, traditional Catholic practices are positively despised when not feared by the new elites of educated intellectuals who aspire to live in a modern, European society and view religion as a factor of backwardness.

In fact, the Catholic religion more than any other institution was seen as having the main responsibility for the backwardness of Brazil among many of the new positivist intellectuals. Toward the end of the nineteenth century, with slavery abolished (1888) and the empire replaced by the First Republic (1890), even the hierarchies of the Church urged a renovation, initiating a process of romanization (Azzi 1979), as they attempted to eradicate magical practices and impose the authority of priests. This context of religious reform also affected the way in which Candomblé and other similar forms of ritual practice were seen in Brazilian society. Forms of popular religious expression that were traditionally framed as Catholic—like the *lavagens*, were now seen as "public Candomblés" (*Candomblés a céu aberto*), and persecuted by both the police and the church (Sansi 2005).[11]

On the other hand, the word *fetichismo* starts to appear in Bahian newspapers around the 1860s in cases of police persecution of Candomblé cults but is much more infrequent than the traditional terms, *feitiço* and *feitiçaria*, that had always been systematically used in these cases.[12] At this point, it is important to make clear that when the authorities were persecuting *feitiçaria*, they were not solely or primordially singling out what they saw as another culture or religion; they were fighting against specific practices of sorcery and spiritualism that they perceived as criminal. As Maggie has explained in *Medo do feitiço* (1992), policemen and judges in the late nineteenth century did not persecute *all* magical and spiritualist practitioners as such, but rather persecuted them when they used magic and spiritualism for *evil* purposes and fraud. Analyzing court cases of the early republican period, Maggie concludes that all the discussion is built around a common belief: the existence of spirits that can be incorporated and the possibility that some of these spirits produce evil charms, *feitiços*. Writers like Xavier Marques, in *O feitiçeiro* (1897), or João Do Rio, in *As Religiões do Rio* (1904), explicitly assess that it was not only African sorcerers but in particular their hypocritical white clients who sustained the belief in sorcery: they were slaves of their superstition and lower passions, they were "ruled by the sorcerer" (Marques 1975 [1897], 17). For them, it was not only the Africans who were barbarians but also their white clients: they were entrapped, bound to sorcery. And the result was that Brazil was a backward country that could never move forward to modernity.

In this context of intense national crisis, Raimundo Nina Rodrigues wrote his classic book, *L' animisme fétichiste des nègres de Bahia* (1935 [1896, 1900]), in which he planned to study the persistence of African fetishism in Brazil.[13] For Rodrigues, the antisorcery laws could not be applied to Africans because they were a different race with a primitive mentality. Candomblé was not only *feitiçaria*, but also a fetishist cult, a religion—a primitive religion, adapted to the primitive minds of their practitioners, but religion still, and it had to be observed, and researched, as a resistant African culture. For Rodrigues, the fact that whites followed Candomblé was even more repulsive than for Marques or Do Rio, because it showed racial degeneration. Looking for the pure African fetishism, the researcher had to leave aside everything that had the mark of mixture—racial, cultural, or religious—because mixture was degeneration.

The genial paradox of Nina Rodrigues is that, despite the general criticism that his racist approach received afterward, he became the founder of a school of research that defended the African cultural autonomy of Candomblé as a different African culture that was encrusted in Brazilian society. His disciple, Arthur Ramos, reframed his theory, hiding its racist backbone and replacing it with a culturalist argument: on the one hand he put the culturally pure African religions and on the other hand the culturally mixed and syncretistic cults, which would inevitably degenerate toward sorcery; on the one hand, we have good *fetichismo*, on the other hand, bad *feitiçaria* (Ramos 1934; Dantas 1984).

These assumptions are still common among many contemporary researchers, and they are behind the suspicion many have in regards to sorcery. The paradox of Nina Rodrigues is the paradox of generations of intellectuals from outside the core of Western civilization, who have faithfully followed European theories that radically separated the world into two—the West and the rest—when they lived in situations in which they were both, and maybe something else.

Sorcery, Fetishism, and the Trap of History

At the same time that Brazilian intellectuals started to use "fetishism" to define their local Afro-Brazilian cults, the use of the term began to fade in some parts of Africa. Peter Pels asked why the English term "witchcraft" replaced "fetishism" in the ethnography of British eastern and central colonial Africa in around 1900 (Pels 1998, 199).[14] One possible answer would be the changing trends in the anthropological literature, but in that case probably "fetishism" would have been replaced by "animism," or even "magic"; the use of the term "witchcraft," as Pels pointed out, seems related to the intricacies of colonial legal practice: British African administrators translated the "problem" by themselves by associating African practices with the European history of witchcraft. By so doing, they were on the one hand dismissing the construction of fetishism as a religious system, a system of power and knowledge that was absolutely impenetrable for Europeans, because it was absolutely other. As far as Africa was an impenetrable, deceitful, and despicable other, only having worth as a provider of slaves, fetishism seemed to fit; but when Africa became a land to be fully colonized and civilized in the late nineteenth century, the image of African beliefs started to change. By seeing African beliefs simply as witchcraft, they were reduced to the status of irrational rural survivals, which could be overcome, like in eighteenth-century Europe, by the enlightened rule of the law. This may not have been the way things really went, and in many ways, as Pels argues, indirect rule produced a subversion of the law, by allowing witchcraft evidence to fulfill certain functions in colonial legal practice (Pels 1998, 200).[15] It could be argued that, paradoxically, this legislation produced a discourse on witchcraft as an "African problem" (see also Ciekawy 1998), which became widespread among its colonial populations, actually gaining momentum in the postcolonial period.

On the other hand, in Brazil, sorcery has rarely been an object of research,[16] precisely because it has been seen as a denigrating term, which indicates syncretism, degeneration, and, worse, criminality. The silence of scholars on sorcery, however, does not correspond to its disappearance in social practice: *feitiçaria* is not a thing of the past in Brazil. The openly belligerent antisorcery discourse of the new Pentecostal churches in Brazil shows not only that the belief in sorcery is still very much present but that the belief in a modernity without sorcery is still strong: we only have to look at the incredible power of seduction of the prophetic discourses that pledge to unbind Brazil and finally embrace the progress of the developed countries, praying for the end of sorcery, envy, and corruption (see Maggie, this volume). The quickness with which these churches proliferate in the Atlantic—from Brazil to Africa and from there to the peripheries of the big cities of the north, where immigrants from the south move searching for prosperity, progress, liberation—shows how these discourses are nothing new; they are only working on a seed that had already been sown, something that was already there.

This would be the provisional endpoint of our particular history of sorcery discourses in the modern Atlantic. I started looking at the history and uses of some key terms to understand the transformations of an Atlantic discourse of sorcery. We have seen first how the loose and ambiguous discourse of Portuguese *feitiçaria* and *feitiço* appropriated practices, terms, and persons in the early modern colonial world, reinventing itself as the Atlantic complex of the *mandinga*. On the other hand, the Portuguese *feitiço* was transformed into the African *fetisso*, which in the discourse of Protestant European travelers like de Marees or Bosman became the center of African religion, later called "fetishism" by de Brosses. These terms, in their turn, were dismissed in the late-nineteenth-century colonial world and replaced by notions of witchcraft that are still common in Africa today.

But "witchcraft" is not exactly a return to the early modern complex of *feitiçaria*. As we have seen, *feitiçaria* in the early modern Portuguese colonial world was not described as exclusively African but as a universal phenomenon. There could be, and there were, particularly powerful forms of sorcery that apparently came from Africa, like the *mandinga*; but their actual origin was less important that their particular historicity, the fact that they worked in a certain historical circumstance; and they were used by all sorts of people in the Atlantic world, not just Africans. In this sense, the discourse of *feitiçaria* in the early modern colonial world was not so strongly bound to Africa, Africans, and African beliefs, as "witchcraft" was in the late nineteenth century and in many ways still is today. This is partially a result of the discourse of fetishism, which placed African beliefs in a situation of radical alterity from Europe, and from History with a capital H. In this sense, although modern notions of witchcraft in Africa appeared to make African beliefs more manageable than they would be in terms of fetishism, the spell of the fetish seems difficult to shake: witchcraft, still today, like fetishism in Bosman's time, is often described as the curse of Africa, which makes it stuck in its past, unable to develop, to gain its place in history. This curse can also be extended to Latin American countries stuck in their colonial past, where the postcolonial elites are entrapped by sorcery, "out of History."

The Africanness of witchcraft is in fact still difficult to disentangle, even for anthropologists and historians, because it has become so entrenched in local discourses that it cannot be simply dismissed; however, it is not enough to take these local discourses for granted, because they are the result of a long and convoluted history of exchange, appropriation, imposition, and subversion.[17]

Notes to Chapter Two

1. Even today, *mandinga* is synonymous with the devil in Argentina.

2. The first mention Sweet found to *bolsas de mandinga* was in 1601, in the words of the Jesuit father Balthazar Barreira, in Guiné, in reference to the bags that Muslim priests made for "tricking people" (Sweet 2003, 181).

3. In eighteenth-century Minas Gerais, 71.8 percent of the accused were black (Nogueira 2004, 7).

4. However, the first Christian king of Congo, João, also had a moment of weakness in his old age. The chronicler João de Barros explains how the priests requested him to renounce his large harem and keep only one wife, as a Christian. But the king was not ready to accept it, and this provoked a conflict with his son Alfonso, who was a devout Christian. According to de Barros, some people in the king's court, inspired by the devil, conspired against Alfonso and told the king that Alfonso had become a powerful sorcerer, thanks to the Christian priests, and that he flew at night from the distant city where he lived to his father's harem, to have sex with his father's wives. To test if this was true, the king played a trick: he sent a *feitiço*, a charm, wrapped in a cloth to one of his wives, whom he suspected. The messenger who brought the *feitiço* told her that it was from her lover, the prince, and that he sent it to protect her from the king—since he was intending to kill all his wives. The wife, shocked by this story, ran to tell her husband the king about it. This was enough proof for the king that he was ill advised and that his son was loyal. This is the first and more specific reference to a *feitiço* in de Barros (1553).

5. La Courbe, a French traveller, talks about these *tangomagos*, saying that "[t]hey always wear a large Crucifix around their neck and call themselves by a saint's name, although for the most part they are neither baptized, nor show any evidence of Christian religion" (Brooks 2003, 153). Another traveller, Olivier, talks about a certain Dom Joan of Rufisque, who had "several wives [. . .] He prayed two Missionaries [. . .] to baptize his children [. . .] I was astonished to see that this man was very devout, having always a large Rosary in his hands, & several images of Our Saviour, of the Virgin, & of the Saints around his bed. The same with his wives or concubines, who carry'd also large Rosaries around their necks" (Brooks 2003, 153).

6. "A Mina há noventa annos que hé descoberta. Nunca em todo este tempo se coverteo huma alma, nem se tratou disso [. . .]" (Brasio 1952, 97).

7. In the words of De Marees, "They weare strange wreathes, which they call *Fetissos* (which name they derive from their Idolatry) for when they eate and drinke, then they power meat and drinke upon them: and first gave them to eate and drinke" (Purchas 1605, 267). He also says that "[t]hey have also a Priest, who in their speech they call a *Fetissero*, hee upon their Sabbath day sits upon a stole" (Purchas 1605, 290).

8. The same definition is given by the *Encyclopédie Française* of Diderot and D'Alembert some fifty years later. I quote the first edition of 1751-72, p. 598: "Fétiche, f, F. (Hist. mod) Nom que les peuples de Guinée en Afrique donnent à leurs divinités. Ils on une fétiche pour toute une province, & des fétiches particuliers pour chaque famille. Cette ici est un arbre, une tête de singe, un oiseau, une quelque chose de semblable, suivant leur fantaisie."

9. For example, Kidder and Fletcher, English travelers in Bahia in 1839, say, "You can scarcely look into a basket in which the *quitandeiras* [the women who sell food in

the street] carry fruit without seeing a 'fetisch.' The most common is a piece of charcoal, with which, the abashed darkey will inform you, the 'evil eye' is driven away" (Kidder and Fletcher 1857, 136).

10. "Entretanto, aquele mísero culto fetíchico, tão grosseiro e tão ridículo, é credor de maior soma de bens reais de que certo monoteísmo barbaro que ajeza a humanidade, sob a vigilância do látego divino e tem as mãos cruentas de sufocar auroras e garrotear idéias" (Barreto 1990, 30).

11. *Lavagem* literally means 'cleaning,' and in Brazil it refers to the cleansing ceremonies usually performed at Catholic churches by Candomblé devotees.

12. "O *fetichista* Grato, africano que foi preso pela polícia em uma casa do Conceição do Boqueirão, no meio do seu laboratório para prever a sorte, e que era pai de terreiro de seu candomblé foi deportado pela polícia para a costa da África, na barca portuguesa D. Francisca." *O Jornal da Bahia*, July 17, 1859; "Chico Papae, gransacerdote do *fetichismo*, fallecido ha mais de 5 annos, na rua da Poeira." *O Alabama*, July 23, 1870; "A sacerdotisa do *fetichismo* enche a casa de mulheres de toda laia e de rapazes de vida solta, os quaes são attraidos por ali, mais por causa de umas creoulinhas, escravas sem subordinação da mesma, do que pelos seus embustes." *O Alabama*, March 11, 1871:3. I thank Luis Nicolau Parés for providing these data.

13. "A persistencia do fetichismo africano como expressão do sentimento religioso dos negros baianos e seus mestiços, é facto que as exterioridades do culto catholico apparentemente adoptado por elles, não conseguiram disfarçar nem nas associações hybridas que com esse culto largamente estabeleceu o fetichismo" (Rodrigues 1935, 15).

14. The French colonies may have a different story; even today, the terms *fétichiste* and *fétiche* seem to be present in everyday French in former colonies like Benin. Unfortunately, I have not found any research on this subject.

15. Likewise, it is arguable to what extent the Witchcraft Act really ended up "witchcraft beliefs" in England (Davies 1999).

16. An exception would be Maggie (1975, 1992).

17. On this point, we could recall, for example, Ashforth's affirmation that we have to take witchcraft in Africa "literally," and not "metaphorically," as he claims that most of the literature on the "Modernity of witchcraft" does (Ashforth 2005, 114). Perhaps the question is a bit more complex: looking at the history of the different uses of this term may be more difficult, but also more interesting, than distinguishing between literal and metaphorical meanings.

3

Sorcery in Brazil: History and Historiography

LAURA DE MELLO E SOUZA

From Folklore to History

WITCHES AND THE DEVIL are strong presences in the Brazilian imaginary, but until the 1980s the study of sorcery in Brazil was relegated to the realm of folklore. It is in this category that we may consider the work of Luis da Câmara Cascudo (1972), as well as the more sophisticated essay by modernist writer Mário de Andrade, *Música de feitiçaria no Brasil* (1983), which was written in the 1930s. Marked by the wave of national consciousness that followed the abolition of slavery (1888) and the institution of a republican form of government (1889), these works emphasized African and indigenous influences, without giving much attention to the European traditions with which they had melded in Brazil.

When, in 1981, I chose sorcery as the subject of my doctoral dissertation, entitled *O diabo e a terra de Santa Cruz* (Souza 1986), I had little idea of what lay in store. The first surprise was in realizing the marked role that European tradition had played: in the documents of the Inquisition, especially in the second half of the sixteenth century and the first decades of the seventeenth, I found variations, with different degrees of complexity, of what I had read in studies of witchcraft in Britain and France and had heard in stories that were told to me as a child. Later, as the eighteenth century approached, there were increasing numbers of hybrid practices, which I naively, and with some reluctance, considered syncretistic. The nature of sorcery thus mimicked the process of colonization: first, it was defined according to the preexisting beliefs of the European colonizers whose systematic presence began in 1549, mainly along the coast. It then began to show the influence of autochthonous practices, some with a certain degree of syncretism, such as indigenous *santidades*—the most significant of which,

41

found in Jaguaripe, was brilliantly studied by Ronaldo Vainfas in *A heresia dos índios* (1995). Finally, during the seventeenth century, especially near its end, the mark of African cultures became more and more pronounced, and forms peculiar to the colonial period appeared, such as *catimbós, pagelanças, calundus,* and *bolsas de mandinga.*

The latter seemed to me to synthesize the contact between cultural traditions that had occurred during the process of colonization: they reinvented a thousand-year-old form, European body pouches, under a name that invoked the traditions of a specific African people—the Mandinga. These pouches utilized, side by side, objects from the Christian cult and from the veneration practices of tribal peoples, fragments of European and Luso-American daily life: consecrated particles, pieces of *pedra d'ara* (sacred stones from the Catholic Mass altar), papers inscribed with Koranic verses, fish and animal bones, bits of powder, arrowheads, human nail parings, and locks of hair, to cite only a few of their ingredients. In the 1990s, Daniela Calainho, in her dissertation, *Metrópole das mandingas* (2000), showed that these pouches were used not only in Brazil; they also appeared under the same name in Portugal, where they generated a lively commerce. These *bolsas de mandinga* constituted a powerful expression in the cultural plane of the colonizing process (Souza 1986); they transcended racial and cultural miscegenation in the Atlantic world to embody personal experiences and trajectories and experiences marked by uncertainty (see Sansi, this volume).

Defended in 1986, my dissertation focused more on individual magical practices than on collective ones. In this sense, what I studied was not witchcraft per se but sorcery: everyday rituals performed in order to bring success in affairs of the heart, to bend the will of others, to ensure good health and success, to see into the future, and to soften the harshness of life that, in a slave society, the masters reserved for the slaves. Following ideas current in Spain and Portugal, I adopted the idea that, in Iberian sorcery, satanic elements were insignificant: the kind of witchcraft with nocturnal flights, secret meetings, devil worship, infanticide, orgiastic banquets, and frenzied dances was almost nonexistent. When such elements did appear, they did so in isolation, unrelated to a more coherent context: women returning with divinations and rites common in the European world thus said that they flew to Portugal at night to buy spools of thread, buttons, and other articles unavailable in the colonies.

Some examples can perhaps help to better understand this question. At the end of the eighteenth century, a certain Goody Lianor claimed she was able to go from Bahia to the motherland in a single night, which made of her a suspect of witchcraft. During the same period, a woman called

"Crocked Mouth," who had been locked in jail and stigmatized as a devil's sorceress, "claimed she saw what was said and done in Lisbon." Around 1758, in Grão-Pará, part of the Amazon region, Isabel Maria de Oliveira prided herself in taking people from Belém to the Metropolis, using some glass rings she had bought at the Terreiro do Paço in Lisbon. Possibly as a means of causing envy among her acquaintances, she also claimed to have the gift of transporting people to wherever they wanted to go. For this, all she needed was to get into a canoe with a black rooster, but she could not utter the name of Jesus or Mary, nor could she take gold or silver coins (Souza 1991–92). The concept of nocturnal flight, of such complex significance in the European world, found itself, in the Portuguese empire, reduced to an expression of the relationship between the center and the periphery.

For all these reasons, I avoided establishing distinctions between witchcraft and sorcery, ignoring the common Portuguese adage that "a witch is born a witch; a sorceress learns her trade" (Bethencourt 1987). My study focused primarily on acquired knowledge, on techniques transmitted from one person to another, without examining collective rituals of possession or attempts to communicate with the beyond. Instead, I examined popular religious practice and the way that it informed magical practices, for they seemed to me to be fundamentally interrelated. In everyday life in Brazil, even today, the experience of religion is inseparable from that of magic. This historical continuity shall be taken under consideration but, in some cases, can also be misleading, as we will see later, in the case of the Calundu.

During the first three centuries of Brazilian history, as popular religious and magical practices developed, they were indelibly marked by the specificities of colonization: our religious practice was peculiar to our colonial past, as Gilberto Freyre astutely observed in *Casa grande e senzala* (1933). More specifically, the particular characteristics of that colonial past have been shaped by slavery, by race, by vast geographic distances, and by the insurmountable gap between metropolis and colony. In the end, *O diabo e a terra de Santa Cruz* became an ethnography of magical and religious practices; its denseness, in terms of description, frequently impeded more detailed analyses of culturally hybrid forms and their deeper meanings. I sought to avoid the discussions then in vogue in Europe, which, in my view, were reductive—whether because they categorized witchcraft as a mental construction or because they sought to understand the persecution of witches in terms of a mismatch between church and state. This led me to a focus, perhaps excessive, on the concrete practices that had existed, which seemed to me to be a less subjective area of investigation. Unlike most European historians, I had little interest in the mechanisms of persecution, favoring instead the subjects themselves. Moreover, to the extent that magical practices continue in Brazilian society to this day, the idea that the witches' Sabbath and analogous manifestations were expressions of fearful imagination or constructions of the elite to justify the creation of apparatuses of repression seemed to me out of place. I was, however, captivated by analyses such as that of Carlo Ginzburg's *I benandanti* or that of Danish historian and folklorist Gustav Henningsen, whose "The Ladies from the Outside" commented on the educated elite's incapacity, with the advent of the modern era, to comprehend popular practices that had existed since time immemorial (Ginzburg 1966; Henningsen 1990).

During the 1980s and the beginning of the 1990s, when I returned to the theme of sorcery in my book *Inferno Atlântico—demonologia e colonização*, extremely influenced by the studies of British historian Stuart Clark, magical-religious practices became a window through which I sought to understand the past of the land that later came to be known as Brazil (Souza 1993; Clark 1984). If readings of the work of Gilberto Freyre, so often misguided, had led to exotic and anecdotal interpretations of that past, it was important to try to put it back on track—an effort undertaken by many historians of my generation—and, beyond emphasizing its atypicality, to carefully scrutinize the combinations observed between different traditions and to recognize their European influences.

But my reflections over the past were often oriented by evidence from the historical period in which I lived; not as survivals, a notion that Jean-Claude Schmitt (1976) rightly criticized in a classical article, but by experiences that could be detected in the everyday life of my country. Indigenous practices remained confined to certain regions and, especially in rural or jungle areas, occasionally made the papers—as in a celebrated case from the 1980s, when a well-known ornithologist, Augusto Ruschi, was temporarily cured of a poisonous toad bite by an indigenous *pajé* (healer). Afro-Brazilian practices, however, especially those of Candomblé, became increasingly present in the everyday life of Brazilian cities, even in São Paulo, which, according to Reginaldo Prandi (1991), was the most important in this process of expansion.

Interweaving past and present, I thus traced an explanation of Luso-American magical practices over the first three centuries of colonization. My utilization of rich documentation from the courts of the Holy Inquisition in Portugal constitutes, I believe, a significant contribution to the field of historical ethnography, emphasizing the decisive role played by European traditions, which, owing to the heavy weight currently given to African traditions, had been neglected. However, I did not add much to understanding the mechanisms that favored the mixture of such disparate cultural elements. If the process of colonization was decisive, it was necessary to understand the internal logic that led to syncretism, to acculturation, or, in more contemporary terms, to cultural hybridity. In this sense, the introduction of this book and Sansi's chapter make an important point in considering the variety of semantic transformations put into play when different cultural universes meet. Even if all cultures are more or less hybrid, we still should examine why some traces or aspects of other cultures are incorporated while others are left behind, or better, how different elements from different cultures are dialectically combined in ways that make sense for both.

From History to Anthropology

Over the past decade, studies of magical and popular religious practices have come to emphasize the numerous African cultural traditions involved in the processes of cultural translation and hybridity. The considerable growth of research on the ethnic and cultural diversity of the African continent brought a more nuanced understanding of the importance attributed to the African contribution, as Gilberto Freyre had done in the beginning of the 1930s, or even of African contributions, in the plural, as so many others who came afterward had done, myself included. Magical practices and much of sorcery, as described in the documents of the Inquisition and the Catholic Church, including court proceedings, inquisitorial and church visits, and, more recently, the so-called *Cadernos do promotor* ("prosecutor's book")—came to be seen as confluences of beliefs and practices belonging to specific regions and cultures. A period marked by a hegemonic preference for identifying traces of the cultural traditions of the Yoruba (or Nagô) in Brazil gave way to an enthusiasm for discovering the legacy left by Bantu peoples. As suggested by Joao José Reis (this volume), such preferences may have been partially oriented by political reasons. The contemporary importance of Afro-Brazilian cults in the northeast, generally speaking, and in Bahia, in particular, with its renowned *ialorixás* ("priestesses")—Mãe Senhora, Mãe Menininha of Gantois, Mãe Stella of Opô Afonjá—and its "organic" intellectuals—Jorge Amado, Dorival Caymmi, Vinicius de Moraes, and Carybé—contributed greatly to the initial predominance of studies of Nigerian influence. But an equally crucial factor was the importance that these cults had taken on over the course of the nineteenth century, a period during which they eclipsed older ones of Angolan origin, because of the northward shift that was occurring in the Atlantic slave trade at that time. Whereas previously slave traders had exploited Central African regions, such as Angola, in the nineteenth century the most intense activity occurred in the Niger delta region. The importance of the Yoruba during this period is attested to by oral tradition and collective memory of the groups that controlled or frequented the Afro-Brazilian religious temples or *terreiros* and is also suggested by police and newspaper records. But as the number of historical studies of sorcery grew—my own, as well as those of Luiz Mott and Daniela Calainho—evidence of an Angolan presence became stronger (Mott 1986, 1993, 1994; Calainho 2000).

In this sense, I consider the discovery of the Inquisition proceedings against Luzia Pinta to be a milestone. The documents related to her case are found in Lisbon, in the Arquivos Nacionais da Torre do Tombo (Inquisition of Lisbon, Case No. 252, Vol. 26). Luzia Pinta was a Calundu practitioner who lived in the region near Sabará, Minas Gerais, in the late 1730s. The term *calundu* and its plural form, *calunduzes*, appear frequently in documents of this period, as well as *calunduzeiro* and *calunduzeira*, referring to its practitioners. The term was applied to a variety of African and Afro-Brazilian magical and religious practices, such as gatherings characterized by dance and drumming, but at times it was also used to refer to customs that did not seem to involve any sort of ritual: potions made with herbs, food offerings to idols, the preparation of small packets of bones, hair and nail clippings.[1]

The documents of the Luzia Pinta case, however, yielded information that suggested that Calundu was a complex ritual, with such strong similarities to today's Afro-Brazilian religions that it became apparent that this Angolan woman constitutes a forerunner of contemporary *babalorixás* ("priests"). At the time, I traced a genealogy without questioning the details of ritual practice from the eighteenth century to today, without examining the changes in social context over time, without realizing that to see it in this way brought to the forefront the controversial question of progress and continuity, diminishing the transformative power of history. Luzia Pinta became a central figure in my book, *O diabo e a terra de Santa Cruz* (Souza 1986).

In 1993, ethnohistorian Luiz Mott wrote a brilliant essay about the same *calunduzeira*, correcting some aspects of my analysis and emphasizing the Bantu heritage of Luzia's ritual practice: in his view, the Luzia Pinta case constitutes the "oldest manuscript description of an Angolan Calundu [...], rooted in the *xinguila* ritual of the Angola nation." According to Mott, the rituals described in the proceedings against Luzia, quite different from what is known today as Candomblé Angola, bear witness to the character of Bantu rituals as they existed before they were coopted and contaminated by the Yoruba religious complex of the *orishas*, a sort of deity related to ancestrality and/or natural forces in Yoruba and other Afro-Brazilian rites. He describes Calundu Angola as "the primary matrix of the rituals that are today called Umbanda," in which persist, alongside "the orishas and ceremonies lent by Candomblé as one more trace of Umbanda syncretism with African, Portuguese, Amerindian and Brazilian roots" (Mott 1994, 74 and 81).

From Anthropology to History

In an essay published in 2002, I suggested that both Mott and myself, despite the contributions of our work, had fallen into the trap of what Marc Bloch (1941) has called "idolizing the origin"—we believed that the point of departure explained the genesis of the process, that there was a coherent nexus between Mãe Stella and the *calunduzeira* of Sabará, between Umbanda and Calundu Angola. At the time, I proposed an analytic framework that took Calundu more as a constellation of assorted practices than as an established, well-defined ritual. This approach was based on linguistic studies, such as those of Yeda Pessoa de Castro, and on period documents, including literary works, such as the late seventeenth-century work of Gregório de Matos and the early eighteenth-century work of Nuno Marques Pereira, as well as on official records such as those of the Catholic Church and the Inquisition.[2] I was also influenced by João José Reis's admonishment about the risks of reading backward in time—whether in relation to Afro-Brazilian rituals or African cultures, as both the one and the other have undergone transformations over time (Reis 1988, 58-9). The preliminary results suggested that, in comparing the genealogies, Candomblé was a term that had always been used in relation to magical and religious practices, while Calundu was utilized in a variety of ways, "going beyond the field of beliefs and behaviors, passing into the area of moods, and, finally, to the soul, the psyche of the individual" (Souza 2002, 297). They also suggested that it is impossible to say that Calundu eventually became Candomblé and that they may actually have been distinct phenomena that were repeatedly grouped together by the authorities as though they had a single point of origin.

In general terms, *calundus* could be isolated, ordinary magical practices performed in public or collective rituals held in private spaces, supervised by a religious specialist and involving spirit possession. The latter required special garments, whose description in the Inquisition proceedings against Luzia Pinta is rich and varied: strange outfits unlike those used in the area where she lived, "like an angel" with a long ribbon tied around her head and the ends dangling in back, and "various inventions in Turkish style, with a half-moon shaped turban on her head and a small sword in her hand," or wreaths of feathers or plumes in her ears. Calundu required a certain spatial organization: Luzia was separated from the audience, on a sort of stage that was covered by a canopy, accompanied by percussion instruments. Calundu also involved ritual trance: Luzia became "as though out of her mind, for at this time came to her the illness of her land, which they call *calundus*"; standing still, with eyes turned toward the ceiling, she began the divination after a brief curtsey, when the "divining winds" came into her ears.[3]

With regard to isolated practices, I found them dispersed in thirty-two cases registered in the capitancy of Minas Gerais between 1734 and 1782. I divided them into three categories: obvious Calundus (fifteen cases), possible Calundus (four cases), and disperse elements of Calundu (thirteen cases). As I wrote at the time, all the cases in the first category were designated by or identified with the term "Calundu," "and, in most cases, they referred to dances, nearly always accompanied by musical instruments" (Souza 2002, 308-14). Frequently, they were associated with magical/curative practices that seemed to be independent of the ritual, involving the manipulation of objects—pans, bowls, mats, mirrors, crucifixes—in combination with traditional knowledge of the natural world: snails, herbs, trees, magical powders, and skulls, which are common to so many cultures. As for the possible Calundus, these involved dances, drumming, bending the will of others, communication with spirits of the dead, which were related to more than one set of beliefs—which I illustrated, according to the sources, with two models—that of Luzia Pinta, in Sabará, and that of a couple, Ivo Lopes and Maria Cardoso, who lived nearby in the town of Mariana, also in the captaincy of Minas Gerais. Luzia Pinta took part in a ritual that was quite similar to some rituals of what nowadays is called Candomblé. On the other hand, the techniques of magical cure used by Ivo Lopes and Maria Cardoso are very different from that and in some aspects very enigmatic, including a sort of hopscotch and the use of bird feathers to clean the ears in order to introduce—like in the case of Luzia—the "winds of divination." Ivo and Maria's practices are close to Calundu because of their use of disperse elements, in particular divination. In other possible Calundu cases, the verbs utilized are not always the most appropriate, the dances being "invented" or "worshipped," and elements foreign to the coherent nucleus begin to distort the most typical features of the ritual.

In the category of disperse elements of Calundu were cases involving the manipulation of objects and animals, the invocation of spirits, and the causal investigation of pathologies (*feitiços* that caused illnesses), suggesting, as I wrote, a "transition to a distinct magical complex whose characteristics, while similar to those of Calundu, perhaps presented their own unique character. These elements did not always reveal themselves in an obvious way; rather they arose in isolated, apparently meaningless ways" (Souza 2002, 312). This category seems to suggest the decomposition of a more cohesive ritual system, in which, not rarely, there is a shift from magical/ritual curing practices to those of a malevolent nature. The negative side of the practices is more accentuated, perhaps due to the impact of the dismissive attitude of the agents of the Court of the Holy Inquisition, who had denounced them to the Lisbon Court and, there, classed them as Calundus in the *Cadernos do promotor*.

From History to Memory

Thus far, in the attempt to historicize the magical-religious practices of Brazil's colonial past, I have focused on deconstructing and reconstructing the so-called African traditions, criticizing the idea of an easy genealogy linking Candomblé to Calundu. I will now turn to the European heritage and the witches' Sabbath.

In urban areas of Brazil and even in rural ones, the idea of witches as ugly old women who flew on brooms and brewed repulsive potions in boiling cauldrons figured prominently in the imagination of children and even adults whose cultural referents were predominantly European. They were, however, the stuff of children's stories: the Enlightenment, the disenchantment of the world, the twilight of folk culture had drained them of their magical, threatening, demonic content that had relegated them to the imagination of children—components, for Philippe Ariès (1973), of the most conservative human societies.

To the extent that studies of sorcery began to increase in Brazil—which occurred, from the historical point of view, in the beginning of the 1980s, as we have seen—the idea of cultural hybridity gained predominance, especially in combination with practices of African origin. When endowed with a primarily individual character, Luso-Brazilian sorcery thus expressed itself in a varied gamut of procedures that invoked traditions brought by African slaves, absorbing them, as in the case of the *bolsas de mandinga*, or revising them as time went on and the initial practices became more distant—which, in the view of purists, constituted a sort of degradation. When collective, Brazilian sorcery showed its specific face by way of adopting African rituals of possession, mainly those from the Niger River region and the Bantu area, especially when these rituals arrived in the Americas before the close of the eighteenth century.

A question remains that as far as I know has never been adequately answered. Why did history not coincide with memory? Why were the witches that existed in the Brazilian imagination European, if historical evidence documented a different kind of sorcery, one that was predominantly African? Was popular memory entirely sideswiped by the ideology of colonization, with Brazil having become, in its dreams and fantasies, a larger Portugal?

The problem became much more complex when viewed as more than just one of socially conditioned memory. If a cultivated poet such as Bernardo Guimarães registered in his verse, during the second half of the nineteenth century, the presence of the witches' Sabbath in the collective unconscious of the Brazilian elite, portraying, in *A orgia dos duendes*, the classic figure of the nocturnal witch so pervasive in European culture, there is documentary evidence attesting to the incorporation of this same imaginary by the poorer classes (Souza 1993, 181–95).

I will examine just one more example, one I have already discussed in another essay.[4] In 1758, the wandering missionary Manuel da Silva, a Jesuit priest who was traveling through the backlands of Piauí, took note of the confessions of two women, one mulatto and the other a Guegê Indian, thus bringing to light incidents of witchcraft involving two other mulatto women, one a freedwoman and the other a slave of a military commander, José de Abreu Bacelar. Piauí at this time was one of the most unsettled and poorest areas of Portuguese America. Administratively speaking, it belonged to the state of Brazil, and ecclesiastically it was part of the archdiocese of Maranhão, which administratively belonged to another part of the Portuguese Empire, the state of Grand Pará and Maranhão. Unlike the Spanish colonies, the Portuguese territories in the Americas did not have courts of the Holy Inquisition. Thus, all suspects of crimes against the faith were denounced to commissaries and, in their absence, to members of the orders or regular clergy. In the case we are discussing, the accused women appeared before the missionary priest and confessed their crimes. Their confessions were sent to Lisbon and added to the *Cadernos do promotor*, which registered denouncements and free confessions that had not become official cases of the Inquisition.

Joana Pereira de Abreu, a slave, was the first to confess, describing how Cecília, a mixed-race freedwoman, had taught her a certain rite on the eve of the Feast of St. John: she should renounce the Catholic faith and stand nude at the door of the church in the village of Moucha, where she lived, and tap it three times with her buttocks, walking backward and uttering the name "Tunda." She was then to walk naked to a graveyard and wait for a youth who, "after she had gotten down on her hands and knees," would possess her from behind.

The first part of the testimony referred to acts that occurred in the village of Moucha. The second part had to do with a later period, when, after having been bought by the military leader Bacelar, Joana went to live on the plantation of Cajazeiras and to frequent, along with three other mulatto women, among them her sister, Josefa Linda, a place close to Moucha called Enforcado. Despite its distance from the plantation, the women arrived quickly, without knowing how they had gotten there: "I am taken there I know not how," Joana confessed. Upon arrival, they met Mistress Cecília—almost always referred to this way in the document—"seated on a bench or a three-legged chair." There were large numbers of women, "of all colors and classes," who had come from far and wide, supposedly by the same quick and mysterious means that had brought Joana and her companions. The individuals of the male sex, presumably, were demons. The participants greeted each other, made reverences and cursed, and, incited by Mistress Cecília, who would say, "Let's enter our new life," they surrendered themselves to the "infernal exercises of the demons, until the cock's crow." At times, Mistress Cecília and some other women would remain with their backs aligned against those of their male companions, as in the European descriptions of satanic dances. Finally, Mistress Cecília would call them back to reality, with the words, "Our new life has ended, so we can leave." Joana and her friends traveled the sixty or seventy leagues that separated them from their home on the Cajazeiras plantation, without feeling distance or physical exhaustion. "And if they opened the doors for us, which were closed, I know not how."

The second testimony came from Custódia de Abreu, a Gueguê Indian, who, like Joana, divided her statement into two parts. In the first, she talked about erotic games she played with Josefa Linda, who thus trained her for the acts that she would later practice with the devil. Associated with these games was the adoration of the devil and various acts of disrespect before images of Christ on the cross and of Our Lady of Carmen, as well as disrespect to the sacraments, to the saints, to the Virgin Mary, to the clergy, and to the church. The most curious aspect of this was that they referred to Christ as a rogue and Our Lady as a strumpet. In the second part of her confession, Custódia told of her submission to the devil, who appeared under various forms, performed torpid acts with the Indian and Josefa Linda, and stomped on the Host, which she had stolen for him during mass. At the end of her tale, she mentioned that the women of Moucha associated with the devil, whom they called "Tunda," and, as mentioned, they would go at night to the door of the church and tap it with their buttocks, and then go "to the graveyard in search of the bones of pagan children."

The last testimony by women of Cajazeiras closes with a brief presentation by Maria Leonor, a white girl of fifteen who lived with her widowed mother in the house of the military commander, her uncle. Joana had told her "to see if she was interested," that in Moucha "there were women who took Tunda with the devil." If her statement can be believed, the episode had no effect on the girl: the only sin she admitted to was that she "had learned with one of the family's slave women to recite *I Believe in God the Father* backwards."

The Piauí case involved Indians, mulattoes, and whites—the latter of which included the Jesuit missionary, who was simultaneously inquisitor and scribe. The content of the confessions is impressively European, but the allusions to Tunda send up a red flag: perhaps this was the original nucleus, which the missionary failed to understand and was thereafter eclipsed by the descriptions of a more sabbatic character, induced (or deduced) by him based on fragments.

Was the Jesuit responsible for the sabbatic tone of the written version of the confessions of the mulatto women of Piauí? If so, why did this transformation take on such significance and root itself in the secular memory of the Brazilian people?

One last piece of empirical evidence may help to better understand how the pathways linking history and memory are shaped. In 1775, a denouncement arrived in Lisbon about a group of wealthy landowners of Portuguese extraction who lived in Minas Gerais because of mining interests and who had become involved with a black sorcerer, known as Antonio Angola. Mônica, matriarch of the family, was a credulous soul and given to solving her daily problems by resorting to what were officially considered superstitions and hoaxes. Her house was always full of faith healers who had reputations of being sorcerers. Illnesses, in Mônica's view, could be cured by spells. Her son-in-law, Henrique Brandão, was Portuguese and officially attached (*familiar*) to the Holy Inquisition; thus one would have thought that he would have denounced such acts against the Catholic faith. But, quite the contrary, he personally went with his mother-in-law to Paraopeba, to bring the black sorcerer back to their home and remain there, "to help bring them health and wealth."

The most spectacular of all, however, was a public display by the sorcerer in the town of Macacos. Antonio Angola appeared at midday, dressed in red and wearing on his shoulders "a pallium, covered with feathers of various birds, laid on top of jaguar skins and a headdress with diverse feathers, and carrying in his hand other plumes." João Coelho de Avelar, another Portuguese, accompanied the black man, carrying in his hand a pot full of roots steeped in boiling water, prepared and blessed by Antonio Angola himself. Using a monkey's tail, which he dipped into the infusion, he sprinkled the liquid onto the heads of those present, suggesting they drink it to rid themselves of hexes (*feitiços*) and obtain good fortune. The procession stopped at some houses that the black man declared to be afflicted by *feitiços* and, when asked where they had come from, he

> responded from above, giving to understand that they came from the house of Maria de Ceytas, the wife of Manoel da Silva Lopes, which led to the conclusion that the aforementioned Mônica, mortal enemy of Ceytas, planned to destroy her by creating the rumor that she was a sorceress, because [Mônica] was her mortal enemy because of an inheritance from Ceytas's parents, and that [Ceytas] was an honorable woman, even if she was mixed-race.

To remove the *feitiços* from the afflicted houses, Antonio Angola demanded payment, asking loudly for "alms for the Calundu," while he "hyssoped the houses with the said hyssop of monkey's tail." In this way, he received payments of chickens, gold, even jewels: the wife of Manoel Lopes dos Santos, Mônica's sister, "having no gold with her, removed her earrings and gave them to the Negro."[5]

That Portuguese citizens, one of them involved with the Holy Inquisition, who resided in the most urban region of Portuguese America would follow a procession accompanying an African sorcerer seems quite as extraordinary as the account of mixed-race women in the backlands of Piauí participating in satanic gatherings. Popular memory has fixed upon the European image of the witch, not only because the dominant ideology was European or because Europeans were missionaries and colonizers, but because this image was shared.

On the other hand, today, metropolises such as São Paulo are experiencing an impressive growth of Afro-Brazilian cult houses because these beliefs have been present in Luso-American cities for centuries. The pathways of memory and cultural miscegenation—or syncretism—were diverse and reflected the social roles of the actors involved, returning us, once again, to the problem of cultural circularity, accentuated in social contexts such as that of Brazil, which has absorbed various and complex cultural traditions.

Perhaps the day will come when we, scholars of sorcery and magical practices, will find it necessary to locate the precise region that gave birth to traditions that in the past we generically described as European. But this will only happen when Brazilians' uneasy consciences with respect to Africa and slavery are finally appeased. From the scholarly perspective, this possibility seems to me pertinent and interesting. From the ideological and political point of view, however, there is the risk of being interpreted as endorsing the view of the conquerors, and because of this, it remains in the distant future.

From the cultural, political, and ideological point of view, thus, the study of sorcery in Brazil opens a Pandora's box of problems that are much bigger and more complex than in Europe. We cannot, however, turn our backs—and we never wished to do so—on what is developing on this continent. In the end, one of the good things about globalization—and, as we know, there are not that many—is that it lends specific research projects a sense of belonging to a more general body of knowledge.

Notes to Chapter Three

This chapter and all quoted text in it was translated from Portuguese by Lisa Earl Castillo.

1. For further discussion on Calundu, see also Reis (this volume).
2. Yeda Pessoa de Castro (2001, 192) for *calundu*; page 196 for *candomblé*; pages 266-7 for *lundu*; and page 267 for *macaca*. See also Pereira (1939, i, 123) and Cascudo (1972, 211-2).
3. All of these quotations are from the Inquisition proceedings against Luzia Pinta mentioned above, with special emphasis on the part referring to her confession, which was taken in Lisbon on June 7, 1743. See also Souza (1986, 267-8 and 352-7) and Mott (1994); about the feathers, see Mott (1994, 76).
4. All the data of this case derive from Instituto Arquivos Nacionais, Torre do Tombo (IANTT), Inquisition of Lisbon, *Caderno do Promotor* no. 121, book 313, folios 125-7. This document was transcribed and kindly ceded by Luiz Mott, who also wrote on the case (Mott 2006).
5. All of the quotations from this case derive from IANTT, Inquisition of Lisbon, Cadernos do Promotor, no. 129, book 318, folio 247.

4

Candomblé and Slave Resistance
in Nineteenth-Century Bahia

JOÃO JOSÉ REIS

THE EXPRESSION *"candomblé"* emerges for the first time in written record in 1807, and by the mid-nineteenth century it had already become the most frequently used term to denote religions of African extraction in Bahia. It referred both to a wide range of religious practices privately performed by ritual specialists and to groups of initiates hierarchically organized by a cult head around a temple or *terreiro* where a sort of "convent life," to use Roger Bastide's formula (Bastide 2001; see also Lima 2003), was observed. Public and private ceremonies were also held, especially spirit possession rituals to the sound of drums and the performance of dances usually in honor of African (and sometimes locally born) spirits, ancestors, or gods. Private practices such as divination, healing, and amulet making to protect from spiritual and physical ailments represented perhaps the most salient and widespread dimension of Candomblé life in nineteenth-century Bahia.

The term *candomblé*, although of Bantu extraction, meaning prayer, became in the course of the nineteenth century a trademark of primarily Jeje (Gbe-speaking) and Nagô (Yoruba-speaking) groups from West Africa, who represented the majority of slaves imported into Bahia during the last decades of the slave trade, which ended in 1850. Clearly the different Jeje and Nagô groups combined to create what can perhaps be largely considered a New World religion, even though much of what it included came from Africa. I concur with the idea that Africans remade or created anew much of their culture in the New World, but I will not concentrate my narrative on the dynamics of culture change. My subject here is Candomblé viewed not from a cultural formation perspective but rather from the dynamics of social relations, and more specifically slave-master relations.[1]

I will focus on the relationships between Candomblé and slavery, namely, how Candomblé helped slaves to cope with and even overcome slavery. In that sense, I address the old question of slave resistance. The connection between religion and resistance is a major theme in the study of American slave societies. The three most important slave movements in the antebellum U.S. South—Gabriel Prosser's in Richmond, 1800; Denmark Vesey's in Charleston, 1820; and Nat Turner's in Southampton, 1831— were in part or entirely inspired by Christian messages. In the Caribbean, African slaves used Obeah magic to improve their chances of successful uprisings in the seventeenth and eighteenth centuries, and, following the nineteenth-century creolization of the slave population, both cultural and demographic creolization, Christianity came to be the predominant language of slave resistance. The most important examples were the 1820 rebellion in Demerara and the 1831 rebellion in Jamaica—later known as the Baptist War—both major slave revolts that boosted the abolitionist movement in England. At the same time, the literature on U.S. slavery has paid close attention to the interplay between slave religion and day-to-day resistance, where Christian morality justified small acts of deviation from the norms of the slaveholding order (Egerton 1993; Oates 1975; da Costa 1994; Genovese 1974, 1979; Raboteau 1978; Sterling 1988).

The theme is not new in the literature on African religion or slavery in Brazil, where, for instance, the role of Islam in the nineteenth-century Bahian revolts has been discussed since the turn of the twentieth century. Popular Catholicism has also been studied both as an instrument of collective, violent revolt and primarily of day-to-day resistance. Historians have at the same time studied the way "traditional" African religions were used on a daily basis by slaves in their effort to cope with and even attack slavery. Roger Bastide constructed much of his classic study on the formation of the Afro-Brazilian religions around the idea of micropolitical resistance to slavery and African cultural resistance to seigniorial religious values. More recently, Luiz Mott, Laura de Mello e Souza, and James Sweet also addressed the involvement of Calundu and other African and Afro-Brazilian magico-religious practices with the struggle of slaves against masters, police, and Church authorities.[2] Closer to the subject of this paper, other historians have covered the role of Candomblé specifically in advancing slave resistance in nineteenth-century Bahia. Rachel Harding, in particular, wrote a book in which Candomblé is forcefully viewed as a major aspect of resistance to masters' hegemonic cultural values and modes of domination. I myself have discussed Candomblé as a tool of both slave negotiation and conflict from the end of the eighteenth through the nineteenth century.[3]

Candomblé's basic features were brought to Brazil by African captives, but the religion expanded its clientele and membership considerably in the course of the nineteenth century. At the same time that African religion was creolized, so to speak, and perhaps because of it, African-born slaves ceased to be the only group embracing or practicing it. Indeed, African freed persons made up the bulwarks of nineteenth-century Candomblé. Freedmen and women represented the vast majority of both Candomblé leadership and its rank and file, which can be ascertained by merely counting those who were denounced in correspondence to police authorities and in newspaper reports as well as those actually accused of participation and/or arrested by the police in Candomblé public and private ceremonies. Candomblé also recruited *mestiços* and whites—primarily, although not exclusively, as clients—including individuals who belonged to the slave-owning elite and even Catholic priests. In that sense, although Candomblé represented in many respects "a refuge in thunder" for exiled African slaves, as Rachel Harding (2000) argues, it went way beyond that. In other words, Candomblé was not simply a slave religion, which is one primary reason why it is somewhat complicated to discuss it only in terms of slave resistance. Candomblé would rather seem to be a set of beliefs and practices that implied resistance by different groups and individuals to predominantly Western values, in particular Catholic conventional doctrine, as well as medical and other allegedly scientific procedures. However, both Catholic devotees and secular intellectuals were often given to Candomblé practices, and they did not cease to be Catholics or moderns for this reason. Indeed, people in Brazil regularly circulated through different cultural codes without necessarily making this movement a banner of resistance to anything in particular, or of tolerance to different faiths, but rather of useful additions to their struggles against misfortune of all kinds, be it diseases, failed love, or business and political affairs. Religious life unfolded in complex, hybrid ways as one drew near the periphery of the various systems of knowledge, where myths, rituals, and symbols could be more freely shared or negotiated. And Candomblé did become a superb tool of negotiation for a wider cultural and social space disputed by Africans and their local allies.

Slave masters were among those who often sought Candomblé—just as they had sought Calundu during Brazil's colonial era—for a number of spiritual and material needs. (And when I say masters, I have in mind that blacks and mulattos, including African freed persons, and even a few slaves themselves could also own slaves.) Slave owners could share with their bondmen and -women similar attitudes toward the spiritual world and the mechanisms to deal with it, including witchcraft procedures. Being a male, white, Catholic slave master represented no impediment to seek a cure for himself or family members with an African healer following the failure of other methods such as conventional medicine or Catholic prayer and masses to patron saints. Unexpected results were reached sometimes. In 1864, a master in Salvador, Bahia's capital, consulted a famous African diviner and healer about curing his wife only to find out that her lingering illness was allegedly caused by witchcraft dispensed by one of his domestic female slaves. The latter was brutally punished by her master.[4] Situations such as this one make it difficult to automatically attach the resistance paradigm to Candomblé practices. In that respect, I would disagree with James Sweet (2003, 120, 135) that even when condemning other slaves to the wrath of masters, African diviners challenged slavery because their judicial methods were being chosen over the masters'. In this case, I would rather argue that slave control and domination benefited from masters' acceptance of African ritual norms.

An additional problem to considering Candomblé as slave resistance is the fact that slave masters could be Candomblé priests or priestesses themselves. Francisca da Silva, also known by the name of her title, Iyá Nassô, the legendary founder of one of the most traditional Candomblé houses in Bahia, the Ilê Iyá Nassô Oká (popularly known as Casa Branca), and her husband owned fifteen slaves, the majority of them women, between 1832 and 1837.[5] Marcelina da Silva, also known as Obatossi, a former slave of Francisca and her successor as head of the religious community, owned eighteen slaves between 1844 and 1878. Several other Candomblé priests, diviners, and healers possessed slaves as their most valuable property. As the case of Marcelina illustrates, these slaves were themselves often initiates of the Candomblé houses led by their masters and mistresses (Castillo and Parés 2007; Reis 2008).

Yet I would argue that Candomblé, especially divination and medicinal practices, may still be considered an important tool of slave struggles every time slaves used it to challenge or at least ameliorate their subaltern position in society. In 1879, a certain Senhorinha, who lived in Salvador, was slowly killed by her slave Elias, who introduced certain leaves into the wine she used to drink. Senhorinha was not a mean mistress, for in a will apparently written a long time before she died she manumitted three slave children, a treatment that perhaps Elias wanted for himself as well in return for his good services.[6] Episodes such as this one explain why, although far from being unanimously accepted, the concept that Candomblé and slavery did not make a good mixture was widespread among masters, police, and political authorities in nineteenth-century Bahia. The more than thirty known slave uprisings and conspiracies that shook the region in the first half of that century, and in which the Nagô nation played a leading role, were possibly inspired by warrior gods, such as Ogun, the god of iron and war, who became increasingly popular in Yorubaland at the most intense phase of the Bahian slave trade from that region in the 1820s through the 1840s.[7]

There is at least one case for which evidence exists of Candomblé involvement with a slave uprising, namely, the Urubu revolt of 1826. This revolt began with the gathering of fugitive slaves from Salvador in a *quilombo* (runaway slave settlement) on the outskirts of the city, a place known as Urubu. The plan was to attack the capital on Christmas eve, kill the white population, and attain freedom. The revolt was aborted ten days before it was to take place by *capitães-do-mato* (bush captains, fugitive slave hunters) who attacked the *quilombo*. The slave hunters were initially repelled but returned with reinforcements and defeated the rebels. Three Africans died, some were taken prisoner, and most fled into the bushes.[8]

The police found a Candomblé cult house on the site where the *quilombo* had been implanted. Among the confiscated objects were "dance paraphernalia used by blacks," as well as loose cowry shells (commonly used for divination), rattles, drums, "a cardboard crown decorated with sea shells" (probably part of the ritual attire belonging to a royal Orisa, the general term for Yoruba gods, such as Shango or Ogun), statues of "cows painted red, a red hat with three feathers," and so on. The clothes, torsos, and wands found were also predominantly red, which suggests that this was a Candomblé dedicated to Shango—the mythic *alafin* or king of Oyo, the powerful northern Yoruba kingdom—whose color symbol is red. Urubu seemed to be one of these places in the suburbs of Salvador where *quilombos* and *candomblés* melded. Its very name, Urubu, or "vulture," may have derived from the presence on the site of African cult houses, since around them vultures abounded, attracted as they were by the remains of animals sacrificed to African gods and ancestors. These birds are part of Yoruba mythology because they are believed to carry sacrificial offerings to their proper destination. Verses of Ifa, the Yoruba divination system, confirm this:

> Vulture, come and eat sacrifice
> So that sacrifice may be acceptable to the gods.
> One does not always realize that without vultures,
> One cannot perform a sacrifice.[9]

It seems that the site of the rebel *quilombo* was full of Nagô/Yoruba religious symbolism, but it does not wholly prove that the Candomblé house found there participated organizationally in the uprising.

The only other occasion that I know in which Candomblé and a *quilombo* were involved in a violent clash with the police was an incident that took place far away from the capital city, in the southern Bahian littoral village of Barra do Rio de Contas, in 1859. The chief of police reported that an African religious meeting place had evolved into a large *quilombo* and was attacked by armed men led by the local district police officer (*subdelegado*), resulting in four deaths—one national guardsman and "three on the part of the resisters, among whom an African woman who fought with a firearm, and was killed in the conflict, another one being wounded."[10] Here again our source, the chief of police, is too vague on the role of Candomblé in the *quilombo*, but the relationship between the two was clearly recognized.

Accusations that slavery and Candomblé did not match up abound in police records and newspaper reports. In 1853, a *subdelegado* who arrested a Hausa freedman by the name of Cipriano José Pinto in São Francisco do Conde, a village in the Recôncavo, the main sugar plantation region of Bahia, and confiscated and destroyed his Candomblé ritual objects argued that the existence of a "great number of Africans" in the area made his cult house a dangerous venture. The authority defined his raid as a preventive measure against "the bad results that could eventually obtain from (the operation of) similar clubs."[11] In Pinto's Candomblé cult house, the police officer found a long list of votive objects, animal sacrifices, and papers written in Arabic that were reminiscent of those used by the 1835 Muslim rebels in Salvador.[12] The policeman feared that the Candomblé cult house—probably a Hausa Bori venture—would eventually become a seditious "club," that is, an organization dedicated to promote revolts among local plantation slaves. Nothing indicates, however, that Cipriano Pinto had this in mind, despite his Muslim writings. The relationship between Candomblé and slave resistance followed more often a less dramatic path and acquired the dimension of day-to-day resistance to slavery.[13]

In both 1826 and 1859 violence resulted from police repression of a *quilombo*-cum-Candomblé gathering, but only the first case is known to have involved a concerted conspiracy with plans to defeat slavery. Generally, the association between a *quilombo* and Candomblé did not imply collective, armed resistance but rather peaceful slave flight and festive gatherings. In the beginning of the nineteenth century, Bahia's newly appointed colonial governor the Count of Ponte decided to severely repress the *quilombos* and Candomblé houses that abounded in the suburbs of Salvador. The governor's report to Lisbon, written in April 1807, read

Seeing that slaves frequently and repeatedly escaped from their masters in whose service they had been engaged for years ... I became curious ... about where it was they went. I soon learned that in the outskirts of this capital and in the thickets that surround it, there were innumerable assemblages of these people who, led by the hand of industrial charlatans, enticed the credulous, the lazy, the superstitious, those given to thievery, criminals, and the sickly to join them. They lived in absolute liberty, dancing, wearing extravagant dress, phony amulets, uttering fanatical prayers and blessings. They lay around eating and indulging themselves, violating all privileges, law, order, public demeanor.[14]

This was not a completely new phenomenon. Roger Bastide (1971, i, 193, 220) suggested that Calundu and *quilombo* were associated in the minds of whites. He probably had in mind a seventeenth-century satirical poem by Gregorio de Mattos in which such connection is made.

The same connection continued to be made in Bahia way into thse nineteenth century, and, what is more telling, urban dwellings where candomblé rituals were performed were associated with *quilombos*, which was a typically rural or at least suburban phenomenon. In 1869, the newspaper O *Alabama* defined as *quilombos* the residential buildings occupied by Africans in a street of the populous São Pedro parish, in the heart of Salvador, where, besides sheltering numerous people squeezed inside small rooms, "the drums, dances and cries boil until late at night" (*"fervem constantemente os tabaques, as danças e as gritarias que se prolongam até alta noite"*) in rituals dedicated to African gods or honoring recently deceased Candomblé members. The newspaper also complained about the foul smell of animal sacrifices emanating from those buildings.[15]

The image of Candomblé cult houses as *quilombo* was more than metaphorical and was justified by the frequency with which slaves left the service of their masters to attend all kinds of religious ceremonies or to consult with diviners and healers, either in Candomblé *terreiros* (that is, cult houses) or in their residences. In February 1859, in a site known as Quinta das Beatas, where Candomblé houses thrived, forty-two persons were arrested, among them seven fugitive African slaves. Later in that same year, the police chief announced a large operation in the capital and the interior to close down *terreiros*. The police chief had in mind particularly African funeral ceremonies, sometimes lavish festivals organized under the pretext of seventh-day Catholic Mass ceremonies for the deceased's soul, which attracted "people of all colors and conditions" born in the country, not only Africans as it should be expected. This kind of mixture was considered appalling by many watchful individuals in the political and social hierarchy, who thought that some sort of social separation helped to keep public order and enhanced European civilization in the tropics. One element in the mixture, namely, slaves, was especially undesirable. "The majority of the slave flights," wrote the police authority, "originated in these drumming sessions (*batuques*), in which they (the slaves) stayed for days, and fearing a deserved punishment (by their masters) they abscond to very far, and sometimes commit suicide."[16] Suicide was perhaps considered by some slaves a last, permanent flight to the other world, which for many meant Africa, a journey for which they undoubtedly negotiated with their gods and ancestors, who normally condemned that style of death.

In December 1864, the police attacked a *terreiro* headed by the African freedman Paulo Vieira in a site called Campo Seco, again on the outskirts of Salvador, and confiscated four drums, several ritual costumes, two pots, and other containers filled with infusions of rotten leaves, "with which the said African Paulo Vieira used to cure severe deceases, divine and exorcise the devil from the bodies of the ignorant, extorting for that end not small amounts of money."[17] Of the twenty-two individuals "of both sexes" arrested, nine were African freed persons and four were Creole slaves, two of whom had been astray for some two months from masters who lived in Inhambupe, a village in the interior of Bahia. The other two slaves were not considered fugitives yet, and they may have negotiated with their masters some break time, an arrangement usually unwelcome by police authorities.[18] In April 1862, for instance, the chief of police took measures to guarantee that masters "watch over their slaves' behavior and see to it that they retire [to their houses] before curfew, sleep at home and do not wander through the streets."[19] A few masters did tolerate short-term flights that lasted, say, hours, as long as they did not become a routine. In 1869, Amaro Gomes Vieira asked the police for the release of two of his slaves who had been jailed in the *Casa de Correção* ("house of correction") after having been arrested for being "in a house of entertainment that the people call Candomblé."[20] Masters usually asked the police to punish slaves arrested for this kind of transgression, but this was not the case with Vieira. That masters did not accept systematic escapades, however, is illustrated by a letter written in November 1874 by Felipa Laura Maria da Conceição to Bahia's police chief, in which she complained that her African slave named Maria was a chronic runaway who often disappeared to go to Candomblé houses, "disobeying her and refusing to perform even a few domestic tasks." When Felipa Conceição penned these words, Maria had already been arrested, and her mistress asked the police chief to punish the rebel slave woman with three dozen strikes with the ferule on the palms of her hands before returning her back to captivity.[21]

Ceremonies to the gods or to the dead could last for days, during which time masters simply had their slave labor force withheld from them, which was more than a simple nuisance for the ordinary workings of the slave order. In April 1873, in the district of Saboeiro, a Candomblé house that gathered a large number of devotees and noisy visitors from all walks of life, including "fugitive slaves," had been beating the drums for days and loudly enough to disturb the neighbors.[22] Slaves systematically challenged the authority of masters to attend these Candomblé assemblies, out of devotion, desire, or for the fun of it, to socialize with social peers, to see or seek lovers, and so on. Women represented the majority of these runaways, thus adding a gender dimension to this kind of trouble—to say the least—for slavery. In 1870, O Alabama proclaimed that slave women dared to risk "leaving home without the authorization of those who govern them" so that they could participate in the New Yam festival, dedicated to the Yoruba god Orisala, which lasted for a couple of days and opened the annual cycle of public religious ceremonies in many Bahian terreiros.[23]

Women such as these mentioned by the newspaper were probably full members of terreiros, meaning that they were initiated priestesses. Although the majority of highly placed Candomblé devotees were freed persons, some slaves played important roles in the religious hierarchy, but they were usually men. In 1828, a slave owned by a member of a powerful Bahian family, that of the baron of Pirajá, figured as guardian of the drums in a Jeje terreiro attacked by the police in Nossa Senhora de Brotas, a semirural parish of Salvador. On this occasion, this slave, whose name is unknown, led others in a visit to the justice of the peace who ordered the police raid to complain against his action, which resulted in the arrest of many Creole and African slave and freedwomen. A leader in the Candomblé, the drummer was also a feitor, or overseer, which means that slaves holding sensitive, privileged positions in the slaveholding system could also break the norm. In this case, however, resistance was not precisely against master control but against the state represented by a petty police officer known for his tyranny against African Candomblé goers (Reis and Silva 1989, 48-50). Many years after this incident, in 1864, I found Batula, the Creole slave of another baron with the title of Rio Vermelho, who also held the post of drummer in a very active Candomblé house led by the Angolan priestess Ana Maria, the cult head, and by pai ("father") Francisco, its head drummer. Besides promoting trance sessions to receive the gods with dances and drumming, the couple exorcised spells, arranged marriages, and cured the sick, usually charging very high fees.[24] One can imagine that part of this money was redistributed to members of the Candomblé hierarchy, which in this case included a slave drummer.

Many slaves probably bought their freedom with money earned from providing religious services. José Zacarias, for instance, a reputed diviner in Rio Fundo, a Recôncavo parish, was in 1798 accused of divining for "many vile and poor, but also upright people," from whom he received "large sums with which he has extinguished his misery and captivity."[25] Zacarias was certainly not the only enslaved ritual specialist who achieved freedom this way.

If they were *quilombos,* Candomblé houses were rather special ones in the sense that the majority of their leaders and even members were not slaves but free or, in their majority, freed African-born persons or their descendants.[26] I could identify only two slaves performing the role of Candomblé leaders in nineteenth-century Bahia. One was an Angolan slave by the name of Antonio, described by a militia captain in 1807 as "president of the candomblé terreiro" (*presidente do terreiro dos candombleis*). A successful Candomblé cult head, healer, and diviner, Antonio lived away from his mistress, actually in a different town, on land that belonged to a sugar plantation, the Fazenda Boa Vista, in Santo Amaro, where he had established his *terreiro.* There he gathered "numerous people from some neighboring *Engenhos* [sugar plantations] on the eve of holy days and Sundays." In spite of being young, according to a police report he "demanded that others ask for his blessings and obey him, even the elderly." Antonio would probably soon buy his freedom with the money he received for his service, or, on the contrary, he may have decided that he would keep his slave status to benefit from the protection it implied, especially if he was on good terms with his mistress, as seemed to be the case.[27]

The other enslaved cult head I found in the archives was Manuel, who also lived away from his mistress and who was accused in 1871 by *O Alabama* of having founded a *terreiro* on Caminho do Inferno (Hell Road!), in the vicinity of Salvador. Manuel divined, cured witchcraft victims, promoted and destroyed marriages, reconciled lovers, and, most importantly, oversaw and performed spirit possession ritual dances to the sound of drums, which indicates the existence of a complex religious community under his command.[28]

In both cases, the enslaved priests had developed exceptionally loose or special relationships with their proprietors, managing to live completely on their own. One can guess that either their owners feared or appreciated their slaves' power as manipulators of mysterious spiritual forces and their knowledge of poisonous herbs or they just allowed their bondsmen to live and work unhindered as long as they paid their owners part of what they earned as religious leaders. This was a common arrangement between slaves for hire and masters, especially in the urban setting. For most slave owners it did not matter if their men and women obtained money by performing witchcraft or by performing some other kind of craft.

For most Bahian masters, slave membership in Candomblé temples was a problem more than a solution. And the name of the problem was slave flight, if not for good, for an extended period. Slaves could abandon the company of masters for several months to undergo initiation rites. The police received constant complaints from masters who accused Candomblé cult heads of keeping slaves imprisoned in the *terreiros*, where they were allegedly drugged and put to work for them. There were of course strong and complex ritual reasons, with secular implications, for slaves to follow the rules of sometimes despotic priests besides those of their masters. The *Alabama* told the story of a master who urged the police to search a Candomblé house in the Campinas district, outside Salvador, where his slave woman had been "cloistered" by force with several other initiates to undergo ritual obligations that would last between three and six months. Forewarned about the police raid, the *terreiro*'s chief priestess quickly hid elsewhere the group of female novices, except the one the police wanted, who was properly dressed (initiates spent much of their seclusion time naked or seminaked) and delivered to the officers. The newspaper reporter described the small room (*camarinha*) where the initiates had been lodged as extremely filthy and fetid (they ate and defecated on the room's earthen floor, for example), so much so that the women could only stand it because they had been drugged to the point of loosing control over their senses and willpower. Herbs that altered one's perception might have been part of the initiation process, which, as in most rites of passage, could be in certain respects as painful as slavery itself.

According to *O Alabama*'s report, after the time spent in seclusion the initiates—whether slave or free—would still "serve as slaves to the people who had bought them in the saint," most likely referring to patrons who had paid for the usually considerable expenses involved in the initiation rites to become a priest/priestess dedicated to a specific African god/goddess or "saint."[29] Nina Rodrigues (1935, 85) described the phenomenon in the 1890s:

> Having finished the period of initiation, the daughter-of-the-saint [female initiate] ends up belonging to the mother of the *terreiro* who did her [the initiate's] saint and can only return to her family and go back home after a true purchase. The price paid by the husband, lover, or family for the daughter-of-the saint varies according to the resources they possess. Purchase arranged, the daughter-of-the-saint is taken with great ceremony to the door of her house and solemnly delivered to the buyer.[30]

Rodrigues's ethnography was written a few years after slavery was abolished, otherwise he would probably have included slaves and masters among the characters involved. The description, however, suggests that the painful experience of initiation represented a radical rupture with the secular world, which included slavery. Under seclusion, neophytes were taught total subordination to the gods (or "saints") they would serve for the rest of their lives. When isolation was suspended, they had to learn all over again the conventions of the outside world, from the language they spoke to the modes of subordination that they experienced before entering the initiation room. In other words, slaves had to learn to be slaves for a second time. However, they would never be the same persons again, if for nothing else because they were now to serve, dedicate their time and resources, to more than one master, so to speak.

One can only imagine the pressure under which slaves had to live. It is not hard to guess why some may have committed suicide, as the chief of police pointed out. Maybe, however, the idea that slave bodies possessed by African spirits became free bodies is not only poetry, "a stunning contestation of subalternity," as Harding (2000, 156) writes. More to the point, it can be argued that as a form of temporary flight from conventional reality, possession represented a temporary flight from slavery as well. In any case, after initiation, slavery as it existed before suffered a significant blow. Slaves did not seek a religious pledge necessarily as a strategy to fight slavery or even aspects of it but for other equally deep personal needs—for example, the need to fulfill a family devotional tradition or to overcome a serious disease. Whatever the starting point, however, the end result radically affected slaves' relations with masters.

In 1872, José Luis Bananeira complained to the chief of police that a young Creole woman who was born a slave in his house and manumitted under the condition that she serve him until his death disappeared from his company and for six years "was given to the relaxation and depravation of the drumming sessions (*batuques*)." Bananeira was in his eighties and alleged he was living in poverty because he had freed all his eleven slaves unconditionally, except Gracinda, who certainly considered his decision unfair. Gracinda lived outside Bananeira's control with a man by the name of Manoel Inácio de Oliveira, probably her lover, who worked for the city transportation company and according to Bananeira took her regularly to a place called Jaburu, in the Island of Itaparica, to a Candomblé house where she may have been initiated and where she had to fulfill ritual obligations regularly. Oliveira would then be the person responsible for hiding the fugitive, a conditionally freed woman, but also the person who promoted her affiliation to Candomblé. "Since she did not want to pay the rightful services to the supplicant," her master wrote, he asked the chief of police to arrest her and suggested that she be punished by forcing her to clean the House of Correction—where slaves and petty criminals were deposited—in Salvador, "until she is corrected and rented out to someone else," the fruits of her labor accruing to him.[31]

Bananeira's accusation against Oliveira was mild compared with allegations that an African priest known as Candeal was trying to sell someone else's slave who was now under his spell. Candeal headed a Candomblé *terreiro* in the Our Lady of Brotas parish where he had interned Auta and other young women to undergo initiation procedures that would last one whole year. The accusation came from an African freedwoman, Maria Perciliana Bandeira, Auta's owner. According to her, Candeal had already forged papers as proof of his alleged ownership of the slave woman so he could pursue his wicked plan successfully. It is possible that Maria Bandeira fabricated the accusation of theft in order to prompt the police to rescue her slave from Candeal's initiation room. Again, the point here is that initiation rites competed with the master's command over his slaves.[32]

These are stories about slaves who fled from their masters, sometimes for long periods of time, to attend Candomblé ceremonies, during which time they simply suspended their lives under captivity, at least as far as the supply of labor to masters was concerned. These slaves, according to an expression commonly used at the time, had become *inutilizados*, or useless for their owners. There were other ways of becoming an *inutilizado* slave. In 1861 an African freedwoman of the Nagô nation by the name of Constança was accused of "rendering useless" several slaves on a sugar plantation through her ability to manipulate strong medicine. She was apparently sought after by slaves who had lost their will to work in the cane fields or who had gained the will to boycott their master's production. The owner of the property, João de Argolo Ferrão, a powerful planter belonging to a traditional aristocratic family, had his version of Constança's activities. He accused her of fatally poisoning her own husband, a field laborer, and another man who was a sugar master (the person who oversaw the sugar-making complex process) and proclaimed that the African woman "used Candomblés and all these means seized upon by these idolatrous people to instill terror and credulity into the willpower of those who go to her house for divination [. . .] and thus apply her herbs and poisonous drinks to those she for some reason dislikes, and those she wants to eliminate . . ." The sugar planter complained of the "financial loss [*prejuízo*] that the undersigned suffered in two of his best slaves, one of them being his sugar master and a slave of high price and merit."[33]

We do not need to believe entirely Ferrão's version of this affair; he might be secretly fearing for his own life at the hands of slaves instructed and given poisonous potions by the African freedwoman. He certainly feared Constança's ability to hurt, to provoke pain, disease, and ultimately death. In other words, the planter believed in witchcraft as a force that militated against his slaveholding interest and therefore that challenged slavery itself. However, as much as Ferrão's slave property was hurt by Constança's acts, the death of slaves through poisoning by other slaves or freed persons cannot be automatically considered resistance against masters or, more broadly, against the slaveholding order as it has often been considered by historians. By destroying masters' property, the slave system was harmed and therefore this was resistance, so the argument goes. Souza (1986, 206, 208-9), for instance, warns that, instead of attacking masters' interests, "mutual accusations of witchcraft sometimes reflected tensions among the slaves themselves," although she does not always follow her own good warning, and Sweet (2003, 166-71) almost never does.[34] I would emphasize that, in cases such as these, some measure of intention to harm masters' interests should inevitably be evinced to identify slave resistance. Otherwise any conflict among slaves that resulted in the death or wounding of one or more of them would equally be deemed resistance—and violence within the slave community was the most frequent variety of slave violence (Machado 1987). In the case of Constança's doings, I can imagine both things happening: there were slaves who sought her to appease or even confront their masters and others who sought her to solve problems, including relations with personal enemies, by means of drugs they themselves drank or served to their foes.

Take another example. In 1807, a Jeje freedman by the name of Francisco Dossu, an itinerant, successful healer and diviner, was arrested during a witch-hunting operation motivated by a Muslim slave conspiracy in Salvador. Dossu was no social rebel, but he confessed that he healed and divined for "many white, mulatto and black people." It was up to his African lover to tell the police that Dossu also worked on the dark side of the medicinal business and that out of jealousy he had used a poisonous concoction to kill a Creole woman and her lover, the latter a sugar master on a Recôncavo plantation.[35] Because it has nothing to do with slave/master relationships, this story shows that conflict within the slave community—or the larger plantation laboring community, which included freed persons as well as slaves—could be decided by what was at the time defined as *feitiçaria*, or sorcery. There is not much in Constança's or Dossu's stories—which are unfortunately stories told by white opponents—

to define them unconditionally as slave resistance, although the authorities considered them as potential threats to local slavery.

Other *feitiçaria* procedures, conversely, were more directly pointed at slavery, for they were employed, as Souza puts it in her analysis of the phenomenon in colonial Brazil, "to prevent bad treatment inherent to the slaveholding system" (Souza 1986, 207). In 1882, again in the Recôncavo, this time in the town of Cachoeira, the local district officer informed the chief of police in Salvador that seventeen persons had been arrested in a site called Campinhos, in the house of a certain Maria Mina, an African freedwoman. According to the police officer, she was locally "known as a witch and against her there were several complaints from property owners about the evil caused by the superstition that she knows how to instill in slaves and ignorant persons, who, in the pursuit of happiness, deviate themselves from their duties by means of witchcraft."[36] Maria Mina, whose ritual objects were destroyed by the police, clearly deviated slaves from their duties to masters and therefore became an accessory to slave resistance.

The belief that sorcery could help slaves obtain manumission or break the willpower of and even kill their masters was widespread. One result that slaves regularly hoped to obtain from consulting with professed *feiticeiros* was embodied in expressions such as *"amansar senhor"* ("taming of the master"), *"abrandar o ânimo do senhor"* ("soften the willpower of the master"), and so on. The concept was not entirely new, as the studies by Souza (1986, 206–8) and Sweet (2003) demonstrate for the colonial period in details unfortunately unavailable in my nineteenth-century sources. Sweet mentions a 1646 episode involving a certain Domingos Umbata who, in order to protect two slave women from their mistresses' bad mood, recommended baths in water containing certain crushed leaves, a rattle, and a cougar's tooth. Half a century later, in 1702, a Jesuit priest reported that in the Bahian Recôncavo Angolan slaves used certain potions to appease their masters' mood. All over the Luso-Atlantic world, slaves used different means to reach the same goal. Some resorted to wheat roots, others to scraps from their masters' shoes soles, and still others chose powders made from human skulls to prepare the appropriate taming ingredients. The same year Domingos Umbata charmed slave mistresses, a Bahian *mulata*, Beatriz, filled her female owner's pillow with small amulets containing pieces of birds' feathers and beaks as well as pieces of seashells to ensure that her mistress treat her well and even "love" her. Souza shows that both witchcraft to tame masters and witchcraft to obtain freedom were not always of purely African origin but often derived from European or hybrid

European, African, and Indigenous magicoreligious traditions. Whatever their cultural sources, these procedures were used by slaves to improve their lot under slavery.[37]

In nineteenth-century Bahia, the taming of a master could mean controlling his wrath against slaves who stole from him, disobeyed, idled, or escaped. As we have seen, slaves often absconded to attend Candomblé ceremonies, and they subsequently returned to slavery and to an irate master who needed to be dealt with. In 1853, an African slave woman accused of poisoning the coffee she served to her masters' family on the island of Itaparica declared that she had only mixed cowry shell powder with lemon because "she was told it was good to soften masters."[38] The slave woman certainly knew that cowries, besides being used as currency on the coast of Africa, had important ritual functions, such as being instruments of divination, and could therefore help her reach the expected results. A report in O *Alabama* confirms that a major reason for slaves to seek Candomblé priests entailed efforts to break the spirit of masters. In 1868, the newspaper made a list of people who attended a Candomblé house in Salvador, which included—besides sexually unhappy married women and unsuccessful businessmen—"slaves who went to ask for ingredients to soften the willpower of their masters."[39] The master's taming procedures fit well with Harding's argument that "[t]he use of ritual, magico-phamacopoeic means to alter the extreme inequalities of power in colonial and slave-based societies must be understood as a principal form of black resistance to slavery in Brazil" (Harding 2000, 78). I certainly agree with her on this point.

Here is another good story. Domingos Pereira Sodré, known as *pai* (father, as Candomblé priests were usually addressed) Domingos, a freedman from Onin (present-day Lagos, Nigeria), was accused in 1862 of being a Candomblé priest who, among other things, divined and prepared concoctions to tame masters. The *subdelegado* who arrested Sodré wrote that the diviner sold slaves "drinks and mixtures" for them to "be able to tame their masters," which led to "the loss of many Africans who are today useless (*inutilizados*), their masters not being able to count on their labor."[40] If we are to believe in this verdict, Sodré's witchcraft promoted efficient slave resistance. Slaves purportedly abandoned or slowed down the work they owed their tamed, perhaps drugged masters believing that no harm would fall upon them for this behavior.

The concept of taming masters belonged to elementary sorcery protocol, of course. The tamed victim was one who submitted to the will of the person who commissioned the *feitiço*. In the case of the slave who tamed the master, the expected result was a reversal of the power structure. In a sense this can be considered counter-witchcraft, for slavery itself was seen by many Africans as a by-product of spells deployed against its victims. This was a well-known formula, often associated in the Atlantic slave trade circuit with Africans' perception of whites as cannibal witches.[41]

In addition, witchcraft directed at controlling masters' willpower may perhaps be seen as a strategy of resistance in the realm of paternalist domination typical of nineteenth-century Brazil. Resistance in this context implied that the resolve of the slave appeared as that of the master.[42] After all, *enfeitiçar* ("to bewitch") also means to seduce or to control the will of others—in a sentimental dimension, to tie one person to the other. Under paternalist cultural and ideological pressure, slaves often worked hard to create bonds of affection with masters through witchcraft or other means, including good behavior and steady work, but having failed this—or not even having tried—they struggled to untie their lives from those of their masters, through either a successful permanent flight or a negotiated manumission, if we rule out homicide and suicide as solutions. The services offered by Domingos Sodré and many other Candomblé priests supplied such a demand in Bahia.

Indeed—and more directly related to overcoming slavery—witchcraft could be used toward obtaining freedom. Accusations of this kind abounded. In 1848, a *subdelegado* denounced free Africans of the Nagô nation who worked in the navy arsenal of trying to induce enslaved Nagôs into "using witchcraft to obtain freedom" ("*fazerem feitiço e tratarem de liberdade*"). Unfortunately, details about specific witchcraft procedures are not offered by the sources. All we know is that a complaint from a master who owned thirty slaves specified that a free African by the name of Lucas, probably the *feiticeiro*, was "trying to lead astray" his bondmen, who refused to comply; for this reason some of them were attacked and wounded with clubs by Lucas's associates.[43]

Pai Domingos Sodré also worked in this branch of witchcraft, but for willing slaves. His potions could presumably weaken the will of his slave clients' masters when the time came for them to negotiate manumission terms, namely, the cost of freedom, if any, and conditions of freedom. Reporting on additional damage to the seigniorial order, the chief of police wrote that slaves stole money and valuable objects from their masters to give to Sodré to obtain "their freedom through sorcery." The police chief claimed that Salvador was full of "speculators" like Sodré and promised unrelenting repression against them "to guarantee other people's property and prevent sad consequences." He was keen on this point when he wrote, "these superstitions are much more damaging in a country in which a large part of its wealth is employed in slaves."[44] What the police chief did not realize was that Sodré led a manumission society, a kind of savings institution that lent slaves money to buy their freedom. At least part of what slaves stole from their masters almost certainly ended up in the manumission society's funds controlled by Sodré. However, Sodré did not bewitch masters or lead a manumission society out of ideological or moral opposition to slavery; he was himself a slave owner, and probably familiar with antidotes to medicines such as the ones he prepared to pacify other masters. Not only slaves were among his clients, but "people with necktie," that is, those in good standing, the socially elevated, whites, and so on, as reported by a contemporary.[45]

A slave owner himself, Domingos Sodré represents well the ambiguity, the ambivalence of Candomblé vis à vis slavery, for his experience, just like that of his religion in a wider sense, lay on the threshold between slavery and freedom. Candomblé served a wide range of devotees and clients, irrespective of their social backgrounds, including both slaves and masters (Reis 2001). Because it was staffed primarily by freed and free persons, Candomblé served as a showcase for slaves eager to achieve freedom, in addition to helping them to reach that goal through a series of ritual procedures often seen as witchcraft or *feitiço*. But because its leaders had to negotiate a breathing space in a hostile environment, they rarely attacked slavery head-on. In many ways slavery represented just one among other misfortunes against which Candomblé priests had to fight when healing the lives—the souls and bodies—of slave clients specifically. In that sense, Candomblé was often only marginally concerned with the question of slavery. The slaveholding system, however, almost always suffered from the interest slaves invested in Candomblé, for even when it only fulfilled spiritual needs that were unrelated to their pursuit of freedom, it still challenged slavery by simply competing with masters for their time, labor, and resources. In other words, slaves necessarily tested slavery when they associated their lives with that of Candomblé, which means that Candomblé cannot be easily separated from slave resistance. However, instead of converting this last sentence into a model or a paradigm, the best path to follow may be to interpret all the possible complexity and angles involved in each specific story emerging from the archives.

Notes to Chapter Four

1. On the process of African culture formation as creolization in the New World, see the classic essay by Mintz and Price (1992 [1976]) and more recently Price (2003). See also Trouillot (1998) and the valuable collection by Stewart (2007).

2. For a definition of *calundu*, see Sweet (2003, 144-5). See also Souza (this volume).

3. On the themes covered in this paragraph, see Rodrigues (1935); Machado (1994); Souza (1986); Sweet (2003); Bastide (1971); Mott (1988b); Harding (2000); Reis (1989, 1993, 2001, 2008); Graden (2006); Silveira (2006); Parés (2006).

4. *O Alabama*, January 12, 1864.

5. Iyá Nassô is the title for the priestess responsible for taking care of the *alafin*'s (king of Oyo) personal Shango.

6. *A Tribuna da Bahia* 4 (67), October 10, 1879.

7. On the expansion of Ogun's cult in nineteenth-century Yorubaland, see Ajayi (1974); Barnes and Ben-Amos (1997); and Peel (1997). See also, on what he calls "the Era of Ogun," Matory (1994, esp. 13-22). On the Bahian slave revolts, see Reis (1993).

8. For details on the 1826 revolt, see Reis (1993, 55-9).

9. See Wande Abimbola (1977, 210-11).

10. Arquivo Público do Estado da Bahia (hereafter APEBa), *Polícia. Correspondência expedida*, vol. 5726, Chief of Police to the President of Province, April 28, 1859, folio 320.

11. *Subdelegado-suplente* of Monte parish, Gustavo Balbino de Moura e Camira, to the *delegado* of São Francisco do Conde, March 15, 1853, Soares (1992, 139).

12. On this revolt, see Reis (1993).

13. Graden (2006, 128-31) suggests but does not fully demonstrates the role of Candomblé in the abolition of slavery as such in Bahia. On daily resistance of the subaltern, see Scott (1990), whose theory of everyday forms of resistance is understandably based on studies about U.S. slavery.

14. Count of Ponte to Viscount de Anadia, April 7, 1807. In *Anais da Biblioteca Nacional do Rio de Janeiro* 37 (1918): 450-1.

15. *O Alabama*, May 6, 1869. The edition of August 24, 1869, also refers to a *terreiro* (i.e., *candomblé*) as a *quilombo*.

16. APEBa, *Polícia. Correspondência expedida*, vol. 5726, Chefe de Polícia to the President of Province, April 28, 1859, folio 320.

17. *Diário da Bahia*, December 15, 1864 (vol. 14).

18. APEBa, *Polícia*, maço 3139-28, Chief of Police to the President of the Province, n.d., and *Subdelegado* Sinfronio Pires de Franca to the Chief of Police, December 12, 1864.

19. *Diário da Bahia*, April 23, 1862. Edict by the Chief of Police João Antonio de Araujo Freitas Henriques, April 21, 1862.

20. APEBa, *Polícia*, maço 6335, Amaro Gomes Vieira Lima to the Chief of Police, n.d.

21. APEBa, *Polícia*, maço 6497, Felippa Laura da Conceição to the Chief of Police, November 14, 1874.

22. APEBa, *Polícia*, maço 5819, Chief of Police A. Ferreira Espinheira to *subdelegado* of the Santo Antonio parish, second district, April 17, 1873.

23. *O Alabama*, November 24, 1870. For a short description of this ceremony, see Querino (1955, 52-3). See also Graden (2006, 121-2).

24. *O Alabama*, November 8, 1864.

25. Arquivo Nacional Torre do Tombo, Inquisição de Lisboa, *Cadernos do Promotor, 1797-1802*, n. 134, folio 6. I thank Luiz Mott for this reference.

26. On the profile of Candomblé leaders, see Reis (2001).

27. APEBa, *Capitães-Mores. Santo Amaro, 1807–1822*, maço 417-1.

28. *O Alabama*, June 1, 1871.

29. *O Alabama*, November 11, 1871.

30. Echoes of this procedure survived in postemancipation era rituals and have been studied by Parés (2010). See also an earlier study by Herskovits (1966).

31. APEBa, *Polícia*, maço 6337, José Luis Bernardino to the Chief of Police, ca. April 1872.

32. APEBa, *Polícia*, maço 6244, *Subdelegado* Antonio Joaquim Rodrigues Pinto to the Chief of Police, January 29, 1876.

33. APEBa, *Polícia*, maço 6328, João de Argolo Ferrão to the Chief of Police, January 31, 1861.

34. For Haiti, where slave poisoning became epidemic in the years leading up to the Haitian revolution, see Fick (1990, esp. chap. 2). At least in this case there are clearer connections between poisoning and concerted, collective slave resistance.

35. APEBa, *Capitães-mores. Santo Amaro, 1807–1822*, maço 417-1, Capitão-mor in São Francisco do Conde Joaquim Ignacio de Siqueira Bulcão to Capitão-mor in Santo Amaro Antônio Joaquim Pires de Carvalho e Albuquerque, São Francisco do Conde, June 25, 1807.

36. APEBa, *Polícia*, maço 6503, Delegado José Antonio de Jesus to the Chief of Police, May 15, 1882.

37. Sweet (2003, 164-5, 166-7, 185); Souza (1986, 206-209, 265). See also Souza (2002, 293-317).

38. APEBa, *Polícia. Relatórios para a Presidência, 1849–54*, livro no. 5689, Relatório dos sucessos, violências, e crimes que tiveram lugar na Província durante o mez de Setembro de 1853, folio 344v. In this case, doctors at the Faculdade de Medicina da Bahia concluded that arsenic had been used by the slave cook. Certainly the vomiting and dizziness suffered by those who consumed the coffee were not caused by the shell's powder; however, that could have been the information passed on to the slave by whoever prepared the substance.

39. *O Alabama*, September 2, 1868.

40. APEBa, *Polícia*, maço 6234, *Subdelegado* Pompílio Manuel de Castro to the Chief of Police, July 27, 1862. See also Harding's discussion (2000, 94) of this case as a strategy of slave resistance.

41. See Miller (1978, 413); Palmié (2002, 176-81); Sweet (2003, 162-63).

42. On paternalism in the world of slaves and dependents in nineteenth-century Brazil, see Chalhoub (2003).

43. APEBa, *Polícia*, maço 3113, Chief of Police João Joaquim da Silva to the President of the Province, March 21, 1848; and Querino Antonio to the Chief of Police, n.d. Free Africans were captives confiscated as contraband after several laws passed in Portugal and Brazil between 1815 and 1850 to restrict or completely abolish the trans-Atlantic slave trade. Wards of the state, they were usually employed in public and charitable institutions, such as the navy arsenal and the Santa Casa, respectively, or had their services auctioned to private employers. For Bahia, see Florence (1989, 58-69, and 2002).

44. APEBa, *Polícia. Correspondência expedida, 1862*, vol. 5754, Chief of Police João Antonio de Araújo Freitas Henriques to *subdelegado* of São Pedro parish, July 25, 1862, folio 215.

45. See a detailed narrative of Sodré's story in Reis (2008).

5

Chiefs into Witches: Cosmopolitan Discourses of the Nation, Treason, and Sorcery; The Pondoland Revolt, South Africa

KATHERINE FIDLER

ON A COLD MOONLIT NIGHT, a mother and daughter sit next to a fire. The mother, Manene Xokozela, is pregnant with her second child. A sudden noise, and three men burst through the door and push their way into the house. While the daughter watches, her mother attempts to fight off the attackers with a hoe, but they prove too strong for her. The woman falls to the ground, and her attackers fall upon her with the most mundane of farm tools: sticks, hoes, and axes. Her body is broken—mutilated beyond recognition—and her unborn child ripped from her body. Finished with their work, the men disappear into the night. One of the accused, Lagingqama Mguyelwa, later boasts to his friend that "Manene was killed in a bad way [. . .] and we did well by killing her because [the reason] my mother is so black and I am so black is on account of Manene."[1] He is convinced that Manene was a powerful witch and that her violent death would only benefit his family and the general community.

Several months later, in an adjoining district, a scream echoes across a valley in the early morning hours. An old woman runs from her hut, chased by a shadowy figure. She trips and falls to her knees. The figure, illuminated by the moon, stands over her and, with an ax, rains blow after blow upon her body. Her aged body is broken: her skull fractured, her spine snapped, her face disfigured, and her tongue ripped out. In the mind of her killer, a witch was dead and the death of a wife avenged.[2]

In the 1950s, witches and their familiars roamed the hills of Pondoland. It was a time of great uncertainty for the people in this small region in South Africa. Their world was changing in dramatic and often frightening ways. Faced with a state determined to dictate the terms of their economic, social, and political lives, in conjunction with a series of severe food shortages due to sustained drought conditions, the inhabitants of Pondoland confronted a chaotic world.

How were the people to make sense of this chaos? What images and vocabularies could they draw upon and deploy? What steps could they take to alleviate the chaos? Beginning in the 1930s, the judicial archives for Pondoland record a significant increase in witch killings.[3] As accusations of witchcraft and sorcery (*ukuthakatha*) increased, a dissident group, hostile to the ambitions of the white government, grew in strength. This group—known as the Congo Movement (alternatively known as *i-Kongo* or "the Congress") employed tropes of witchcraft and sorcery as they sought to create a nation separate from that of apartheid South Africa.

In 1959, the Congo declared war on the representatives of the government, white and black, whom they identified as responsible for the calamities that they and their families faced. Prominent among the list of grievances was the belief that the white officials, in collaboration with the government-appointed headmen and chiefs, exercised a malevolent sorcery that was to blame for the deteriorating conditions that many inhabitants of Pondoland faced. For the next two years, 1959–61, the hills of Pondoland burned as Congo insurgents attempted to right a world gone horribly wrong. Burning the kraals and mutilating the bodies of persons suspected of government collaboration, the insurgents drew upon the potent and often ambiguous language of witchcraft and sorcery.

This chapter explores the different ways in which participants in the insurgent movement called the Congo Movement in 1950s South Africa implemented and deployed concepts of witchcraft and sorcery as part of their fight against the apartheid government. Building upon archival and oral research, I will argue that the Congo insurgents in Pondoland used the language and imagery of witchcraft and sorcery in new and innovative ways to construct a nation that simultaneously drew upon familiar local concepts and sought to enter the Western arena of governance and civil society. Participants in the Pondoland insurgency created a political order that drew upon idioms of everyday life—particularly witchcraft—and languages of nationalism, human rights, and popular protest. The Congo implemented images of witchcraft and sorcery as part of its identification of traitors to the nascent nation.

The role of witchcraft and sorcery in African societies has long been a favorite topic for anthropologists and historians alike, and the image of the witch and the sorcerer remains potent in the popular imagination. In the 1950s and 1960s, much of the scholarly work on the subject argued that the continued belief in witchcraft and sorcery among African societies reflected a degree of conservatism or "backwardness."[4] This view of witchcraft and sorcery continues to influence many people to this day. A recent blog, featured on the Web site of the South African newspaper *Mail and Guardian,* by a professor of philosophy at the Nelson Mandela Metropolitan University, refers to the belief in witchcraft and magic as "something that is essentially pre-modern in so far as it reflects a mindset that has not even accepted reason as the basis for civilized living" (Olivier 2008). Additionally, even as journalists and politicians attempt to present a less judgmental view of the place of witchcraft and magic in African society, most articles place the term in quotations, thereby reflecting a continued unease with the "reality" of such beliefs and practices.

However, an increasing number of scholars are challenging the opinion that the belief in and practice of witchcraft and sorcery are fundamentally opposed to the development and advancement of modern society.[5] In the introduction to a collection of essays on ritual and modernity in Africa, the Comaroffs state that witchcraft "far from merely being a homeostatic feature of precolonial societies" has the ability "to counter the magic of modernity" (Comaroff and Comaroff 1993, xxv). Echoing their contention, Peter Geschiere states, in his study of witchcraft and politics in postcolonial Cameroon, that

> rumors and practices related to the occult forces abound in the more modern sectors of society. In Africa, the dynamism of these notions and images is especially striking: they are the subject of constant reformulations and re-creations, which often express a determined effort for signifying politico-economic changes or even gaining control over them. In many respects, then, one can speak of the "modernity" of witchcraft. (Geschiere 1997, 3)

The relegation of witchcraft and the occult to the realm of the premodern, traditional, and backwards obfuscates the multivaried ways in which people deploy a belief in and practice of witchcraft in the field of contemporary society. The task is clear: How can we understand the ways in which people adapt their belief in the potency of witchcraft and magic to address the challenges posed by a rapidly changing society in which new technologies and political imaginaries must be explained? I suggest that we approach the Congo insurgency and the tropes of witchcraft and sorcery that insurgents implemented during its course as an example of rural cosmopolitanism. Framing a study of the way in which Congo insurgents adapted their belief in magic and witchcraft during their struggle against the malevolent forces of Bantu authorities as a moment of a rural cosmopolitanism serves as a preliminary exploration into the dynamism of sorcery and magic ways of contemporary African society.

The concept of rural cosmopolitanism finds its roots in the historiography of Subaltern Studies.[6] Subaltern historians such as Ranajit Guha (1983) and Shahid Amin (1995) have asserted that the rural revolutionary was not conservative, concerned only with the retention of tradition. Instead, these scholars argue that the rural insurgent possessed an "embryonic" form of political consciousness (Guha 1983, 11). This recognizes the political agency of rural men and women but continues to work on an assumption of the existence of a scale of political consciousness. This scale implicitly places Western secular nationalism as the highest form of political consciousness. According to this rubric, rural insurgents, while possessing a form of political consciousness, have yet to achieve a fully formed political consciousness because they continue to hold onto religious beliefs and traditional practices that cannot be reconciled with the secularist tenets of Western nationalism.

Analyzing rural insurgency as a moment of rural cosmopolitanism moves away from the scale of political consciousness present in the early works of Guha and Amin. It acknowledges that people living and working in a rural environment are shaped by the demands and experiences of that environment. However, the framework of rural cosmopolitanism also posits that, particularly in a world in which time and space are compressed owing to a variety of technological developments, rural insurgents will, rather than discarding or adopting one set of beliefs in favor of another, adapt and deploy both traditional and modern concepts and practices to create new political and social imaginaries. The implementation of tropes and images of magic and witchcraft during the course of the Congo insurgency is thereby not at odds with the desire of the Congo Movement for recognition as a nation and its use of nationalist, secular images.

After a brief discussion of the development of the Congo Movement and the course of the insurgency, I will interrogate the different ways in which Congo insurgents actively drew upon a language of witchcraft and sorcery as part of the creation of a new political imaginary of a Pondo nation-state. This political imaginary sought neither to return to traditional values nor to conform to the political and social platforms of large-scale nationalist movements such as the African National Congress (ANC) or the Pan-African Congress (PAC). The use of diviners (*igqira*) and the belief that government collaborators drew their power from sorcery were not at odds with the creation of a nation-state that explicitly drew upon such Western political features as democratic participation, civil rights, and the separation of executive and judicial powers. Instead, insurgents (re-)adapted the existing images and rhetoric of witchcraft and magic while simultaneously incorporating elements of "modern" governance to create a political and societal imaginary that challenged the binary distinction typically made between premodern and modern.

Sorcery and Witchcraft in Pondoland

Located in the former Transkei region of the Eastern Cape, Pondoland is home to the Pondo peoples, a Xhosa-speaking group with a long history of resistance to colonial rule.[7] Throughout the nineteenth century, the Pondo consistently, and for the most part successfully, resisted British incursions only submitting to British rule in 1894.[8] The belief in witchcraft and sorcery was integral to Pondo society. A people intimately connected to the land on which they lived, natural and man-made phenomena were imbued with various meanings. In her 1933 ethnography of the Pondo, Monica Wilson (1961) described in great detail the different ways in which the Pondo used tropes of magic to understand their world. Magic was something that could be used legitimately or illegitimately. Diviners (*igqira*) and herbalists (*amaxhwele*) learned the different ways in which plants could protect people from sickness, and war doctors (*inyanga yempi*) used a variety of medicines to protect warriors from afflictions such as *iqunqu*—an illness that caused madness in warriors recently returned from battle.

However, people could also use magic for evil purposes, and throughout the twentieth century, the Pondo believed strongly in the ability of witches and sorcerers to cause significant damage to individuals and to the community. In his study of magic among the Azande, anthropologist Evans-Pritchard (1937) contended that the Azande believed witches exercised power through qualities intrinsic to their being, in contrast to sorcerers, who exercised power through the external use of potions and spells. This distinction between witches and sorcerers is useful to a point when analyzing Pondo society. The Pondo commonly believe that witches possess particular intrinsic qualities that allow them to bewitch their victims, while sorcerers possess the skills and knowledge necessary to use particular potions in a way that can inflict harm upon people and animals. Consequently, witchcraft is inherently evil, while sorcery is a kind of medicinal practice used for evil purposes. However, it is important to note that the Pondo do not differentiate linguistically between "witches" and "sorcerers" (Wilson 1961, 275). The words *umthakathi* and *igqwira* describe both witches and sorcerers and are used interchangeably, while the word *uku-thakatha* describes the practice of witchcraft or sorcery. As a result, while sorcery and witchcraft held different legal positions under colonial and apartheid rule—witchcraft being explicitly illegal—people generally saw little difference between the two practices.

The Hardships of the Twentieth Century

Throughout the early twentieth century, as contact with whites increased, the Pondo connected Europeans with a rise in the practice of witchcraft and sorcery both explicitly and implicitly. The epidemics of East Coast fever that so often decimated the cattle population of not only the Pondo but all the inhabitants of the Eastern Cape were frequently seen as the "result of an orgy of *uthakatha* (witchcraft and sorcery), or that they are sent by the Europeans" (Wilson 1961, 273). Members of Pondo society believed that Europeans possessed an intimate knowledge of sorcery and witchcraft that they would use to inflict damage on Pondoland and its inhabitants. One of Wilson's informants, a woman identified as Geza, contended that "all really dangerous *ubuthi* (materials of sorcery) came from European towns" (Wilson 1961, 294).

Perhaps unwittingly, white government officials also contributed to an increased sense of secrecy surrounding the practice of witchcraft and sorcery for malevolent ends. Convinced that the belief in witchcraft inhibited natives from becoming "civilized," magistrates and judges prohibited accusations of witchcraft in civil and criminal courts and were reluctant to recognize witchcraft as a defense in murder trials.[9]

> The law says that the court is entitled to take this belief (witchcraft) into account [. . .] However, I think that I cannot do better than to repeat what was said [. . .] in the highest court in this land [. . .] "It is important to emphasize that the prevalent belief in witchcraft is a very great blight on upon the native people in the Union."[10]

As a result, of government prohibitions surrounding the discourse of witchcraft, the Pondo believed "that the cause of the increase in sickness since contact is due to the Government prohibition of killing those who commit sorcery or witchcraft. Old men spoke bitterly of how sorcerers and witches work their will with impunity" (Wilson 1961, 275). This belief would resonate throughout the 1940s and 1950s as inhabitants of Pondoland faced increasing environmental, social, economic, and political hardships as the racial policies of apartheid took effect.

After the election of the Nationalist Party in 1948 and the entrenchment of apartheid policies of segregation, the Pondo developed a particularly hostile stance toward the South African government. Pondoland was among the first areas in which the apartheid government attempted to introduce the Bantu Authorities Act (1951). Designed as a means by which to categorize, control, and separate the black African population from the white, the Bantu Authorities Act effectively retribalized peoples in the Transkei.

While much of sub-Saharan African and indeed the colonial world began the conflict-ridden process of decolonization in the 1950s, South Africa entered a period of rigorous segregation based on race with the election of the Nationalist Party in 1948. Determined to permanently enshrine its apartheid policies of racial separation, the white domination Nationalist Party embarked on an aggressive campaign known of "tribal restructuring" in Pondoland and surrounding areas in the Eastern Cape beginning in the early 1950s. Building on a series of Native Land Acts dating back to the 1920s, the Nationalist Party sought to divide black Africans according to their "tribe" and confine these tribes to Bantustans.

The Bantu Authorities Act served as the cornerstone of apartheid and had a significant and immediate impact on the peoples of the Eastern Cape and Pondoland specifically. The government first introduced the Bantu Authorities Act in the region of the Eastern Cape, then known as the Transkei, of which Pondoland was a part, in 1956. The Bantu Authorities Act disrupted existing lines of succession to the paramount chieftaincy by empowering persons more amenable to the ideology of the apartheid state (Crais 2002; Evans 1997; Southall 1982). White Bantu Affairs Commissioners held the responsibility of selecting chiefs who would sympathize with the policies of the Nationalist Party—particularly the segregation of peoples according to race and tribe. The Bantu Authorities Act also restructured the ways in which people could access land and other means of employment. An additional component of the South African government's policies regarding the African population were called "rehabilitation schemes." The South African government devised rehabilitation schemes as a way to modernize African farming through techniques such as cattle culling, fencing, and villagization. People throughout Pondoland and the Transkei hated rehabilitation, and, as Sean Redding has argued, the chiefs' acquiescence to the government rehabilitation schemes led to renewed suspicion among many people about the prevalence of witchcraft and evil magic in Pondoland throughout the 1950s (Redding 2006, 179).

By the mid-1950s, many Pondo believed that the land suffered from an array of evil influences. In addition to the suspicion elicited by the rehabilitation schemes and political policies of the Bantu Authorities Act, the region suffered a series of severe droughts in the early 1950s that made the production and harvest of staple crops difficult. Drought conditions did not cease after one or two years and, with each passing year, it became increasingly difficult for families to produce enough food to provide basic subsistence. To compound the difficulties faced owing to these drought conditions, the white government did not institute any form of tax relief. Throughout the twentieth century, increasing numbers of families fell into considerable debt and were unable to pay the government taxes.[11]

In an effort to compensate for this loss in income, many men entered into the migrant labor cycle. For upwards of six months at a time, they traveled to work on the sugar plantations of Natal or in the gold and diamond mines of Kimberly or to perform menial tasks in the urban centers of Johannesburg and Cape Town. However, even when the income earned from migrant labor made it back to the families left behind in Pondoland, people continued to fall into greater debt as prices increased and access to the basic means of production decreased. To add to the financial strain of the period, many of the young men who remained behind turned to stock theft and other forms of hooliganism. The result was a complete disregard for existing age gradations in Pondo society.[12] Throughout the 1950s, local magistrates and commissioners repeatedly noted in memos addressed to the central government in Pretoria that the elders were no longer capable of exercising any authority over the youth.

It was in this atmosphere of extreme environmental, economic, political, and social instability that the inhabitants of Pondoland increasingly came to associate government collaborators with the practice of witchcraft. The Xhosa word for the tax known as the "general rate" was *irhafu yempundulu*. This translates to a "bloodsucking" tax and can be interpreted as a tax wielded by people using evil magic to subjugate the population (Redding 2006, 183). In 1957, the ANC distributed a pamphlet addressed to chief Kaizer Matanzima, a primary supporter of the Bantu Authorities Act, accusing him of witchcraft. In this pamphlet, chiefs collaborating with the Bantu Authorities are compared with wizards with the implicit threat that "the people know how to deal with wizards when they cause trouble among them."[13] The degree of influence exercised by the ANC in the development of the Congo Movement or the insurgency is debatable. In fact, there is very little evidence that the ANC had any interest in the Congo Movement. What is clear is that ANC leadership knew that, in order to rally support in the region, making connections between government collaborators and witchcraft would provide a potent image for the residents of Pondoland. The Congo Movement would also draw on the image of the witch as it developed their policies throughout the 1950s.

The Emergence of the Congo Movement

The formation of this movement first appears in the archival record in early 1947 in the district of Mount Ayliff.[14] Composed primarily of men in their thirties, the movement was mainly motivated by two concerns: stock culling and the appointment of chiefs. In a confidential memo addressed to the chief magistrate on July 10, 1947, the magistrate of Mount Ayliff states that "[t]he dissatisfied element is a fairly strong one [. . .] possibly so strong now that the whole district is against the rehabilitation schemes. Their wishes are clear, namely that they want the rehabilitation scheme stopped and that they are prepared to fight to retain their stock."[15]

An additional concern that preoccupied the minds of the original members of the Congo Movement concerned the perceived collusion between certain chiefs and white government officials. In anonymous letter written by members of the Ama-Xesibe tribe in Mount Ayliff district in mid-1947, a member of the nascent movement stated

> that a person who creates discord in a community is an undesirable element. We submit that this policy of the Government [rehabilitation schemes] is to be deprecated. Again we [. . .] detest the policy of chief Gaulibso Jojo who disregards the opinion and interests of his people [. . .].[16]

Chief Gaulibso Jojo was known to have supported the government's rehabilitation scheme that aimed, in part, to reduce the frequency of livestock sickness through periodic culling of black African cattle stock.

During its early years, members of the Congo Movement openly rejected the use of violence and instead sought other means to voice their concerns. "During April 1947 it was decided to abandon the idea of fighting the [rehabilitation] scheme by force and to make some other plan for opposing it. It was decided to collect some money and to engage attorneys."[17] Over the next several years, the Congo Movement remained relatively quiet, but there are clear indications that, particularly after the election of the Nationalist Party in 1948 and the attempts to implement the Bantu Authorities Act after 1951, the movement began to spread throughout the region, attracting ever-increasing numbers of dissatisfied men.

By the mid-1950s, in response to the actions of the Bantu Authorities, particularly the interference of white government officials in the succession of the paramount chief to the Pondo, the Congo Movement developed a more explicit political program. Congo members believed that the Bantu Authorities Act represented a material threat and that the implementation of its policies was a manifestation of plague that had come to permeate the countryside. An anonymous letter addressed to chief Quisling Douglas Ndamase in 1961 highlights this belief:

> At the inception of this century, we see [a] plague consolidating itself in preparation of a fresh onslaught [...] Verwoerd, your "father" came with his colleagues and puppies. In his Bantu Authorities you have been one of the chief protagonists who have publicly [capitalized] on it. This is shown by your fleecing the people in buying your cars [...] Your masters have given you three farms which have to be tilled by the voiceless peasant [...] I hereby demand that you resign from the chieftainship [...] denounced any connection with Bantu Authorities. We abhor this system, so you must if you identify yourself with the people, stop all [...] dealings. Stop prospering at our expense.[18]

Their response to this threat was to organize a plan designed to remove Bantu Authorities from the region and to counteract the sorcery that they connected with the government-appointed chiefs. As conditions continued to deteriorate throughout the 1950s, the Congo Movement incorporated increasing levels of violence into its protest strategies. The violence that the movement chose to implement was a violence used against a witch or a sorcerer. Official communiqués between native commissioners and magistrates, letters written by black Africans, and interrogation reports, in conjunction with recorded interviews with participants, point to an increase in the use of tropes of witchcraft and sorcery during the course of the insurgency.

The Outbreak of Insurgency and "Smelling Out" Evil

Beginning in 1958, white traders and representatives of the South African police record meetings of upwards of 5,000 men throughout the region.[19] These groups, or cells, elected officials and collected dues and funds for the retention of lawyers. In 1959, leaders of the Bizana cell of the Congo wrote a constitution outlining their aims as a nation. The constitution, later ratified by other cells throughout Pondoland, asserted the political and legal power of the movement. Judicial cases were no longer to be taken to European courts and could instead only be heard by the courts set up by the Congo leadership. The constitution also attempted to address the problems of hooliganism and stock theft by prohibiting beer drinks—an activity long seen as encouraging the lawless activities of the youth.[20]

During the meetings of the Congo, members also discussed which government collaborators they would target. Congo members called upon men and women versed in traditional medicines (diviners and herbalists) to help purify Pondo society. Using a variety of techniques, diviners and herbalists assisted Congo leaders (also referred to as "the Mountain" or *Intaba*) in identifying persons suspected of collaborating with Bantu Authorities. The Congo suspected that government collaborators, particularly chiefs and headmen, employed sorcery and other forms of malevolent magic to fortify their powers. Congo leaders also looked to diviners who could call upon specialized forms of medicine to both protect insurgents from the weapons of the government and to "smell out" those people actively encouraging the spread of the evil throughout the hills of Pondoland.[21] Government-appointed chiefs and headmen were among the first targeted as collaborators. Not only were these men subverting existing lines of succession to positions of power, but they also had "sold the land" to the government. Congo members saw these men as possessing and deploying significant degrees of magical power and in turn believed that they had to use magic to counteract the sorcery wielded by these men and white officials.

War doctors (*inyanga yempi*) were employed by Congo insurgents to help smell out the collaborators; they also used medicinal herbs to help fortify insurgents against the weapons and tactics of European counterinsurgent operatives. These same war doctors helped to fortify Congo members going on raids against government collaborators.[22] Congo leaders saw themselves as going to war with a government that they believed drew much of its extraordinary power through materials of sorcery (*ubuthi*) and the curses of witchcraft and through the special powers it had through the use of sorcery and witchcraft.

The belief that government collaborators had access to the materials used for sorcery is further elaborated in a statement given to police by Mvulu Venda. A member of the Congo Movement, he gave information to the South African police about a meeting in 1961. During this meeting, Congo members discussed the employment of a woman near the town of Umtata who was a "witch-doctor." Members planned to "engage this doctor who has medicine which will be used to make the chief (Matanzima) blind and this will enable a party of people to attack the chief and slay him."[23] Congo members saw chief Matanzima, commonly perceived as in collusion with Bantu Authorities, as exercising a kind of sorcery counteracted only through magic. The chief had burned over 120 kraals of those people who opposed his rule in the late 1950s, and people commonly believed that he was "faster than lightning."[24]

The association of chief Matanzima with lightning is particularly important given the place of lightning in Pondo beliefs about witchcraft. In Pondo society, lightning was not merely an evil omen. Lightning was a tool of witches and sorcerers. One of the ways that a witch could send curses was through the *impundulu* or lightning bird. An *impundulu* lived on the other side of the sky and only appeared when summoned by a witch in order to cause sickness and/or death or to cause chaos in a community (Wilson 1961, 282). Sorcerers were also reputed to wield the power to cause lightning to strike whenever they wished. Persons killed by lightning were buried apart from the community, and a house struck by lightning was subject to a series of elaborate purification ceremonies by an herbalist (*amaxhwele*) to rid the space of the evil influences that had entered it through the bolt. To associate a person with lightning was to accuse him or her of sorcery or witchcraft or, at the very least, to accuse him or her of affiliating with a sorcerer or a witch.

To claim that chief Matanzima was faster than lightning was a very serious accusation that would have resonated with people throughout Pondoland. Members of the Congo would have regarded him as a particularly dangerous figure given his connection with Europeans, who, as discussed earlier, had long been associated with the material of sorcery. In a letter addressed to chief Matanzima and signed only by "the Congo," the association between the chief and the practice of sorcery is clear: "It is immaterial to us where you doctored yourself, we are sure to see you this time."[25] To effectively counteract his powers, they would have to fortify themselves using a variety of magical substances.

Once members of the Congo had identified a collaborator, they would organize a party of men to go to the house and burn out the man and his family. The act of burning and mutilation has a long history in the region. Described as an *impi*—the Xhosa word for "army"—these men, fortified with medicines to protect their bodies from sorcery, would march out under the cover of darkness toward the kraal of the collaborator. As they approached the kraal, the war bugles would sound and women standing on the ridges would sound the war cry. The target of the attack—the government collaborator—would have been well aware of the force that approached.

Once the *impi* reached the kraal of the intended target, the men would surround the structure and call out the name of the man they intended to kill. Shouting, *"Tahisa, tahisa"* ("burn, burn"), Congo members would then attempt to forcibly remove the collaborator while setting his kraal on fire.

Many of the men targeted by the Congo escaped. Warned by sympathetic friends, they watched their kraals burn from the safety of hillside foliage.[26] However, those unlucky enough to fall into the hands of the insurgents suffered the fate reserved for witches and sorcerers: an extraordinarily violent death. Fire purified evil influences, and the Pondo saw fire, followed by an act of mutilation upon the body of the victim, as the most effective way of disrupting and dispelling the evil influences of sorcery or witchcraft.

The Congo Movement identified the paramount chief as the primary government collaborator. A supporter of Bantu Authorities from the beginning, Botha Sigcau had attained the position of paramount chief with the support of the white government after a protracted succession battle. People throughout the region commonly assumed that chief Botha Sigcau received medicines from a local diviner and herbalist, Khotso Sethuntsa. Although no one accused Khotso of sorcery, most people in the region believed that the famous medicine man knew how to use and had used the materials necessary for sorcery (*ubuthi*). Rumors circulated that Khotso used this knowledge to help protect his friend, Botha Sigcau, from the wrath of the Congo by supplying him with medicines that would turn him into a dog or a chicken (Wood and Lewis 2007, 214).

His brother, chief Vukayibambe Sigcau, was also a government collaborator. Not only had he "sold his people" to Bantu Authorities, a term commonly used in connection with the government-appointed chiefs and headmen, but he had also opened fire on a group of men, women, and children several days before his murder. This last act, the killing of his own people, was the catalyst for the Congo's decision to murder him. During the meeting on November 20, 1961, a man named Mkatazo, the man alleged to later wield the ax that would kill the chief, stated, "we have decided that an informer should have his throat cut and thrown over a cliff."[27] Clifton Crais, in his analysis of the insurgency in Pondoland, has noted that this was the way that Pondo chiefs would kill witches before the white government made witch killings illegal (Crais 2002, 179).

In the early hours of November 21, 1960, under the cover of darkness, a group of more than two hundred men arrived at the Vukayibambe kraal of ten huts and proceeded to set fire to all the structures. As they were burning it down, they pulled the chief from the building and proceeded to kill him with an ax strike to the back of his skull. As the chief lay dead in front of his burning kraal, his attackers proceeded to mutilate his body: his right hand and left ear were chopped off, and the fingers of his left hand were severed just above the knuckles.[28] While Congo insurgents did not throw chief Vukayibambe's body off a cliff as they had threatened, the circumstances surrounding his death serve to demonstrate that members

of the Congo made an explicit connection between government collaborators and witches. As with chief Matanzima, the insurgents saw that chief
Vukayibambe was a traitor who exercised a malevolent power: only an
evil man, a sorcerer, would fire on his own people, the people whom he
had pledged to protect as chief. The only way that this malevolence could
be counteracted was to treat him as a sorcerer and to kill him in the same
fashion that witches and sorcerers had been killed before Europeans outlawed such actions.

While Congo insurgents sought to punish government collaborators as
witches and exacted the same punishment upon their bodies as chiefs had
once done to men and women accused of witchcraft and sorcery, they also
sought to construct a nation that embodied ideals of Western governance
such as democracy and public participation. How do we understand this?
As suggested earlier, the framework of "rural cosmopolitanism" proves a
useful analytic and theoretical tool.

Rather than folding themselves into the nationalist discourse of the
ANC, Congo insurgents saw themselves as creating a nation.[29] Drawing
upon a history of strong regional identity, Congo leaders drew up a constitution that institutednot only a judicial and bureaucratic system but also
a tax system.[30] They even petitioned the United Nations for recognition
of their national sovereignty in early 1960 (Mbeki 1984, 42). Envision-
ing themselves a nation, Congo leaders conceptualized the government-
appointed chiefs and headmen as usurpers and traitors. On the hillsides,
in the new judicial arenas of the Congo, the leaders of the Congo tried,
convicted, and condemned these men (frequently in absentia) as traitors
to the people.

However, instead of couching the discussion of the traitorous actions
of men like chief Kaiser Matanzima, chief Botha Sigcau, and chief Vukayibambe Sigcau in a discourse of secular law, a discourse typically associated
with Western post-Enlightenment justice, the men of the Congo chose the
discourse of witchcraft and sorcery. In a discussion of popular justice in
Africa, Clifton Crais contends that too "neat" a distinction exists between
"traditional" kingly and chiefly courts and the "modern" courts of European colonial officials. He instead argues for the term "peoples' courts"
that act as "complex and creative bricolages that appropriate critical signs
from various sites, contest the dominant order, and become spaces within
which people imagine, communicate and enforce ideas and visions of society and morality" (Crais 1998, 49). The image of the peoples' court as
bricolage is useful when discussing the interplay among the creation of
a nation-state, treason, and sorcery. As the Congo developed a political
imaginary of the nation, they also developed a language flexible enough

to incorporate sorcery as a legitimate explanatory device for treason. The traitors were guilty of betraying their nation through the exercise of *uku-thakatha*, and as such they were to suffer the fate of witches and sorcerers: burning and mutilation.

The Emergency Years

For over two years, the hills of Pondoland burned. When one talks with people who witnessed the violence of the insurgency, there is a sense of an impending apocalypse. Every night, fires dotted the hillside, providing a visual reminder of the evil that the Congo insurgents sought to erase. The air crackled with fear and tension: who would the Congo identify as a collaborator, whose kraal would be burned the next night? Supporters of Bantu Authorities fled their homes with their families, seeking refuge with local commissioners. Congo insurgents, determined to overthrow Bantu Authorities and purify the land of the evil that it encouraged, cut telephone lines, erected road blocks, and constructed homemade bombs to use against the military forces sent into the region. The South African government, recognizing that the movement threatened to destabilize the entire region, called in mobile police forces and the South African Air Force to help contain the movement. In a statement given by the South African police force in 1960, Sergeant Leonard Eugene Muller describes the atmosphere at the time:

> The owners of the kraals (huts) burnt are all supporters of tribal authorities. The Bantu people are not in favour of tribal authorities [...] we had to get in reinforcements as we could not enter locations alone. At the height of disturbances, the S. A. Air Force was called in to assist. At that time, Bantu men were always found in large groups and armed. We often encountered road blocks and they did not want to assist [...] in any manner. Women also took part—sending out war cries wherever police entered locations. [...] Police could not enter locations alone.[31]

By the end of 1961, the South African government had virtually crushed the Congo insurgency. Motivated by a concern that the insurgency might spread like the Mau Mau rebellion had several years before in Kenya, the government used helicopters, tear gas, and torture to subdue the population. Thousands of people were arrested, at least twenty-three were executed, and an untold number were tortured by the paramilitary.[32] The hills of Pondoland no longer reverberated with the war cry.

Over the next several decades, the Transkei would become a hotbed of

ANC and PAC political activity, but the nation imagined by members of the Congo would not survive. However, the desire to build a nation on their own terms continued to resonate with many people in the years following the suppression of the insurgency. Throughout the 1960s, rumors of the rise of the Congo appear sporadically in the records of government officials: anonymous letters sent to local Bantu affairs commissioners accuse the government of employing magic and sorcery against the inhabitants of Pondoland.

Conclusion

Over the next several decades, the region plunged into a deeper state of poverty. To this day, as South Africa seeks to enter a new phase of financial and social success on a global stage, much of Pondoland lacks a basic infrastructure. Many homes do not have running water, sewage disposal, or electricity. Diseases such as HIV/AIDS and antibiotic-resistant tuberculosis are on the rise, and much of the population remains unemployed and dependent on subsistence agriculture.

If the material success of Pondoland and the surrounding region seems to have fallen off the agenda in the new South Africa, most South Africans have also forgotten that the Pondoland insurgency ever happened. In the years following 1994, historians have largely rewritten the history of South Africa. The history of the antiapartheid movement is of great public interest, both within South Africa and internationally. However, these histories focus almost exclusively on the actions of the ANC. There is almost no mention of the events in Pondoland in the late 1950s in any official account of the struggle against apartheid. Will this new official history—a history couched in the rhetoric of "modern secularism"—ever find room in its narrative for a movement that challenged the legitimacy of apartheid with the use of concepts such as magic and sorcery?

Perhaps part of the answer lies in the fact that people remain profoundly uncomfortable with a movement that implemented images of the lightning bird and punished traitors as witches and sorcerers while simultaneously exalting the virtues of democracy and human rights. As mentioned in the beginning of the chapter, people throughout South Africa, and indeed much of the Western world, cling to the assumption that the belief in witchcraft and magic is a marker of primitive or backward cultures. The violence committed against people accused of witchcraft, while often brutal and inexcusable, remains universally condemned, while official political policies of inaction and "quiet diplomacy" resulting in the deaths of hundreds of thousands of people and the persecution of minorities attract little attention in the international media.

The kind of political and social imaginary posed by the Congo Movement stood in sharp opposition to the vision of the ANC. The Congo was able to navigate the tensions between the poles of tradition and modernity to create a society that sought recognition on an international level through recourse to the United Nations, while implementing the language and imagery of witchcraft. Government collaborators were deemed traitors, and traitors were understood to possess a magic associated with witches and sorcerers. As such, these traitors were subject to the same fate as witches, and the hills of Pondoland burned by night. This is by no means an outright justification of the actions of the Congo during the insurgency. Congo insurgents implemented brutal forms of violence in the name of ridding their society of evil. However, the brief life of the Congo does serve as a reminder that other political and societal imaginaries did exist during the antiapartheid struggle. The secular nationalist vision of the ANC was neither the only option or necessarily predetermined to be the victor. The Congo Movement, far from being backward or primitive, was truly cosmopolitan in its attempt to create a society that wove together images of nation-state, magic, human rights, and witchcraft as it sought to throw off the repressive yoke of the apartheid government.

As South Africa struggles to find its place on the world stage, it is clear that the ANC-dominated government remains uncomfortable with the continued belief in magic and evil that permeates much of the South African countryside. The Congo Movement may have failed, but the belief in magic and witchcraft remains a potent force in the everyday life of many people in a democratic South Africa.

Notes to Chapter Five

1. Cape Archives, Cape Town (hereafter CA), Grahamstown Supreme Court (hereafter GSC), 1/2/1/792, Case 273, Bizana district, 1957.

2. CA, GSC, 1/2/1/805, Case 34, Flagstaff district, 1958.

3. CA, 1/ECO, 6/1/28, Confidential Memo from the Magistrate of Engcobo district to the Secretary of the Engcobo Civic Association, February 8, 1930.

4. Anthropological studies conducted in the 1950s and 1960s—particularly the works of Max Warwick (1965) and Victor Turner (1954)—stressed the conservative tendencies of witchcraft accusations. These studies effectively placed witchcraft solidly within the traditional realm, thereby reproducing the binary of traditional and modern.

5. Examples of the new trends in scholarship on witchcraft, magic, and the occult include Ciekawy and Bond (2001), Jean and John Comaroff (1993), and Crais (2002).

6. The concept of rural cosmopolitanism allows us to escape the urban/rural and modern/traditional divides present in the majority of literature concerned with emerging nationalisms, labor migration, and global cosmopolitanism. Rural cosmopolitanism instead suggests that rural peoples draw upon and employ vocabularies and images from a multiplicity of sources as part of an effort to engage with and insert themselves into transnational discourse. Far from adopting wholesale such modern concepts as nationalism or secular law, rural cosmopolitans engage in a kind of syncretic exercise that at once fuses, adapts, and molds seemingly dissonant concepts (such as witchcraft and treason) into a unique vision of society and governance.

7. The major work on nineteenth- and twentieth-century Pondoland is *The Political Economy of Pondoland, 1860–1930* by William Beinart (1982).

8. In the years immediately preceding the incorporation of Pondoland into the Cape Colony, rumors abounded about the strength of the Pondo army. In 1886, the Cape Mounted Riflemen were mobilized in response to reports of a Pondo army numbering 15,000 men (Beinart 1982, 33).

9. For a discussion on a similar dynamic in Zimbabwe see Maggie (this volume).

10. CA, GSC, 1/2/1/811, Case 146, Charge: Murder; Accused: Fumanekile Matadi; Deceased: Nobanga Solani, 1958.

11. CA, Chief Magistrate Transkei (hereafter CMT), 3/609, Confidential Memo from the Magistrate, Engcobo District, to the Chief Magistrate, Umtata, September 24, 1919.

12. By the early 1960s, approximately 160,000 native men per year entered the employment of labor agents. Many of these men would leave the region for work on the mines and plantations: 1/QBU 7/1/72, Minutes of the Magisterial Conference in Umtata, August 9–10, 1960.

13. CA, CMT, 3/1471, November 9, 1957. It is also worth noting that just as the terms "witch" and "sorcerer" were used interchangeably, so were "witch" and "wizard."

14. CA, CMT, 3/1480, Statement made by Joseph Mangqoba of Mount Ayliff district, June 15, 1948.

15. CA, CMT, 3/1480, Mount Ayliff district, July 10, 1947.

16. CA, CMT, 3/1480, Mount Ayliff district, July 10, 1947.

17. CA, CMT, 3/1480, Mount Ayliff district, July 10, 1947.

18. CA, CMT, 3/1471, 1961.

19. CA, CMT, 3/1478, Statement by Keith Hilton Wicks concerning a meeting in Flagstaff district, January 4, 1961.

20. CA, 1/BIZ, 6/47, 1959.

21. CA, CMT, 3/1054, Statement by Mvulu Venda of Mcuncuzo Location, Cofimvaba, November 15, 1961.

22. CA, 1/BIZ, 6/47, Unrest in Bizana district National Emergency: Disaffection in the Lusikisiki district, p. 18.

23. CA, CMT, 3/1054, Statement by Mvulu Venda of Mcuncuzo Location, Cofimvaba, November 15, 1961.

24. CA, 1/COF, 9/1/44, Statement by Gilbert Hani to the South African police, 1962.

25. CA, 1/COF, 9/1/44, Anonymous letter, 1960.

26. Eyewitness accounts of these burnouts can be found in the CMT and in individual magistrate records.

27. CA, GSC, 1/2/1/939, Case 376, State v. Mkatazo and Twenty-Nine Others, 1961.

28. CA, GSC, 1/2/1/939, Case 376, State v. Mkatazo and Twenty-Nine Others, 1961.

29. CA, 1/LSK, 1/1/16, Case 700, State v. Themba Njolweni and Seven Others, August 28, 1961.

30. CA, 1/BIZ, 6/47, Constitution of the Congo.

31. CA, 1/BIZ, 1/1/14, 1960.

32. It is unclear from the records how many people were executed for offenses related to the insurgency. While the official inquiry into the disturbances lists the number as twenty-three, there is a considerable amount of evidence indicating that more people, tried under the ordinary crime of murder, as opposed to treason, were executed for offenses connected to the movements of the Congo. For obvious reasons, the South African government at the time was reticent to record the exact conditions under which suspects were interrogated, but official documents of complaint against representatives of the South African police indicate that manhandling of suspects was routine.

6

Charlatans and Sorcerers: The Mental Hygiene Service in 1930s Recife, Brazil

DANIEL STONE

DURING THE 1930s, a body called the Mental Hygiene Service (*Serviço de Higiene Mental,* or SHM) led an unprecedented attempt to regulate religious practices involving spirit possession in the Brazilian city of Recife. This institution was created by Ulysses Pernambucano, cousin and close confidant of the renowned sociologist and writer Gilberto Freyre (1933). After the revolution of 1930, Pernambucano was given the opportunity to reshape Recife's asylum and the services associated with it. As part of his reforms, the SHM was conceived as a body that would counteract mental illness by investigating and disseminating information about its potential causes. Pernambucano and his colleagues believed that participation in religious practices that involved spirit possession was one of the most important factors contributing to increasing rates of certain psychiatric conditions in the city's population. To these psychiatrists, spirit possession was not simply to be dismissed as a form of deception or charlatanry; it was both a possible sign and a potential cause of mental illness. Although this was a perspective shared by much of Brazil's medical establishment, it was only in Recife that representatives of this medical elite attempted to create a specific system of evaluation and regulation in the hope of curbing what they saw as the harmful effects of these religious practices. During the course of their work, the SHM initiated a series of investigations into Xangô, the generic term used to describe Afro-Brazilian religions in Recife.[1] They also became involved in granting licenses to Xangô temples, extending and changing a system of regulation that had previously only applied to spiritualist groups.[2] Despite this unique set of circumstances, the activities of the SHM and the general context in which they worked

95

have received relatively little attention in scholarly attempts to understand how the Brazilian state sought to regulate these religious practices.

In this paper, I will examine the work of the SHM, addressing two issues that relate to wider debates about sorcery and Afro-Brazilian religion. In the first instance, I will analyze the ways in which fears about sorcery and the charlatan were encoded in medical and legal discourses in Brazil historically, with the aim of building up a nuanced picture of how the figures of the charlatan and sorcerer were condemned publicly. I wish to use the work of the SHM to highlight features of these discourses that have not previously been discussed at much length as well as to demonstrate how the SHM drew on these ideas in novel and unexpected ways.

Central to this is a reexamination of the way in which practices categorized as forms of charlatanry or *curandeirismo* were condemned.[3] Yvonne Maggie persuasively argues in this volume and elsewhere that the terms of the Brazilian penal code of 1890 reveal an underlying belief in the power of magic (Maggie, this volume). She suggests that the new articles of this penal code "revealed, on the part of the authors, a fear of spells and the necessity of creating a method and institutions to combat those that produce them" (Maggie 1992, 22).[4] As such, legal processes against *curandeiros* and charlatans often developed from accusations of witchcraft and did not necessarily involve a condemnation of the belief in magic itself. However, I will argue that legal and other forms of public condemnation of these practices were often more ambiguous. In particular, I will emphasize that the condemnation of certain practices often reflected a common fear concerning the ability of particular individuals to manipulate or hold sway over others. This fear could be configured in ways that might imply a belief in magic but also in ways that rejected this very notion. In this paper, I will explore the complex attitudes and intertwining of different ideas about the power of the charlatan or sorcerer through an examination of the work of the SHM.

The second feature of the SHM's work that I wish to focus on here is the degree to which the body was concerned with the investigation and regulation of spiritualism. The activities of intellectuals linked to the SHM have largely been analyzed in relation to their ideas about Xangô. Beatriz Góis Dantas briefly but insightfully explored their work in her influential book *Vovó nagô papai branco: usos e abusos da África no Brasil* (1988). She saw the SHM in the context of a broader effort by various Brazilian intellectuals to define and defend what they saw as legitimate forms of Afro-Brazilian religion. In this case, intellectuals associated with the SHM contributed to the prestige of certain *terreiros*, heralding them as representatives of a truly African religion.[5]

The study and regulation of Xangô was certainly of central importance to Pernambucano and his followers. However, practices deriving from spiritualism were the principal target in their battle against forms of charlatanry and what those linked to the SHM viewed as the dangerous practice of spirit possession.[6] Significantly, the SHM used an analytical schema that effectively exempted religious groups that they viewed as African from the criminal responsibility it attributed to those professing to engage in spiritualist activities. The SHM's approach toward Afro-Brazilian religions departed from the idea that since both leaders and followers shared the same primitive mind-set, deliberate fraud or manipulation could not be taking place. However, despite recognizing that possession was a central part of these religions, those linked to the SHM did not appear to condemn Xangô as a dangerous cause of mental illness.

The extent to which the SHM focused its activities on combating spiritualism is also relevant to a broader discussion about the historical development of debates about religion and charlatanry in the northeast of Brazil. Dantas and other authors have argued that the focus on the idea of a pure African tradition was a peculiar aspect of intellectual debates about the legitimacy of religious practices in the northeast of Brazil, orienting questions about religious probity and responsibility to the idea of fidelity to an African tradition defined as Yoruban or "Nagô" (Giumbelli 1997a, 273). In contrast, it has been suggested that medical and juridical debates about charlatanry, magic, and possession in Rio de Janeiro centered on the legitimacy of spiritualism. According to Emerson Giumbelli, these priorities were set in a series of exchanges among spiritualist federations, the police, and the press (Giumbelli 1997a).[7]

Although organized spiritualist associations emerged more slowly in Pernambuco than in other urban centers such as Rio de Janeiro and Salvador (Sá 2001, 241), by 1923 the city was home to two prominent associations of spiritualist groups.[8] These federative groups sought to define their "true" or "high" visions of spiritualism against the popular adoption of their ideas by those mediums whom they considered to be engaged in unorthodox or unethical practices. The notion that these federations embodied a legitimate and responsible form of the religion was also shared by the authorities. In 1928, affiliates of the *Cruzada Espírita Pernambucana* had acquired an exemption from the legal requirement for every spiritualist center to take out a license with the police (Queiroz 1999, 97). During the 1930s, meetings at spiritualist centers were also frequently advertised in many of Recife's newspapers, as was news of developments in the international world of spiritualism (Sá 2001, 264).

It is therefore important to consider that the SHM actually went against the tide of public opinion in condemning spiritualism and attempting to identify value in Xangô. In this paper, I will demonstrate that, despite gaining an officially sanctioned recognition for "African sects," the SHM did not succeed in significantly changing public attitudes toward Xangô in the short term.[9] Far from it, their actions actually generated considerable controversy and may even have helped to provoke the radical repression of Xangô in Recife following the installation of the Estado Novo in 1937.[10]

Legal and Medical Approaches to Magic and Spiritualism

Article 157 of the first republican penal code of 1890 represented the first attempt to codify state approaches to spiritualism. This text is central to Maggie's suggestion that the provisions of this code could be interpreted as the very embodiment of a belief in magic. The article stated that it was prohibited "to practice Spiritualism, magic and its spells, use talismans and cartomancy to provoke feelings of hatred or love, inculcate the cure of curable or incurable illnesses, in sum, to captivate and subjugate the credulity of the public" (cited in Giumbelli 1997a, 79).[11]

Maggie suggests that this text demonstrated a concern with identifying those who used supernatural powers to cause harm to others. She emphasizes that the code did not condemn the use of spiritualism or even magic per se; rather it proscribed its use for harm. The code thus meant that the state could be implicated in identifying and prosecuting the sorcerer. For Maggie this meant that the organs of the state not only reflected but shaped the belief in magic and provided a channel through which accusations of sorcery or witchcraft could be made. According to her analysis, the state "involved itself in questions of magic and intervened in the combat of sorcerers, regulating accusations, creating special trials and specialized personnel" (Maggie 1992, 23).[12]

However, Giumbelli has provided a subtly different reading of this same article. He argues that the condemnation of spiritualism or magic may have less to do with a belief in their actual supernatural effects than with the ability of practitioners to ensnare or to deceive the people who accept their power—as the text puts it, "captivate and subjugate the credulity of the public." Giumbelli, then, argues that the principal concern expressed in this text is with the power of illusion, the pretence that these practices were effective, and the harm that believing in this might cause (Giumbelli 1997a, 79–82).

In practice, these readings of the article do not appear to be mutually exclusive. Attitudes toward those who claimed to employ magic could reflect both perspectives. Indeed, the importance of these two interpretations is clearly reflected in the work of a very significant figure in the study of Afro-Brazilian religion—the Bahian criminologist Raimundo Nina Rodrigues. Working in Salvador, Nina Rodrigues was the first Brazilian scholar to approach the study of what is now commonly referred to as Candomblé from a self-consciously scientific perspective.[13] He defined Candomblé as "fetishist animism"—a primitive form of African religion (see Sansi, this volume)—arguing that a religious "sentiment" that originated from African slaves and their descendants had come to infect all social classes (Rodrigues 1935, 186). In fact, he expressed this idea in quite startling terms in a phrase that is also quoted by Maggie in a more recent work: "all classes, even the so-called superior classes, are capable of becoming black" (cited in Maggie 2001, 58).[14]

So as Maggie suggests, Nina Rodrigues's criticisms of legal approaches to Candomblé were aimed at unveiling the extent to which all sections of Brazilian society shared a belief in sorcery. According to Nina Rodrigues, even police actions to repress Candomblé were imbued with the fundamentally primitive fear of magic. Indeed, in referring to Article 157 of the penal code, he wrote that it represented nothing more than "the translation into law of the state of mind that, originating amongst the inferior classes of our population, has been conquering even the more civilized ruling classes with its superstitious preoccupations" (Rodrigues 2004, 283).[15] However, while Nina Rodrigues was certainly reacting to a widespread acceptance of the power of the sorcerer and of magic, he also acknowledged that the suggestion that Candomblé involved the exploitation of credulous followers formed an important part of the rationale behind attacks on the practice. He suggested that such an objection to the religion was illogical: "It is a deficiency in the law to intend to protect those who consciously let themselves be exploited; more than this, this form of sorcery, presupposes the equal social responsibility of sorcerers and their clientele" (Rodrigues 2004, 282).[16]

Reflected in this statement is Nina Rodrigues's distrust of the idea that all humans shared the ability to reason in the same way. What was rational for Africans constituted an aberration in European society, determining what Nina Rodrigues referred to as an "ethnic criminality" (Rodrigues 2004, 306).[17] But Africans could not be treated as if they adhered to or were capable of understanding the same moral and juridical conventions as Europeans. This is why, Nina Rodrigues argued, they should be subjected to a different legal code, one that was more appropriate to their own stage of moral and juridical development.

Nina Rodrigues was also interested in the phenomenon of possession. In contrast to the general view of this practice, he argued that it was not always a case of simple pretense (Sansi 2003, 194). It was akin to a form of hypnosis, or sleepwalking, provoked by the context of the ritual. He also suggested that those most susceptible to being possessed in fact suffered from hysteria. In this he actually went against the predominant view, which was that black people could not suffer from hysteria (Corrêa 1998, 118). Without going into more detail here, it is important to underline Nina Rodrigues's role in defining possession not simply as a form of pretense but as the expression of a mental illness that was in turn linked to a biological predisposition. On the other hand, he attempted to establish the principle that Africans should be exempted from the legal responsibilities of supposedly more capable, civilized citizens.

Both of these ideas were central to later attempts made by members of the medical establishment to come to terms with practices involving spirit possession. However, by the late 1920s and early 1930s, a new paradigm for understanding the relationship between mental illness and biology had begun to take shape with the growing popularity of the mental hygiene movement in Brazil. The concept of mental hygiene was originally elaborated by the North American Clifford Beers, a former psychiatric patient who established a Mental Hygiene Society in Connecticut as early as 1908.[18] The popularity of this movement in Brazil accompanied a general questioning of explicitly biologically based ideas about race that was in turn linked to the emergence of a more optimistic assessment of the country's future. Brazil's population was no longer seen as inevitably doomed to a future of degeneration caused by racial mixture, as the traditionally pessimistic view would have it. Doctors and hygienists were increasingly emphasizing the importance of environmental factors such as poverty and poor hygiene in explaining physical differences. Thus many of the problems Brazil faced could be overcome by better standards of hygiene, nutrition, and education.[19] Similarly, the mentally ill were no longer simply seen as individuals whose biological predispositions led them to insanity. As with other diseases, good hygiene, in other words, prevention, was the key.

However, while the concept of mental hygiene refocused psychiatric practice toward addressing what were interpreted as the environmental triggers or causes of certain conditions, it did not do away with the ideas of hereditarianism or predisposition altogether.[20] Thus, in confronting the problematic popularity of spiritualism, medical scholars working in Rio de Janeiro stressed that a medium's ability to become possessed reflected an underlying pathology.

Encapsulating this approach is a study produced by two psychiatrists, Leonídio Ribeiro and Murilo de Campos, both of whom were involved in the mental hygiene movement. In *O Espiritismo no Brasil*, published in

1931, spiritualist phenomena are explained away as simple products of the unconscious imagination. These authors argued that many of those who frequented spiritualist centers were "hereditarily predisposed to mental afflictions," inherently weak and susceptible to forms of suggestion (Ribeiro and Campos 1931, 63).[21] As such, the book emphasized the importance of some form of inherent predisposition in determining the susceptibility to enter into a trance in certain individuals. For these two authors and for much of the medical establishment, spiritualism was a dangerous practice that exacerbated the symptoms of already mentally unstable people.

Giumbelli highlights another important component of this approach to spiritualism. Campos and Ribeiro objectified a model of the practice in which poor, ignorant, and mentally unstable people were exploited by the director of the spiritualist center. This person, who was presumably more intelligent, would use suggestion and hypnotism to induce a trance in a mentally weaker, predisposed subject (Giumbelli 1997a, 207). The director was thus guilty of deliberately encouraging the delusions of the medium in order to extract money from a wider clientele. Thus the model of spiritualism elaborated by doctors saw poor people as the victims not only of dangerous delusions but also of powerful indoctrinators, cunning individuals who consciously sought to exploit the mentally fragile. A focus on individual pathology—predisposition and the inherent mental weakness of the subject—was combined with a concern about the exploitation of those seeking a cure, and a moral judgment about the manipulators who committed these crimes.

The SHM's approach to spiritualism appeared to have been influenced strongly by this approach.[22] However, at the same time, members of the SHM drew inspiration from the work of Arthur Ramos, a Bahian doctor who, during the 1930s, followed in Nina Rodrigues's footsteps in addressing Candomblé as a primitive form of African religion.

Ramos argued that while Nina Rodrigues had demonstrated tremendous foresight in his work, he had been constrained by the ideology of his time. It is possible to see Ramos's work as an attempt to bring the anthropological concept of culture to bear on Nina Rodrigues's studies, replacing his racial determinism with a more optimistic assessment of the mental capacities of black people.[23]

Using Lucien Levy Bruhl's concept of the "prelogical mentality," Ramos argued that what the medical establishment considered to be illegitimate forms of medicine should not always be treated as a conscious attempt to deceive or exploit others. This argument was made in an article published in 1931 and became central to the SHM's work. In *O Problema psicológico do curandeirismo*, Ramos asserted that the medical authorities needed to draw a distinction between what he saw as two related but distinct phenomena: *curandeirismo* and charlatanry (Ramos 1931). Points two and three of the article's conclusions demonstrate the general thrust of his argument:

> II—The charlatan is the conscious transgressor of a code of class who should suffer the penalties that the law applies. The *curandeiro* is an involuntary charlatan whose conduct obeys different psychological determinisms.
>
> III—These motives are the prelogical elements of the primitive mentality that we find in the medicine man of savage societies. The persistence of this mentality in the *curandeiro* of our time is observable in certain environments in Brazil that received a direct influx of the Negro or Indian. (Ramos 1931, 980)[24]

From this perspective, those involved in Afro-Brazilian religions were simply culturally backward. Crucially, they shared a primitive mentality with their followers, and hence they should not be seen as engaging in conscious acts of charlatanry. By contrast, charlatans were those who deliberately sought to exploit the credulity of others. Ramos thus suggested that a proper system of regulation would distinguish between these two groups and would involve the gradual education of *curandeiros* (Ramos 1931, 980). Having explored these two contrasting visions of how to interpret and approach the issues of spirit possession and *curandeirismo*, the rest of this paper will address how these ideas were put into practice by the SHM.

The SHM and Spiritualism

The SHM was a central element of the reforms introduced by Ulysses Pernambucano in 1931 and was considered to be the analytical hub of all the clinical services and institutions he had created.[25] It was also supposed to provide some form of pastoral support to the families of psychiatric patients, advising them on mental hygiene and monitoring the patient outside of the hospital (Pernambucano 1932, 48). More broadly, it was charged with tackling the causes of mental illness by imparting information to the public. It did this through a monthly bulletin, radio broadcasts, and numerous themed weeks such as an annual antialcohol week. Despite its rather grandiose aims, the SHM did not appear to have a large staff, consisting of a director and a varying number of assistants.[26]

Perhaps the most significant intervention of those linked to the SHM was their attempt to bring their medical knowledge to bear on the process by which the police awarded official licenses to spiritualist centers. Following an agreement with the Department of Public Security (*Secretaria de Segurança Pública*) made on October 15, 1933, licenses would only be granted to mediums after authorization by the SHM (Ribeiro and Lins 1935, 74). This authorization would depend on the psychological examination of the medium in question. The conditions of the license also included an undertaking not to breach the penal code and to accept regular visits from functionaries of the SHM (Cavalcanti 1934b, 143). Perhaps the most notable innovation in this agreement was the idea that licenses should be offered to what they termed "African sects" as well as to spiritualist centers. However, despite both types of religious groups apparently being subject to the same demands, it is clear that the SHM approached these different categories in distinct ways.

Emblematic of the differences between mainstream attitudes toward spiritualism and the SHM's approach to the religion is the way in which the latter employed the term "low spiritualism" in its texts.[27] As well as alcohol and syphilis, "low spiritualism" was described by Pernambucano as one of the "directly accessible causes of mental illnesses" (Pernambucano 1932, 47).[28] In this regard it may appear that Pernambucano shared the concerns of many spiritualists who applied this expression to those who they thought to be engaged in immoral or unorthodox practices. However, the attitudes of those linked to the SHM mirrored those of Campos and Ribeiro in rejecting spiritualism as a whole. For them, low spiritualism was the general manifestation of the growing popularity of a doctrine that was fundamentally spurious and dangerous.

This approach was apparent in two academic articles published by doctors linked to the SHM in 1932. In one of these pieces the authors rejected the distinction between spiritualism and low spiritualism altogether: "The practice of that which is commonly called "low spiritualism" or simply "spiritualism" has spread to such a degree amongst the lower classes of the population that it now constitutes a sanitary problem and a problem for the police that is difficult to resolve" (Borges and Lima 1932, 38).[29] A second article applied a statistical analysis to the numbers of patients entering Recife's asylum suffering from what were termed "episodic deliriums" (Araujo 1932, 134).[30] It was suggested that the growing percentage of cases over the years 1925-30 was due to the "peculiar development of Spiritualism in our milieu" (Araujo 1932, 134-35).[31] Those suffering from the delirium were identified as "uncultured individuals"[32] who in many cases exhibit an "intellectual debility."[33] It was further asserted that this "inferiority makes possible, in the case of spiritualism, its deformities and various popular superstitions, the acceptance, on the part of the individual, of the supernatural character of the phenomena observed [during the session]:

such that these are able to act as a powerful cause of psychopathology" (Araujo 1932, 137).[34]

This form of analysis was pursued in more detail by a technical assistant with the SHM named Pedro Cavalcanti who completed his medical dissertation based on the psychological examinations of various mediums (Cavalcanti 1934a). Summarizing his study in a brief academic article, he concluded that "the majority of mediums are constituted by the mentally feeble" (Cavalcanti 1934b, 143).[35] However, spiritualism and associated practices could also be implicated in greater dangers to public health. Referring to the "manifestations" of these mediums, Cavalcanti stated that "a large part of the population admires and gives credence to them as being "manifestations of spirits" (Cavalcanti 1934b, 143).[36] Cavalcanti also sought to remind the reader of the potential dangers of such beliefs, invoking the memory of two millenarian movements: "Examples of mass mystical manifestations (Padre Cicero in Joazeiro) and anti-social reactions (Antonio Conselheiro in Canudos) are well known amongst us" (Cavalcanti 1934b, 143).[37]

Here spiritualism and its associated practices are defined as phenomena that, while dangerous for the mental health of the individual, also have the potential to cause social unrest. Underlying this analysis is a concern about the credulity and volatility of the nation's poor and uneducated masses. Nevertheless, despite an immediate focus on the psychiatric evaluation of poor, largely uneducated mediums, the SHM clearly set itself against the practice of spiritualism as a whole. This is made evident in the only two surviving transcripts of radio broadcasts made by the SHM in 1932 on the local radio station, the *Radio Club de Pernambuco*. The second of the two transcripts concluded with the following statement: "Spiritualism is a dangerous mental habit; it can lead to madness; you should avoid it."[38]

These broadcasts were interpreted as an attack on spiritualism as a whole by at least one important listener—Oscar Moreira Pinto, a director of the Radio Club—who complained to Pernambucano in the following terms: "Considering that amongst the members of this association there are many adherents to the 'religion' of spiritualism, we impress that no dissertation should take the form of a religious attack, and that low spiritualism, responsible as it is for great ills, should be combated scientifically."[39]

The director of the Radio Club was clearly appalled by an approach to spiritualism that appeared to condemn the religion as a whole rather than focus on attacking its illegitimate forms, which he referred to as "low spiritualism." This serves to illustrate the widespread acceptance of spiritualism among the city's elite and hints at conflicts produced by the SHM's approach to the religion.

In order to better comprehend the impact of the SHM's work it is necessary to reflect on the nature of public attitudes toward practices frequently condemned as low spiritualism during the 1930s in Recife. Although the expression "low spiritualism" is employed in both newspapers and erudite works as if its meaning were self-evident, an important feature of its use seems to be its flexibility. Indeed, in Recife's newspapers it often appears alongside a variety of other pejorative terms such as *macumba, catimbó,* and *magia negra.*[40] These newspaper reports provide an important window into public attitudes toward magic and charlatanry.[41]

More often than not the articles that describe the practices condemned in this way, or relate the stories of police raids on these "centers," do not refer to specific allegations. The people in question are simply denounced as engaging in nefarious activities defined by one or more pejorative terms. However, at times the language used in these articles points toward an interesting coincidence between fear of magic and a concern with the exploitation of the mentally fragile or credulous. For example, in 1930 an article in the *Diário da Tarde* reported the case of a forty-four-year-old woman called Maria Francisca das Chagas whose involvement with practices identified as "false spiritualism or *catimbó*" had apparently caused her to attempt suicide.[42] After seeking the advice of a medium named José Ribeiro, Maria had started to see visions that told her that if she wanted to get better she should cover her head in kerosene and set herself on fire. Maria eventually carried out the instructions of the spirit and was admitted to the hospital in critical condition. The article does not claim that the spirit is a real entity, asserting that its instructions "certainly had an origin in an element of mental imbalance."[43] In this case then, Maria was led astray by a medium who was either maliciously attempting to make money or whose incompetence caused her to experience dangerous visions. The piece exemplifies the common association made between low spiritualism and the provocation or exacerbation of a psychiatric disorder. However, the title of the article also makes an interesting association between the psychiatric concept of suggestion and magic in asserting that it was "fetishistic suggestions" that caused the poor victim to attempt suicide.[44]

A similarly ambiguous but more complex exposition of the power and malevolence of a sorcerer can be found in reports of police actions against the *terreiro* of a Xangô priest named Noberto. In 1932, the *Diário da Tarde* explicitly accused Noberto of exploiting "the credulity of the humble and good people" of his neighborhood.[45] In fact, his most serious crime was that of having "dishonored a poor young woman whom he cravenly deceived saying that he was carrying out a treatment to make her happy."[46] This seems like a clear-cut example of fraud, but the preceding description of the police raid suggests that Noberto was able to marshal more mysterious powers. The police who were sent to arrest Noberto were apparently quickly overcome by the atmosphere of his *terreiro* and "entered into the 'function,' 'enchanted' by the African melodies and by the beat of the drums."[47] The article reports that at one point the officers sensed a chill in the air, and one named Ildefonso "felt something strange make his legs tremble and his heart beat."[48] The clear implication is that some powerful occult force was at work.

Less than a year later, the same *terreiro* was again raided by the police. This time the report in the *Diário da Tarde* accused Noberto and his followers of having carried out "an interminable series of terrifying and appalling things" including separating couples, persecuting people's enemies, and causing the breakup of marriages.[49] No explanation was given of the mechanisms through which Noberto achieved these goals, but we must presume that he was being accused of using magic.

The object of quoting these articles is to illustrate the ambiguous way in which the actions of those identified as *macumbeiros*, *catimboseiros*, or practitioners of low spiritualism could be represented. Although these people are accused of exploitation and fraud, it is often unclear whether or not they also mobilized supernatural powers in the realization of immoral acts. More generally, while these articles continue to condemn certain practices as forms of charlatanry, lists of objects seized from the house being raided are always introduced as evidence of the crime—"objects of *catimbó*." Why were such objects considered dangerous? Was it because of some intrinsic power or because they served to evoke certain ideas in others? Perhaps the answer could be both. A police document from 1938 refers to objects taken from the *terreiro* of one of Recife's most famous priestesses in a police raid. Fortunata Maria da Conceição—the so-called Bahiana do Pina—had requested that some of her belongings be returned to her, claiming that she had ceased to practice low magic. Responding to her request, the police commissioner described these objects as having been "apprehended together with the material of low-magic belonging to the petitioner [...] a measure that has been applied to all those who possess images for the effects of suggestion."[50] Thus while Fortunata's images were to be used for the effect of suggestion, they were also categorized as "material of low magic." The actions of the police in confiscating these objects could be interpreted either as a campaign against harmful magic or as an attempt to put a stop to forms of charlatanry or exploitation enacted through suggestion. But it is important to underline that in both cases the objective of the police would have been configured in terms of the need to prevent Fortunata from using these objects to manipulate or exploit others.

The SHM's approach to the regulation of religious practices involving spirit possession was not entirely at odds with a more generally accepted understanding of how a sorcerer or *curandeiro* could exploit credulous people. Accordingly, the *Diário da Tarde*'s response to the SHM's agreement with the police suggests a certain receptiveness to aspects of their arguments. An article reporting on this accord condemned those that "consciously exploited the credulity and ignorance of others, seduced by the easy profits that this offered."[51] According to the article, the clients of such people were not only "fanatics and ignorants," at times they were also "mentally ill."[52] Indeed it was asserted that "it is alarming the number of insane and mentally unbalanced that is produced by low spiritualism and *low magic*."[53]

However, there is a significant difference between the arguments that were advanced in this article and those put forward by the SHM. Those guilty of such offences are identified by the newspaper as "the so-called fathers of the saint" (*paez de santo*), a phrase that would probably have led the reader to imagine practices considered to be African in origin.[54] Moreover, the target of the police repression described in this article is not spiritualism per se but low spiritualism and low magic. Thus this article was not criticizing spiritualism; rather it was condemning its low forms and other types of magical practice. This approach foreshadowed some direct criticisms of the SHM's work that will be examined below.

The SHM and Afro-Brazilian Religion

Xangô is not mentioned directly as an object of study in the SHM's official publications until 1933.[55] However, personal contacts between certain *terreiros* and those associated with the SHM probably predated its establishment; informally, those linked to the SHM had been attempting to acquire some form of legal recognition for certain groups since 1931 (Cavalcanti 1935, 243).

As part of their agreement with the *terreiros*, members of the SHM were able to attend ceremonies in order to pursue their studies and, presumably, to make sure that nothing untoward was taking place. Yet despite this, the SHM never published material that condemned possession within Xangô in the same terms that were used to describe the phenomenon in spiritualism. Similarly, while the leaders of Recife's *terreiros* were subjected to IQ tests, the SHM did not publish the results of such examinations in a form comparable to Cavalcanti's study about mediums that was quoted earlier.

Ramos's ideas about the conceptual difference between the charlatan and the *curandiero* were central in defining the SHM's approach to Xangô,

and his words were frequently paraphrased or even quoted directly. Gonçalves Fernandes, a technical assistant with SHM, went on to write three
books about forms of Afro-Brazilian religion. In the first of these, *Xangôs
do Nordeste*, he asserted that "[a]mongst the priests, one clearly observes
medical-sorcery. This *curandeirismo*, of magical-fetishistic origins, attaches
itself to pre-logical elements of the primitive mentality, and should not be
confused with charlatanry, which is the voluntary, conscious and responsible transgression of a code of class" (Fernandes 1937, 117).[56]

In light of what has been said about the way in which the SHM approached spiritualism, it should be possible to appreciate the wider significance of this assertion. These Xangô priests were not the conscious
exploiters one could encounter in spiritualist centers; they were representatives of a primitive African culture who were merely seeking, albeit in a
misguided way, to practice their religion. According to Fernandes, it was
thus futile to oppose the "medicine man" with "police violence." Only a
"continuous and persistent work of education" could make him disappear
(Fernandes 1937, 118).[57]

In common with other authors, notably Ramos, Fernandes attributed
the presence of supposedly immoral or commercial practices in Recife's
terreiros to the intermingling of Xangô with spiritualism, Catholicism, or
what were assumed to be other Amerindian traditions. This is epitomized
in his description of a religious group apparently known as the "Sect of
Caetana worshiping the Three Maji Kings" (Fernandes 1937, 140).[58] He concluded his account of a ceremony with these words: "The poverty of the
ritual in the Caetana centre reflects the predominant catholic-spiritualist-
caboclo influence, very little remaining of the African root" (Fernandes
1937, 140).[59] Fernandes also invoked a distinction between the collective
and spiritual aims of African religion and the commercial and individual
motivations behind what he considered to be more syncretic practices. He
suggested that in the Sect of Caetana "there does not exist the impulse to
worship the gods as a spiritual obligation." Rather, what drove the followers
were "solely magical concerns for immediate results" (Fernandes 1937,
144).[60]

However, despite the characterization of Xangô as a more positive and
spiritual religious practice, the SHM still faced a potential contradiction
in its analysis of the religion. How could they reconcile their characterization of spirit possession as a cause of mental illness and the tool of wicked
charlatans with their assertions about the fundamentally benign nature of
many of Recife's Afro-Brazilian religions? Interestingly, Fernandes seemed
to suggest that the most trusted of their informants, Pai Adão, hardly
tolerated possession at all: "In Adão's *terreiro* I never witnessed a fall of the

saint [...] This would be very difficult. Adão's scruples do not allow mystification. A whole year passes without even one of his initiates manifesting a deity" (Fernandes 1937, 64).[61]

This statement is somewhat ambiguous and may reflect the author's understanding of what constituted possession. Fernandes's use of the term "fall of the saint" in the first instance may suggest that he only recognized or was concerned with the more dramatic episodes when a person would fall to the ground as he or she was possessed. Possession was seen by Fernandes as a dangerous sign of instability and a potentially harmful act. Thus he dedicated a chapter of a book published in 1941 to the topic of "Spiritual-fetishist possession, mediunity and crime" (Fernandes 1941, 119–29).[62] This text referred to numerous examples of crimes or misdemeanors committed by those who were possessed or under the influence of a certain spiritual leader. However, Fernandes appeared to suggest that possession was less common in what he considered to be the more orthodox African temples. The first sentence of this chapter described "spiritual-fetishist possession," or the "state of the saint" as "frequently observed in the more diluted Afro-Brazilian cults—cheap spiritualism in the main, more difficult to see in the old Bahian 'terreiros' and [those] of Recife" (Fernandes 1941, 121).[63]

Fernandes thus projected the dangerous act of possession onto the supposedly less pure, more syncretic religions, while Pai Adão's apparent reluctance to allow the mystical and spectacular act of possession was a sign of the sincerity of his religious practice. In fact, this would suggest that those linked to the SHM were not able, nor indeed did they seek, to resolve the tension between attempting to protect Afro-Brazilian religions and their vision of spirit possession as evidence of pathology.

This apparent asymmetry in the SHM's approach to Xangô and spiritualism did not go unnoticed. Soon after the coup that brought the Estado Novo into existence in November 1937, Carlos de Lima Cavalcanti, the state governor who had supported Pernambucano in his reforms, was replaced by the zealously Catholic Agamenon Magalhães. In January 1938, a large number of spiritualist centers and terreiros were closed by the police at the order of the new state government. Many of the terreiros that were targeted were those that had been registered by the SHM and documented in their publications.[64] An article appearing in the conservative Catholic magazine Fronteiras in early 1938 applauded the police repression as a "work of hygiene—mental and social" and blamed the SHM for having fostered a climate of tolerance in which such practices could thrive.[65] The piece also noted that references to Xangô were absent from the SHM's texts, which linked possession to mental illness. It accused the body of inconsistency and asserted that "In not so remote times of common sense, the xangôs were comparable to spiritualist sessions, one of the most important causes of mental disturbance."[66]

This opinion reflects the contradictory legacy of the interventions of those linked to the SHM. While seeking to document and register cults that they considered benign, they also provided the conditions for their identification by the authorities as well as some of the arguments that would justify their eventual persecution.[67] Likewise, the principle of subjecting mediums to psychiatric tests was initially accepted in new legislation concerning the police registration of spiritualist centers in 1938 (Sá 2001, 330). Later still, the law that recognized the authority of the first Federation of Afro-Brazilian Cults created in 1951 required that leaders of *terreiros* be subjected to a psychiatric evaluation.[68]

Perhaps the most significant and certainly the boldest cultural intervention of those linked to the SHM was the First Afro-Brazilian Congress, which took place in November 1934. The event, organized by Freyre and Pernambucano together, united academics, artists, and priests in a six-day series of lecturers and cultural activities that included visits to witness ceremonies in some of the city's most famous *terreiros*.[69] At the time it was viewed with disdain by many conservatives and was associated with left-wing, even communist activity (Levine 1975, 190).[70] Indeed, it seems that in the minds of the conservative elites, communism and primitive African witchcraft were linked in an amalgam of antisocial forces. A government document from 1939 outlining the state's actions to repress "African sects" attributed their profusion to

> the intransigence of the authorities and to the effect of propaganda from certain intellectual elements, who, in their subtle interference, sought to form, among the individuals of color of our popular classes, a proselytism that is offensive to our culture and, moreover, encourages ideas that cause the disintegration of our civilization. (Magalhães 1939, 158)[71]

What precisely were these intellectuals being accused of encouraging among the black population of Recife? Does this text refer to communism, or is it suggesting that these intellectuals shamefully celebrated primitive, backward practices that should have no place in civilized society? Notwithstanding the symbolism of the Brazilian nation and "civilization" that is deployed here, this language seems to invoke the dynamic of an intelligent manipulator exploiting the ignorance and credulity of the poor and leading them to ruin. As an editorial in Magalhães's newspaper, *A Folha da Manhã*, put it, "The Afro-Brazilian Congress and those that inspired it, some of exceptional intelligence, ruined many good people, who were illiterate and of less strong character" (Campello 1938, 1).[72]

The Charlatan and the Sorcerer

Throughout this paper, I have drawn certain parallels between the figures of the charlatan and the sorcerer. In particular, I have suggested that fears about the actions of both were configured in a similar way. The sorcerer, it was presumed, was able to use supernatural powers in order to realize his selfish or immoral acts, while, through the invocation of powerful ideas and suggestions, the charlatan was also capable of manipulating and undermining the will of other people. Moreover, both were able to awaken strange passions and desires, even to motivate irrational and dangerous behavior.

But if there was a common understanding of the need to identify and combat the work of the sorcerer or charlatan, does this mean that all those who commented on, condemned, or were involved in prosecuting these individuals shared the same overarching belief in magic? This is a provocative question. It might even be argued that, in their desire to distinguish between the dangerous and exploitative charlatan and the innocent *curandeiro*, those linked to the SHM were merely recoding fears about sorcery using psychiatric language. Furthermore, it is certainly true that the SHM acted as a sort of power broker, becoming an important focus for those religious leaders who wished to condemn others or assert their own authority through claims made to members of the body. In this sense, the SHM's interventions could be seen as part of a tradition of legal regulation, which, as Maggie suggests, enacted accusations of witchcraft that often reflected rivalries between different groups (see chapter 8, this volume). I would suggest that the concerns of those who professed a rational scientific approach had much in common with the supposedly "irrational" beliefs they were rejecting. However, this does not mean that they were therefore equally implicated in the belief in witchcraft. The actions of the SHM were certainly not "inside" the logic that Maggie suggests underpins accusations of witchcraft since they rejected the notion that spirits or magic existed and could have an actual effect on people. Rather the ideas and histories discussed here reflect a more complex and ambiguous situation in which differing approaches to the problem of what was variously referred to as *curandeirismo*, charlatanry, or sorcery (*feitiçaria*) intersected, producing new ways of understanding supposed threats to the individual and society.

To some extent Maggie's overarching theoretical approach can be criticized for reducing the complex interaction of ideas and agents to a single objective—the task of identifying the sorcerer—guided by a simple and straightforward logic and common belief in magic.[73] For Maggie, the belief in witchcraft structures the activity of all those individuals involved in the legal process. However, Maggie also sees the possibility of a context in which this was not the case—colonial Rhodesia (see chapter 8, this volume). Maggie suggests that here the colonial authorities sought to overcome the belief in magic by outlawing accusations of witchcraft, espousing what is by implication a "rational" approach to these beliefs. Maggie's suggestion that some societies are in thrall to the power of the spell, while others stand outside this, risks reproducing the very divide between modernity and primitivism that has historically been at the center of attempts to push Africa to the margins of modernity and history—to a distant primitive world (see the introduction to this volume). Except this time it is Brazil that suffers in comparison to other supposedly more enlightened places.

Indeed the maintenance of a clear distinction between the rational and irrational, science and magic, modernity and primitivism was a concern that was central to the work of the SHM. It is possible to argue that in studying Xangô and portraying it as a primitive religion that was destined to die out, the doctors of the SHM achieved a certain confirmation of their own identities as scientists and as representatives of the modernity that they believed would eventually prevail over these primitive beliefs. To members of the SHM, the religious leaders they studied represented an authority that was totally different from their own. Figures like Pai Adão were seen as guardians of a primitive religious knowledge whose authority flowed from a supposedly static tradition rather than from the progressive application of scientific knowledge. In both cases, the reality may have been very different, but this was the symbolism that seemed to define these relationships for members of the SHM.[74]

In contrast, it appears that in spiritualism the doctors of the SHM confronted an alternative vision of modernity. While spiritualism was broadly accepted as a modern and scientific discourse, for members of the SHM it was nothing less than a pseudoscience that was enchanting the poor ignorant masses, creating ever larger numbers of mentally deranged people. Worse still was the possibility that, with its spurious claims to scientific authority, spiritualism was infiltrating the African cults and polluting their traditional culture, creating new syncretic forms of religion that were neither African nor European, modern nor primitive.

In seeking to describe a pure African tradition persisting in Recife's suburbs and poor neighborhoods, the interventions of those linked to the SHM have a broader significance in the longer trajectory of relations among the state, elites, and Afro-Brazilian religion—the transformation of

Xangô into a celebrated item of culture was beginning. However, it is also important to bear in mind that the immediate impact of the SHM's work was quite limited. In the short term, the body only succeeded in creating a narrow space in which "Africanness" effectively defined religious legitimacy. The SHM did not establish a broad consensus that so-called African religions should be tolerated. To the contrary, the increased visibility of Xangô and its association with certain intellectuals, most clearly expressed in the Afro-Brazilian Congress, was used to justify its repression, creating, or perhaps merely revealing, interesting semantic associations between communism and witchcraft. Significantly this was not the case with spiritualism as represented through the officially sanctioned federations. Despite initially suffering under the intensely Catholic regime that came to power in the state of Pernambuco in 1938, and after some disputes with the government, spiritualist federations were able to continue functioning with a legal situation that was much the same as before (Sá 2001, 324–38). As such, the contrast drawn by Giumbelli between the southeast and northeast of Brazil in terms of the privileged position of spiritualism in the former and the ascendancy of the concept of Afro-Brazilian religion in the latter may be somewhat overdetermined.

Nevertheless, Giumbelli is right to suggest that in the longer term Afro-Brazilian religion would become synonymous not with pathology but with culture. Perhaps ironically, intellectuals such as Ramos and those linked to the SHM were espousing a vision of these religions that eventually removed them from the ambit of medicine or psychiatry (Giumbelli 1997a, 215). Emblematic of the transformation that took place in the work of those doctors who began their study of Afro-Brazilian religion in the 1930s is the trajectory of René Ribeiro. During the 1930s, he worked as an intern with the SHM but later went on to produce an anthropological study of Recife's Afro-Brazilian religions under the guidance of Melville Herskovits (Ribeiro 1978). The ideas proposed by this North American ethnographer shifted anthropological approaches toward possession in Recife. In accordance with Herskovits's cultural relativism, Ribeiro now asserted that possession was culturally "normal" and indeed a vital ritual element in Xangô (see Ribeiro 1956). This position differed radically from the approach espoused by another member of the SHM, Fernandes, only a decade earlier. Ribeiro himself suggested that his time working within the SHM had been crucial to the success of his later research, allowing him to be seen by his informants as a "sympathetic confidant" (Ribeiro 1978, 6).[75] From this point of view, we can see that the SHM also played an important role in opening a dialog between intellectuals and representatives of the religion that would prove central to the reconfiguration of Xangô as a form of culture.

Notes to Chapter Six

1. I use the word "Xangô" to refer to the religious practices that were being described by intellectuals in Recife. The use of the word "Xangô" frequently implies an attempt to delimit a specific body of practices that is seen as more African than others. Today "Xangô" is broadly assumed to be equivalent to the term "Candomblé," which is employed more widely in relation to Afro-Brazilian religion in Bahia.

2. The doctrine of Kardecist spiritualism was initially expounded in Brazil by literate elites who had absorbed the teachings of Allan Kardec. Kardec was the pseudonym of the French writer Hyppolio Denizart Rivail. Beginning with *The Book of Spirits*, published in 1857, Kardec produced a number of writings based on the idea that the spirits of the dead could communicate with the living through mediums. Kardec's work grew from a desire to investigate the phenomena of spinning tables or talking boards, which had fascinated the European and North American public during the 1850s. He accepted that these phenomena should be seen as evidence of the existence of spirits and argued that humanity could learn through communication with higher, more evolved spiritual entities.

3. Owing to the specific questions surrounding their meanings, the Portuguese terms *curandeirismo* or *curandeiro* will be used in this paper. The terms *curandeirismo* and *charlatanismo* (charlatanry) are frequently used interchangeably. The word *curandeiro* could also be translated as "healer" (Harding 2000, 77). However, during the nineteenth century, representatives of the medical establishment used *curandeirismo* to refer to healing practices associated with poor and often black people. The term was therefore employed to delimit practices considered to be illegitimate but did not necessarily suggest the conscious attempt to commit fraud or invent cures that had no therapeutic value. Rather it expressed disdain for both the supposed ignorance of *curandeiros* and their clientele (Xavier 2003).

4. "os artigos revelaram, da parte dos autores, temor dos malefícios e necessidade de se criar modos e instituições para o combate a seus produtores" (author's translation). Maggie also makes this argument in this volume.

5. A *terreiro* is the temple/house in which religious ceremonies take place.

6. Those associated with the SHM used various expressions to refer to instances of spirit possession. Notably, the word "trance" was used mostly, if not exclusively, in relation to spiritualism (see Cavalcanti 1934b, 135), or to religious groups they considered to reflect a mixture of spiritualist practice and Xangô (Fernandes 1937, 127). "Possession" or even "state of the saint" (*estado do santo*) was predominantly used in relation to Xangô (Fernandes 1937, 111–5). Although it is clear that members of the SHM saw a difference between instances of "trance" or "possession" in Spiritualism and Xangô, they did not seek to make explicit comparisons between the two. It is possible that the use of the word "trance" in relation to spiritualism reflected the extent to which members of the SHM thought such states to be the product of deliberate artifice. Throughout this paper I have used "possession" or "spirit possession" for consistency, employing the term "trance" only when this was used by the authors of the texts I am discussing.

7. More broadly, the northeast of Brazil is assumed to be home to a more powerful tradition of African religion, whereas the south and southeast of Brazil are often portrayed as having been regions in which these African roots were diluted by practices such as spiritualism, producing new forms of syncretic, but symbolically

"whiter" religions. The extent to which spiritualism influenced or was influenced by other traditions forms the basis of a much larger debate about how racial, class, and ethnic identities could be expressed through the configuration of religious practices. The emergence of *Umbanda* in Rio de Janeiro has been seen as an attempt to socially "whiten" Afro-Brazilian religions, doing away with the more "African" elements of ritual practice and incorporating elements of spiritualism (see Brown 1986). Adherence to Kardecism might well have been a way of asserting an elite identity, but it seems unreasonable to suggest that the adoption of elements of spiritualism necessarily implied a social "whitening" of Afro-Brazilian practice. The SHM's own studies testify to the diversity of the different practices and techniques adopted by various *terreiros*. Both spiritualist federations and the SHM were concerned with the profusion of different practices and the intermingling of what they identified as separate traditions, albeit for very different reasons. In this context it is not necessarily useful to see categories such as "Afro-Brazilian religion" and "spiritualism" as reflective of two readily identifiable and distinct bodies of ideas and practices. In fact they may be better understood as terms that are applied by different individuals or groups to assert or contest the legitimacy of various religious practices at different times.

8. The *Centro Espírita Regeneração* was founded in 1904, informally providing support and guidance to establish other spiritualist centers. In 1915 this body ceased to exist and became the *Federação Espírita Pernambucana*. *A Cruzada Espírita Pernambucana* was founded in 1923, also with the intention of offering affiliation to other groups (Sá 2001, 311).

9. *Seitas africanas* was the expression used in numerous of the SHM's publications. See, for example, Cavalcanti (1935).

10. The Estado Novo was an authoritarian regime implanted in Brazil by President Getúlio Vargas.

11. "Praticar o espiritismo, a magia e seus sortilégios, usar de talismãs e cartomancia para despertar sentimentos de ódio ou amor, inculcar cura de moléstias curáveis ou incuráveis, enfim, para fascinar e subjugar a credulidade pública."

12. "imiscuiu-se [...] nos assuntos da magia e interveio no combate aos feiticeiros regulando acusações, criando juízos especiais e pessoal especializado."

13. Nina Rodrigues was a criminologist and scholar who occupied various posts in the medical establishment in Bahia including the chair of criminology (*medicinalegal*). His first study of Afro-Brazilian religions, *O animismo fetishista dos negros baianos*, was published in serial form in *Revista Brasileira* in 1896 and published in French as a book in 1900. His second work on this subject, *Os africanos no Brasil*, was not published as a single volume before his death in 1906. Both books were republished during the 1930s when Nina Rodrigues's ethnographic work was championed by the criminologist and ethnographer Arthur Ramos, whose work I discuss below.

14. "todas as classes, mesmo a dita superior, estão aptas a se tornarem negras."

15. "a tradução na lei desse estado de espírito que, partindo das classes inferiores da nossa população, vem conquistando para as suas preocupações supersticiosas mesmo as classes dirigentes e mais cultas."

16. "é uma inépcia da lei pretender proteger quem cientemente se deixa explorar; mais do que isso, a feitiçaria assim organizada pressupõe a mesma participação, na responsabilidade social, dos feiticeiros e da sua clientela."

17. "criminalidade étnica."

18. As Eleonora Haddad Antunes suggests, the popularity of the movement increased greatly after the First World War. The *Liga Brasileira de Higiene Mental* was founded in Rio de Janeiro in 1923 (Antunes 2002, 88–93).

19. This description can hardly hope to account for the complexity of discussions about race and hereditarianism in Brazilian social thought at this time. This represents an extremely simplified summary of the arguments put forward by Thomas E. Skidmore (1993).

20. For a discussion of the extent to which the mental hygiene movement accommodated and was aligned with eugenics see Antunes (2002).

21. "predispostos hereditariamente às afecções mentais."

22. Ulysses Pernambuco had studied medicine in Rio, graduating in 1912, and had been an intern at the *Hospício Nacional de Alienados*.

23. Giumbelli argues that Ramos did not view spirit possession as the expression of a biological predisposition but as the result of a more transient psychological state. (Giumbelli 1997b, 55–6).

24. "II—O charlatão é o transgressor consciente de uma codificação de classe e deve soffrer as penalidades que lhe dita a lei. O curandeiro é um charlatão involuntario cuja conducta obedece a determinismos psychologicos bem diversos."

III—Estes moveis são os factores pre-logicos da mentalidade primitiva, como os encontramos no homem medicina das sociedades selvagens. A persistencia desta mentalidade no curandeiro de nossos dias torna-se evidente em certos meios, do Brasil, que receberam o influxo directo do negro e do indio."

25. Apart from an institution to house the criminally insane (*manicômio jurídico*), the services were divided into those orientated toward the treatment of mental patients with more severe psychiatric conditions (*alienados*) and those who were deemed to require only occasional care (*não alienados*). The first group of patients was further divided between those who were suffering with acute conditions, treated in the psychiatric hospital, and those with chronic conditions, who were treated in a colony located outside the city. For those patients diagnosed with less severe illnesses, an ambulatory service and an open hospital were available (Pernambucano 1932, 10–11)

26. Among those who occupied the role of "technical assistant" (*auxiliar tecnico*) were Pedro Cavalcanti, Gonçalves Fernandes, and René Ribeiro. All three were medical students when they worked for the SHM and went on to develop interests in the study of forms of Afro-Brazilian religion. See Ribeiro (1978); Fernandes (1937, 1938, 1941); and Cavalcanti (1935)

27. In Rio de Janeiro, Giumbelli argues that the term "low spiritualism" (*baixo espiritismo*) emerged from conflicts between spiritualist centers and federations. Along with the term "false spiritualism" (*falso espiritismo*), it was used to label those centers believed to be engaged in unethical or doctrinally unorthodox practices. By the 1920s "low spiritualism" had become the more common expression, appearing frequently in police reports to describe objects and practices that were deemed to be criminal. Giumbelli argues that, rather than refer to a specific set of objects or practices, the most important feature of its meaning is the suggestion of intent to delude or exploit (Giumbelli 1997a, 221–9).

28. "causas de doenças mentais diretamente acessiveis."

29. "A pratica daquilo que se convencionou chamar o "baixo espiritismo" ou simplesmente "espiritismo" se alastrou tanto nas baixas camadas da populaçao que já constitúe um problema policial e sanitario dificil de resolver."

30. "delirios episodicos."

31. "desenvolvimento peculiar do espiritismo em nosso meio."

32. "individuos incultos."

33. "debilidade intelectual."

34. "Esta inferioridade torna possivel no caso do espiritismo de suas deformações e das varias crendices populares a aceitação por parte do individuo do carater sobrenatural dos fenomenos que observa: estes são assim capazes de agir como causa desencadeante da psicopatia."

35. "a maioria dos mediums é constituida por debeis mentais." Cavalcanti also asserted that at least one of those cases analyzed was of possibly "normal intelligence" (*inteligência normal*). He suggested that this person was an indoctrinator rather than a medium (Cavalcanti 1934b, 142).

36. "grande parte da população vive a admirar e a acreditar nelas, como sendo, manifestações dos espiritos."

37. "São conhecidos entre nós os exemplos das manifestações misticas (Joazeiro do Padre Cicero) e as reações anti-sociais (Canudos de Antonio Conselheiro) das massas."

38. "O espiritismo é um perigoso habito mental; pode conduzir á loucura; devem evital-o." Arquivo Público Estadual Jordão Emerenciano (hereafter APEJE), Diversos Fundos, Saúde Pública 1930–1932, Copies of radio lectures, anonymous, 5 February 1931.

39. "considerando que no quadro social desta associação, existem muitos sectarios do espiritismo "religião" nos empanhamos para que nenhuma dissertação tenha o cunho de ataque religioso, devendo haver o combate scientifico ao baixo espiritismo, responsavel que é de grande males." APEJE, Diversos Fundos, Saúde Pública 1930–1932, Oscar Moreira Pinto to Ulisses Pernambucano, January 26, 1931.

40. This is hardly an exhaustive list of the numerous colloquial terms used to signify witchcraft or *curandeirismo*. The most commonly applied of these in Recife at this time appears to have been the expression *catimbó*.

41. The newspaper consulted in this research was the *Diário da Tarde*, which ran from 1928 until 1939. The title was owned by Carlos de Lima Cavalcanti and was a vehicle for promoting his political aspirations before he became governor following the revolution in 1930. During his governorship the paper served as a mouthpiece for his administration.

42. "falso espiritismo ou catimbó." "Alta Noite, Quando Ella Dormia, Diziam-lhe As Visões: 'Se Queres Ficar Bôa, Deita Kerosene Na Cabeça e Ateia Fogo . . . ,'" *Diário da Tarde*, February 6, 1930, p. 3. All subsequent notes related to this case refer to the same article and page.

43. "certamente tinham como origem algum principio de desequilibrio mental."

44. "suggestões fetichistas."

45. "credulidade daquella gente humilde e bôa." "Acabando Com a 'Macumba' Em Beira-Mar," *Diário da Tarde*, December 19, 1932. All subsequent notes related to this case refer to the same article.

46. "deshonrado uma pobre moça a quem illudiu covardemente, dizendo estar fazendo um tratamento para ella ser feliz . . ."

47. "entraram na 'funcção,' 'enlevados' pelas toadas africanas e pelos rufos dos tambores."

48. "percebeu que alguma cousa extranha lhe fazia tremer as pernas e palpitar o coração."

49. "uma serie interminavel de coisas espantosas, apavorantes . . ." "Afogados—refugio dos macumbeiros africanos," *Diário da Tarde*, August 1, 1933.

50. "apreendidas juntamente com o material de baixa-magia, pertencente a requerente [. . .] medida esta que vem sendo aplicado a todos que teem imagens para efeitos de sugestão." APEJE, Secretaria de Segurança Pública/Delegacia de Ordem Política e Social, Fortunata Maria da Conceição—Baiana do Pina, 1938 (21.913), Ildefonso Vasconcelos to Secretário de Segurança Pública, August 18, 1938.

51. "exploram, conscientemente, a credulidade e a ignorancia alheias, seduzidos pelos faceis lucros que dahi auferem." "Para a efficiente repressão ao 'catimbó' e ao baixo espiritismo," *Diário da Tarde*, November 26, 1933, p. 6. All subsequent notes related to this case refer to the same article and page.

52. "fanaticos e incultos"; "doentes mentaes."

53. "É alarmante o numero de psychopathas, de desequilibrados mentaes produzido pelo baixo espiritismo e pela *baixa magia.*"

54. "os chamados *paez de santo.*" Pai de santo means "father of the saint" and is normally identified with Xangô priests.

55. Cavalcanti referred in passing to the "African sects" (*seitas africanas*) he had observed in a certain neighborhood in Recife, asserting that these would be the subject of a later work (Cavalcanti 1933, 59).

56. "Entre os páis de terreiro observa-se franca feitiçaria-medica. Este curandeirismo, de origem magico-fetichista prende-se a fatores pre-logicos da mentalidade primitiva e não deve ser confundido com o charlatanismo, que é a transgressão voluntaria, consciente, e responsavel de um codigo de classe."

57. "homem-medicina"; "violencia policial"; "um trabalho continuo e persistente de educação."

58. "Seita de Caetana em adoração aos 3 Reis Magos."

59. "A pobreza do ritual do centro de Caetana reflete a influencia predominante catolico-espirita-coboclo, muito pouco restando da raiz africana."

60. "Não existe [. . .] o sentido de cultuar aos deuses como obrigação spiritual"; "mas unicamente preocupações magicas para exitos imediatos."

61. "Neste terreiro de Adão nunca presenciei uma quéda de santo [. . .] O escrupulo de Adão não permite mistificações. Passa-se ano inteiro sem que um dos filhos sequer manifeste o orixá." Pai Adão, Recife's most venerated *pai de santo*, developed a personal relationship with Gilberto Freyre and was also well-known to scholars and religious leaders in Salvador.

62. "Possessão espírito-fetichista, mediunidade e crime."

63. "possessão espírito-fetichista"; "estado-de-santo"; "de observação frequente nos cultos afro-brasileiros mais diluidos—espiritismo do barato na maioria, mais dificil de se ver nos velhos "terreiros" baianos e do Recife."

64. A list of the *terreiros* raided was provided in an article appearing in the *Diário de Pernambuco*. Most, if not all, of the *terreiros* identified in the SHM's various publications were among these. "Fechados pela policia varios 'xangôs,'" *Diário de Pernambuco*, February 13, 1938, p. 12.

65. "obra de hygiene—mental e social." "A Repressão dos Xangôs," *Fronteiras* 7, n. 1–2, January–February 1938. All subsequent notes related to this case refer to the same article.

66. "Nos tempos não muito remotos do bom senso, os xangôs eram equiparados ás sessões espiritas, uma das mais importantes causes de disturbios mentais."

67. As such, while the SHM was criticized for having encouraged Xangô, the official decree that prohibited the city's African sects (*seitas africanas*) from functioning also stipulated that the objects taken in police action against those who did not comply with the order would be taken to the SHM's own museum. ("Secretaria da Segurança Publica, Portarias do Sr. Secretario da Segurança Publica," *Diário do Estado*, January 26, 1938, p. 15.) The SHM's small museum of 130 pieces was described by Ribeiro in an article in 1935. It consisted of three sections: one containing records about spiritualist centers, a part dedicated to the artistic production of mental patients and documenting old techniques for the restraint of the mentally ill, and an "African section" (*uma seção africana*) consisting of objects donated by some Xangô temples after the First Afro-Brazilian Congress (Ribeiro and Lins 1935, 75). According to an article published in the SHM's regular bulletin in the same year, the museum was already established as a repository for "cult objects apprehended by the police" (*objetos de culto apreendidos pela policia*). "O Estudo das Religiões do Recife," *Boletim de Higiene Mental*, 3, n. 9-12, September–December, 1935.

68. "Those responsible for the functioning of 'terreiros' are subject to proof of moral competence and a psychiatric examination, in which shall be established their complete mental health" ["Os responsáveis pelo funcionamento de 'terreiros' ficam sujeitos à prova de idoneidade moral e a exame psiquiátrico, em que seja constatada a sua perfeita saúde mental"]. "Lei N° 1166," *Diário Oficial*, September 11, 1951, p. 3,870.

69. Notably, Pai Adão did not participate in the congress, despite having been closely involved in its organization alongside Freyre. Soon after Adão's death in 1936, Freyre wrote that this was provoked by a disagreement over who should participate in the event. Adão had apparently proposed that only he and a man named Martiniano Eliseu do Bonfim, a renowned oracle or diviner from Bahia, should be present to represent their religion. Freyre could not accept the exclusion of representatives from all other Xangô groups. Freyre, "Pae Adão," *Diario de Pernambuco*, April 28, 1936, p. 3. Martiniano was Nina Rodrigues's informant and continued to be a figure of great importance to intellectuals studying Candomblé in Salvador during the 1930s.

70. Pernambucano left his role as director of the state asylum and associated services in 1935 but continued to work within the organization. He was subsequently arrested in 1935 and held for forty days under suspicion of being involved in the attempted communist coup of that year. Under Magalhães's administration he was harassed and forced out of any official posts (Hutzler 1987, 32).

71. "As seitas africanas, notademente, a principio em pequeno número, tiveram nos últimos tempos, grande desenvolvimento no Recife, para o que contribuiram a transigencia da autoridade e a influência da propaganda de certos meios intelectuais, visando esta, na sutilêza da sua interferência, a formação entre os individuos de côr das camadas populares, de um proselitismo infenso à nossa cultura e portanto, propicio às idéias dissolventes da nossa civilização."

72. "O Congresso Afro-Brasileiro e seus inspiradores, algumas de excepcional intelligencia, estragaram muita gente bôa, mas de poucas letras e menos fortaleza de caracter." In fact, the author of this article seemingly made a much more powerful claim about the former political elite's involvement with Xangô, suggesting that "the 'father of the Saint' most skilled at preaching in the *terreiros* to the sound of the drums" was none other than the previous governor Carlos de Lima Cavalcanti ["o 'pae de Santo' mais habil em predicar nos terreiros ao som do batuque"]. Considering the context of

the article, it seems unlikely that Campello was actually accusing Cavalcanti of being a Xangô priest. Rather he was using a powerful metaphor to condemn the former governor's perceived tolerance of the religion. However, the ambiguous nature of this statement was probably not unintentional.

73. A similar criticism of Maggie's approach is also made by Giumbelli (1997a, 34–35).

74. Leaders in some of the most powerful and intensely studied *terreiros* in Brazil have often presented innovations in ritual practice or the structure of their temples as a return to or rediscovery of older African practices. For a discussion of this dynamic in relation to the history of the famous *terreiro* of Axé Opó Afonjá in Salvador, see Sansi (2003, 214–6). In Recife, Adão is widely thought to have contravened the previously female line of accession in his *terreiro* when he assumed the leadership of the group after his return from Africa. He also introduced a number of modifications to the rituals, justifying them as a return to lost African traditions (see Ribeiro 1978, 108). The logic of uncovering deeper sources of knowledge also appealed to intellectuals who were seeking out the purer, most authentically African practices. As I argue generally here, it is also significant that in their attempts to deploy scientific knowledge about possession, the SHM tapped into longstanding fears about the ability of one individual to control or harm others through unseen powers.

75. "confidente-simpatizante."

7

From Enchantment by Science to Socialist Sorcery: The Cuban Republic and Its Savage Slot

STEPHAN PALMIÉ

ONCE THOUGHT TO have been laid to rest in the 1970s, the anthropological study of witchcraft and sorcery has rebounded with extraordinary vigor. Part of this is owing to its ostensible unmooring from the functionalist paradigm that, in its most classical Africanist instantiations, tended to reduce occult practices and their persecution to convenient gauges of social strains internal to small-scale social formations (Marwick 1964). Likewise, the Durkheimian strategy of approaching the seemingly counterintuitive increase of occult practices under conditions of modernization as symptomatic of the breakdown of traditional social orders has fallen into disrepute.[1] Mary Douglas herself (1970, xx) summarily closed the door on both interpretations in calling "the proposition that an increase of witchcraft accusations occurs as a symptom of disorder and moral collapse" in seemingly closed, homeostatically integrated systems "superbly untestable."

Among other things, this was so because these systems were never closed or homeostatically integrated to begin with. If, in puzzling over the rise of initiatory associations devoted to magical practices in early twentieth-century Azandeland, Evans-Pritchard (1937, 513) had conceded that "new situations demand new magic," then what came into light in the course of the past decades was precisely this "newness" that Evans-Pritchard himself had attributed to what some of us might nowadays be inclined to call the globalization of local social worlds and moral economies in the Anglo-Egyptian Sudan. Ironically, what appeared to Evans-Pritchard as a question-begging anomaly difficult to integrate into a finely wrought analysis of Azande notions of mystical causality has now become the subject par excellence for a renewed anthropological interest in the occult worlds emerging on the peripheries of global capitalism.

Perhaps prefigured by Taussig's (1980) interpretation of devil pacts and money baptism as a folk analytics critical of the effects of capitalism on the lives of what he called "neophyte proletarians,"[2] but certainly fully articulated in the contributions to Jean and John Comaroff's *Modernity and Its Malcontents* (1993) and Peter Geschiere's (1997) *The Modernity of Witchcraft*, the *nouveau regime* in anthropological studies of witchcraft has turned the tables on the tradition for which *Witchcraft, Magic and Oracles* set an ambiguous precedent.[3] This is so because the explanatory premium is no longer placed on the persistence of locally endemic traditions of witchcraft and witch-hunting. What has come into focus instead is the nature of the modernity (or modernities) that appears to be driving a pandemic of sinister signification, thus rendering "the parochialism of witches [...] an increasingly global phenomenon" (Comaroff and Comaroff 1999a, 286; cf. Geschiere, this volume). No longer an anomaly to be relegated to footnotes or appendices, the coincidence of witchcraft *and* modernity now has become an analytically priority, if not a priori.

Obviously, and whether we are dealing with Andean miners' devil pacts, colonial East African vampire firemen (White 2000), Latin American organ-stealing rumors (Scheper-Hughes 1996), witchcraft-driven helicopter gunships in Mozambique's independence war (West 2005), or postapartheid South African zombie labor forces (Comaroff and Comaroff 1999b), the new agenda dovetails with the belated entrance of the concept of "modernity" itself into the purview of an anthropology critical of its own foundations in, and long unwitting complicity with, larger discursive regimes premised on and gyrating around what Michel-Rolph Trouillot (1991) called the "savage slot." Indeed, a good deal of the fascination the subject of witchcraft and sorcery held for anthropologists and historians in the past was unquestionably owed to the unacknowledged play of some of the very "asymmetrical counterconcepts" (Koselleck 1985) that had made modernity thinkable in the first place. That occidentalist visions of Western rationality have always been propped up by the exuberant irrationality of a non-Western other is no innocent matter, however.[4] As Randall Styers (2004, 223) puts it in a scathing polemic about the rise of the category of "magic" in Western social thought,

> scholarly debates over magic regularly turn on questions of social order. Issues of class, authority, and social control have been central components of theoretical formulations of magic commonly configured as the province of women, children, foreigners, primitives, and other deviants. The

rhetoric of magic's self-seeking, irrationality, and futility reverberates with broader gender and racial ideologies, both lending its weight to those ideologies and taking on greater resonance through them. Magic is invoked as a marker of social difference, and by highlighting magic's preoccupation with power, the efforts of socially marginal actors to obtain or exert power is overtly stigmatized. At the same time, with the theme of power deflected onto magic, the forms of control exercised by the dominant classes are eclipsed and naturalized. [. . .] modern theories of magic have regularly conformed with the interests of dominant groups, both in configuring an unruly and benighted colonial periphery and in stigmatizing marginal groups within the domestic population.

Matters are, of course, rather more complicated than that. Elites are, after all, not unknown to have deployed mystical resources to cement their power. Yet the syndrome Styers is diagnosing here is easier denounced than remedied. As Douglas (1970, xxiii) pointed out quite some time ago, classic structural functionalist interpretations of witchcraft aiming to counter such conceptions by revealing the constructive role that witchcraft beliefs served in managing conflict thrived on a charitable liberal relativism that tended to primitivize the political dimensions of non-Western forms of sociality and therefore (by implication) left the savage slot pretty much intact. If this is so, however, it may well be worth asking whether our current concerns with the neoliberal New World disorder and the dialectics between occult global economics and local economies of the occult once more merely reproduces the syndrome, in politically revalorized form, at a higher level of analysis (Englund and Leach 2000).

Take here Paolo Israel's (2009, 158) checklist of the "conceptual operations" necessary to transform the occult into a privileged domain "in which to explore crises of capitalist modernity and their counter-hegemonic discourses and moral economies produced by a vernacular standpoint." Thus goes Israel's recipe:

(1) Abstract from the inherent truth-value of occult rumours and witchcraft talk, considering them as discursive genres market by moral intentions and a metaphorical texture. (2) Connect the rumours to some "hard" politico-economic reality constructed with objectifying methods of social and historical analysis. (3) Presuppose an unthematised "political unconscious" as the point of mediation where reality (as understood by the scholar) is articulated into representation (as expressed metaphorically by witchcraft discourse or rumor) [. . .] (Israel 2009, 158–9)

In other words, if witchcraft was once about the misrecognition of social contradictions inherent in traditional social systems or produced by their disintegration in the course of modernization, it is now about much of the same on a global scale where local experiences of misfortune and inscrutable dangers produced by the harsh realities of neoliberal capitalism are misrecognized (or critiqued, depending upon one's analytical preference) as the work of witchcraft and sorcery. While the truth of witchcraft once lay in local structural tensions for which there was no other institutional solution, it now appears to lie in global structural tensions for which there is also no other solution.

I do not wish here to add to an emerging critique of the literature that anthropologists and historians have spun around the theme of magic and modernity in the past quarter of a century or so. But I would like to make a point about the nature of the epistemic objects around which this literature has taken shape. Given that such objects tend to become accessible to us only through discourses about them (after all, the nature of the occult is that it is occult), and given also that words certainly can kill, perhaps we might do well to consider the economies of signification within which such objects take shape and do their (sometimes truly deadly) semiotic work. In other words, rather than concentrate, a priori, on the metaphorical functions of witchcraft-talk as either folk analytics or mystifications (which is not to say that discourses on the occult do not serve such functions), it may be worth focusing on the productivity—the pragmatics and illocutionary functions—of such discourse in constituting its own referents in the form of "moral artifacts" (Fields 1982) that, once they enter into social circulation, are ignored only at one's own peril.

Focusing on such objects and artifacts themselves not only allows us to attend to their sometimes rather paradoxical careers, as they transform in alignment with the historically changing publics and projects within which they perform their cultural and political work (and that they, in turn, help crystallize). It also enables us to guess at the extent to which their semiotic productivity entails the "creative destruction" of alternative economies of signification within which people, under different circumstances, might try to comprehend their social worlds and envision their futures. This is by no means to foreclose the question of how and why the specific objects and artifacts so constituted attain credibility and experiential salience—and therefore extradiscursive relevance and tangible force. But it is to bracket the question of what occult representations may—or may not—be really about and to start instead at an empirically accessible level, namely, that of talk and that which is talked into being.

In the following, I will sketch the career of one such moral artifact talked into being in Cuban public discourse since the beginning of the twentieth century when proponents of a scientific national modernity first objectified it as manifestations of "black wizardry" to be exterminated in securing the nation's future. There are significant ironies involved in telling this story. For if black wizardry initially served both as a launching pad for Cuban versions of science and modernity and as a stage on which republican elites violently instantiated their visions of social control, then perhaps the properly objectified and patrimonialized cultural heritage left by the victims of republican persecutory campaigns is nowadays similarly serving the revolutionary Cuban state as a stage on which (changing) visions of socialist consciousness, citizenship, and internationalism are enacted and performed into being.

What is more, if the resurgence of occult economies in the midst of the failed promises of prosperity and plenty held out by millennial capitalism has been attributed to the experientially occult nature of global neoliberal economics (from the perspective of its victims and their anthropologists, that is), then the Cuban state's recent promotion of Afro-Cuban religious traditions from a remnant of capitalist false consciousness to an ideological weapon in the fight against just such forms of consciousness ought to give us reason to pause.[5] Is global capitalist sorcery here being fought with more sorcery—as a witchcraft and modernity interpretation might suggest? Is the Cuban state merely conjuring with a newly discovered source of rationalizations—secondary elaborations of belief in socialism as a premise for authentic Cuban nationhood, as we might say with both Max Weber and E. E. Evans-Pritchard? Are we facing an instance of "extraversion" (Bayart 1993)—this time in tune not with classical modernization theory (whether of bourgeois or Marxist tenor) but with the instrumentalization of cultural heritages in the service of local versions of global identity politics? Or has black wizardry perhaps always functioned as an essentially empty category to be filled with varying political and moral content? As will become clear, I favor the latter answer.

Whatever role witchcraft and wizardry played and continue to play in the minds and actions of Cuba's *clases populares* (as current official language has it), so much is clear: Cuba's very own savage slot became radically reconfigured over the course of a long second half of the twentieth century. How Afro-Cuban tradition (itself arguably a product of postcolonial modernity) transformed from a liability of the Revolution to one of its declared assets is a long and involved story that I can only begin to sketch here. But it needs to be put into proper historical context. So let me turn back the clock about a hundred of years.

Human Sacrifice

In the course of a period of at least two decades of massive, often violent repression, beginning in late 1904, Cuban social science and Afro-Cuban religions came to enter into mutually constitutive relations. In November of that year, a twenty-month-old female toddler named Zoila Díaz disappeared from her parents' homestead in a rural town south of Havana. Within days, three elderly Africans were arrested and charged with having killed and disemboweled the child. A theory about their motive emerged early on, and although it was never proven in court, it led to the execution of Domingo Bocourt and his alleged accomplice, the creole Victor Molina. Being a "locally known" *brujo* or African wizard, Bocourt, so the reasoning went, had aimed to cure an African woman of a magical harm (*daño*) done to her by the whites in the period of slavery by application of the girl's blood. Selected to procure the victim, Molina, in turn, had killed the girl and had extracted not only the blood but various organs from her body, which he intended to fashion into charms to be sold commercially.[6]

The story is as fascinating in its dramatization of themes pertaining to the abuse of dehumanized bodies for economic purposes—a key feature of slavery if there ever was one—as it is obscene in its political implications and concrete results. Neither was it an isolated case. Between 1904 and the early 1920s, some two dozen incidents involving the death or disappearance of children were publicly interpreted as *brujería*-related crimes and repeatedly elicited not just vociferous bursts of public outrage but also mob violence and attempted or consummated lynchings of presumed black *brujos*. In public discourse, the term *brujería* came to flourish as a highly inclusive category, metonymically condensing a variety of practices by means of a superimposed metaphorical scheme in which Afro-Cuban cultural otherness and the violent murder of children interacted to form a novel complex that exhibited stunningly expansive tendencies. *Brujería* proliferated—if in the form of a growing ubiquity of signs perceivable as symptoms of its presence, or created in the course of measures to eradicate it. Particularly in the aftermath of the so-called race war of 1912—the violent military campaign to smash the *Partido Independiente de Color*[7]— Havana's urban police increased raids on Afro-Cuban cult groups in attempt to stem what was felt to be a rising tide of African witchcraft that complemented black political unrest in a dangerous manner. The copious evidence of African-looking ritual paraphernalia thus produced seemed to indicate a sinister process insidiously unfolding behind closed doors or under cover of darkness.

By the time of the second U.S. occupation, the American forces could not help but face up to the problem. In the wake of the so-called "niña Luisa" case in Alacranes (province of Matanzas) in 1908, the commanding officer of the American occupation forces in Matanzas saw fit to report to his superiors the results of his confidential investigations into the beliefs and practices "responsible for most, if not all, of the child-murders that so frequently occur in Cuba." "One of their beliefs," Colonel O.J. Sweet concluded, "is that the blood of a child is a sure cure for some diseases. The higher and nobler the birth of the child, the greater and surer the efficacy of its blood."[8] What particularly perplexed Cuban observers was that none of these practices seemed to be traceable to the colonial period. Instead, if Cuba appeared to be in the throes of an epidemic of ritual crime, such atrocities were entirely contemporaneous with—indeed, as Bronfman (2004, 39) writes, represented an "inherent but inexplicable" feature of—Cuban republican modernity. As a commentator in El Día put the matter in 1918, "Until after the triumph of the revolution blacks raised white children without eating or abusing them." Now that national independence had been achieved and Afro-Cubans were endowed with full citizenship rights, they "have begun to drink the blood of white children" (cited in Bronfman 2004, 39).[9]

As the latter quote indicates, it is of course not difficult to see to what interests the construct of brujería spoke. As Helg (1995, 1996) argues, the concept of brujería and the techniques of repression it suggested well served a new Cuban elite bent on avoiding having to address the problem of persisting racial inequality under a nominally color blind constitution. Similarly, Chávez Álvarez (1991) suggests that the "niña Zoila" case dramatizes, in symbolic form, the turn from the "violent mechanism of slavery" to the "violence of racial discrimination," which was vital to the political economic order characterizing the U.S.-sponsored first Cuban republic. In his view, brujería focused, and thereby rendered more effective, general strategies of racializing social inequality.

Helg and Chávez are certainly right in situating the case within its larger political—and political economic—context, including, not incidentally, the role of U.S. interference in the economic and political affairs of the Caribbean region. Sharing important structural features with the North American obsession with the sexual defilement of white women by black men, the image of the disemboweled bodies of white female children sacrificed to African deities for the sake of healing illiterate ex-slaves invoked not only a symbolical inversion of the projected future of the Cuban nation—suggesting the ravage of white republican progeny as an atonement for the clinging evil of a slaveholding past. It also constituted a national embarrassment with respect to Cuba's accreditation as a civilized state.

Ever since the 1820s, Cuban critics of slavery had condemned Spain's policy of building up its last prosperous colony by condoning the illegal import of Africans instead of white metropolitan laborers. Now, it seemed, the Cuban republic labored under the lasting heritage of a misguided colonial development scheme, and its unintended social, cultural, and—most painfully for contemporary nationalist thinkers—biological results. The very presence of an African and African-descended population within the social and political space defined by the new Cuban state posed a vexing ideological problem. As in many other Latin American nations, the reception of European scientific racism and positivistic social thought by local intellectuals and the political elite since the late nineteenth century had created an obsessive awareness not only of the existence of an African population but of the "racially mixed" status of the better part of the national population—an awareness that appeared to call for attempts on the part of self-conscious modernists to rid Cuba of its racial stigma by discursive and/or physical means.

Here then was a second arena in which the "niña Zoila" case and its successors came to perform "cultural work." No doubt, the early twentieth-century witch hunts served the overt political purpose of discrediting Cuba's black electorate and justifying the manner in which landless rural Afro-Cubans were shuttled back into coercive labor regimes different from slavery only in the formal legitimating structure undergirding their exploitation. But to say as much is to stop short of the larger analytical task of relating concrete technologies of repression to the ideological templates that not only inform them but within which instances of repression, in turn, come to function as cultural performances reproductive of situated projections of identity and moral community. As I shall argue, the concept of *brujería* acquired its tremendous power as a device for constructing overtly racialized notions of Cuban national self-hood precisely at a moment when Cuban versions of European science came into their own. The conjuncture was not fortuitous. The vision of social progress and scientific control of human affairs that animated Cuban intellectual life in the early republican period was deeply imbricated in the construct of an atavistic other whose very body—indeed, whose anatomy and visceral structure—would serve as the theater within which apprentices of an international sorcery would perform their cures of the Cuban national organism.

One of the obvious problems they encountered was that *brujería* was legally intractable. Indeed, a critical defect of the old Spanish criminal code—still in force in the early republican period—was that it failed to provide for legal measures to be directed against the evil that Cubans now found themselves facing. While the Spanish colonial government had outlawed the male secret society *abakuá* since 1876 as a seditious and criminal organization, banning its ceremonies as acts of "unlawful association," no such legal grounds existed for the persecution of practitioners of other Afro-Cuban religions at the time of Zoila Díaz's death. Moreover, the Cuban constitution explicitly guaranteed freedom of religion and peaceful association for legal ends, thus, among other things prolonging the lease of life of many of the old *cabildos de nación*—legally inscribed voluntary associations of Africans and their descendants organized along the lines of New World constructions of African ethnic identity. Although Cuban witch-hunters went as far as to try to resurrect Spanish slave law to cast people engaged in African-derived practices as criminals, they fared particularly badly in cases in which the victims of police raids were civic associations, and—to the dismay of the officers in charge—could usually produce written permissions from the municipal government to stage "festivities according to the African custom." In more than one sense, the rule of law—itself a curious hybrid of Spanish penal legislation and republican constitutional guarantees—provides a key to the inability of republican persecutors to achieve their goals of eradicating the "African savagery" in their midst. Inscribed within one and the same legal framework, Afro-Cuban cult groups and the executive organs of the Cuban state were technically constitutive of each other. The "Africanity" of the one not only mirrored the "Westernness" of the other. They were deeply implicated in each other.

Writing in 1921, Fernando Ortiz seems to have recognized this strange collusion between the modern state and its African deities. "The governmental aim [. . .] of transforming the *cabildos* into modern associations failed completely," he lamented, arguing that while the socially positive functions of the *cabildos* had been repressed, a "savage animistic fetishism under a Catholic advocation" now subsisted under reglementations "adapted to the demands of legal formalism. And the authorities were satisfied. How much better would have been a contrary outcome! How much better would it be if we today had mutualist cabildos and public dances with African drums, and not temples of *brujería*, of clandestine or tolerated nature!" (Ortiz 1921, 30). By then, Ortiz was already on his way to a fundamental revaluation of Afro-Cuban culture as a vital part of Cuban national culture (cf. Palmié 1998). Still, it was he who initially put the legally intractable phantom of *brujería* on the map of a regime of knowledge geared toward constituting the odious racial and cultural other as an object of scientific elimination.

Captured by Science

By the time Ortiz first entered the debate on *brujería* in 1906, he had become closely associated with the "nouva scuola penale" of Cesare Lombroso. Lombroso's positivistic theories of delinquent behavior as a function of physiologically determined (and anatomically detectable) moral atavism—that is, individual regression to biologically older, animalistic psychological states conflicting with the stage of moral evolution of the delinquent's social milieu—had strongly impacted not only European but Latin American thought on the scientific rationalization of social control. This new criminological idiom—allowing for the establishment of a correlation between delinquency and physiology on the one hand and an evolutionary scheme of collective moral progress on the other—paved the way to a conceptual refiguration of long-standing elite constructions of black deviance into scientifically circumscribable indices of "Africanity." For many a Latin American modernist, this was an appealing solution. It was not through massive physical repression but through the scientific policing of the population and through the transposition of conceptions of deviance and crime into an idiom of physiological or psychic abnormality that eruptions of Africanity into the public sphere would become knowable as "racial atavisms" and, therefore, subject to rigorous measures of social hygiene (cf. Stone, this volume). Particularly in the Cuba case, the metaphor of hygiene—with its implications of scientifically enforced cleanliness and transparency—provided a powerful rhetorical tool for the objectification of *brujería* as a noxious agent, a social pathogen. This solution was especially compelling, because the successful eradication of yellow fever through the sanitation campaigns conducted by the American occupational forces between 1900 and 1902 had been based on the Cuban physician Carlos Finlay's earlier discovery of its vectors and could thus be claimed as a triumph of Cuban science. Hence the scientific savagery of Ortiz's early vision of a medical-criminological regime based on positive knowledge:

> The first [measure] in the defensive struggle against the *brujería* has to be to finish off the *brujos*, to isolate them from their faithful like those afflicted with yellow fever, for *brujería* is by its nature contagious, and while these [i.e., the *brujos*] enjoy more or less compete liberty to continue their parasitism, it will subsist, and will attempt to maintain those who sustain it in the intellectual passivity necessary for that they continue to support it even happily. Once those swindlers are gone, their feasts, dances and savage rites ended, their temples destroyed, their impotent deities confiscated, all the tentacles of the *brujería* which chain its believers to the barbaric

bottom of our society cut, then, free of hindrances, they will be able to alleviate their still not de-Africanized minds of the weight of confused superstitions, and rise to successive zones of culture. (Ortiz 1973, 242)

The complex intertextuality between physiological and moral discourses, and the enormous semantic productivity of the metaphoric linkages between ethnography and epidemiology, sanitation and punishment, science and domination that Ortiz established in *Los negros brujos*, immediately impacted a wide discursive field. Ortiz's positivistic regime of knowledge production initially foisted itself not only on "empirical" data but also on secondary recensions of "atavistic bodies," "African customs," and Afro-Cuban practices that he had merely culled from newspaper reports while still in Spain and fused into the authoritative product of a truly "Cuban" contribution to the world of science. Nevertheless, as the public reception of *Los negros brujos* shows, once removed from the genre of reportage to that of science, the veracity of the data so produced and the questionable referential functions of the theories built on them turned into a nonissue: a certainty on which other forms of discourse began to build and which was soon fed back into those genres from which it had, originally, taken off. In an ingenious comparison between the texts of a verdict rendered upon the alleged authors—who meanwhile were lynched (or fusilladed in flight, if you will)—of the 1919 killing of "la niña Cecilia" in Matanzas, Chávez Álvarez (1991) has shown in detail how the very wording of the incriminatory document indicates beyond doubt the wholesale transfer of entire passages from *Los negros brujos* to a legal text ostensibly describing a crime that took place fourteen years after the book's first publication.

More obviously yet, Ortiz's diagnostic and therapeutic suggestions amply fed back into the journalistic discourse from which they had taken their initial departure. In the context of the so-called "niño Cornelio" case of 1913, Havana's *Diario de a Marina* reprinted a letter to the editor of the periodical *El Día*. Signed "x.x.," it suggested the following measures against *brujería*:

(a) perpetual deportation for all those who are justifiably considered to be *brujos*, regardless of sex or race.

(b) males and females are to be confined separately in different localities so as to render impossible their coming near each other.

(c) the localities to be designated for their deportation could be the keys or islets which surround our island, or any other territory bought by the state for this purpose, and in these places the vigilance necessary to avid the escape of the confined will be enacted.

(d) in these banishment territories arable land will be distributed among the confined, who will there be at liberty to, and have access to the means of, work.

In summary: what is needed is to organize colonies of *brujos* and *brujas*, absolutely, and definitively closed off to the outside, while giving them freedom within the territory they inhabit, and the means to subsist by labor, but impeding them from escape and reproduction.

Another commentator in *El Día* offered rather more severe variations on a theme by Ortiz. As in the animal kingdom there existed the threefold distinction among tame, tamed, and wild beasts, he suggested, so humanity divided itself among the civilized, civilizable, and refractory. If, in both cases, the third category universally merited extirpation, Cubans would do well to face up to the example given by the nation whose civilizing efforts it had benefited from so much in the past.

The Americans, insuperable people in as far as practical sense is concerned, have given to us a good object lesson and grand proof in respect to that problem occupying us now. It is known that [the U.S.] is the most tolerant country of the world, the great "country of tolerance" par excellence: there all sects—however excitable they may be, are respected. Well then, the so-called "Moros of Mindanao and Jolo" (in the Philippines) were, are, an equivalent to the Cuban "brujos": in their barbarous practices, in as far as they eat children, cut the throat and mutilate Christian maidens, with which they attain the heavenly reign (of their heavens, that is). And what did the Americans do? Well, they publicly, officially, and without unnecessary qualms, gave the order to exterminate them. And general Wood [well-known to Cubans as the head commander during the second occupation], obediently and happily "diminished them" (as the Mexicans say) with gusto. And at this very moment, under the present American administration, we just read the following (fresh off the press) what the New York Herald of the 22 of the past month of June tells us in respect to those Philippine equivalents to the "brujos": "As the government of President Wilson is convinced that the troglodyte crimes of the "Moros of Jolo" and the septentrional part of Mindanao represent a formidable threat for the civilized natives and resident Americans, as well as that any solution given to the Philippine problem has nothing to do with the extirpation of a savagism "immune to Christian teachings," it has been decided in Washington [that it is necessary] to "destroy which one cannot regulate." (*El Día*, April 13, 2007)

The author added that even "illustrious anthropologists" nowadays maintain that practitioners of *brujería* do not constitute a race but a species. The trajectory of reduction Ortiz had suggested in commending "the progressive immunization against the microbe of *brujería*" (1973, 248) had run its full biotic course: in a metaphoric progression running across diverse fields of inquiry, the *brujo* had evolved from microbiotic to simian incarnations, from feral to indomitable stages, and from republican civic status to that of a product of nature—a different species, noxious, parasitic, and irredeemable. And it is surely not accidental that the verb *linchar* entered Cuban Spanish as an American loanword at just that time, and in precisely this context.

Hence the task of criminal anthropology: to penetrate beneath the surface of criminal appearances and develop a regime of knowledge capable of rendering the *brujo* transparent to the gaze of science in order to forestall cruder and politically more costly forms of violence. Perhaps the most symptomatic figure in all of this was Israel Castellanos, at the time professor of criminology at the University of Madrid. In his prize-winning memoir *La brujería y el ñáñiguismo desde el punto de vista médico-legal*, Castellanos (1916) declared the *brujo*'s body the theater in which the nascent science of Cuban criminology would perform its most significant feats. Emulating the taxonomic and procedural regime of an anatomy of the criminal body, Castellanos dissects the *brujo*'s physiology in search of typologically salient features—few as they surprisingly turn out to be: the "simian cleavages" of his brain, the smallness of his ears, the asymmetrical implantation of his eyes, the tendency to cover his small—by "racial standards"—lower jaw with a beard, his longevity. Castellanos's pompous memoir, in fact, reads like an awkward attempt to prove the physiological normalcy of the handful of convicted *brujos* who did not escape the calipers of Cuban amateur anthropometrists. Of course, for Castellanos, this somewhat embarrassing fact indicated nothing less than that he was on the right track. For the semiotics of the *brujo*'s body apparently involved a cunning attempt at biotic simulation. The *brujo*'s body was as polymorphous as the civic status of Cuba's African or African-descended population remained polysemic under the republican regime. And both were in need of fixing.

This bizarre exercise in conjuring up a textual simulacrum of the physiologically invisible *brujo* was not a mere aberration, a quirk of scientistic opportunism. Not only the prize Castellanos's memoir won from Havana's *Academia de Ciencias* but the very heuristics and methodology upon which it was based bespoke the working of a much more widely dispersed regime of knowledge, a form of semiosis that—in reinscribing relations of dominance and inequality upon human bodies in the form of relations between civilization and savagery—constantly strove to materialize its object, only to annihilate it. Visualizing the *brujo* was the first step. Sanitary measures would follow. As a site of both lynch justice and criminological science, the *brujo's* body was little else than a scenario within which a variety of discourses, afloat in early republican Cuba, found or created their reified referents.

Castellanos's efforts to "make science" from the stuff of black Cuban bodies bear a striking resemblance to the semiotics of police investigations in the aftermath of raids productive of "instruments of *brujería*." Not surprisingly, officers barging into tenement buildings or private homes often found themselves faced not only with a multitude of people engaged in activities of unclear portent but with a profusion of objects of even stranger aspect (Bronfman 2004). Carted off by the police in vast quantities, duly cataloged, and usually included in legal files and press reports in the form of long descriptive lists, such objects came to perform a double function in the making of *brujería*. On the one hand, the catalogs of items confiscated by the police precisely because of their strange appearance and ostensibly nonintelligible function reveal a peculiarly archaeological mechanism of interpretation that assigned ritual value to what, in fact, were simply ill-understood heaps of decontextualized objects. Although such lists undoubtedly contain what must have been perceived by the victims of the raid as ritual objects, the main purpose was not to understand their meaning but to create evidence of something that had no meaning—and, indeed, could have none—in the eyes of their original owners/manipulators: *brujería*. We might call this the enunciatory function of such loot. Yet these sadly jumbled remains of sacred objects and assemblages, reassembled according to a bizarre new logic together with unrelated mundane articles at the hand of cataloging police clerks, underwrote the reification of *brujería* in yet another way. This was so because they not only objectified the presumed existence of the referent of *brujería* but also served as palpable signs for the effectiveness of the reconnaissance strategies with which law enforcement and scholarly agencies pursued what otherwise seemed to elude them. Not accidentally, many of these objects wound up in the newly founded Anthropological Museum of the University of Havana, where they underwent yet another set of semantic transformations circling around the idea of *brujería* at the able cataloging hands of Dr. Luis Montané, a former disciple of Broca. Then and there, they assumed their second function as signs not of *brujería* but of the productivity of a science they served to constitute.

Here we might note a rather intriguing parallelism of practices. Part of the catalogs of crimes laid at the doorstep of Cuba's *brujos* was the desecration of graves to obtain human body parts. Bones or dirt from the graves of specific persons does, indeed, play a significant part in the rites of the *reglas de congo* to this day. Such remnants of the dead serve to animate complex objects—known in Cuba today as *ngangas* or *prendas*—by installing the spirit of the dead in a relationship determined by the object's owner's power to "feed" and manipulate it for his or her ends. Possession over the remains of a person, to this day, represents the key to accessing the power of his or her spirit. It is a relation surrounded by sinister images of slavery, wage labor, and dependence (cf. Palmié 2006). But just as modern-day *brujos* constitute their priestly competence on the domination of one or more *muertos* (spirits of the dead), so did the science practiced by Castellanos and his colleagues in the *Museo de Antropología* constitute itself on the grounds of the bodily remains of dead *brujos*. As Castellanos (1916, 22) himself opined, the fact that the brains of the garroted authors of the Zoíla crime (sacrificed as they had been to the fetish of modern republican statehood) wound up—along with innumerable other objects—in the able hands of the illustrious Dr. Montané was a sign of auspicious portent regarding the future of Cuban science. As contemporary priests of *palo monte* might say, the *Museo Antropológico* had turned into a giant *nganga*, animated by the enslaved remains of the powerful dead.

A Hundred Years of Solitude

In late November 1994 I picked up a copy of the newspaper *Juventud Rebelde* somewhere on the streets of Havana. It carried a notice pertaining to the upcoming festivities for Santa Bárbara on December 4—a popular occasion for rituals in honor of *Changó*, a deity associated with the day of this saint. Reflecting the current party line on Afro-Cuban religions, the author was at pains to point out that the legends of white children abducted on that day and sacrificed by black wizards to African idols not just referred to a *thing* of the past. Rather, he argued, they harkened back to a previous stage of Cuban society when ideologies of racial otherness still effectively served to mystify the fundamental class antagonism alienating the Cuban nation from a realization of its common Latin-African cultural heritage. The implication was that the specter of African *brujería* had always been an epiphenomenon of capitalism—an ideological phantasm dividing the Cuban working class along racial lines and securing imperialist domination. Hence its obsolescence in a society in which socialism had eradicated the class antagonisms it had served to mystify and so realigned social thought with material reality.

If so, however, why disabuse a socialist readership—fully thirty-five years after the triumph of the revolution—of the notion that frightful things might happen on the night of December 4? Should it not have been evident to the readers of *Juventud Rebelde* that the drums echoing throughout the poorer and notably blacker barrios of Havana that evening were testimony to the revolutionary working class's righteous celebration of the culture of what Castro called *"un país latinoafricano,"* not incidentally, on the eve of Cuba's entry into the Angolan war? "If, under capitalism, the bourgeoisie declared the values created by the dominant classes [to be the] cultural patrimony," the Moscow-trained anthropologist Guanche (1983, 475) had written in 1983, "under socialism it is necessary to valorize the creations of the old dominated classes and, with the proletariat in power, to consider as cultural patrimony the totality, positive or identificatory of what is Cuban, in the material and spiritual traditions of the [national] culture." As Argüelles Mederos and Hodge Limonta (1991, 143) phrased the official consensus obtaining in the early 1990s,

> for the practitioners of these cults, the Revolution has meant not only so-
> cial liberation, but also a certain revalorization of their cults through the
> consequent policy of the Party and Revolutionary Government, and the
> granting of importance to the preservation of the cultural values to which
> the syncretic cults associate themselves in [respect to] the music, dance or
> instruments which enrich Cuban folklore.

If so, again, why even point out, in so many words, that there was nothing sinister about such ceremonies and that phenotypically white children need not be locked up at home after dark? For Alejandro, a graduate student and recent convert to Pentecostalism who never failed to strike up a conversation in English with me whenever we ran into each other on the street, matters were rather more straightforward. "Why," he asked me, fully aware of the focus of my research, "do you keep going to these witch-craft parties [meaning Afro-Cuban religious ceremonies]? They kill people, you know."[10]

To be sure, neither Alejandro's disapproval of Cuba's African cultural heritage nor such academic paeans to the revolution's policies of cultural revalorization would have been thinkable only ten years earlier. Up until the late 1980s, the Cuban revolutionary state's declared politics of scientific atheism would certainly not have allowed Alejandro to openly express his views of the dangers posed by witchcraft parties in a manner that implied his own belief in the diabolic nature of such rites. More significantly, perhaps, they would also have forced those Cuban ethnographers still active after the demise of the short-lived *Instituto de Etnología y Folkore* (1961–73) to argue that their task consisted in "salvaging" remnants of Cuba's prerevolutionary popular religious heritage before its aesthetic or otherwise edifying manifestations melted away, along with its mystifications, under the glaring sun of socialist rationalism. While no longer proposing that it was the goal of practitioners of Afro-Cuban religions to ensure that "in the midst of the revolutionary process there persist in our fatherland a horrible and mysterious chunk of fifteenth century equatorial Africa," as a contributor to *El Militante Comunista* had written at the heyday of the "revolutionary offensive" of 1968 (Anonymous 1968, 45), in 1983 Jesús Guanche (1983, 65) thus argued that it was Cuban anthropology's responsibility to demystify and creatively assimilate those aspects of Afro-Cuban religious culture worth "conserving in the form of positive values created by the popular traditional culture, as a testimony to the periods our people has lived through from the origin of national sentiment to its consolidation as a socialist nation." For as his colleague Rogelio Martínez Furé (1979, 267) had proposed only four years earlier, the

> development of a country's folklore can be stimulated in an intelligent and scientific manner. So-called negative folklore (superstitions, taboos without scientific basis, idealistic concepts about supernatural forces that govern men's lives, practices of *curanderismo*, coprolag[n]ia, xenophobia, etc.) can be gradually eliminated, while enriching and employing positive folklore (everything that aids the harmonic development of society, that contributes to the reinforcement of the links of solidarity among men, that exalts the traditions of struggle against the forces of oppression, as well as humorous folklore, empirically beneficial pharmacopoeia, and all artistic forms that flourished around popular religious conceptions, but which possess cultural value independent of their idealistic content, of which they can be purged so as to give them a new, revolutionary social function.[11]

Little more than twenty years after Martínez Furé published this master recipe for getting rid of Afro-Cuban wizardry—this time not through the physical elimination of its proponents but through strategic secularization and patrimonialization of their religious practices—the tides had turned again. Limitations of space will not allow me here to even begin to speculate about the effects the so-called "special period in times of peace" that was announced upon the disintegration of Cuba's economic ties to the Soviet bloc in 1991 may have had on the relations between the Cuban state and its black wizards.[12] Still, Argüelles and Hodge's monograph *Los llamados cultos sincréticos y el espiritismo*, published the same year, amply demonstrated that Marx's dictum that social being determines social consciousness was now boomeranging back toward those Cuban ideologues who were once prepared to escort Afro-Cuban deities to the graveyard of those collective representation that history had come to pass by. Conceding that even "under the conditions of socialism there exist subjective and objective factors that permit the reproduction of religious practices and beliefs in some sectors of the population" (Argüelles Mederos and Hodge Limonta 1991, 10), they eventually admit that the puzzling "increase of the membership of these religious groups" may be due to the influx of "persons who feel the 'need' of expressing religious beliefs with a mythical-magical-superstitious conception of the world without this necessarily implying their distancing themselves from the revolutionary process" (Argüelles Mederos and Hodge Limonta 1991, 217). Their careful wording notwithstanding, the question now had become this: Can a revolutionary engaged in building a socialist society afford to entertain beliefs of a mythical-magical-superstitious character? Can a *militante comunista* feel a need to express religious belief? The answer given by the Fourth Congress of the Cuban Communist Party in the same year that Argüelles and Hodge's book appeared in print was an ambiguous but nonetheless legally binding, yes. And so it came to pass that the Cuban state once more entered into a mutually constitutive relation with its "African wizards"—some of whom, by then, turned out not only to be socially white but to have occupied politically responsible positions for quite some time (Argyriadis 1999, 274).

It may well still be too early to judge the lasting effects of such incorporative legal gestures, coming as they did in the continuing absence of an effective body of civil legislation regulating religious practice (something that had not existed in Cuba since the U.S. military government had forced Cuba to separate church and state in the first republican constitution of 1902). Yet what clearly compounds the situation is that whatever policies the Cuban state nowadays decides to pursue in regards to Afro-Cuban religious practices, their object is no longer confined to the island's jurisdiction but flourishes in a score of countries in the Americas, as well as—documentably—Spain, Italy, Germany, the Netherlands, and France. What is more, Afro-Cuban religious debate nowadays no longer takes place within the confines of localized cult groups that the state can recognize at will. It has taken on virtual dimensions to a degree at which a random Google search for "Santeria" can pull up 2,750,000 sites, while even such more specific terms as "Lucumí," "Regla de Ocha," or "Oricha" will generate 183,000, 44,800, and 136,000 hits, respectively.[13]

The issue is thus not just that a mere eleven years after the publication of Argüelles and Hodge's still somewhat perplexed conclusions, researchers affiliated with the same Center for Psychological and Sociological Research would have issued policy recommendations including, for example, "the gradual substitution of narrow, dogmatic, prejudiced, unilateral and antidialectical conceptions of the so-called 'scientific atheism' with dialectical, open, flexible and logical ones," "more frequent references to religion in the media," or "increase of human and material resources for religious organizations" (Roa del Rey and Castañeda Mache 2002). Nor is it that Martínez Furé nowadays sports luxurious African clothes and regales his audiences at public events with Afro-Cuban liturgical chants that—as the ritual necklaces he wears indicate—may or may not hold merely folkloric significance to him. What is at stake here is not even the exquisite historical irony that the founding member and director of Santiago de Cuba's research center *Casa del Caribe*, Joel James Figarola, would see fit to assert that in the most "profound sense," the "Cuban nation constitutes—in its history, in its reality, and in its perspective—a great and exceptional *nganga*" (James Figarola 2006, 27; cf. Routon 2008): a power object, in other words, that allows contemporary Cubans to conjure with and harness the force of the dead (that is, in James Figarola's sense, their own history) to the building of their own new futures, although the real rather than metaphorical presence of such objects in any Cuban citizen's home might have constituted a crime less than sixty years ago and a potential index of antisocial tendencies as late as the beginning of the last decade of the twentieth century. Rather, what really is at issue here is that socialist Cuba has begun to openly capitalize on the presence of its African deities as a country-factor advantage—not only in the literal economiic sense, which has already seeded popular speech with neologisms such as "santurismo," "ochatur," or "diplosanteros," but also in regard to what, at first glance, appears a truly mind-boggling rhetorical, but possibly also ideological, *volte face*.

The latter moment found its most visible expression in the staging of the Eighth Global Orisha Congress in Havana's *palacio de las convenciones* in July 2003 that had been organized under the auspices of the *Asociación Cultural Yorubá*—a state-backed association of practitioners of Afro-Cuban religion based in a beautifully restored nineteenth-century palace facing Havana's American-built capitol. Presided over by the U.S.-based Nigerian *babalawo* and cultural entrepreneur Wande Abimbola, this event united some seven hundred priestly delegates from about ten different countries in deliberation about the future of their partly shared faiths and practices as a world religion. But it also featured a rousing speech by Cuba's minister of culture, Abel Prieto, who reminded the audience that their traditional African religiosity was not only entirely compatible with socialist modernity but that it represented a powerful antidote against the ideological poison emerging from Hollywood and other sites of global capitalist cultural production. Apparently including the several dozen U.S.-based delegates in his definition of *tercermundistas*, Prieto concluded that it would behoove "all of us" to stave off such dangers by heeding the call of those African deities, which, as he chose not to mention, had once been launched on the path toward their current global dissemination by the Cuban revolution itself. For had it not been for the post-1959 exodus from that island, which spread Afro-Cuban religious practices across much of the Western world, chances are that the event at which Prieto uttered such momentous words might never have taken place (cf. Frigerio 2004; Argyriadis 2005; Palmié 2005).

But Prieto's glib instrumentalization of Afro-Cuban religion as emblematic of what Cuba's "multiracial, but monoethnic" and "culturally hybrid" (Martínez-Echazábal 1998; Argyriadis 2005) socialist nation could contribute to the making of a novel post–cold war internationalism was not merely rhetorical window dressing. Uttered almost exactly a century after the "niña Zoila" case, his speech was also an exercise in what Povinelli (2002) in an Australian context calls the "cunning of recognition" or Bayart (1993), in the African case, an instance of Gramscian "tranformismo." As Carlos Martí, head of the Union of Cuban Writers and Artists put it, the *Asociación Cultural Yorubá*, although "there still exist few institutional linkages, has added its name to the call we have made for a global antifascist front" (Castañeda 2003). By the same token, however, these linkages to the state—resulting as they do for members of the association in tangible benefits, such as permits to stage ceremonies, access to sacrificial animals, hard currency, or foreign travel—have rendered the *Asociación* rather more an agent of a state-controlled projection of Afro-Cuban religion and its role within a socialist legal culture than a corporate actor in its own right. For although the Orisha Congress certainly united a large number of Havana's luminaries in Afro-Cuban religion, it excluded at least two groupings who have, since the mid-1990s, not only boycotted the *Asociación Cultural Yorubá's letras del año* (that is, yearly divinatory predictions for Cuba and the world) but consistently issued dissenting versions on the Internet (cf. Argyriadis and Capone 2004; Routon 2006).[14]

I do not want to enter here into the lively debate about whether the *Asociación*'s predictions merely add divine ratification to what is policy anyway, a debate that—it should be mentioned—resulted in a political skirmish spanning the Florida straights when Miami-based *oriaté* (ritual specialist) and high-profile *Santero*-politician Ernesto Pichardo accused the *Asociación Cultural Yorubá* of being a "subversive foreign organization" whose U.S. members and contacts ought to be put under surveillance by the U.S. Department of Homeland Security and investigated by the U.S. Treasury Department's Office of Foreign Assets Control for illicit transactions with Cuba (Pichardo and Forbes 2006; Routon 2006).[15] But it needs to be noted that since Cuban law prohibits two or more legally inscribed bodies to execute the same functions, the recognition of the *Asociación Cultural Yorubá* legally preempts all further claims from its rivals.

On the other hand, to phrase the matter as a question of cooptation by recognition (or Gramscian transformist hegemony, if you will) may be to miss the point that such incorporative moves on the part of the Cuban state—even in the absence of legally well-defined "institutional linkages"—constitute cultural performances in their own right. No less than the technologies of repression unleashed against practitioners of Afro-Cuban religion in the name of scientific modernity a hundred years ago, the socialist state's courting Cuba's African deities for their legitimating powers, both at home and abroad, deeply implicates it in the religious irrationalities it was only too recently willing to eradicate. In fact, only slightly overstating the case, we might say that what nowadays increasingly looks like a localized case of a survival of socialist tradition in the midst of global neoliberalism is now being absorbed into a rapidly internationalizing Afro-Cuban religious modernity far more rationalized in Max Weber's sense than anything the revolution could nowadays ideologically muster.

Coda: The Remembrance of Futures Past

Even that, however, is not the bottom line. For since the cultural program of the Eighth Orisha Congress did not include a visit to the sprawling Calixto García hospital complex, few of the delegates might have suspected that the socialist modernity into which Prieto strategically inserted their beliefs and practices included the *Museo de la Cátedra de Medicina Legal de la Universidad,* where the section "criminal ethnography" still houses, among an amazing jumble of objects, ritual and secular, the skulls of "African wizards"—garroted in far too insufficient numbers, as Israel Castellanos once complained, to allow for scientific analysis. Of course, as the Cuban museologist Luis Alberto Pedroso (2002, 138) has argued, the tables have turned insofar as the exhibits at the *Museo de la Cátedra de Medicina Legal* are now in themselves worthy of preservation as an illustration "of a museographical concept of which no other examples are left."

The structural inversion could not be more perfect. For now those sorry objects—and artifacts—of a brutal ideology of scientific progress and modernity have become the data for a version of Cuban science that, in aiming to transcend that past, repeats it by other means. Reposing there for a hundred years of solitude, perhaps these skulls are best thought of as silent witnesses to precisely the kind of indigenous Caribbean modernity a republic enchanted by science could then not countenance—and arguably has yet to come to terms with today. If the Cuban nation is indeed the great *nganga* that some of the engineers of its newly mystically enhanced socialist internationalism make it out to be, then one does well to remember whose mortal remains animate and give power to the histories and futures it purports to bring into being.

Here is a symptom of the dilemma: to this day, the grave of Remigio Herrera, a.k.a. *Adechina*, the last African-born *babalao* (priest of the Ifá oracle) in Cuba, still remains unmarked in the cemetery of Regla (an industrial municipality on the eastern rim of the Bay of Havana). As Pedro Cosme Baños, the director of Regla's Municipal Museum, tells me, this is so decidedly not because of a lack of recognition on the part of Cuban scholars and officials of the foundational role of *Ño* Remigio in establishing the tradition of Ifá divination in Cuba, and thereby laying the groundwork not only for the *Asociación Cultural Yorubá* and its *letras del año* but for the global Orisha movement itself. Rather it is because Cosme and his colleagues fear (not altogether unrealistically) that if it became known where *Adechina* was buried, practitioners of *palo monte* or other *reglas de congo* would likely waste no time in digging up his bones, and so—one presumes—install that part of Cuba's newly discovered national history in a *nganga* of their own. Could such blatantly sorcerous privatization of the Cuban nation's patrimony, let alone mystical resources, be countenanced by a state that, at least rhetorically, has styled itself the socialist purveyor of occult weapons against global capitalism? One wonders.

But in the absence of a marker on *Ño* Remigio Herrera's grave, and given the destruction of Regla's old slave cemetery containing the remains of his unknown predecessors, which was bulldozed in the early years of the revolution to make way for a school building constructed on its site (another future, then!), the *Museo de la Cátedra de Medicina Legal* would appear to be a logical place to start searching for the pasts in which contemporary Cuba's futures would likely seem to be implicated. What such excavations—and I mean this in a literal rather than Foucauldian sense—could bring to light might tell us a good deal about how exactly a particular regime of knowledge and governance managed to obscure its—historically no less specific—origins in the symbolic and practical violence that has, by now, rendered Cuba's republican and revolutionary former savage slot coextensive with the country's global mission and socialist future.

Notes to Chapter Seven

An earlier version of this essay was published in Kirsch and Turner (2008). The parts in question are reprinted here by permission of Ashgate Publishers. I would like to thank Paul Johnson for helping me to sharpen my argument on the conjunction of sorcery and socialism. All translations are mine.

1. To wit, Max Gluckman's (1963) famous and—from a contemporary perspective—famously misguided interpretation of Mau Mau as an expression of the "magic of despair" exemplifying not a return to "pagan tradition" but a "release of nihilistic courage to revolt."

2. Perhaps somewhat rashly, at least in the Colombian and Bolivian cases that his book was based on. After all, not only did wage labor emerge in Andean mining regions as early as the late sixteenth century, but Colombian plantation workers became "rural proletarians" once the independence of Gran Colombia brought slavery to an end some 150 years before Taussig's book was published.

3. Ambiguous because Evans-Pritchard himself was all but interested in the sociologistic elaborations his seminal contribution to the study of witchcraft was to trigger.

4. This is evident, for example, in the somewhat embarrassing fact that the entire "rationality debate" in anthropology and Oxbridge philosophy foisted itself on the distinction between "African traditional thought" (as epitomized by Zande witchcraft beliefs) and "Western science" (as epitomized by Popperian neopositivism).

5. If Todd Sanders (2008) is right in arguing that much of the anthropological literature on capitalist modernity and the occult proceeds from the assumption that capitalism does bad things to good people and then proceeds to tautologically restate this assumption in the form of ethnographic evidence, then the Cuban state's current promotion of practices and beliefs that it formerly denounced as witchcraft as an antidote to capitalist consumerism and its ideological aberrations clearly pushes against the limits of such interpretations.

6. This and the following sections draw on material presented in Palmié (2002, 201-59). See also Bronfman (2004) and Román (2007).

7. An all-black party founded by disgruntled Afro-Cuban veterans of the Liberation Army. See Helg (1995).

8. U.S. National Archives, Record group 199, Prov. Govt. Cuba, Conf. Corr. 1906-9, case file 248.

9. As Lara Putnam (forthcoming) argues, what Román (2007) calls the "genre of the *asesinato ritual*" literally emerged in the course of 1904 and from an amazingly dense form of pan-Caribbean journalistic intertextuality that transformed older topoi

of child sacrifice in Haiti by fusing them with antisemitic blood-libel genres. As she makes clear, the origin of the Zoila story lay not in Cuba but in St. Lucia where the so-called Monchy murder in the spring of 1904 of an apparently white child by black men for allegedly occult reasons elicited instantaneous and virtually global journalistic response. As she concludes, "there is every reason to believe that ritual child murder was the most recent European addition to the lore of obeah and *brujería*, rather than the last lingering vestige of African belief."

10. Wirtz (2004, 429) reports the continued vitality of similar rumors for Santiago de Cuba.

11. Similar programmatics can be found in Navarro (1998 [1978]) and López Valdés (1985, 3 f.). One of the most interesting examples is that of Mirta Aguirre's "prologue" to Lourdes López's unpublished "Estudio de un babalao"—a 1975 report on the conversion of a former *babalao* (priest of the Ifá oracle) named Gabriel Pasos to socialism conceived as a form of therapy—where Aguirre notes the following:

> The direct attention given to Gabriel Pasos by the [members of the] Party nucleus of [his] work center came to play a very important role in this period of defanaticization. These *compañeros* worked patiently and systematically with Gabriel, discussing his anxieties, doubts and even personal problems, aiming to provide him with a collective solution. This ideological work of the *compañeros* with the ex-*babalao* has had—and continues to have—positive results. Although we cannot affirm that he has ceased to believe, he is on his way to doing so, for his incorporation into revolutionary tasks is improving day by day. (cited in Menéndez 2002, 42f)

12. See Argyriadis (1999, 2008), Hagedorn (2001), Ayorinde (2004), Wirtz (2004), Holbraad (2004), and Moret (2008) for such speculations. Hearn's (2004) brief ethnographic study of the interface between the state and practitioners of Afro-Cuban religions in the context of urban community development programs in Havana remains a notable and highly welcome exception.

13. Searches performed August 3, 2008. I have tried to control (to a certain degree) for Spanish spelling so as to rule out sites originating in Nigeria and the Anglophone Americas. To give just one example, while the Hispanophone "oricha" produced only 136,000 hits, the Anglophone "orisha" generated 409,000.

14. The divination ceremonies determining the *letra del año* appear to go back to the turn of the twentieth century, although it is not clear whether the tradition was ever monolithic and its pronouncements uncontested among Cuba's *babalaos*. Since 2001, the *Asociación Cultural Yorubá* has been circulating its version both in print (distributed free of charge in the streets of Havana) and over its government-sponsored Web site http://www.cubayoruba.cult.cu.

15. Pichardo won a U.S. Supreme Court case legalizing animal sacrifice for members of his Church of the Lukumí Babalú Ayé (cf. Palmié 1996).

8

The Logic of Sorcery and Democracy in Contemporary Brazil

YVONNE MAGGIE

The Problem

IN 1998, I decided to leave behind what had been the central concerns of my academic investigations for many years: the belief in sorcery and in the powers of the occult to produce evil in Brazil during the republican period (extending roughly from the 1890s to the present day). My decision was based on a sense that, in a country with such great inequalities, there could be no point in continuing to spend time studying religions that proudly claim an African origin (Batuque in Belém and Porto Alegre, Xangô in Recife, Candomblé in Bahia, Umbanda and Macumba in Rio de Janeiro and São Paulo) or analyzing offerings laid out on street corners or investigating criminal procedures in which the state meddles in the affairs of magic in order to "distinguish" the true *pai-de-santo* (the highest position within the spiritual hierarchy of the *terreiros*) from the charlatan (*charlatão*) or the sorcerer.[1] I felt that all this was peripheral to Brazil's most crucial question, namely, the production and reproduction of social inequality.

Yet during the last four or five years I have been asking myself if it is not precisely witchcraft and a belief in the powers of the occult to produce evil that are part of the problem.

Economists and political scientists may regard suggesting that a belief in witchcraft might be an important factor in the perpetuation of social inequality to be both a false hypothesis, produced by a professional bias derived from my status as anthropologist, and a disregard for the stinging critiques of modernization theory. In their introduction to this volume, Roger Sansi and Luis Nicolau Parés comment upon recent interest in understanding the persistence and even effervescence of sorcery beliefs in contemporary society, claiming that until recently it was commonly believed that they would be inevitably defeated by modernity. It was thought, they claim, that sorcery, "as an irrational traditional belief, should disappear in an enlightened, modern, and rational society."

Similarly, in this volume, Peter Geschiere states that there is "some urgency in arriving at a closer understanding of this strange convergence of witchcraft and the modern," exhorting us to try to understand "the quite enigmatic convergence of witchcraft and modernity." But why should the convergence of beliefs in witchcraft and modernity be "strange" and "enigmatic"? It can only be enigmatic for those who hold that since the West left witchcraft as it embraced the Enlightenment, so should everyone else. One might even argue with Keith Thomas (1991) that it is more difficult to understand the demise of witchcraft beliefs than their persistence, especially after the noble insights of Evans-Pritchard (1937) so many years ago. Secondary elaborations are always around to console the believer and denounce the skeptic. Evans-Pritchard's analysis of witchcraft, oracles, and magic among the Azande in no way suggested any contradiction between sorcery and science, or "common sense," as he called nonmagical interpretations of events. Indeed one of the most important contributions of his classic ethnography was to demonstrate that there was no conflict between witchcraft and commonsense interpretations of misfortune since they provided answers to distinct questions. Science and commonsense can explain *how* events occur but not *why* they occur when they do. The famous example of the falling granary is cited ad nauseam to make this point: the action of termites explains how a granary collapses, while witchcraft explains why it falls when it does and upon whom.

Interestingly enough, the anthropological and sociological literature on possession, witchcraft, and sorcery in Afro-Brazilian religious groups has not been characterized by perplexity at their coexistence with modernity. Perhaps this is because such beliefs are so socially widespread that the anthropologists have not generally seen them as a problem.

So when I look at Brazil in this chapter, I do not ask why beliefs in magic, witchcraft, and sorcery have remained so strong. Nor indeed do I seek to "interpret" them in terms of their possible social and intellectual functions. They may indeed be as Ndjio suggests "(desperate?) efforts by various social groups to come to terms with massive social, political, and economic shifts that harm their own interests or are not profitable to them" (Ndjio, this volume), but this would be to understand them as somehow ancillary to social problems, external to the social fabric in some way. I prefer to argue, in what may be seen as a truly traditional anthropological perspective, that knowledge of any kind is not simply an innocent tool for explanation, nor, from a functionalist perspective, is it around to give vent to sorrow, anger, and resistance. It is much more than that, for it is itself constitutive of these emotive terms and their genesis. I will argue that such beliefs only express what they *are*. The Afro-Brazilian Candomblé does not engender resistance. It is in its very existence the antithesis to the rational bureaucratic order that the Brazilian state outwardly proclaims. It does not express envy and jealousy. It *is* those things. As we shall see, the emphasis on protection from mystical attack does not express a lack of trust in colleagues and family; rather it is that mistrust.

So I do not start with any perplexity over the coexistence of witchcraft beliefs and modernity (see Geschiere, this volume). Nor do I take a dispassionate stance in relation to a set of beliefs that, I argue, not only provide an explanation for misfortune but may also engender it. How can we be firm in our defense of human rights and turn a blind eye to the suffering of those who are accused of sorcery or all those who live in fear of the mystical attack of family, colleagues, and neighbors? The most valuable power of Afro-Brazilian ritual specialists is to provide protection for their followers and for those millions of Brazilians who may not be good Catholics or Protestants or Jews or whatever but who share a belief in the influence of the spirits and the power of their enemies to harm them through sorcery.

Witchcraft and Afro-Brazilian Religion in Brazil

In 1896, the forensic doctor and loyal follower of Cesare Lombroso, Raimundo Nina Rodrigues (1862–1906) published a series of essays that would later form a book called O *animismo fetichista dos negros baianos* (The Fetishistic Animism of Bahian Blacks).[2] One of the most interesting aspects of this book is that although Rodrigues set out to study the beliefs of black Bahians, he ended up showing that they had become disseminated throughout Bahian society as a whole. He put it this way:

> It may be said that, in Bahia, members of all social classes, even the so-called upper class, can become black. The number of whites, mulattos and individuals of all skin colours and shades who seek out black sorcerers in order to solve their afflictions and their misfortunes, and those who publicly profess belief in the supernatural power of talismans and magic spells, as well as those larger numbers of people who mock them in public yet consult them in secret—such a number would be incalculable, were it not simpler to say that, as a general rule, it encompasses the entire population with the exception of a minority of enlightened spirits who

understand the true value of those psychological manifestations. (Rodrigues 1935, 186)[3]

Although Nina Rodrigues does not enlighten us as to the identity of the small number of "enlightened spirits," it is reasonable to assume that he and his family were part of them. Throughout his book, Rodrigues gives many examples of how upper-class whiter Bahians were involved in magical manipulations, such as the immense fetish that appeared in front of the Bahian parliament, the specialist in spells whose temple was disguised as a fashion shop so that her genteel clients would not be suspected of involvement in sorcery, or the author himself who was offered magical assistance to become a federal deputy should he so desire.

A few years later, the Rio de Janeiro journalist, Paulo Barreto (1881–1921), who wrote under the pseudonym of João do Rio, argued in a similar vein that witchcraft and sorcery were legion in the city, "our addiction, our delight and degeneration" (2006 [1904], 50).

> For three months—he wrote—I lived among sorcerers whose existence people tend to ignore until pain or ambition drives them to seek such fellows out, and it is my sense that we will profit more by studying those who seek consolation, than by examining the merchants of such foolishness [...] We are dependent upon witchcraft [...] it is we who guarantee its existence as a businessman cares for his actress lover. (2006 [1904], 50)[4]

The actress lover as metaphor for the Afro-Brazilian religions evokes the unmentioned yet implicit presence of their symbiotic counterparts, the faithful wife and the Roman Catholic Church. It is as if the *terreiros* were as much a part of the religious life as mistresses were of the life of love and sex.

The next generation of anthropologists, who were imbued with notions of cultural relativism and interested in drawing attention to the positive contribution that slaves and their descendants had brought to Brazilians culture, paid much less attention to witchcraft and sorcery, concentrating instead on the great public rituals in honor of the divinities of Yoruba origin (*orishas*). Thus, for example, Rodrigues's disciple Arthur Ramos (1934), Edison Carneiro (1948) and the French ethnographers Roger Bastide (2001), Pierre Verger (1985), were able to argue for the continuity between Africa and Brazil. For these authors, many of whom become members of their *terreiros* and occupied ritual posts within them, often as *ogãs*,[5] witchcraft was to be found less in the great and traditional and most African of the *terreiros* and more in the syncretic ones, which were often run by European immigrants. They concentrated their efforts in describing the great public rituals in honor of the *orishas*, leaving aside the more private treatment of sorcery and witchcraft, and in this way ended up lending scientific authority to the native belief that sorcery is something that others do.

An important exception is the work of Georges Lapassade and Marco Aurélio Luz (1972), who, in the wake of the countercultural movement in Europe and Brazil, argued for the positivity of witchcraft and sorcery in the *terreiros* of Rio de Janeiro, which, they claimed, were in countercultural opposition to the bourgeois establishment.

Other functionalist interpretations claimed that religions of African origin helped rural migrants adapt to urban life (Camargo 1961; Lopes 1971; Ortiz 1991) or asserted regional, national, or even racial identities (Bastide 1973; Luz 1995; Brown 1986; Dantas 1988; Matory 2005).

My own work took another direction. In my first book *Guerra de orixá: um estudo de ritual e conflito* (1975), I analyzed the internal dynamics of an Umbanda *terreiro* in Rio de Janeiro, narrating its birth, life, agony, and death in just over four months. This revealed a delicate balance between charisma and routine, which, when disrupted, resulted in conflict, witchcraft accusations, and the formation of new *terreiros*, somewhat along the processes of fission in African segmentary societies.

My second book, *Medo do feitiço: relações entre magia e poder no Brasil* (1992), grew out of a concern that arose during the writing of the first. Many contemporary writers seemed to take it for granted that the Afro-Brazilian religions were confined mainly to poorer and darker Brazilians. Yet as my research developed, I was constantly drawn back to the observations of Nina Rodrigues and João do Rio. The *terreiro* that I studied brought together people of all colors, men and women, young and old, rich and poor, all of them united by a common belief in spirit possession, the knowledge that spirits can interfere in our lives and that people can bring suffering to others through magical manipulation (*ebó, despacho*). João do Rio suggested that instead of studying the "merchants of foolishness," we ought to study those who "go there seeking consolation." This is what I did. Looking at criminal cases against charlatans, *macumbeiros*, and "false or low spiritualists" (*falsos ou baixos espíritos*) in the first half of the twentieth century, I found that the Afro-Brazilian belief system was shared by the police, magistrates and lawyers, and those they accused or defended.[6]

The Republican Penal Code of 1890 condemned the illegal practice of medicine and *magia* and *sortilégios*, magic and sorcery. The combat against sorcery was regulated by three articles—156, 157, and 158—of this code. Article 156 prohibited the practice of any type of medicine (*medicina*), the "art of dentistry" (*arte dentária*) or pharmacy, the practice of homeopathy, dosimetry (*dosimetria*), hypnotism, or "animal magnetism" (*magnetismo animal*) "without prior certification according to laws and regulations." Article 157 prohibited the practice of Spiritualism (*espiritismo*), magic (*magia*) and its spells (*sortilégios*), and using charms (*talismãs*) and cards (*cartomancias*) to bring about "feelings of hatred and love, or to promise the healing of curable and incurable diseases in order to fascinate public credulity." Article 158 prohibited "administering, or simply prescribing substances from any of nature's domains as cures for internal or external use, and thus practicing the so-called trade of medicine men (*ofício denominado de curandeirismo*)." After years of intense debate, a new penal code went into effect in 1942 that contained the same prohibitions. What was and still is being punished is a certain way of practicing spiritualism, which is considered to cause evil. Not every Spiritualist, medicine man, or witch doctor (*espírita, curandeiro ou praticante da magia*) is punished, only those who are supposed to have used their powers for evil, those who used magical spells (*magia e seus sortilégios*).

As we know, the battle against witches is a moral imperative of the belief in witchcraft. Thus the first step in complying with this imperative is bringing accusations against those who supposedly use supernatural powers to harm people. The criminal procedures that I analyzed are institutional forms created to regulate the accusations, decide whether the individual is a charlatan or witch or not, sentence the guilty, and free the innocent.

Criminal procedures against supposed witches and charlatans are always initiated by an accusation. The code of 1890 and subsequent laws encourage accusations against individuals and religious associations "when they serve illicit ends." Without an accusation there can be no case, as demonstrated in this letter to the chief of police:

> I have the honour of addressing you even though I have never had the honour of meeting you. Because we know that your Excellency is a champion of morality and of justice, I appeal to your Excellency in writing that you may bring to an end this abuse [illegible] sorcery and fortune-telling that infest this city; the victims are many. We shall report a fact that will allow your Excellency to understand the full shamelessness of these people.
>
> There is a certain Rocha or Costa on Senador Pompeu street, a black man from the Mina Coast [*preto mina rica*] who lives at the expense of ignorant victims: seeking out the black man on the advice of others, a woman consulted him about her missing husband, whom she wanted back. The sorcerer (*feiticeiro*) told her he could make the husband come

home through an advance payment of 300$000. Then the woman began to cry and said she couldn't [pay him] because she didn't have money, and that if he would make her husband come home she would get the money from *him*. The black man said that wasn't necessary because she could pay with her body. He pointed to the woman. She left in desperation, and came and told us about it. I was indignant and promised to send a letter to your Excellency denouncing him. There are others in worse conditions, too many to describe. However, I give your Excellency the number and the house so that you can catch *in flagrante delicto* the immoralities practiced there. It is a shame. There is one on the Monqueiras Alley in front of number 49 [...] these are sorcerers (*feiticeiros*) who say that they could do away with the Republic if they wanted to; certain women use the place for indecent purposes and de-flowerings. That one on Monqueiras calls himself Cipriano and is known as Bedê, and there is another known as Diogo Mina. These are terrible killers; they give tips on the *bicho* [the Brazilian version of the numbers racket] for a certain percentage. On behalf of the poor ignorant victims of such nonsense, we ask you to look into these matters. In time I shall supply your Excellency with lists of these people and of numbers runners and fortune-tellers.[7]

Such accusations were always anonymous and there must have been many missives like these, because the lawsuits always allude to many complaints having been filed with the police. After the accusation, the police would send their findings to the judge. Whether pronounced innocent or guilty, the fact is that, from the beginning of the republic until 1942, the accused would be "morally" convicted in any event, since he or she was obliged to remain in jail for the duration of his or her trial unless he or she had the money to pay bail—a rare occurrence. Six months was the maximum penalty for the crime, and the accused could spend up to six months in prison before the trial's conclusion. Thus, as with witchcraft accusations in seventeenth-century Europe, the accusation itself was already a condemnation of the defendant, regardless of whether he or she was finally pronounced guilty or innocent.

From the period covered in *Medo de Feitiço* (1890–1942) to the present day, there are numerous examples in which the entire legal system (judges, lawyers, police, and prosecutors) becomes involved with magic. This involvement occasionally leads to the employment of so-called experts who are called to distinguish objects used for "good" magic from those used for evil. Such experts were usually police officers-cum-diviners, who determine whether a defendant might be a dangerous sorcerer or a legitimate priest. What is interesting about these investigations is that none of those involved, whether judges or lawyers, feel the need to translate the terms of the accusation; all of them seem perfectly familiar with them. The very technical terms that are used in the lawsuits are analogous to those used in witchcraft. To analyze present-day criminal lawsuits as well as those from the 1890s is to become perplexed regarding the exact meaning of terms such as *despacho* (meaning judge's decision or dispatch, while also meaning a magical spell), *consulta* (meaning a consultation with a spirit or a lawyer), *sessões* (meaning either court sessions or rituals held every week in the *terreiros*), and, finally, *trabalho*, which means simply everyday work but also the placing of a magical spell. The parallelism between the magic-religious and legal procedures is so strong as to make it impossible not to imagine a very close relationship between the two institutions.

A comparison of the system I have described with that of the British colonies of Africa clearly demonstrates what I believe to be the most significant aspect of the Brazilian system, namely, the fact that it does not challenge the reality of witchcraft. The Southern Rhodesian Witchcraft Suppression Act of 1890 was based then on the premise that it is a crime to suppose the real existence of witchcraft. Those indicted in Rhodesian courts of law were the ones who had accused someone else of witchcraft, not those who were accused of witchcraft. Article 3 proclaims that

> Anyone who accuses another of the use of unnatural means causing any illness to any person or animal or causing any injury to any person or property, in other words, anyone who wishes to accuse or indicate any other person as a magician or sorcerer shall be guilty of an offence and subject to a fine of no more than 100 pounds or prison for a period of not more than three years or corporal punishment not greater than 20 lashes or any of two or more of these punishments. (Crawford 1967)

For Africans living under the rule of the British empire, we can well imagine that the law must have been seen as totally alien since, for them, witchcraft was as natural and true as summer rain.

Recent events confirm such speculation. The Witchcraft Suppression Act that remained in force in Zimbabwe even after its independence was radically changed in June 2006.[8] The state now must prosecute those who are accused of using supernatural powers to harm others, not those who accuse them. Those convicted are subject to either a fine or up to five years of prison.

The change in the law in Zimbabwe did not come about without debate. "Witchcraft is not an area that lends itself to police scrutiny," said Wayne Budzijena, the Zimbabwean Republic Police spokesman. "How do you verify an evil spell? This is a matter of spiritual faith, not a matter of empirical evidence." Nonetheless, the arguments of Justice Maphios Cheda prevailed:

> The strongly held conviction of belief in witchcraft and traditional healers [. . .] cannot be wished away. We should amend the century-old Witchcraft Suppression Act in keeping with the popular thinking and beliefs of the majority in this country. Although many highly educated Zimbabweans tend not to believe in such phenomena, they acknowledge the belief is part of their cultural background.[9]

The fact that the Brazilian law that condemns those found guilty of witchcraft and charlatanism has not changed suggests that Brazilian jurists, magistrates, prosecutors, and witnesses (not to mention the accused themselves) would have as much difficulty in understanding the Rhodesian Witchcraft Suppression Act as the people of Zimbabwe. Like the denizens of Southern Rhodesia, all those involved in Brazilian lawsuits believed in magic and considered it their duty to punish those who were supposed to have utilized it. Whereas the British colonizers sought to suppress the belief in witchcraft, the Brazilian elite, who were entangled in it, sought to administer it to their own satisfaction.

The criminal procedures analyzed in *Medo do feitiço* showed the fascination that magic held throughout Brazilian society. But it is not just the criminal lawsuits of the first half of the century that allude to this Brazilian fascination with magical powers. A more recent case is illustrative of how a belief in witchcraft remains very much alive and widespread (in addition to a number of ways of dealing with accusations).

Seu Sete da Lira: An Emblematic Case

In August 1971, at the height of the military dictatorship and at the beginning of the "economic miracle," the city of Rio de Janeiro was shaken by an event that resulted in the imposition of censorship on TV stations and the creation of a national organization to protect Afro-Brazilian religious groupings named the National Deliberative Council of Umbanda-CONDU (*Conselho Nacional Deliberativo de Umbanda*): the emergence in Rio de Janeiro of a spirit called Seu Sete da Lira who attracted as many followers as critics.

On August 29, a spirit called Seu Sete da Lira, embodied in the medium Cacilda de Assis, appeared on two of the most popular television programs, the variety shows of Flávio Cavalcanti and Chacrinha. Seu Sete da Lira was an Exu spirit of Umbanda. Identified by many people as the Catholic devil, he is in fact a trickster who, lacking any kind of morality, is believed to be able to bring about what more morally inclined people might define as both good and evil. Exu is the messenger between the gods and between the gods and men. But it is dangerous to invoke his powers, since he does not always fulfill his promises and may cause damage to those who invoke him, especially if they fail to fulfill their side of the bargain. He is represented in many forms, one of them being that of a philanderer (*mal-andro*), wearing a white linen suit, straw hat, and white shoes. Some of his representations more closely resemble those of the devil, and he may be depicted as having goat's feet or a forked tail and holding a trident.

All *Cariocas* (natives of Rio de Janeiro) over the age of forty remember Seu Sete and his medium Dona Cacilda de Assis, with her *terreiro* of gigantic proportions in the working-class suburb of Santíssimo in the western part of Rio. They will remember the fascination for Seu Sete, how cars bore bumper stickers on which were written "Seu Sete da Lira" in red with the name of the Exu and the number 7 in black drawn in the center (black and red are the colors of Exu). These same cars also carried the hypernationalist sticker appropriate to the years of military rule: "Brazil: Love It or Leave It" in the Brazilian national colors of green and yellow.

Newspapers reported that up to 30,000 people attended the weekly sessions of this Exu and that the medium performed amazing cures. The nearly two thousand mediums who worked at Seu Sete's *terreiro* at the time were made to punch in and out of the temple on a time clock. The rituals were performed in an enormous tent where the thousands attending jostled against one another in anticipation of her appearance, Dona Cacilda would enter in a trance state possessed by the spirit of Seu Sete da Lira, smoking a huge cigar and sporting a pair of black trousers, a red and black cape, and a black top hat.

The songs were in samba rhythm, and the musicians played the drums characteristic of Umbanda and Candomblé rituals (*atabaques*) as well as accordions and electric guitars. In the *lira*, as the séance was called, the musicians played on a stage in the style of the *trio elétrico* of northeastern Brazil.[10] Possessed by Seu Sete, Dona Cacilda walked up and down the surfaces of very long tables, which resembled the walkways of fashion shows, sprinkling *cachaça* (Brazilian sugar cane liquor) onto the delirious participants beneath. An entourage of assistants (*cambonos*) dressed in red shirts and black trousers followed the Exu, carrying replacement bottles of *cachaça*.

In these *liras*, the atmosphere was one of euphoria. At midnight, everybody sang Seu Sete's hymn—"Seu Sete, King of the Lira, cure my pain /

Seu Sete Saracura, cure my pain." Luxury automobiles were parked near the huge tent. What follows is an account of the ceremony published in the June 1971 issue of *Realidade*, one of the most respected magazines of that period:

> At a certain moment in which a crowd has gathered, an onstage orchestra begins to play slow music and the audience begins to sway their bodies, arms locked together, palms of the hands raised. Suddenly, the orchestra changes the rhythm to that of a noisy *batucada* [insistent drum beat] and everyone claps to the same beat. A woman dressed as a man appears. The light, which only a short while earlier had been dimmed, comes back up at the precise moment of Seu Sete's entrance, giving the impression that he has come out of thin air, from nothing, to great applause and cries of "Miracle!" There are people of every type: poor, rich, famous artists [. . .].[11]

Two of the most popular TV hosts, Flávio Cavalcanti and Chacrinha, invited Cacilda onto their programs. In trance, she brought her Exu Seu Sete as guest of honor. The presence of an Exu in full possession of the female medium's body turned those transmissions into what the then Brazilian equivalent of *Time* magazine described as a delirious event (*Revista Realidade* 1971). When Dona Cacilda possessed by Seu Sete was aired, audiences went into a trance. In some cases, the excitement that spread among audience members called for medical assistance, and confusion spread among viewers in general. The scene was apocalyptic. Women fell into a trance, while Chacrinha himself wept and had to be comforted by his friends. The streets around the Globo and Tupi television studios were filled with shouting people in a trance. It was nearly impossible to enter or leave the studios, and studio hallways were filled with people who wanted to see, touch, or hear Seu Sete.

Over the course of the next few days, newspapers describing the events reported suicides committed by individuals possessed by the spirit of Seu Sete.

But all was not euphoria. The country's mainstream newspapers characterized Dona Cacilda as a profiteer of doubtful morals, accusing her of illicit monetary gain. The income tax service began an inquiry into her financial affairs. Meanwhile, the Catholic Church was one of the most relentless critics, labeling all the spiritualists (*espíritas*) as *macumbeiros*. The politicians who had been elected largely by *umbandistas* went on the defensive.

Accusations against the *macumbeiros* and their definition as evildoers were identical to those that I had found in the early criminal records. The

debate surrounding the television broadcast engendered a sense of identification between individuals and groups who would otherwise never have
even talked to one another. The Catholic Church, the *umbandistas*, spiritualists, and many *pais-de-santo* were forced to relate to each other through
the accusations that were made after the appearance of the medium on TV.
Politicians also entered the fray. Some deputies demanded greater regulation of the procedure of accusation of "low or false spiritualists" (*baixos ou
falsos espíritos*), those who practiced black magic (*magia negra*). The debate
was intense. But no one called into question the existence of spirits and
magic. They all shared the belief that spirits and supernatural powers exist
and that they may be utilized either to bring about good or evil. Thus, while
some believed Dona Cacilda should be prosecuted for being an evil *ma-
cumbeira*, others admired her and considered her to be a true medium and
healer. Just as in the lawsuits of the first half of the twentieth century, the
beliefs in spirit possession and witchcraft went virtually unquestioned.

The accusations against Dona Cacilda also brought about political and
aesthetic outpourings. The English counterculture group Living Theatre,
led by Lapassade and Luz, came out in support of Dona Cacilda, proclaim-
ing her and her spirit as liberators of the body. The same group accused
other movements, such as the self-proclaimed conceptual artists who held
the Sundays of Creation at Rio de Janeiro's Museum of Modern Art, of being less interesting and less efficient than the cultural manifestations of
the Carioca *terreiros*.

This case shows how various segments of society became involved with
one another through the accusation of a famous medium but also how
these segments were hierarchically positioned. From the Penal Code of
1890 until today, the field of possession cults is organized according to
events such as these, during which accusations against some religious
practitioners exclude them to the advantage of others.

The case of Seu Sete—a spectacular example of the simultaneous seduction of acts of black magic or *macumba* and witchcraft as well as repression
against them—demonstrates that the belief system in question is shared
by people of all classes in Brazil and that, from the moment in which the
accusation is made, people and things are placed in relation by approxima-
tion, by contiguity. Thus, the accusation against Exu, as well as the accusations against the *terreiro* I studied in *Guerra de orixá*, in addition to those
of the courts in *Medo de feitiço*, succeeded in creating relationships among
distinct religious groups, the state, the political and artistic elites, cult participants, and *pais-de-santo* of all types.

By the time I had concluded my research, I found myself in agreement
with Evans-Pritchard that, although it may be at the core of our contempo-

rary way of thinking, belief in spirit possession and witchcraft do not affect the less "exotic" aspects of Brazilian life. As I mentioned at the beginning of this chapter, like Evans-Pritchard, I recognized that the logic in witchcraft was not incompatible with the common sense interpretation of events basically because they ask and answer distinct questions. Following this argumentation, I felt that the widely shared witchcraft cosmology would be irrelevant to the course of general social, political, and economic activity.

But Evans-Pritchard also sought a relationship between the accusations of witchcraft and the political system of the Azande. The accusations are carried out by factions that invest in accusations as a way of destroying their enemies and in order to increase their power. Thus, in addition to being a form of knowledge that runs parallel to other forms of knowledge, witchcraft is also a constituent part of the political process. It is important to point out that, among the Azande, no one admits to using supernatural powers to bring about harm. Similarly, during the first half of the twentieth century, in Rio de Janeiro, witches were made real and brought into the public eye through accusation and incrimination, resulting in long, drawn-out investigations that sometimes condemned and occasionally acquitted the unfortunate accused.

Today, looking at the same data, I ask myself whether the belief in witchcraft that is pervasive among people of all social classes might not also be part of less apparently exotic areas of social life.

Questioning Relativism

The question I ask, therefore, is, what are the consequences of our immersion in this logic, this addiction to witchcraft; this vice (*vício*) as João do Rio described it? Is not this the reason we are always directed toward the search for malicious motives that lead people to act this way or that, on the assumption that evil is ubiquitous? Is not the iniquity and huge social inequality hard to overcome because we are immersed in a battle of mutual accusation that impairs our ability to maintain our gaze on the social problems we are supposed to be solving?

I do not wish to make antirelativistic claims after the manner of a certain variety of anthropology from more powerful countries because I believe it was the discovery of relativism that led us to conceive the universality of mankind.[12] But in examining the consequences of this logic that permeates our society, I cannot help but remember Pierre Verger, one of the most extraordinary scholars of the Afro-Brazilian cults.

The French ethnologist and student of African and Afro-Brazilian religion who arrived in Brazil with a camera and lived his life in a simple house in Salvador amid the poor replied to the delicate question of his friend, the anthropologist John Ryle, as to whether he had ever gone into a trance. Verger replied, "*Hélas*, I am too French for that" adding that "reason kills everything—all the opportunities for pleasure, for relaxation, for true sentiment." In an extraordinary article (1998), John Ryle subtly described the courage it took for him to ask Verger that question, and, later, when he insisted on a response, Verger retorted with an air of sadness, "You want to know if I believe in the *orixás*? [. . .] I live *as if* I believed." John Ryle compares Pierre Verger's attitude to that of the aging Sir Edward E. Evans-Pritchard, whom Ryle also knew when he was a student at Oxford. Evans-Pritchard recalled that when he was among the Azande people, he lived as if he believed; like the Azande, he became immersed in witchcraft. But he added that when he returned to Oxford, he again would become a son of the Enlightenment.

John Ryle's comparison leads us to think about the nature of belief. The attitudes of Sir Edward Evans-Pritchard and Pierre Verger may surprise ultrarelativistic present-day souls who cannot make moral comparisons between one belief system and another. Pierre Verger spent most of his life among the *terreiros* of Brazil, bequeathing an extraordinary legacy of photographs and writings about their rituals and practitioners. Although a son of Oxalá, he never converted to the belief, because, having been raised in a society dominated by Cartesian logic, he was unable to take such a radical step.[13] Evans-Pritchard, by his own admission, lived in those two worlds as if they were parallel.

Other Consequences

Many scholars have pointed to an analogy between beliefs in witchcraft, and favoritism and patronage in Brazilian society (DaMatta 1981, 1985; Fry 1998). Fry proposed going a step further when he asked whether, beyond being mere resemblances or reflections of the political order, "they are not in fact constitutive of that cultural order" (1998, 466).

In *Medo do feitiço* I pondered over the relationships between Brazilian society at large and its legal machinery during the first half of the twentieth century. I concluded that the logic of witchcraft was located at the very heart of our contemporary way of thinking. However, I did not interrogate the consequences of my findings any further. Today, however, as I look around myself and at a number of incidents in the country's political and social life, I ask myself whether it is not witchcraft and the logic associated with it that keeps us from escaping from the collusion of favoritism, patronage, and factionalism. Or better still: if witchcraft itself is, indeed, central to our way of thinking, how do we get out of this vicious circle and search for other ways of unveiling causalities?

Today I think that this is the reason why politics now as in the past continues to be so closely related to accusations of witchcraft as in the beginning of the twentieth century. As we have seen, Nina Rodrigues noticed this relationship in Bahia at the end of the nineteenth century. Another classical example comes from the State of Alagoas in 1911, when the reigning political clan, the Maltas, was accused by a rival clan through their newspapers of favoring certain *terreiros* in exchange for providing spiritual protection and bringing harm and suffering to their enemies.[14] The police persecution that followed led to the arrest and, in some cases, even to the death of two *pais-de-santo*. The sacred drums of the *terreiros* whose leaders had been accused of conspiring with the Malta clan were burned in a public square, and ritual objects were put on display at the local Literary Academy (*Academia de Letras*). To this day, the Historical and Geographical Institute of Alagoas (*Instituto Histórico e Geográfico de Alagoas*) exhibits a fine collection of objects confiscated during that period.[15] It is interesting to observe that the cards that identify and describe the objects were prepared in the heat of the moment by one of the persecutors, which clearly indicates his familiarity with the *terreiros*.

A more recent case occurred in 2000, during the government of President Fernando Henrique Cardoso, who was a sociologist and associated with a more "Weberian" rational-bureaucratic style of government. For three months, Brazil was caught up in a scandal surrounding the fact that the leader of the government and former president of the senate and senator for the state of Bahia, Antonio Carlos Magalhães, was accused of tampering with an electronic voting panel in the senate. The possible existence and public dissemination of a list of names of those who might have been involved in the fraudulent act haunted all of the parties involved. Antonio Carlos Magalhães, maybe one of the most important senators, was accused of using unconstitutional means to protect himself and his allies from the accusations. The public followed the controversy with inordinate intensity, as an embodiment of the struggle of good against evil. Who would prevail in the cross-examination of the accused parties and witnesses? Who would win and destroy the enemy? Who had lied? Experts in electronics were called in to unravel the questions, and they practically turned into oracles, deciding against the defendants, who were finally forced to resign. The causes and consequences of the senators' acts were never very clear to those who followed the daily news reports.

The reader may feel that this example reveals only a parallelism between politics and witchcraft, but I should like to argue that witchcraft *takes the place* of politics. Let me explain. When the accused senator began to realize that he might actually be found guilty, images of him began to appear on television and in the most-widely circulated newspapers. In these, he was surrounded by *mães-de-santo* from his home state of Bahia, the base of his political support, and the *locus classicus* of Afro-Brazilian religion. While some would argue that the relationship between the senator and the *terreiros* of Salvador points to his strength which derives from the protection of the *orishas*, for others, this strength derives, as they say in Bahia, from the fact that he is the "son" of the powerful *orisha* Exu. In the end, however, neither the *orishas* nor the powerful *mães-de-santo* of Bahia were powerful enough to save him from the accusations and the Bahian senator was forced to resign.

This case illustrates the difficulty inherent in moving away from the logic of witchcraft to a logic within which there is room for doubt. The country remained glued to television sets for three months in order to find out who would win and who would lose, in other words, whose magical power was the strongest.

To conclude and returning to my comparison between Zimbabwe and Brazil, perhaps the path Brazil will take in relation to witchcraft and sorcery will be the inverse of that followed in Zimbabwe for the reason that the very anti-relativistic thoughts I have expressed are certainly not only in my head or in those of a few "enlightened spirits." I would argue that they are also present in the millions of Brazilians who are migrating from the Catholic Church and the *terreiros* to the ever-growing neo-Pentecostal alternative.

Walking along the roads of Brazilian cities, in particular in the poorer districts, the researcher will no longer find, as she would have done thirty years ago, innumerable offerings (*ebós*), usually of candles, dead chickens, manioc flour, palm oil, cigars, and cane spirit, at intersections. The absence of these visible signs signals the retraction of magic and reflect what seems to be a decline in the demand for the magic of Afro-Brazilian religion, as Patrícia Birman shows in her chapter in this book. The belief in Exu, the *orisha* representing evil and the principal recipient of the *ebós*, has been transformed into the Christian devil.

In the hundreds of cases against charlatans during the twentieth century that I analyzed, the Christian devil was totally absent. Instead, I found a belief that was shared by rich and poor alike in the supernatural power of certain individuals to harm others.

The migration of people and Afro-Brazilian spirits to the evangelical and neo-Pentecostal temples reveals a significant cosmological transformation in Brazil that becomes evident in the significant difference between the Christian devil and Exu. The former is believed to punish those who stray from the true path of Christianity, while the latter may be bought off by anyone to bring about suffering to others. The Christian devil operates on the basis of a universal moral code. Exu classically has no moral sense at all.

The growth in evangelical and neo-Pentecostal Christianity dates from the mid-1980s. From 1990 to 2000, the percentage of Catholics fell from 83.3 to 73.7 percent, while the evangelicals increased their share from 9.1 to 15.4 percent.[16]

It is tempting to suggest that the gradual movement away from Catholicism and the Afro-Brazilian religions is a form of belated Reformation in Brazil. After all, neo-Pentecostal theology, termed the "theology of prosperity" (*teologia da prosperidade*), preaches the autonomy and responsibility of each individual under the aegis of a protecting Jesus and the Holy Spirit (Lima 2007). Affliction ceases to be interpreted in terms of the magical machinations of enemies and becomes punishment for lapsed faith.

Notes to Chapter Eight

In this article I shall use the terms "witchcraft" and "sorcery" interchangeably. The terms have various meanings, and "sorcery" is more widely employed to define a belief in the existence of people who make conscious use of supernatural powers in order to bring about evil, while "witchcraft" is a belief in the existence of people who are not conscious of their power to practice evil. However, in order to understand the logic of accusation, I do not find the distinction to be a useful one. I have explored the contrast at length in Maggie (1992). Thanks to Edgar Miller for the translation of the essay and quotations, and to Steve Berg and Peter Fry for a final revision of the essay.

1. *Pai* or *mãe-de-santo* can be translated as "father" or "mother of the Saint" or as "father" or "mother in sainthood." The term is used to refer to leaders of *terreiros*, and it conveys the notion of ritual kinship as discussed by Vivaldo da Costa Lima (2003). *Terreiro* literally means "yard" but also the sacred spaces where the Afro-Brazilian rituals of Candomblé and Umbanda are celebrated; they are often situated in peripheral areas of the city. For a discussion on the efforts to distinguish between the *pai-de-santo* and the charlatan in the 1930s in Pernambuco, see Stone (this volume).

2. Widely regarded as the father of Brazilian anthropology and forensics, Raimundo Nina Rodrigues was a physician from the state of Maranhão who lived in Bahia. A professor at the School of Medicine in Bahia, he wrote about the religious life of Africans and Creoles in Brazil, influencing a generation of scholars who studied Brazilian blacks, including physician/anthropologist Arthur Ramos. For an analysis of the ideas and importance of Nina Rodrigues, see Mariza Corrêa (1998).

3. "Pode-se afirmar que na Bahia todas as classes, mesmo a dita superior, estão aptas a se tornarem negras. O número de brancos, mulatos e indivíduos de todas as cores e matizes que vão consultar os negros feiticeiros nas suas aflições, nas suas

desgraças, dos que crêem publicamente no poder sobrenatural dos talismãs e feitiços, dos que em muito maior número zombam deles em público, mas ocultamente os ouvem, os consultam, esse número seria incalculável se não fosse mais simples dizer de um modo geral que é a população em massa, à exceção de uma minoria de espíritos superiores e esclarecidos que tem a noção verdadeira do valor exato dessas manifestações psicológicas."

4. "Vivi três meses no meio dos feiticeiros, cuja vida se finge desconhecer, mas que se conhece na alucinação de uma dor ou da ambição e julgo que seria mais interessante como patologia social estudar, de preferência, aos mercadores da paspalhice, os que lá vão em busca de consolo. Vivemos na dependência do feitiço [. . .] somos nós que lhe asseguramos a existência com o carinho de um negociante por uma amante atriz."

5. *Ogã* is a position within the *terreiro* hierarchy that is said to have been created in Brazil specifically to guarantee protection by powerful and influential individuals against police persecution and its routine invasion of temples for purposes of rounding up quacks and witch doctors.

6. *Macumbeiro* designates the practitioners of Macumba, the term most frequently used in Rio de Janeiro to refer to the Afro-Brazilian religion. When used in the form of an accusation, it carries the pejorative meaning of sorcerer.

7. Arquivo Nacional, Rio de Janeiro, Box 6, C21, 1892 (Maggie 1992, 31): "Tenho a honra de cumprimentá-lo apesar de não ter a honra de conhecê-lo. Como sabemos que V. Exa. é amigo da moralidade e da justiça, iremos, por meio desta, fazer um apelo a V. Exa. para fazer cessar este abuso [illegible] feitiçarias e cartomancia que infesta esta cidade, as vítimas são muitas, vamos relatar um fato que indicará a V. Exa a que ponto chega o abuso desta gente. Na Rua Senador Pompeu existe um tal Rocha ou Costa, preto mina rica, que vive às custas das ignorantes vítimas, tendo uma senhora ido consultá-lo sobre o marido que achava-se ausente e querendo fazer voltá-lo foi procurar o tal negro a conselho de outras pessoas. O tal feiticeiro disse-lhe que fazia o trabalho para ele voltar para casa porém mediante 300000$ pagos adiantados. Aí a senhora caiu em prantos e disse-lhe que não podia pois não os tinha, que fizesse o marido voltar para casa que dele mesmo tiraria o dinheiro. O negro disse que não precisava isto pois ela tinha no seu corpo com que pagar e ali apontou para a senhora, ela saiu desesperada e relatou-nos o fato, fiquei indignado e prometi, por meio de uma carta, denunciá-lo a V. Exa. . Há outros em piores condições, seria muito longo, porém dou a V. Exa. a numeração e casa porque serão apanhados em flagrante pelas imoralidades ali praticadas. É uma vergonha, existe um na Travessa das Monqueiras defronte ao número 49 [. . .] estes são feiticeiros que dizem que acabam com a república se eles quiserem, certas mulheres fazem ponto para as pândegas e defloramentos. O tal da Travessa dos Monqueiras chama-se Cipriano conhecido por Bedê, outro conhecido por Diogo Mina, esses são terríveis matadores, dão palpites de bicho mediante porcentagem, pedimos providências para essas pobres vítimas ignorantes que caem nestas baboseiras. Com vagar darei a V. Exa. listas desse povo e bicheiros e cartomantes."

8. I am grateful to Professor Terence Ranger for his patient critique of my paper at the "Sorcery and the State in the Lusophone Black Atlantic" workshop in London during January 2007. His criticism has helped me in rewriting this essay. I should also like to acknowledge his generosity in sharing with me information about legal

changes in Zimbabwe in 2006. Thanks also to my friend John Ryle for finding the sources that allowed me to describe these changes.

9. Lebo Nkatazo, "Zimbabwe outlaws practise of witchcraft," *News Zimbabwe*, April 24, 2006. http://www.wwrn.org/article.php?idd=21276&sec=39&con=62. Accessed November 7, 2009.

10. Carnival revelers follow the *trio elétrico* (a truck carrying live musicians broadcasting music over loudspeakers) through city streets during Carnival.

11. "Numa determinada hora em que se concentra uma multidão, uma orquestra que fica no palco começa a tocar uma música lenta e as pessoas começam a 'ondular' o corpo de braços entrelaçados e palmas da mão para cima. De repente a orquestra muda o ritmo para uma barulhenta batucada, todo mundo bate palma na mesma cadência e surge então uma mulher travestida de homem. A luz, que se apaga poucos minutos antes, volta a se acender no exato momento em que Seu Sete aparece, dando a impressão de que ele veio do ar, do nada, e as pessoas aplaudem e gritam 'milagre!' Há gente de todo o tipo: pobres, ricos, artistas famosos."

12. For a deeper understanding of the debate about cultural relativism in the contemporary world, I suggest reading Geertz (1996, 2001). I also recommend reading Peter Fry's article (2000) on the struggle between tradition and modernity in Mozambique.

13. Oxalá is one of the Yoruba *orishas* worshiped in Brazil.

14. For a description of this case, see Rafael (2004).

15. For a similar process of museification of Afro-Cuban ritual objects obtained through police repression see Palmié (this volume).

16. For 1991 and 2000 census data, see the Instituto Brasileiro de Geografia e Estatística site, http://www.ibge.gov.br/home/estatistica/populacao/censo2000/tendencias_demograficas/comentarios.pdf, accessed on October 19, 2009.

9

Naming the Evil: Democracy and Sorcery in Contemporary Cameroon and South Africa

BASILE NDJIO

Introduction

TAKING A LEAF out of the works of Peter Geschiere (1995, 1996), Jean and John Comaroff (1993, 2001), and Adam Ashforth (1998, 39–67, 2005), who were among the first anthropologists to link contemporary African discourses on occultism to modern political and economic processes in sub-Saharan Africa, this article aspires to explore the connection between the proliferation of witchcraft[1] discourses in contemporary Cameroon and South Africa and modern developments, most notably the adoption by these two countries of liberal democracy.[2] More precisely, the present article seeks to understand why the democratization process on which both Cameroon and South Africa have embarked since the early 1990s has resulted not only in the propagation of "spiritual insecurity" (Ashforth 2005) or "occult economies" (Comaroff and Comaroff 1999a) but also in the superfluity of witchcraft discourses in these two countries. Does the power of such discourses on occultism reflect the contradictory consciousness of a people who still cling to an essentially magical view of the world or whose worldview is still rooted in an essentially religious cosmology, as earlier generations of anthropologists generally understood African witchcraft?

The main argument is that both the wide complex of witchcraft accusations and prosecutions that arose from 1993 onward in Cameroon and the current widespread witch-hunting campaign in South Africa, instead of being a thinly disguised hysteria of the superstitious people (Arata 1990; Glover 1996) or a residual survival of a traditional thinking (Minnaar 1992, 1997)[3] should be rather viewed as (desperate?) efforts by various social

165

groups to come to terms with massive social, political, and economic shifts that harm their own interests or are not profitable to them. In this respect, the paper will show, for example, that one of the main stratagems or tactics devised by both embittered Grassfields customary rulers from the western region of Cameroon and disappointed black South Africans consists in producing moralizing discourses that misrepresent as dangerous witches or sorcerers their fellow countrymen who have either embraced the social and political changes of the early 1990s for the case of Cameroon or have been able to exploit to their own advantage the end of the white-dominated apartheid system in South Africa.

Yet in the two countries, the production of witchcraft discourses has different meanings or follows different trajectories. In postmonolithic Cameroon,[4] witchcraft accusations leveled at the so-called forces for change (*forces du changement* in the local vernacular expression) by proponents of the CPDM (Cameroon People's Democratic Movement) regime appeared as a technology of power that enabled members of the dominant classes not only to "africanize what is alien and alienating" but also to "appropriate and assimilate what is otherwise puzzling and confusing," as Kiernan (2006, 5) would put it. That is why it can be interpreted as a conservative reaction to modern changes that initially undermined their dominant position. In postapartheid South Africa, the pervasive witchcraft discourses appeared rather as what James Scott (1990) would call the commoners' "hidden transcript" of resistance to the new forms of economic inequalities in social relations, and especially to a political and economic system that excluded and victimized poor black South Africans.

This study is divided into three parts: the first section broadly discusses the superfluity of discourses on occultism and sorcery in contemporary Cameroon and South Africa. The research will demonstrate that in Cameroon the proliferation of such discourses coincided with the dramatic spin of the oppositional policy of the early 1990s that turned into a nightmare for both the holders of political power and the customary rulers connected to the unpopular CPDM regime of President Paul Biya. Concurrently, in South Africa a similar proliferation was rather the result of both the "political transition" of 1994 and the African National Congress- (ANC-) promoted Black Economic Empowerment policy, which over time have been disappointing for many black South Africans.

In the second part, the paper will show through the discussion of the reemergence in 1993 of the traditional sasswood ordeal, locally known as *gru,* how some traditional rulers from the Grassfields region of West Cameroon, who were very concerned with the steady loss of their authority and social prestige, artfully made use of the idiom of witchcraft to curb the impact of the democratization process that undermined their political and symbolical power in favor of prodemocracy leaders and influential members of the newly emerging civil society movement in this country.

The third section of this paper discusses the witchcraft frenzies that South Africa has been witnessing since the official end of the apartheid system in the early 1990s. We will show that contrary to Cameroon, where the so-called evil forces are mostly the young "combatants" who formerly symbolized the "forces for change," in postapartheid South Africa, those who are generally suspected of being pernicious sorcerers or witches are rather the new politicobureaucratic elites, most notably members of the newly emerging class of the black bourgeoisie.

Democracy or Demoncracy?

Since the advent in the early 1990s of what came to be known throughout the continent as the democratization process, there has been a growing tendency among Africans to believe that the emergence of the so-called liberal democratic society so dear to many apostles of neoliberal ideologies has only favored the triumph of witches or propelled the emergence of what Bernault and Tonda (2000) have referred to as "the power of sorcerers" (*pouvoirs sorciers*). For example in July 1995, I interviewed in Douala (the economic capital of Cameroon) a well-known traditional healer who was the leader of one of the groups of witch-hunters who, at that time, were touring many city's neighbourhoods in search of suspected witches who were being held responsible for what some progovernment media generally referred to as "social malaise." During our discussion, the middle-aged man earnestly explained to me that it was not a good idea to democratize the country. His argument was that the democratization process had made the country become more vulnerable to what he called "evil forces." In addition, my interlocutor strongly believed that the political liberalization of the early 1990s had unleashed these evil forces that were now out of control and running riot. In other respects, my interlocutor strongly believed that the democratization process had permitted many witches to take control over the country, which, according to him, had become a "heaven for sorcerers and malevolent spirits." That is why he interpreted the witch-hunt campaign—backed by local administrative authorities, traditional rulers, and politicians connected to the ruling CPDM—as a "salutary operation" and a "public cleansing campaign," which would bring back peace, harmony, and stability to the country.

The above statements are expressive of a growing sentiment among Africans that democracy in Africa has been downgraded to what one informant from Johannesburg once referred to as "demoncracy" (the power of witches or rule by sorcerers and demons) or that in this continent the democrats have been supplanted by the "demoncrats."[5] Indeed, in the wake of the democratization process of the early 1990s that was first associated with the ideas of progress, evolution, modernization, and development, no one would have expected the old-fashioned discourse on sorcery and witchcraft to "become again a way of producing meaning, a social theory to make sense of unexpected and adverse events for which no traditional explanation exists," as Luis Nicolau Parés and Roger Sansi cogently write in the Introduction to this volume. No one, not even the most seasoned social scientists and thoughtful gurus of neoliberal policy, would have forecast that in times of political adjustment and liberal democracy the "outdated" symbolism of occultism would become for both ordinary people and members of the elite classes in Africa a key concept for giving meaning to their predicament, fear, and anxiety.

When one glances through the mainstream literature on the reemergence of witchcraft discourses in contemporary Africa, it seems as if social scientists have been caught unaware by the unexpected turns of the democratization process, which are causing many of them to lose their hair. Indeed, recent anthropological research has noted, sometimes with surprise and disappointment, that in many parts of Africa, political liberalization seems to have given new strength to both occult epistemology and witchcraft governmentality. For in most sub-Saharan African countries, the democratization process has also engendered a social malaise that now finds its expression in a "spiritual insecurity" (Ashforth 2005) of which witchcraft aggressions and occult violence are generally seen as the main causes. As a matter of fact, in many of these countries, this spiritual insecurity has resulted in exuberant witchcraft accusations and witch hunts often spearheaded by disgruntled both urban and rural youth who have given to themselves unlimited rights, not only to crack down on the alleged witches, but also to physically eliminate them in collective ritual killings (Niehaus 2001; Tilly 2003). In other countries, occult anxieties have rather induced an avalanche of witchcraft prosecutions in the various state courts where poor and illiterate people suspected of being sorcerers or witches are regularly subjugated to the inquisitive and authoritative power of magistrates and judges.[6] These representatives of the postcolonial state are often less concerned with dispensing justice than with settling a score with the so-called dangerous fiends who allegedly contrive to make human life intolerable (Fisiy and Geschiere 1996; Geschiere 1994). The new inquisitors of modern times are often assisted in their inquisition both by modern "experts" such as parapsychologists and psychologists and especially by traditional wizards such as diviners, mediums, or witch-doctors who have not only emerged as expert witnesses in state courts but also have been turned into the eyes and ears of the postcolonial power in the impenetrable world of witchcraft and occultism.

For example, in a fascinating study on witchcraft trials in contemporary Cameroon, Fisiy (1998) has shown how since the late 1980s, the state power in this country has been trying to hold back what the state-based elites generally perceive as a "witchcraft threat," by making use of legal, administrative, and political instruments in their struggle (see also Fisiy 1990; Fisiy and Geschiere 1990). Ciekawy (1992) has observed a similar process in coastal Kenya where since the mid-1920s both the colonial and postcolonial powers have launched true juridical and administrative offensives against the supposed proliferation of *utsai* witchcraft in order to strengthen the power of state agents and state institutions in this area. These state crusades mounted against the so-called evil forces were generally premised on the nativist ideologies that witchcraft practices were not only subverting the government's ability to maintain public order and tranquility, but they were also seen as a hindrance to the state's development ambitions (Fisiy 1998).

However, what is singular about the contemporary revival of sorcery accusations and witch hunts in the periphery of the capitalist world system, most notably in sub-Saharan Africa, is that it has emerged within the context of the democratization process and political liberalization that primarily threatened the very foundation of the postcolonial state, and it has undermined the legitimacy of traditional institutions in a significant number of African countries. Indeed, it was at that particular moment in the history of postcolonial Africa that a constellation of authorities and powers (be they state-based elites or traditional rulers) placed themselves at the center of the production of moralizing discourses on occult threat and anxiety, not only in a desperate attempt to discipline and punish "uncivic" subjects, but especially to safeguard their power and authority, which were undermined by popular practices of indiscipline. This is the case with Cameroon, where the radicalization of this politics of the occult somehow helped President Biya's regime to maintain its hegemonic stability even during an uncertain democratization process of the early 1990s.

However, what is striking with the Cameroonian case is the fact that in this country, political liberalization was first marked by the disagreement between the prodemocracy movement on the one hand, and the conventional CPDM regime on the other hand. This antagonism was somewhat compounded by the ambivalent representation of the multiparty system by various social groups in this country (Monga 1998; Takougang and Krieger 1998), while the ruling classes (be they urban politicobureaucratic elites or customary rulers) were reluctant to endorse the oppositional policy because they viewed it as threatening and dangerous for their maintenance of power. The populace, notably socially and economically marginalized youth, rather welcomed the rhetoric of liberal democracy with excitement, which sometimes bordered on fanaticism, because many tended to associate the political liberalization with the dreams of *changement* ("change"), to borrow the local expression.

Yet what was distinctive about the democratization process in Cameroon was the fact that it substantially changed the relationship that subaltern people had so far maintained with their leaders. Indeed, while under the former one-party system or "advanced autocracy" (*autocratie avancée*), as Cameroonians humorously commented, the relationship between the Cameroonian leadership and its subjects was essentially dominated by a theology of worship and deification of the head of state. Under the current multiparty system, it was rather dramatically turned into a dramaturgy of blasphemy, profanity, and sacrilege of the same ruler, who was no longer seen by his subjects as the "Father of the Nation" or "Enlightened Guide." Moreover, in its early years, the democratization process went along with the subversion of the postcolonial power by the commoners, and especially the negation of the authority of postcolonial rulers, as necessary and relevant. This implicitly means that the political changes of the early 1990s made loyalty and obedience to the postcolonial rule not only precarious but also a matter of constant negotiation between the rulers and their subordinates. One of the main consequences of this change in the popular attitude toward the postcolonial power was the local youths' strong opposition to the Biya regime and its conventional ruling CPDM party, which has been in power since 1982.

The civil disobedience movement that came to be known in Cameroon as "ghost town operation" (*opération villes mortes*) exemplified the aesthetics of both indiscipline and subversion against a regime that claimed to be a democratic and humanistic one but that was mischievously depicted in popular literature and music as bestial, ferocious, murderous, sadistic, malevolent, diabolic, and so on. Sometimes, it was sketched as voracious, greedy, and grotesque (Ndedi Penda 1992). From early 1990 up to late 1993, the daily performance of what James Scott (1990, 18) would refer to as the "infrapolitics of the subordinate groups" also went along with the populace's desecration of the state power. It was especially marked by the subalterns' irreverent attitude toward the head of the state, whose countless images and giant portraits that generally invaded the public space were defiled or dishonored by hordes of young freedom fighters and combatants—as the subversive youths were generally characterized—who sometimes did not hesitate to put the president's eyes out on his images with points or nails, pour drinks on his face, tear his picture up and use it as toilet paper, or coat his face with their excrement.

However, the detotalizing project initiated by many socially and economically marginalized Cameroonians did not only affect modern structures of power and domination (such as the postcolonial state and the ruling CPDM party) and their representatives (administrative authorities and politicobureaucratic elites). It also undermined the social prestige and authority of traditional rulers who took sides with President Paul Biya or were engaged in clientelist alliances with his vilified CPDM regime. This was the case with many *fons* (chiefs or customary rulers) from the Grassfields region of West Cameroon, whose populations have a reputation for their strong attachment to their traditional chiefdom and ancestral customs (Geschiere and Ndjio 2003; Tardits 1960). These so-called guardians of tradition not only agreed to perform what James Rush (1990) would call "the dance of collaboration" with the Biya regime and ruling CPDM party. They also allowed themselves to be used as important assets in the government's bid to mobilize ethnic and regional supports in favor of its policy; in contrast the large majority of their subjects were rather favorable to the opposition movement, notably the SDF (Social Democratic Front), which was the main political force in this mountain region (Geschiere and Ndjio 2003; Ndjio 1995).

Although the collusion of these Grassfields chiefs with the CPDM government helped many of them to position themselves as one of the main sources of patronage for urban bureaucratic elites seeking political or administrative promotions, it increased their unpopularity with their people, who ceased to view them as *taloh* (father or protector of the community) and came to view them rather as *fingon* (traitor, collaborator, or turncoat). In addition, as a result of their connivance with the scornful CPDM regime, many of these *fons* became the prime targets of young combatants and freedom fighters who were irreverent enough to call their rulers by their names or destroy their properties. Some of these young "uncivic" subjects even made attempts on their rulers' lives (Mouiché 2005).

It is against this backdrop of popular opposition to different structures of commandment and authority in Cameroon that one can understand why, after 1993, the "moral economy of witchcraft" (Austen 1993, 89-110) became prominent in the postcolonial state's attempt to rehabilitate its power and why since then some members of the ruling classes have been engaging in the construction of collective moralizing discourses about the so-called occult violence.

The Gru *Ordeal and the Political Invention of Witches*

In contemporary Africa, it is often through the metaphor of witchcraft/sorcery that both the rulers and ruled, the poor and rich, the elites and masses, the powerful and weak voice their concern about the spread of violence and insecurity, the precarious balance of power, the new forms of inequalities, the uncertainty of life, the malcontents of modernity, the disenchantment with democracy, and the social and political changes their countries have been going through for almost two decades. If this observation is obvious for many people in Africa who strongly believe that they live in a world plagued by unseen powers and invisible forces capable of wreaking havoc on peace, order, and security within families and communities, for many social scientists it is not. Indeed, up to now very few have been sensitive to the role of both witchcraft epistemology and occult discourses in contemporary struggles for power, class differentiation, access to state resources, social and political demands, and the articulation of new forms of domination and submission in recent histories of postcolonial Africa. It is also amazing to note that in the exuberant scholarly production about the resurgence of witchcraft discourses in this part of the world (as elsewhere), very few experts have paid attention to the way in which both the state-based elites and the socially and economically marginalized Africans have been able to convert their misfortune, plight, suffering, or predicament into a dynamic discourse on occult harm, witchcraft violence, zombification, alienation of the identity, and enslavement of the selfhood by dangerous witches. Cameroon's example is interesting in more than one respect. Indeed, in this country, the uncontrolled oppositional policy of the early 1990s led by the end of 1993 to the political invention of sorcerers by representatives of both modern and traditional powers. Moreover, it urged local politicians, administrative authorities, and customary rulers to entangle ungovernable subjects and irreverent citizens in the nets of occult governmentality that posited them as dangerous witches and agencies of evil forces or associated their insubordination with the postcolonial power and the traditional institution with evilness and malevolent witchcraft. In the Grassfields region, the *gru* ordeal was part of this witchcraft technology of domination used by embittered traditional authorities to discipline their subjects in order to produce respect and obedience to both state authorities and customary rulers.

As a matter of fact, following the controversial presidential elections of

October 1992, which resulted in political unrest in most Grassfields chief-doms—because Paul Biya, the outgoing president and CPDM candidate, allegedly rigged the vote at the expense of Ni John Fru Ndi, the opposition candidate who was the locals' favorite—most Grassfields paramount chiefs, who had the bitter experience of the youth's violent expression of freedom, surprisingly decided by the end of 1993 to stage a vast antiwitch campaign throughout the Bamileke Grassfields. Although the opportunity to perform the *gru* ordeal was not approved unanimously, because at that time many people were much more concerned with the failure of the opposition movement to unseat the current president (Paul Biya) and bring about the long-awaited *changement* than with the threat of mystical aggressions, the folk, however, positively reacted to their *fon*'s decision. More surprising was the fact that many of those who not only passionately campaigned for the holding of a witch-cleansing cult in their village but who were also ready to use violence to compel their fellows who were unwilling to take part to this ritual, were the local youths who formerly stood against their rulers. This was the case with many active members of the local SDF youth wing, who unexpectedly switched from being "lion hunters"[7] to being "witch-hunters." Some of these former radical youths even became the witch finder's aides or disciples, who were often sent off with the suspected witches to search for "witchcraft objects" in the latters' houses. Others preferred to work as security guards who helped to discipline the often massive crowd of excited onlookers during the *gru* ceremonies. Their spectacular turnabout as well as that of many of the folk who formerly associated themselves with the opposition movement was explained by the fact that in the local imagination, the *gru* ordeal had always embodied a promise to restore productivity and self-determination to a divided community, as Apter (1993, 111–28) and Auslander (1993, 167–92) have also noted about the Atinga witch-finding movement among the Yoruba of Southwestern Nigeria and the witch-detection cult among the Ngoni of Eastern Zambia. Moreover, if the local population unexpectedly backed their chief's proposal to stage the *gru* ritual in their community, it was because they (as well as their fellows who live abroad) strongly believed in its efficiency in stamping out evil forces within the community.

The postdemocratization *gru* rite, which unexpectedly resurfaced in 1993 after more than three decades of absence,[8] was only the reactualization of a time-honored witch finding ritual deeply rooted in Grassfields customs. In the precolonial time, this witch-detection ritual was generally carried out when the community was confronted with threats to the social harmony and tranquility that were generally attributed to the dark forces of sorcery and witchcraft. It was the case with some unpleasing events or facts, such as extended drought, crop failure, grasshopper invasions, an epidemic, stubborn or inexplicable illness, frequent miscarriages, and mysterious deaths, which were perceived as evidence of the anachronistic witchcraft-related activities by some members of the community. Thus, the *fon*, who is generally considered "the guarantor of peace and stability," could decide at any time to organize a public witch finding ceremony in which the local populations, except the notables and other close collaborators of the chief, were coerced into participating. This witchcraft cleansing ritual, which often lasted three months, could mobilize up to 20,000 participants. It was generally conducted by the most powerful and reputed witchdoctor in the village, who was entrusted with the task of unmasking malicious and dangerous witches among the ritual's attendants. But it was not uncommon that a *fon* of a particular chiefdom hired a witch expert from another locality or region of the country to perform this ritual when it was proved that the local witchdoctors were not equal to the task or could no longer win the witchcraft battle against witches.

The *gru* ritual, which was generally held in the courtyard of the *fon*'s palace or at the village square, was presided over by the chief, whose imperial presence dramatized both the importance and the solemn character of this rite. In general, the ceremony began with the execution of the *gru* dance by the attendants, who were generally armed with bamboo sticks with which they gave a rhythm to their chants, while professing their noninvolvement in witchcraft-related practices or their ignorance of nocturnal activities. Then followed the procession of the witch finding team, who marched past the attendants in order to detect witches. Each time the witchdoctor stopped in front of a dancer and hit his/her head with his wand, the unfortunate person was immediately removed from the ranks and isolated in a corner or in the middle of the circle, where the alleged witches were requested to stand.

Thus it was on the same premise of securing social order and harmony, and especially of suppressing the diffuse occult dangers so vividly embodied by witches and sorcerers, that both Grassfields customary leaders and local political and administrative authorities legitimized the staging of the *gru* rite, which spread unexpectedly throughout the Grassfields region in the early 1990s. Indeed, the public witch-finding rituals I attended in several Grassfields chiefdoms between 1993 and 1995 aspired to redress disruptions occasioned by so-called malevolent spirits. That is why these events generally attracted a large audience, even if I suspected that many people only came because those who refused to attend the cleansing rite risked accusations of partaking in witchcraft activities, thus exposing themselves and their relatives to physical or psychological violence.[9] In some respects, contemporary witch-cleansing campaigns did not depart from the principles and logics that guided the old mode of *gru* ritual, insofar as they also involved the detection, indictment, examination, and then public humiliation of those who were accused of being witches by witchdoctors who had become over time highly disciplinary and punitive figures in the service of the postcolonial power, as Fisiy and Geschiere (1990) have rightly noted. In several localities in which the *gru* ritual was staged, most of the accused who were cast in the roles of villain sorcerers and subjugated to all sorts of humiliation and harassment were what the official discourses often labeled *opposants* ("political opponents"). This was the case of the revolutionary youths, who had formerly tried to free themselves from the paternalist state's tutelage, or of elderly notables who once challenged the authority of the *fon* in the struggle for control over local people or space.[10] In some cases, the suspected witches—who were generally convicted without any tangible proof of their involvement in nocturnal witchcraft feasts—were elderly women and men from underprivileged backgrounds. These unfortunate people upon whom the repressive structures of both the postcolonial state and the traditional chiefdom exerted their implacable power were generally accused of several sins such as practicing mystical cannibalism and malevolence, using their occult powers to harm their fellows, subverting proper relationships within the community and family, disrupting social order and peace, abusing social reproduction, bewitching or possessing the youth, and so on. For example, in some villages, many middle-aged or older men and women were held responsible for the local youths' violent behavior and especially their unusual disrespectful attitude toward both customary rulers and administrative authorities. They allegedly had mystically taken control over the minds and bodies of these youths, who were turned into mere puppets. For example, in a speech he delivered during the launching of the *gru* ordeal in the locality of Tonga (in the southern part of the Bamileke Grassfields region), the paramount chief of Bandounga voiced this belief that the "deviant" and rebellious youths were under the nefarious influence of some malicious elders. He put it in these terms:

> When the community is divided, when peace and tranquility no longer prevail, when the youths no longer respect their elders and parents, when they begin to call their rulers by their names, destroy their properties, and even make an attempt on their lives, it means that some evil forces have taken hold of [*s'emparer*] them. As the leader of this village, I have to do

something to free my youths from these bad people and enemies to the community. And I have no doubt that the *gru* ordeal will help us to achieve this goal.[11]

Contrary to what Geschiere (1997) has observed in other regions of Cameroon, most notably in the forest areas where local discourses on witchcraft mostly centered on power and inequality, on new forms of accumulation, and on the tension between individual ambition and communitarian control, in the Bamileke Grassfields region, at least in the localities where I followed the *gru* ritual, the emphasis was much more on the destructive use of occult forces, most notably on mystical eating or consumption and zombification of innocent victims by some dangerous members of the community, generally designed as *ndeuh* or *suenga* ("destructive sorcerers or malevolent spirits"). What the locals generally referred to as *touk* or *tok* embodied this destructive sorcery, which was generally opposed to the sorcery of wealth often characterized as *famla* or *sa'ah*.[12]

What particularly marked out the different antiwitchcraft campaigns I observed in the early 1990s throughout the Bamileke Grassfields region and in some towns mostly populated by Grassfields migrants was the fact that they emulated the arbitrary and repressive character of both the postcolonial state and the Bamileke traditional chiefdom—their disciplinary powers, their obsession with order, harmony and stability, and especially their propensity to resort to violence, coercion, constraint, and intimidation to achieve their hegemonic project. For example, those who refused to confess their involvement in witchcraft activities or to surrender their witchcraft materials to the witchdoctors were generally threatened to be submitted to the feared sasswood poison ordeal or to be handed over to the gendarmes, who could take them into custody for several days or weeks. That is why these witch finding cults, which generally dramatized the strength and supremacy of these structures of domination and command, could be appropriately interpreted as what Jean and John Comaroff (1993, xviii) referred to as "the totalizing moments" during which different instances of traditional power and representatives of the authoritative rule of the postcolonial state strove to redress social and political tensions within the community. Indeed, most of the *gru* ordeals organized in the early 1990s accorded with what Ciekawy (1998) once described as "witchcraft technologies of power." By this expression she means not only "a discourse of power that centralizes and hierarchicalizes magical ideas and practices as a way of bringing order to confused and messy circumstances" (Ciekawy 1998, 123) but also different "techniques of power that enable centralising processes and ensure forms of domination for both the colonial and postcolonial states" (Ciekawy 1998, 120).

One of the five instances of these witchcraft technologies identified by the Ciekway is the construction of collective moral discourses about the problem of witchcraft and the necessity to contain it through a vast witch finding campaign. Another important component of these techniques is the conceptualization, categorization, and naming of particular members of the community as witches. In order words, this act of witchcrafting works toward the invention or production of what Ciekawy has referred to as "witch-others" (Ciekawy 1998, 120). As a matter of fact, beyond its disciplinary and corrective techniques, beyond the theatricalization of the accusation and indictment of the unfortunate men and women forced to confess their "sins" under the authoritative surveillance of the agents of the postcolonial state, notably the fearsome gendarmes and sous-prefects who are the incarnation of the state violence, the *gru* ordeal was above all a complex system of production of power/knowledge. For it went along with the superfluity of moralizing discourses on occult aggression and witchcraft insecurity as well as the "invention" of so-called witches.

When in 1996 I returned to the Grassfields region after the dramatic witch-finding campaign that contributed to bringing back peace and order in the area, I was surprised to find that both local chiefs and administrative authorities had succeeded in encapsulating the local populations within the framework of the government-promoted *démocratie apaisée* ("appeased democracy") that marshalled a project to reinforce the state's authority or to extend its scope of domination at the local, regional, and national levels. These postcolonial elites had also been successful in creating submissive and docile citizens who now subjugated their rights to the state authority and the power of the chiefs and sous-prefects. This was the case with many of the young prodemocracy activists who formerly plotted to deconstruct the dominant social and political order and were now engaged in a logic of collaboration and connivance with the CPDM regime: many of them who had left the opposition movement for the ruling party now considered themselves President Biya youths or the *jeunesse du Renouveau*.[13] In this state's totalizing process, even the public space had been turned into what I have called elsewhere "a politically structured space" (Ndjio 2005, 265–94), which was permanently overloaded with signs and symbols that articulated the state authority or represented its power as well as dramatizing its importance.

However, what most impressed me was the resurgence in popularity of Bamileke *fons*, who were now praised as *taloh* ("the protector of the community") or *tagob* ("father of the community") by the same people who, not so long ago, mischievously misrepresented them as *fingon* ("traitor to the community") or called them by their names. Undoubtedly the *gru* ritual had enabled many not only to recover their authority and social prestige but also to secure their political power. Indeed, by adroitly manipulating and perverting traditional mechanisms of discipline and obedience, these Bamileke customary rulers managed to position themselves as protectors of their community.

Black Nouveaux Riches or Nouveaux Witches?

If in Cameroon the democratization of the early 1990s turned into a nightmare for both the state-based elites and traditional rulers connected to the scornful CPDM regime, who found themselves at the mercy of untrammeled and uncontrolled subjects, in South Africa it was rather the so-called democratic miracle that finally turned into a plutocratic mirage for many underprivileged black South Africans, most notably, residents of Soweto, the notorious township of Johannesburg. These socially and economically marginalized groups first deluded themselves into believing that the postapartheid system would put an end to their wretchedness and distress. Indeed, the political liberalization that culminated in the election in February 1994 of Nelson Mandela as South Africa's first ever black president brought about political, social, and economic changes that initially aroused enthusiasm and fervor from many black South Africans for whom the political liberation of their country inaugurated a new age: that of the "millennial optimism," to use Comaroff and Comaroff's catchphrase (2001, 36). As a matter of fact, the new liberal and democratic South Africa that projected an egalitarian country offering all its citizens the same possibilities to achieve their dreams of modernity regardless of their ethnic, racial, and religious backgrounds provided many disenfranchised black populations with optimism, self-confidence, and good expectations about their future, even though many were still experiencing the dramatic effects of the former apartheid system. The expectations were all the more high when during the campaign for the general elections of February 1994, the ANC party, which was poised to rule the country, promised a "better life for all" and a "general sense that upward mobility is the rightful entitlement of all" (Ashforth 2005, 92).

But over time, this so-called democratic South Africa has proved as discriminatory as the former white-dominated regime of apartheid, since it has so far enabled a small minority of black politicobureaucratic elites and their associates to accumulate in short time span huge fortunes that permit them to enjoy a soft and easy life, while many of their fellow countrymen continue to live an empty existence. For example, recent surveys about the rapidly increasing inequality within black South African communities and families have revealed that in these last two decades, "while the income of the top 20 per cent of African households (involving 6 million people) increased by more than 60 per cent over this period, that of the bottom 40 per cent (involving about 18 million people) declined by almost 60 per cent" (Terreblanche 2002, 132–3). Some estimates based on the 1991 and 1996 censuses also showed that, while in 1991 the richest 20 percent of African households earned nineteen times more than the poorest 40 percent, by 1996 the former capitalized more than thirty-one times the income of the latter; and by the turn of the last century, the top group of African households enjoyed more than forty times the income of the poorest 40 percent of families (Terreblanche 2002, 133; Whiteford and McGrath 1994; Whiteford and Van Seventer 1999).

In other respects, the political transition has propelled overwhelming misery, occult violence, upsurge of new forms of individualism, loss of communal solidarities, economic crisis, and the invasion of the country by hordes of foreigners and strangers who allegedly have taken control over the natives' ancestral lands and the wealth of their communities.[14] So does the "democratic miracle" that has engendered what Ashforth once called "spiritual insecurity" and "epistemic anxiety." The former expression accounts for "the condition of danger, doubt, and fear arising from exposure to the action of unseen forces bent upon causing harm" (Ashforth 1998, 63), while the latter rather makes reference to "fear arising from doubt about knowledge of the nature and purposes of invisible forces capable of causing harm" (Ashforth 1998, 64).

With the official end of the former evil apartheid system that could no longer provide an all-purpose explanation of the social, economic, and political marginalization of black South Africans, witchcraft is now considered the major cause of people's continuing suffering and their inability to make the most of the new opportunities for enrichment provided by the ANC-dominated government. For example, in places such as Soweto, many people now strongly believe that witchcraft is the main source of the pervasive spiritual insecurity and the propagation of HIV/AIDS and violence in this poverty-stricken township (Ashforth 1998, 63). There is also a growing tendency among the local residents to resort to the same vocabulary of "witchcraft" or "occultism," not only for explaining the exacerbation of new forms of social and economic inequalities among black people, but also for elucidating why the promising political transition of the early 1990s is now exacerbating conflicts within kin groups and communities.

In this area in which the millennial democracy has been turned into a spectral reality, as I showed elsewhere about Cameroon (Ndjio 2008), the discourse on the occult is entangled not only in the teleology of alienation of the selfhood and enslavement of the subjecthood by devilish folks but also in the eschatology of loss and deprivation endured by powerless black South Africans in the postapartheid South Africa.

All this has led many disappointed black South Africans to equate democracy with what I referred earlier to as "demoncracy" and even to see their country as a witch country. This was the opinion of David, a cab driver from Johannesburg, who thought that he now lived in a world infested by witches.[15] Although he was optimistic about the future of his country, my informant regretted the fact that postapartheid South Africa seemed to dramatize new forms of individualism and selfishness within the black community. The sense of solidarity and brotherhood that was the hallmark of the liberation struggle of the years past was gradually dissipating because black South Africans could no longer stand together as they did during apartheid, when they were united in resistance against the former white-dominated regime. From the middle-aged man who lived in Soweto, as did many black South Africans working in Johannesburg, I learned that black sorcerers had taken over for white sorcerers in robbing the poor and weak of their vital forces, strength, and energy, as well as their luck. They were people who allegedly had vampirized the idealized salvific "political transition," which initially promised a better future to all black South Africans. They did it by perverting, for example, the Black Economic Empowerment policy into a (another?) segregationist and exclusive system that is profitable only to a handful of black elites. My informant strongly believed that South Africa urgently needed a second liberation struggle that would this time help the country get rid of the witches and malevolent spirits, as the first liberation struggle put down the former ignoble apartheid system. As he emphatically put it, "After winning [the] war against apartheid and exploitative white people, I think that we must now wage war against all these witches and malevolent people who are not happy to see all South Africans enjoying a good life as well. We should not let these bad folks bring us back to bad times."

David's comments only echo a sentiment that prevails among many destitute black South Africans who take it as truth that if they and their families continue to be poor and economically marginalized even after the demise of the regime of apartheid, it is because they have been zombified or because someone has cast a spell on them. Yet the critical question that one can ask here is: Who are these so-called evil forces who allegedly have "blocked" the evolution of many black South Africans or have perverted the political transition in this country? What are the social backgrounds of those who are affected by popular discourses about witchcraft aggression and mystical enslavement?

Unlike Cameroon, where many of those who were designated as witches during the *gru* ordeal campaigns of the 1990s were generally the *opposants* either to the Biya regime or the traditional chiefs, in postapartheid South Africa the so-called evil forces are rather the nouveaux riches, who are now dubbed nouveaux witches by many disgruntled black South Africans.[16] In many respects, members of the newly emerging classes of the black bourgeoisie who have turned their lives into a success personify these "demoncrats" that David—the informant from Johannesburg whom I mentioned earlier—held responsible not only for people's misfortune and plight but also for their lack of progress and prosperity. They are the prime targets of the popular mystification of new forms of wealth and the magical interpretation of economic success that contravene conventional, rational, and moral principles. They are also the main victims of the growing popular discourses on illegitimate accumulation and consumption of wealth that transgress dominant social norms, what I have referred to elsewhere (Ndjio 2009) as "magic money" and "ill-gotten money," which can be spent carelessly because they do not originate from hard work, patience, effort, and savings. Nor are they acquired through the legitimate production and conservation of value, as so-called good money. These popular discourses about magic money and ill-gotten wealth take it as truth that those who enjoy an extraordinary social promotion have achieved their success only by making use of the human body as a commodity. It is also widely believed that the fortunes of these new affluent black South Africans generally derive from the ignoble trading of the bodies of their innocent victims to some mystical organizations in return for an immense fortune.

However, the black nouveaux riches are not the only social category to be suspected of making use of occult means in their ambition to gain access to wealth and power. Indeed, in Soweto and many disenfranchised areas where many people are experiencing a substantial degradation in their living standard, their fellows whose living conditions are rather improving or who are thriving in their activities are also suspected of "progressing" at other people's expense.[17] Ritual killings, zombie conjuring, sales of body parts for magical purposes, and sacrifices of innocent victims to some mystical organizations are some of the common forms of witchcraft-related practices that allegedly enable the so-called new witches to strike it rich or to achieve their accumulative project.

It is because of these popular beliefs that in Soweto, as in many places in South Africa, many destitute black populations are now enthusiastically engaged in the ongoing witch-hunting campaigns generally seen as a continuation of the liberation struggle of the past. Many of the former young "comrades" who generally spearhead these antiwitchcraft crusades often chant liberation songs each time they succeed in capturing an alleged witch and put him/her to death or when the police prevent them from executing their victim (Niehaus 1998). These "politics of collective violence," as Charles Tilly (2003) would call it, generally lead to the ritual execution of the alleged witches, who are either burnt alive or stoned to death by an excited mob (Niehaus 2001; Scheper-Hugues 1995). By submitting to a violent death those who are rightly or wrongly designated as witches, these "righters of wrongs" believe that they can overcome the malcontents or "side effects" of the liberal democracy adopted by the pro-ANC government.

Contrary to what I discussed earlier about Cameroon, where the semiotics of occult aggression embodied the fear and anxiety engendered by an uncontrolled democratization process, in postapartheid South Africa the pervasive witchcraft discourses rather address the economic inequities in social relations that are often viewed as a result of witchcraft activities and occult malfeasance. Here the so-called witches are no longer viewed as those who spread terror within the community or threaten social stability and harmony, but rather as those who deprive people of their wealth and vitality. In order words, in democratic South Africa, the all-encompassing and insidious occult idioms seem to express popular mounting disenchantment with a new political and economic system that produces marginalization and exclusion in unanticipated ways, threatens the very existence of the powerless and the poor, and magnifies class differences among black people at a pace and scale never attained even by the former segregationist apartheid system. But at the same time, it offers up fast wealth and easy money to members of the newly emerging black bourgeoisie manufactured by the ANC-lead government through its controversial Black Economic Empowerment policy.

Conclusion

In a recent speech that he made on February 27, 2008, in reaction to a political turmoil that resulted in the main cities of the country in the destruction of state properties and the deaths of about a hundred young demonstrators who were shot by the forces of law and order, President Paul Biya labeled his political opponents *apprentis-sorciers* (literally "sorcerer's apprentices") who had "no qualms about instrumentalizing the youth in their desperate bid to achieve their political ambitions."[18]

Yet the postcolonial rule is not alone in this political invention of witches and sorcerers. Nor are its agents the only representatives of the dominant structures of power that have attempted through the pervasive discourses of the occult to "resolve the paradox posed by the fundamental and enduring opposition between deviance and conformity," as Kiernan (2006, 10) would have put it. This chapter has shown that some disgruntled Bamileke traditional leaders managed to regain their social prestige and authority, not only by perverting a popular traditional witch-finding ritual, but also by manipulating to their own advantage popular discourses on witchcraft aggression.

In this article, I have argued that the reactivation in 1993 of the *gru* ordeal in many Bamileke chiefdoms and in some towns mostly populated by Bamileke migrants was a social and political response to the social and political changes prompted by the democratization process of the early 1990s. In addition, the unexpected renaissance of this traditional ritual in times of social movements (1991–93) embodied the elites' perception of the democratization process as a dangerous and threatening experience because it exacerbated popular insubordination and dissidence against the traditional authority and especially the Biya regime.

If in postmonolithic Cameroon, the discourse on witchcraft was used by some members of the ruling classes as both a weapon of the strong and a technology of power that allowed them to achieve their political domination, in postapartheid South Africa the pervasive of idea of zombification and enslavement of the powerless in "occult economies" were rather harnessed as a "weapon of the weak" (Scott 1985) by the less fortunate black South Africans who failed to jump on the bandwagon of easy money and magic wealth that the Black Economic Empowerment policy yielded. Thus the idioms of witchcraft and the occult enabled these disgruntled black South Africans to explain both their continuous affliction even after the demise of the apartheid system and the stunning economic success of a few in a context marked by pervasive hardship and poverty. These popular discourses on spirit insecurity and occult aggression especially appeared as counternarratives of a rosy democratic South Africa and political transition.

This article also shows that the witchcraft accusations that were generally leveled at members of the new black bourgeoisie who emerged after 1994 were the expression of people's disappointment with the selective manifestation of the millennial democracy and political transition that failed to improve the living conditions of the large majority of black South Africans. That is why, unlike in Cameroon, those who went on a crusade against the alleged witches or who were engaged in the "second liberation struggle" were not the newly gentrified black elites, but rather young pro-ANC comrades and freedom fighters who might feel nostalgic about the former period of political struggle when black people cultivated a strong sense of comradeship, solidarity, and unity against the ignoble regime of apartheid because they endured almost the same distress and plight.

With regard to the ongoing scholarly debate about the modernity of witchcraft in contemporary Africa, this article has shown that even modern discourses on occultism or sorcery always need some traditional bases or instruments and that if these discourses are not traditionally grounded, they will be too modern and alien to the people to be convincing or credible. As for the Cameroonian case, these bases were the popular traditional antiwitchcraft detention that representatives of both the traditional rule and the postcolonial state reinvented in order to achieve their hegemonic project. More important is the fact that this case highlighted the hegemonic production of witchcraft discourses by postcolonial political elites (be they traditional leaders or urban-based bureaucrats), unlike the modernity literature that generally reduces the metaphor of sorcery/witchcraft to popular discourses.

As far as the engagement with the black Atlantic is concerned, this paper shows that African discourses on witchcraft share some similarities with the vocabulary on sorcery and fetishism so pervasive in the Lusophone transatlantic world. Indeed, in both contexts, the deployment of both popular and mandarin discourses on occult malevolence and witchcraft aggression aimed above all at dealing with problems posed by modernity. For in the black Atlantic and in Africa, sorcery accusations as well as witch hunts gained momentum in moments of radical social and political change. In the former, it was the abolition of slavery and the institution of a republican state that brought about this transformation, while in the latter the change came rather as a result of the adoption by many African countries of both neoliberal policy and a multiparty system in the early 1990s. In addition, in both Africa and the Lusophone transatlantic world, both the elites and the commoners made use of discourses on sorcery and witchcraft not only to give meaning to the transformation that their societies were going through but also to alienate a section of the population constructed as dangerous witches/sorcerers (see, for example, Palmié, Stone, and Maggie in this volume). Yet, unlike the transatlantic case in which the invention of the "witch-others" was primarily inspired by a racial or racist policy that not only made black people second-class citizens but also entangled them in both a logic of assimilation of and incorporation in a Western dominant culture, in sub-Saharan Africa, the marking of a cross section of the population as sorcerers embodied either the ambition of the ruling classes to redress social and political tensions within the community, as in the Cameroonian case, or the effort of the socially and economically marginalized groups to deal with the rise of new forms of social inequalities, as in postapartheid South Africa.

Notes to Chapter Nine

1. In this paper, I indiscriminately use the terms "sorcery," "witchcraft," "occultism," and "magic."

2. The present paper is essentially based on field research conducted between 2001 and 2004 in the western province of Cameroon and the township of Soweto (South Africa).

3. For a critique of this approach, see Peter Geschiere's paper in this volume.

4. By monolithic Cameroon, I mean the period when the country was under the one-party system, from 1966 to 1991.

5. The "demoncrats" are those who make use of democracy to achieve their devilish ambitions. The concept also accounts for the nouveaux witches who have perverted the political change in Africa at large.

6. One can draw certain parallels between this engagement of postcolonial African elites in the production of witchcraft discourses and the critical role played by their Lusophone transatlantic counterparts, not only in the deployment of discourses on sorcery and witchcraft, but also in the juridical construction of witches and sorcerers (see Maggie's chapter, this volume).

7. The lion was the symbol adopted by the outgoing president and CDPM candidate during the campaign for the 1992 presidential elections.

8. Prior to the *gru* ordeal of 1990s, this ritual was last staged in 1962. The French-backed Ahidjo regime (1960–82) made use of this traditional witch-finding rite to "pacify" the Bamileke Grassfields region, and especially to crack down on militants of the UPC (Union des Populations du Cameroun), a radical political movement that was then engaged in a liberation struggle in this area. See Fogui (1990) and Joseph (1977).

9. This is what happened to an elderly woman in the locality of Tonga, in the Nde Division. She and her relatives were assaulted by a group of young men who were the aides of one of the *gru*'s performers because they refused to attend this rite on the excuse that it was contrary to their religious beliefs.

10. Acknowledging the fact that the whole *gru* ritual was controlled by the gerontocratic power of the postcolonial state and the traditional chiefdom, it is inexact to consider this witch finding as "an attempt by young males to preempt the mystical power of their elders and the structures of gerontocratic authority," as Auslander (1993, 185) has noted for Zambia. This is all the more true when we consider the fact that in many cases, both the youths and the elders were designated as witches.

11. Personal communication, March 12, 1993.

12. While most of the suspected witches were depicted as *suenga* or *ndeuh*, very few people were accused of being *famlamen* or *gah sa'ah* ("rich sorcerers"). The fact

that very few nouveaux riches had been indicted during the different *gru* ordeal campaigns organized throughout the Bamileke Grassfields region finally convinced the folk in their belief that their chiefs had perverted the *gru* ritual by allowing some rich sorcerers to "whitewash" or "launder" their ill-gotten wealth.

13. The *Renouveau* ("new deal") is the official designation of the President Biya regime.

14. The recent xenophobic assaults that erupted in May 2008 in several cities of the country, most notably in Johannesburg, were the radical expression of this growing resentment of many black South Africans toward migrants from Zimbabwe and Mozambique, who are more and more seen as invaders.

15. David was one of the two cab drivers who regularly drove me from the Melville residential area where I resided during my stay in South Africa in 2004 to the downtown area.

16. This difference has to be nuanced because successful confidence tricksters commonly characterized in Cameroon as *feymen* are also branded as *mokogne* men ("rich sorcerers"), as I demonstrated in previous research on these young nouveaux riches (Ndjio 2006). In addition, there is a growing tendency among Cameroonians, especially those from the older generation, to resort to the vocabulary of occultism or sorcery to explain how these former underprivileged urban youths have managed to turn their lives into a success or to accumulate huge fortunes in a span of little time. The pervasive idiom of *mokoagne moni* ("magic money or wealth acquired by occult means") embodies this popular belief that the deployment of occult forces is an efficient way of creating wealth, especially in times of uncertainty and anxiety.

17. Ashforth (2005, 99) revealed, for example, how one of his close friends, a middle-aged woman from Soweto, was accused by her neighbor of using "witchcraft to take the money that was supposed to go to her [the neighbor]" because she had started building a new house.

18. See *Cameroon Tribune*, February 28, 2008:2–3.

10

Families, Churches, the State, and the Child Witch in Angola

LUENA NUNES PEREIRA

Introduction

WITCHCRAFT ACCUSATIONS against children and adolescents have emerged recently in some African countries, especially in the Democratic Republic of Congo (DRC).[1] In Angola, this phenomenon has been verified particularly among the Bakongo people, becoming an issue of government concern over the last decade, with hundreds of reported cases, particularly in the country's northern provinces, Uíge and Zaire, as well as in those districts of the capital Luanda where the population is mostly of Bakongo origin.[2]

My initial objective will be to determine some of the factors that contribute to the emergence of this phenomenon. De Boeck (2000, 2004, 2005), discussing the Congo's phenomenon, emphasizes the new economic role of children and the alteration in the balance of power between generations following the absorption of children in the informal economy and in diamond exploration. In Angola as well there is an intense involvement of children in the informal economy, principally in Luanda.

I also examine the different actions and conceptions that guide Angolan state institutions, Catholic agencies, and nongovernmental organizations (NGOs). My objective is to analyze how different agents have been constructing different perceptions, discourses, and forms of intervention regarding this issue, defining what I call the construction of the "social problem of children accused of witchcraft." Notions of otherness, relations among state, social groups, and culture, different forms of handling conflicts, and new models of family, church, and community are at stake. As I will demonstrate, the kind of action accomplished by the Arnold Janssen

Centre, a Catholic shelter for street children in Luanda—allowed the production of a consensus concerning the definitions of witchcraft.

Witchcraft and Children: A Description

This account, from around the year 2000, was found in the archives of the Arnold Janssen Centre. About 60 percent of the dozens of boys and young men at the center have been accused of witchcraft.

> My name is A.M.F. I was born in Angola in 1988 in the province of Zaire. My story is very sad. My mother died in 1994 and when she died, I had no idea life would be so difficult for me. It was after this happened that my misfortune began.
>
> In 1995 I was seven years old and lived for a long time in the house of my sister Angélica. I saw how things were changing with me, I ate during the day, but I felt hungry at night. After a while, my sister discovered that I awoke at night to eat the dinner leftovers, and she would hit me, saying I was a witch. My family is composed of my grandparents, aunts, uncles and cousins. And there are a lot of witches. And when the witches heard that I was a witch, they took advantage of me, they used my face to torment people, and that's when people said that I was a witch. In 1996 I left my sister's house and went to my aunt's. Things got worse and they took me to church and in the church they said that I didn't have any spells [*feitiço*] anymore. Also in 1996, my sister Amélia arrived, having left Huambo for Luanda. She also went to live with my aunt and they told her I was a witch. In January 1997 I went to live in my brother Nelito's house and there too things got worse. They treated me as a witch but I was never a witch. They even accused me of killing my mother. They took me to the healers [*quimbandeiros*], and they said that I really was a witch (just look how jinxed I was). When I heard them say that, I kept my mouth shut. I was afraid. I felt that behind it all there was someone who made me be like this. And the same year, they decided to introduce me to a spiritual church [...]

Witchcraft accusations made against children appear to be a very recent phenomenon and have been explained both by elders and leaders of the more traditional churches and by the government and NGOs as the result of the disintegration of the family caused by the civil war in Angola and by the high political instability and economic and social crisis in the DRC.

According to their accounts, children are mostly accused, by their own family members or neighbors, of manipulating forces from the nocturnal world, bringing misfortunes such as diseases, deaths, miscarriages, and economic hardship to members of their families. The accused children are usually between eight and thirteen years old, although very small children are also frequently accused. Behaviors such as aggression, indolence, unrest, and lack of concentration are used to justify the accusation. Symptoms such as excessive hunger, nocturnal enuresis, and disturbed or excessive sleep and disturbances such as epilepsy and somnambulism are also associated with witch children.

The large majority of accused children have lost one or both parents, or their parents have separated and have been taken in by relatives such as aunts, uncles, grandparents, or step-parents (who are frequently the accusers). Reports from child protection NGOs (Perez and Benge 2006; Friedman and N'Senga 2002; Molina 2005, on DRC) suggest that the accusations are related to the tension in families forced to take in children who because of warfare, migrations, or the emergence of HIV-AIDS have lost their closest kin.[3] The accounts of the accused children themselves also reveal the existence of disputes between the maternal and paternal families. The accusations within the families are generally made by the child's maternal kin who accuse the paternal kin of having passed on the witchcraft to the child (the Bakongo are matrilineal).

According to Bakongo elders, children would not be presumed to have the power to manipulate occult forces, since they lack the intention or discernment to voluntarily cause harm to someone else. The most common explanation, found even in the accounts of the accused children, is that children are used by older people, very often already deceased, as intermediaries to do evil. It is precisely the presumed innocence of the child that is supposed to allow this manipulation to occur, since adults—especially Christianized adults—are unlikely to be convinced by a witch to hand over one of their relatives in order to acquire nocturnal power and take part in the witches' feasts.

In the children's accounts, witchcraft is generally transmitted by an adult offering food (a piece of cake, meat, sweets, or manioc) to the child during the day. At night, this adult will return in dreams to demand repayment of the debt. The child becomes trapped in a circuit of malevolent reciprocity by having to pay for what he or she received from the senior by offering the life of a relative. Consequently, the child also becomes a witch and acquires powers only accessible in the nocturnal world, such as the capacity to fly in sardine tins or peanut husks, to know distant places, own cars and pilot aircrafts, or take part in feasts in which human flesh is eaten. Small children become powerful wealthy men in the "night world." Consuming people, provoking sickness and death, is the main way to acquire power.

Nonetheless, the mere acquisition of *feitiço* ("witch power" in Portuguese) by children is not in itself something particularly new in Bakongo cosmology. Children may be chosen by the heads of a lineage to receive a particular occult power while they are still in their mother's womb. This was considered a benign, hereditary power, used to defend the clan (*Kanda*). However, the child acquiring this power would only make use of it on reaching adulthood and assuming the position of family head (*nkazi*).[4]

However, according to popular narratives, witchcraft is currently being transmitted through a process of democratization, in which anyone, including a child, can acquire, manipulate, and transmit this power for any purpose. This democratization supposedly led to the proliferation of child witches. We shall return to this theme later on.

As shown in the account above, healers and pastors confirm or refute the accusations made by relatives and offer solutions to the problem by curing the child. Usually, the children are accused after a family member consults the pastor of a Pentecostal or a *mpeve a longo* church[5] or a traditional healer (*quimbandeiro* or *curandeiro*). The pastor detects the cause of the family's misfortunes in the malign power of a particular child. Thereafter, these children may be subject to abuse by their relatives. Very often they are expelled from home or flee. The same churches promise spiritual treatment capable of curing children involved in witchcraft. Since these churches believe that confession enables the cure, cases of torture are also widely reported.[6] The churches are accused of abusive treatment, subjecting the children to long periods of reclusion, lengthy fasts, and aggressive medications.

Many children admit to being witches, providing highly coherent and fairly standardized accounts of their nocturnal adventures on the way they took the lives of their relatives and very often on the person who passed witchcraft on to them. However, some of them, especially the younger and older ones (under seven and over fifteen) do not admit to being witches. Boys are the most often accused and the most likely to flee from home, especially in the provinces. Girls are apparently less frequently accused.

According to interviews conducted with the social workers from the Arnold Janssen Centre and Bakongo elders, the cases of child witches are usually kept secret within the families. Friedman and N'Senga (2002) argue that the large numbers of children who are abused and expelled are held to indicate the excessive burden that the children represent for the families who try to rid themselves of them by accusing them, exploiting the children's vulnerability, especially the orphans. From this viewpoint, accusing a child of witchcraft seems to be sufficiently strong grounds for what among the Bakongo would otherwise be seen as the grave action of refusing to support and protect a child who has lost his or her immediate kin. This interpretation would seem to be backed by the lower incidence of mothers accusing their own children.

The Portuguese words *feitiço* (spell or witch power) and *feitiçaria* (witchcraft) are used interchangeably with the Kikongo words *kindoki* and *kundu*. The former refers to the occult power of witches or sorcerers but is also attributed to chiefs and not inherently malignant. The term *kundu*, meanwhile, refers to a magical substance carried in the belly and is taken to be hereditary. Sometimes it may also be acquired by consuming people (MacGaffey 1970b). These concepts have been in relation since the Christian influence in the Congo area from the sixteenth century onward. Concerning local usage of the term, it should be noted that *feitiçaria* popularly refers to a power primarily used for malevolent purposes,[7] but it is still molded by the ambiguities derived from these other conceptions. These multiple and related terms and conceptions are the result of the long-term circulation, in the Atlantic space, of Africans, missionaries, objects, and practices involving the control of occult forces (see chapter by Sansi, this volume).

Churches and Kinship in the Redefinition of Witchcraft

The renewed interest in researching witchcraft over the last fifteen years has shown that far from being the residue of belief systems remaining active in populations that have yet to fully assimilate to modern life, witchcraft accusations are strongly linked to urban space and the market economy, making up part of the language of political and electoral disputes and used even by the school-educated and Christianized population (Geschiere 1997; Moore and Sanders 2001). Some authors have approached the relationship between witchcraft and economics through the idea of witchcraft as an "occult economy," (Comaroff and Comaroff 1999a) where the consumption of human lives takes place in a system of spurious reciprocity, which involves a complete disparity in the exchange and in the attribution of value: a piece of cake received during the day is equivalent to a human life at night (De Boeck 2004).

Hence witchcraft can be seen as a metaphoric language to express modernity and how the capitalist system is experienced by people, that is, in the more acute forms of accumulation and exclusion caused by globalization and the neoliberal economy. From this perspective, witchcraft provides an insight into how the intense social and symbolic exclusion promoted by capitalism and its incomprehensible (and mysterious) forms of consumption and exploitation have been dramatically and abruptly implanted in Africa. The very conception of society promoted by witchcraft—that is, society as a zero-sum game in which the success and accumulation achieved by one person imply the failure and impoverishment of many—seems to be congruent with the contemporary experiences of those on the margins of global society.

Here we can draw connections between the accusations against children and the new meanings attributed to childhood, the new roles of children and adolescents in the labor market as well as in the public space. The new representations of childhood have been regarded by the recent bibliography as a global phenomenon, in which new forms of violence and exclusion (pedophilia, sexual abuse, organs traffic, child soldiers) emerged at the same time as the constitution of children as subjects of specific rights in the documents of international law (La Fontaine 1998; De Boeck and Honwana 2000, 2005; Durham 2000).

One observes also the adaptation of kinship networks involving the decrease in the reach of the matrilineal extended family in favor of the nuclear family centered on paternal authority. In the Angolan case, urbanization and continuous warfare have demanded an abrupt adaptation of extended families that migrate to the cities in fragmented form. A labor market has opened up for women and young people, and family networks are shrunk and combined with new social networks, such as neighborhood groups and religious communities. This context creates spaces of autonomy for young people. The weakening of the authority of elders has combined with the emergence of religious leaders with the expansion of Pentecostal churches. However, we need to emphasize the aspects of continuity between previous practices of attributing mystical power and making witchcraft accusations, rethinking the intersections among kinship, family, and church.

Connections are frequently drawn between urbanization and the disintegration of kinship. Colonization, the spread of Christianity, the displacement of populations, and urbanization have led to the loss of political power and the dilution of the systems of succession and land inheritance (Balandier 1963; MacGaffey 1970a). Among today's urban Bakongo, the matrilineal structures have the function of regulating marriages within the group (but outside the *Kanda*, the Bakongo clan), defining the inheritance group, and establishing authority within the family, with the continuance of the system of family chiefdoms centered on the figure of the maternal uncle or granduncle.

Bakongo elders say that the most notable transformation in the structure of Kongo kinship is the tendency to valorize the father's power to the detriment of the power of the maternal uncle (Pereira 2004). Although not reflecting a complete transition from the matrilineal system to the patrilineal system, this process indicates the nuclearization of the family and the shrinking of the so-called extended family. The elders attribute this change to westernization and missionary influence.

Without wishing to underestimate these factors of transformation, it is worth remembering that the paternal side in Kongo societies always played an important role, especially in the access to land by younger children and dependents and the succession to political and spiritual positions (MacGaffey 1970a). This duality between maternal and paternal families is apparent in traditional marriage, when the goods received by the bridegroom's family are divided between the two families. This indicates, therefore, that this tension is not recent but that it has been inscribed in the Kongo system for a long time. Nonetheless, in the urban setting, the father's power has evidently increased further with the predominance of the nuclear family caused by the change in the economic system, which altered the forms of wealth production and distribution (Pereira 2004). The same tension between the paternal and maternal families can be observed in the witchcraft accusations made against children, in which the maternal family accuses the paternal family of aggression by turning the child into a witch.

However, while the factors described above exacerbated the fragility of the family network, they also stimulated the creation of spaces of autonomy for youths with the emergence of children and adolescents as new economic agents, widely absorbed into the informal economy. This dynamic produced new spaces of sociability. One of these spaces in the urban context is the neighborhood networks.

Other spaces of local sociability are those connected to churches. Here we find marked differences in terms of the relationship with the family sphere between the more traditional Catholic church and Protestant missionaries' churches, on one hand, and the Pentecostal and African churches, on the other.[8] The former show a relationship of greater proximity and mutual legitimization in relation to the authority deriving from kinship. By contrast, the Pentecostal and prophetic churches seem to instill a rupture with family-based loyalties. This clash is seen not only in the dispute for loyalties between distinct networks (familiar or religious ones) but especially in the dispute for legitimacy in the mediation with the sacred, an ancient prerogative of heads of family and the so-called traditional healers.

Put otherwise, although the churches present multiple and differentiated relations with kinship groups, accusing children can be seen to form part of the process of Pentecostalism's dispute for religious authority with the relatively weakened family system. Nonetheless, although Pentecostal and prophetic leaders may compete with family authorities, they are far from occupying the space left by a kinship system supposedly weakened by modernization. It is worth pointing out that both spheres find points of practical (ritual) and discursive intercession, as well as an overlapping of roles. My argument is that the churches in general, in Angola and more specifically in the multiethnic space of Luanda, take up a place that competes with, but at the same time complements, the organizations based on kinship. More than a dispute or collaboration, the religious organizations have participated in the reconfiguration of kinship. Leaders of small Pentecostal churches sometimes try to legitimate their religious authority by soliciting followers from their own kinship group, just as family heads look to increase their power within kin groups by asserting their religious skills. Hence, the sociability and organizations based on the churches and on kinship possess a complex and interdependent relationship, rather than one of substitution.

Seeing the issue from this viewpoint helps us to understand the involvement of Pentecostal and African churches in the formulation of witchcraft accusations or in the legitimization of the accusations made by relatives. It also suggests that accusations against children can only be understood in relation to the Bakongo kinship system and cosmology.

De Boeck states that the churches do not make the witchcraft accusations themselves but only sanction and legitimate the accusations originating from domestic space (2000, 2005). The author recognizes the ambiguity of churches as participants in the accusations, simultaneously exacerbating the role of the devil and emphasizing the end of times, while supplying the solution to the accused child's problem through confession and purification rituals. However, he situates the origin of the crisis that unleashed the accusations within the domestic and family sphere and attributes it to the social crisis in the Congo as well as to the increase in the mobility of young people and children and their involvement in economic activities, factors of family upheaval and rupture and the alteration in the power balance between generations.

In the Angolan case, it seems that the crisis (or change) taking place in the family/kinship system and its functions (division of labor, attribution of authority and obligations between members, regulation of gifts and exchanges within and between kin groups) reveals a strong involvement of the churches in terms of formulating these transformations. This is most evident in the churches' emphasis on a more restricted and nuclear family system, looking to redirect the exchanges and reciprocities found within the extended family to the domain of the churches (through tithes and marriages within the church communities). Examining the profound transformations occurring in the kinship-based organizations also means to perceive their vitality. It is evident, for example, in the continuance of the language of kinship in the church organizations (through the categories of brotherhood and community), as well as in the forms of proliferation of churches, which, as pointed out, reproduce the structures of fissions and fragmentation found in kinship and the production of local chiefdoms (MacGaffey 1983; Pereira 2004).

It should also be stressed that we cannot properly understand the activities of Bakongo Pentecostal churches regarding witchcraft accusations without taking into account the wider religious field in Angola, in which more traditional churches (with higher representation among the Bakongo), such as the Catholic, Baptist, and Kimbanguist churches, remain more cautious and skeptical, looking to minimize these accusations. In other words, the formulation of discourses and practices concerning witchcraft is clearly linked to the dynamic of the religious field and the dispute for followers. And this dispute involves an effective redefinition of the family, kinship, and their (new) limits.

If I am right in arguing for the permeability between two forms of Bakongo organization and authority in Angolan space (family and churches), it can be supposed that the dynamic of the transformation of kinship through the idiom of witchcraft does not necessarily mean just loss of and crisis in the kinship networks. Instead, we are witnessing an ongoing rearticulation in which the language of kinship remains pertinent and encounters other spaces for its reproduction.[9]

The Approaches Adopted by the State, NGOs, and Churches to the Child Witch Phenomenon

The phenomenon of children accused of witchcraft is also shaped by the ways specific institutions—Angolan state agencies, NGOs, and different churches—have been constructing a variety of perceptions, discourses, and forms of intervention on this issue. I turn now, therefore, to a comparison of the various discourses and practices relating to witchcraft and cultural difference produced and transmitted by NGOs, the state, and the churches. The forms of producing and framing the phenomenon, as well as the resolution of the crisis provoked by the accusations, can be observed in light of the practices of agents occupying distinct positions.

Here I shall examine two forms of dealing with the matter: the first, the response of government institutions and NGOs observed in Mbanza Congo; and the second, the response of a Catholic Church institution, the Arnold Janssen Centre in Luanda.

THE CHILD PROTECTION NETWORK   In the small city of Mbanza Kongo, in 2000, more than four hundred street children were counted by the government, the majority of them accused of witchcraft by their relatives. In 2003, a partnership among the Angolan National Child Institute (Instituto Nacional da Criança, or INAC) and the NGOs Save the Children-Norway (SC-N) and Christian Children's Fund (CCF) implemented a "child protection network" (*rede de proteção da criança*), which includes community agents who are responsible for detecting and preventing cases of children accused of witchcraft and/or subjected to violence and providing advice to the families and communities involved at the local level. Here not only are accused children reported but also cases of sexual abuse and domestic violence, negligence, child and organ trafficking, and so on. These cases are passed on to government bodies when a local solution guaranteeing protection of the child in the "risk situation" cannot be found.

The NGOs formulating and executing projects on the ground look to reconcile the idea of the child's rights with the attempt to comprehend and readdress the local cultural universe, profoundly rooted in the belief in witchcraft. Recognizing witchcraft as part of Bantu culture, the strategy adopted has been, according to interviews with staff from the NGOs involved, to sensitize and try to resolve problems without "interfering with the beliefs themselves or taking them into account." In other words, their work is supposedly restricted to preventing physical or psychological violence rather than trying to alter or refute the belief in *feitiçaria*. This includes trying to persuade the family of the possibility of curing the child without questioning the belief systems that motivated the accusation.

Nonetheless, the reports on the training workshops (Christian Children Fund 2003a, 2003b, 2003c, 2004) show that the strategy more often adopted was different. The workshops tried to persuade the people involved that the features and symptoms that are supposed to identify child witches are the same as those of badly cared for, badly loved, and unwanted children (aggressiveness, indolence, and so on). A similar strategy involved equating the manifestations ("symptoms") of accused children with the manifestations typical to specific phases of a child in the transition to adolescence, especially a childhood traumatized by warfare. Thus, there was an attempt to dissuade people from accusing children by attributing other meanings to the symptoms.

The training of these community agents led to the creation of thirty-eight child protection committees, involving the participation of leaders, traditional authorities, military personnel, nurses, teachers, students, religious leaders, and so on. Set up alongside these local committees was the Provincial Child Protection Committee, with representation from the national police, the provincial judiciary, the attorney general, and various ministries, as well as INAC as the committee's coordinator.

The Provincial Child Protection Committee assumed the function of initiating prosecutions in cases of abuse and violence that exceeded the jurisdiction of the community committees. The most repressive role of the state aims to discourage overly violent actions on the part of families but, on the other hand, does not offer any material help or attempt any other approach than that of trying to persuade the family by force of law that it cannot mistreat or beat a child.

THE ARNOLD JANSSEN CENTRE   The Arnold Janssen Centre sets itself the task of reintegrating the child with the family.[10] This reintegration is pursued through the organization of family meetings, encouraging the family's attempt to treat and cure the accused child. The cure is achieved through Pentecostal churches or healers, depending on the choice of the child's relatives. The attempt at reintegration means that the crisis precipitated by the accusation is understood as the symptom of a family conflict and leads to the acceptance of solutions more integrated with the family's conceptions of the cause of misfortunes.

The center works with professional staff, designated *agentes sociais* ("social agents," mostly social workers but also psychologists) who attempt to contact the children's families. In all such cases, the social agents encourage relatives to explain the reasons for abandoning the child or for the mistreatment that led the child to leave home.

Once these family members are persuaded to reveal the crisis that led them to reject the child, narratives emerge of family misfortunes, separations of couples and new marriages, and the confirmation by healers and pastors of the malevolent action of the children causing these misfortunes. On the basis of these narratives, the relatives are encouraged to propose a treatment for the child afflicted by the spell. If the accusation was made in church, the pastor may be asked to carry out the treatment through purification rituals, as long as these are not considered aggressive by the center's staff. Some children deny being witches but agree to the "treatment" in order to placate the accusers. This whole process is described in the testimony by one of the center's social agents:

> One of the cases which I followed was a fifteen-year-old boy brought here by his mother. She believed she was unable to stay married to her husband because her son was her husband in her dreams. She brings the children

here because they trusted us as a church centre. The parents come to pray, but the family also has to do the other part. Africans have their treatments for these things. She arranged a man from her neighborhood, who said she had to perform a [traditional] treatment for the son. At first, the kid did not accept this, but then agreed. And so he [the healer] performed the treatment. He rubbed a liquid on the child's body and told him he could not bathe that day, so he'd be unable to do what he did at night. So the boy came back here and on the following day he told us he'd had a dream. He said that there's a chief there in the spell [*feitiço*] where they live, with machetes [*catanas*]. Then a big man appeared, and this man managed to fight the chief. So, the boy finished the treatment, stayed here a few more days, the mother brought him some clothes, she already felt happier. After the treatment, she came to fetch her son. She added that she no longer had those problems that she had in the past. What all this goes to show: the family only accepts the child back after successful treatment. They believe that the child will only extract himself from this evil after a traditional treatment.

In Luanda, compared with Mbanza Kongo, there are no awareness-raising campaigns to prevent witchcraft accusations. The Arnold Janssen Centre's work involves sheltering accused and mistreated children who have fled home or who have been evicted. The work carried out at the center aims to legitimize the traditional family reunions to solve conflicts and at the same time looks to meet the demands to protect the child's rights, as well as community participation and local empowerment, as we see in this narrative by another social agent.

Question: You told me before that you don't believe the child is really a witch. How do you deal with the fact that you have to accept what the family says and look for solutions?

SA: In principle, this is a question of tradition, a real part of the Bakongo people's culture. In African terms, witchcraft [*feitiçaria*] exists. So we cannot turn up and say that the child isn't a witch, because what has caused the family's separation is the accusation. And we have to find a form of uniting this family. This is achieved by mediating the conflict in terms of witchcraft. Clearly, if it [witchcraft] exists, it's because someone gave and someone else can take it away. So the family itself should find someone of their own choice who can remove the witchcraft. And, in our social work, we are going to analyze the way the situation is unfolding. Because they shouldn't give anything that could kill the child. We're supporting the child's rights. The ritual varies, some families who are not linked to tradition any more prefer religious help. Some families who are still closely linked to the tradition prefer traditional treatment. The two types of treatment do the same thing. First they cure this spiritual part with prayers and so on, and then they give medications, which is the traditional part. After the family says that the witchcraft is over, we also do our part, the social work. We normally reach the conclusion that underlying witchcraft, that we don't believe in, is poverty. Sometimes the family had a higher level and then began to decline and soon after the child appears as a witch, because sometimes he or she is sick, is delirious at night, has malaria and they quickly call it witchcraft.

Searching for a solution to the family crises, the social agents, depending on the case at hand, involve families, neighbors, the Pentecostal churches, or the traditional healers. Occasionally, when there is physical aggression or a death threat, they seek out the police or the INAC to contain and prosecute the aggressor. In the case below, the social agents tell about a sixteen-year-old youth who was taken in badly injured. He did not say where his family lived, which led the staff to suspect that he had been accused of witchcraft. Months later, the boy was sought at the center by an older brother, who knew that he had not died. There had been a new case of sickness in the family.

So the brother came here aggressively with a knife, ready to kill his brother, saying the boy was a witch, because at home a child was dying. The next day we went to the community and managed to locate the family's house, and we indeed found the baby seriously ill. They had even taken the baby out of the pediatric hospital; they'd said the illness wasn't going to improve as it was a spell, so they took the baby home. We sought the hospital directors and contacted other authorities linked to children. The director of INAC followed the case as well as the Home Ministry, with the DNIC [the police]. We had to take the baby to the clinic: it was a case of cerebral malaria. Thanks God, it was a case of praying, the baby recovered and after this, to make the peace in the family, we had to get them to meet and find a solution. It was then that the family decided that there was someone who could deal with this question of removing the spell, because if it wasn't removed, the boy could perhaps do something worse. [...] I can't remember the story very well [about how the boy acquired the spell], but it involved a grandfather, grandmothers and uncles who are actually dead in Uíge province; they asked for the boy, because they normally use the life of the person as something that strengthens those who are there in the other world. And in our visible world, when they realize what's happening, they have to perform a ritual which, they say, covers the eye, so the person cannot be taken. A *papá* [healer] was located, who provided a recipe for the treatment. There was a chicken, wine, a basin, candles, a lollipop, matches, a sheet. We took out some money, supported them and bought what the healer requested. There at the place, he did some tricks, only the family and the boy could enter. Beforehand we talked with the healer and told him we wanted the best for the family and the child too. We explained to the healer that we are an institution and there were people there representing the law. So the man became involved with the Centre's work. [The healer said,] "You can be sure I'm only going to take out the boy's evil spirit." We are all African and as long as it wasn't to cause harm, but to recuperate, that's fine. But, if the idea is to harm the boy, then we can also intervene. They have to eliminate [the *feitiço*] from the child and we have to check how we can find other individuals to provide a solution to the case. In these cases, the community leader also has to appear, the family, a neighbor who more or less knows the family's life, then we have the basis for a solution […] The boy in fact stayed two days and the *papá* explained everything that had to be done, the boy complied and we came back, he removed [the spell] and everything's okay. He's a grown-up lad now, he's now fine at home with his family.

The construction of the "social problem of children accused of witchcraft" involves an array of institutions from the state, NGOs, and churches, as well as the multiple agents who pass through these institutions, marginal actors such as traditional healers and Pentecostal pastors, along with international legislation, charters, and conventions on rights, especially those of the child. The different forms in which NGOs, the state, and churches produce discourses and practices concerning witchcraft and cultural difference are worth analyzing comparatively, taking into account their interfaces and the production of cultural codes that bring together the different discourses and conceptions of family, children, rights, and culture.

These interfaces include the ways in which NGOs and the state are involved and influence the actions carried out by churches. For example, the Catholic institutions providing shelter to street children, such as the Arnold Janssen Centre, are funded by international NGOs and supervised by partner institutions from the state, who share some of their premises in terms of helping accused children. The Pentecostal churches and traditional healers take into account certain limits beyond which they will be subject to repressive actions from the state. In other words, although in each of these spaces we find distinct formulations concerning the witchcraft phenomenon and the place of children in this accusatory system, we can also perceive important intersections accomplished by agents, meaning that some formulations are more effective than others.

The social projects implemented by the NGOs working in the protection and defense of children's rights introduce conceptions of the child's human rights into a universe alien to the idea of specific rights for children. Insofar as they approach the issue of children accused of witchcraft as primarily a humanitarian problem, the NGOs have difficulties in dealing with cultural specificity and the transformations that sustain the accusations in the family environment. In their concern to intervene in the local social groups and solve the problem of the accusations, the strategy they assume is a pedagogical dissuasion of witchcraft beliefs.

The NGOs have important connections with government institutions, whether through joint actions in social projects or through the circulation of their staff between the two spaces. Here we can observe situations involving close collaboration but also conflicts over the different possibilities and conceptions relating to the implementation of projects among the local populations. The difficulties encountered by NGOs and the state in dealing with cultural systems that differ from their universalist directives reveal significant tensions that need to be taken into account if we are to understand the current debate on witch children in Angolan society. The main tension resides in considering the child as a bearer of specific rights separate from the family and clan context. The other is the apparently uncrossable chasm between rationalism and beliefs in the power of an invisible world.

A brief outline of the various forms of producing discourses and practices on witchcraft is the following: the Pentecostal and prophetic churches have shaped a new language that reframes local conceptions of occult power within a dualist conception (Meyer 1999). Then they employ witchcraft accusations against children and adolescents, who are a simultaneously weakened and ambiguous social category. At the same time, they offer a solution by treating the witch children through exorcism and spiritual release rituals. These rituals occur in the space of the church with the participation of the community of believers. Hence the pastors rework the interpretation, identification, and cure of witchcraft, developing specific rituals within Christianity that retranslate local roles and practices.

The NGOs read the phenomenon of accused children within the parameter of human rights and social intervention in an at-risk group. Within this perspective, they work to implement awareness-raising actions as a way of reducing the harm suffered by children through educational campaigns, persuading the population that the inadequate behavior presented by the children is a natural part of the adolescent's development or typical of traumatized children, introducing a new understanding of the phases of child development.

Generally speaking, the state adopts a legalist stance, centered on national law and the international charters on children's rights. This perspective tends to focus on the protection of the child's rights, which often results in a failure to consider the sociocultural circumstances that sustain the accusations in the family environment. Thus it tends to approach witchcraft juridically from the viewpoint of the inflicted abuse, pursuing a more repressive action against the family, as well as the Pentecostal churches, which are seen to provoke and legitimate accusations against children.[11]

The Catholic Church, through the work of the Arnold Janssen Centre, focuses on reintegrating the accused child in his or her family. To this end, it attempts to bring together different kinds of practices and logics: social intervention informed by conceptions of social work and the empowerment of subaltern groups, similar to the conceptions of the NGOs; the repertoire of rights, set down in international laws and conventions, similar to the state; the cultural universe of the families in conflict, which includes the explanations based on witchcraft; the ritual solutions proposed by the African churches and the traditional healers; and the Christian conceptions themselves, where the unity and integrity of the family occupies a central place.[12]

The Catholic strategy for trying to solve the crisis engendered by the witchcraft accusations involves strengthening (and also reinventing) the family sphere through meetings and the rituals of reconciliation with the aim of reintegrating the children. Consequently, the social agents from the Catholic center act as mediators in the solutions proposed by the families, recognizing and legitimating them as a central institution. The belief in witchcraft, rather than being an obstacle as the state sees it, or a cultural factor to be tamed by the NGOs, is taken into account by the churches in the resolution of family conflicts.

The social agents from the Arnold Janssen Centre have been the most interesting mediators in terms of analyzing the practices and discourses relating to witchcraft insofar as they combine the distinct practices and logics described above. Thanks to their positioning (professional training, institutional place, and insertion in a specific network of relations) and a worldview that includes Christianity, these social agents have played a fundamental role in the formulation of a specific practical-discursive field on witchcraft that combines various repertoires and logics, thereby achieving greater success in the representation of witchcraft than other agents in other spheres, such as NGOs and the state. Mediation here is taken primarily in the symbolic sense where it is a question of the capacity of particular agents to manage distinct cultural repertoires. This management enables them through a process of cultural negotiation to combine new codes that, contextually, produce meanings that are shared and generalized in a wider universe of relations (Montero 2007).

The Place of the Bakongo in Angola and the Witchcraft Accusations

In this sense, the macrostructural factors (transitions to a market economy and the impact of these factors on kinship as well as wars and displacements) are indispensable but insufficient to explain the emergence of the anxiety that gives rise to witchcraft accusations. While these factors have imposed abrupt social changes that have affected all of Angola's population indiscriminately, they have not provoked the same phenomenon of accusations of witchcraft against children across Angola at the same level as we find within the Bakongo.

Comparing the phenomenon in Congo and Angola, we find the same configuration of social crisis, Pentecostal emergence, and transformation of kinship. Nonetheless, in Congo the phenomenon has a transethnic character and is not specific to the Bakongo, which is the Angolan case. This impels us to seek other factors concerning this Bakongo specificity in Angola. I would like to present another possibility concerning the borderline and ambiguous place occupied by the Bakongo in the Angolan nation as an important element for understanding the ethnic specificity of witchcraft in Angola.

The classic literature tells us that the witchcraft accusation system activates and consolidates the boundaries between groups. It draws distinctions between those inside and those outside, redefining kin groups, for example (Douglas 1970). Clearly rooted in kinship relations, but signaling a crisis in the kinship system, it also signals its vitality and pertinence as a form of social and symbolic organization.

The modern literature on witchcraft, by contrast, insists on its relation to the emergence of the postcolonial state, inseparable from new forms of capitalism and political and social exclusion. As various authors argue (Rowlands and Warnier 1988; Bayart 1993; Ciekawy 1998; Geschiere and Nwamnjoh 1998; Schatzberg 2000), witchcraft has been an effective idiom in terms of expressing popular conceptions of the state through the definition of the state (and witchcraft) as an occult power and the illegitimate appropriations of another's vital force. Witchcraft in this context is interpreted as a critical language addressing the exercise of power in the new African states, which are dominated by authoritarian and closed systems.

This language interconnects traditional and modern systems that constitute themselves mutually, explaining the hybrid formation of contemporary African states.

During my fieldwork, asking Bakongo adults what had caused the inversion in the pattern of witchcraft, which had shifted from being an attribute of older people to being performed and propagated by children, I was very often told that there had been a "democratization of witchcraft." The Angolan state can be described in terms of political closure and the concentration of resources, with low involvement from civil society, which has grown more quickly following the end of the civil war. Witchcraft in Angola, ironically, in contrast to the state, enables democracy, since everyone can appropriate and disseminate it.

It is also possible to translate the insertion of the Bakongo in the Angolan context as a borderline insertion, in the geographic sense (where the Congo region was divided into three colonial and later national spaces) and in the sense of the relative political marginality of the group in Angola since the independence. The *regressado*/Bakongo population in Luanda were then stigmatized for various reasons: political—the identification of the Bakongo group with the National Front for the Liberation of Angola, a group opposing the party in power Popular Movement for the Liberation of Angola (MPLA)—and economic—the development of the informal sector[13] and the significant presence of the group among civil servants working for the state. However, this stigmatization was primarily expressed in terms of cultural difference, where the strong identification with Congo/Zaire along with the introduction of Lingala (the lingua franca of Kinshasa) and cultural practices deemed to be alien to the cultural universe of Luanda were heavily stressed (Mabeko Tali 1995; Pereira 1999).

The notions of "Angolanness" constructed in Luanda took as their counterpoint the Bakongo returning from the Congo since the independence. These Bakongo were constructed as foreigners, and this ambiguity of being both foreigners and Angolans (former exiles, passing continually across borders, sometimes indistinguishable from the numerous Congolese immigrants in Angola) seems to have been a significant factor in determining how witchcraft is configured in Angola through this ethnic bias.

In addition, some local arguments and perceptions rooted in the historical relations between Congo and Angola should be taken into account when examining the local perceptions that link witchcraft to the Bakongo. The multiplication of Pentecostal and African churches in Angola since the 1990s has matched the growth of Pentecostal denominations in other parts of Africa and the world. In Angola, this multiplication followed the process of opening up the state slightly and liberalizing the economy. It was also connected to the pace of return to Angola of the Bakongo exiled in the Congo and Congolese migration. The negative reactions from the Luanda's population, the more established churches, the press, intellectuals, and sectors of the state to the multiplication of Pentecostal influences can invariably be traced back to the supposed (nefarious) influence of the Congo.

The permeability of the border and the sharing of the same cultural identity among the Bakongo from the two countries does not annul the perception of distinctions between Angolans and Congolese who speak Kikongo or the perception of the Congolese influence, especially in the expansion of Lingala and the experiences of the Bakongo in the Congo that are introduced into Angola. More than a cultural influence reflecting similarities in social organization and kinship, belief system, practices, and so on, it is the Congolese experience of religious ferment and correlated practices that are implicated in the construction of the negative nature of the Congolese influence on Angola.

The presence of the *regressados* was a decisive factor in determining the stigmatized form of seeing the Congo. Consequently, all the negative practices associated with the Bakongo can be taken as evidence of the malign influence of the Congo, such as the introduction of illegal trade, African churches, and, more recently, the witchcraft accusations leveled at children. For the authorities and NGOs, these accusations cannot be dissociated from the activities of these churches.

These arguments, which link the arrival of the churches and the witchcraft attributed to children to the Congo, emerge precisely—although not exclusively—from those sectors more closely connected to the state. Hence it seems to me important to examine the way in which the discourse and practices relating to witchcraft are shaped by the Angolan state in terms of the groups that make up Angolan society and the place of the Bakongo in the Angolan nation. I also argue that the process of constructing discourse and practices on witchcraft and the accusation of children (forms of defining, explaining, avoiding, and containing a social problem) are intimately related to the place occupied by the Bakongo in the Angolan space.

Conclusion: The Different Productions of Witchcraft

The witchcraft accusations that emerge from personal relations, expressing tensions in kinship and neighborhood relations, become problems treated in the institutional sphere. The phenomenon presented here of children being accused of witchcraft brings the family into a wider and more heterogeneous circuit where the state, NGOs, and churches interact.

The form in which the state and NGOs deal with the problem in Mbanza Kongo and the forms of treatment pursued at the Arnold Janssen Centre in Luanda demonstrate that the phenomenon of children accused of witchcraft is produced in different ways, containing many intersections. One important difference resides in the form in which the family is positioned in the two cases. In the Mbanza Kongo case, approached in terms of the violence suffered by the child, the family is considered the aggressor and is liable to punishment by the state. In the case of the Catholic Arnold Janssen Centre, the family itself is encouraged to produce the solution to the problem. The beliefs and practices linked to the accusation are taken in this case as important elements in the resolution process.

By making use of codes derived from various systems (discourses based on rights, local cosmologies, social work), the social agents of the Arnold Janssen Centre make this repertoire even more varied and activate the potential efficacy of the treatment, thereby increasing the chances of success in their aim of reintegrating the child. The relative success of reintegration allows the production of a consensus concerning the definitions of witchcraft in the intersection of churches, families, and state institutions.

The borders made evident in witchcraft accusations relate to the borders drawn by the Bakongo between parents and children and between relatives and nonrelatives (or no longer relatives), since witchcraft accusations are directed mostly toward orphaned children. The accusations reveal and are constitutive of tensions that configure the contemporary extended families in the Angolan context.

Relations of reciprocity between relatives also seem to be at issue, made evident in the accusation of incest in the first case related by the Arnold Janssen Centre's social agents. The same applies in terms of the relations between the visible and invisible worlds given that, as related in the second case, when the dead demand the lives of their relatives to maintain their force in the other world, spurious kinship relations are configured, through the draining of vital force between the living and their dead relatives. Instead of the balanced and mutually supportive reciprocity expected between the two worlds, a form of predation is instigated.

However, the accusations are not only connected to the kinship system's internal boundaries but also to the internal boundaries of the nation, by implicating the relations between Congo and Angola, and to the migrations of the Bakongo as traders (simultaneously foreign and Angolan) within the country, selling products and religious affiliation.

Suspicion appears to be the most effective form of organizing these borders and maintaining them at once flexible and ambiguous. A family's suspicion of a child who is simultaneously disdained and seen as dangerous emerges, as well as the state's suspicion of the family and the nation's suspicion of the Bakongo, whose nationality is placed permanently in question. Ambiguity and suspicion generate then the need to produce and continually relocate boundaries.

The emergence of witchcraft in Angolan public debate highlights the redesigning of other borders: between kinship and churches or among the state, family, and rights, repositioning the public and private spheres in Angola. The churches perform a fundamental role in this debate, as well as in the new forms of witch children that are inserted in urban space and their of visibility as subjects with rights.

Notes to Chapter Ten

This work was based on a field trip to Angola in 2006. I would like to thank Mary Daly and Mena Andrade from the NGO Christian Children's Fund. The work was supported by a grant from Fundação de Amparo à Pesquisa do Estado de São Paulo. Text translated from the Portuguese by David Rodgers.

1. Witchcraft accusations against children have been observed also in Nigeria, Ivory Coast, Malawi, and Cameroon, among other countries. In Angola and DRC, the factors involved and their relations are similar.

2. The Bakongo group was originally located on the northern border of Angola with the DRC and is also present in the Republic of the Congo. In the past, this region composed the former kingdom of Kongo, which entered into contact with the Portuguese at the end of the fifteenth century. The Christianization of this part of Central Africa dates from this period. The Bakongo of Angola have undergone an intense sequence of migrations in their recent history, especially following the outbreak of the war of liberation (1961), when a large contingent became exiled in the Belgian Congo (the present-day DRC). Many of those who returned to Angola after independence (1975) became involved in retail trade and were the most prominent figures of the parallel market in Luanda City under the socialist regime. It has been among this group, pejoratively called *regressados* ("returnees") that we find the largest number of cases of children being accused of witchcraft.

3. The civil war, which erupted after the independence until 2002, between the MPLA-led government and the rebel party UNITA, was responsible for the exile or internal displacement of over a third of the population. Half of Angolans live in the cities, and a third in the capital Luanda, which is home to an estimated five million inhabitants.

4. There are references to the expulsion of children considered witches or to their commerce as slaves in the Kongo area at the beginning of the twentieth century (Claridge 1922). About child witches in the early modern period, see Roper (2000). In the anthropological literature, see Brain (1970).

5. In contrast to the few religious denominations that existed during the colonial era, the contemporary religious landscape in Angola has become highly complex owing to the recent proliferation of churches in the Protestant field, especially Pentecostal and African churches, since the 1990s. The Bakongo are almost all Christian in a

country in which Christianity is professed by more than 80 percent of the population. The largest number of religious denominations—Pentecostal or African, the latter also called prophetic or *mpeve a longo* (the Kikongo name for Holy Spirit)—and religious leaders are found among the Bakongo, especially the *regressados*. These churches perform a key role in shaping a language favorable for witchcraft accusations as well as in providing rituals for identifying and curing the accused.

6. The cases of witchcraft accusation in the Congo, Angola, and Nigeria have been receiving growing attention from the media owing to the violence inflicted by the relatives and by the curing rituals employed by the Pentecostal churches. This attention increased a few years ago when cases of children being accused of witchcraft emerged in London since 2001 (see the Introduction to this volume). A number of the children involved and their families were of Congolese and Angolan origin. See Stobart (2006).

7. Portuguese is spoken and understood in different degrees by 75 percent of the Angolan population. Most of my interviews were conducted spontaneously in Portuguese; some of them were conducted in Kikongo, especially in the Zaire province.

8. Even if there has not been a religious census since 1970, it is presumed that the Catholic Church is still the major church in Angola. However, it is likely that, alongside the Protestant churches of missionary origin (Baptist, Methodist, and Congregationalist), the Catholic Church is losing members to the Pentecostal and African congregations.

9. Brazilian Pentecostal churches, especially the Universal Church of the Kingdom of God (UCKG), are expanding impressively among all sectors, classes, and ethnic groups in Angola. Even though these churches are not significantly involved in child witch accusations, they reproduce the same logic of translating the local universe into a language that emphasizes strongly the power of witchcraft (about UCKG and witchcraft in Brazil, see Birman, this volume and Almeida 2009).

10. The center was created in 1997 by Father Horácio, an Argentinean priest (of Guarani origin) from the Society of the Divine Word. It is situated on the outskirts of Luanda, near the outlying district of Palanca, whose population is mostly Bakongo in origin. It offers shelter to boys and young men only and offers a number of social projects, such as psychological support and career training.

11. The Angolan state does not possess any specific legislation on witchcraft, neither in terms of recognizing and judging the intention or action of the supposed witch, as occurs in some other African countries (Fisiy 1998), nor in terms of considering the accuser's act as slander. It criminalizes only cases of violence or neglect. The mechanisms by means of which the Angolan government deals with issues concerning witchcraft in Angola are closely related to the Portuguese colonial period.

12. The Catholic Church presents a variety of positions and views in relation to witchcraft. There are institutional or official prescriptions and disagreements as to how to tackle the phenomenon among a range of agents. It is not my intention to produce a survey of this multiplicity of positions within the Catholic Church. Instead, I have focused on the work of the Arnold Janssen Centre, through the activity of social assistance, as a typical form of Catholic action.

13. Following economic liberalization in the 1990s, Angola—already weakened by the war—fell into an economic crisis. The informal sector spread further, ceasing to be the preserve of the Bakongo. Thereafter, the *regressados* were relegated to a less preeminent role but also were less stigmatized.

11

Sorcery, Territories, and Marginal Resistances in Rio de Janeiro

PATRICIA BIRMAN

Introduction

HOW IS WITCHCRAFT being used in these Pentecostal times? In recent years, the Pentecostal word on acts of witchcraft seems to have spoken louder and more vigorously than any other. In Rio de Janeiro at least, witchcraft accusations have circulated primarily—and with a particular intensity—in places where the Pentecostal war against diabolical evil has been especially concentrated: favelas and other peripheral areas, usually referred to as "communities." Citing cases of witchcraft supposedly originating in Afro-Brazilian cults, evangelical preachers denounce heinous crimes and acts of barbarity that elicit feelings of horror and fear in their audience at church or on the radio and television stations. In this chapter, I describe two cases of witchcraft accusation that interconnect marginality, crime, and the presence of diabolical evil in two communities. To understand these witchcraft accusations better, we need to take into account that residents from both the "community of believers" and the favela where I conducted fieldwork face a series of problems derived from their admin- *imposed identities* istration as territories subject to specific forms of identification imposed by the state.[1] The latter interpellates their inhabitants through categories that produce effects of exclusion and inclusion that interact with the social and political values associated with religions and witchcraft. Although witchcraft is not "a product of the state [but] a mode of appropriation of the latter" (Bayart, Geschiere, and Nyamnjoh 2001, 180),[2] it is intimately linked to the procedures through which the state defines and relates to the populations located on its margins.[3]

From the outset, I wish to highlight the gradual evolution of a close affinity in the Brazilian media and public space between evangelical and lay discourses in terms of their treatment of the theme of evil and violence. By connecting witchcraft accusations with criminal practices and banditry, evangelicals are, in effect, emphasizing what the lay media never tires of drumming into the public conscience: the presence of a powerful internal enemy, the bandit or dealer, who lives in the communities, thereby reinforcing the negative image of these areas as cultural totalities that are sources of danger and violence for society as a whole.[4] Bearing in mind the importance of these negative perceptions for the policies implemented in these urban peripheries, we can observe that the discourses demonizing these territories make up a form of political-religious action that simultaneously responds to the questions of the state and appropriates its categories, combining them with religious conceptions.

A distance of more than ten years separates the situations described in this text, both encountered during research with evangelical groups in urban communities. The first took place in a favela located in the southern zone of Rio de Janeiro, and the second in a territory designated as a "community of believers," four hours away from Rio de Janeiro City. Comparing these two research experiences has allowed me to comprehend the meanings acquired by witchcraft accusations in precise ethnographic contexts: these meanings are invariably associated with Afro-Brazilian devils and the social spaces hegemonically known as territories held to contain homogenous communities, as though these were cultural totalities. In pursuing this comparison, I wish to show how the evangelical war against evil in the favela territories is designed to achieve what is already supposedly in force in the community of believers, namely, a village in which God's law configures public space in a form guaranteed by the state. The community of believers is seen to realize, at least ideally, the imagined order that Pentecostalism strives to instill in all the social spaces in which it has an active presence.

Since the years separating the two research experiences saw the consolidation of Evangelism in Brazil, the situations that I recount—in all their specificities—also illustrate the passage of time and the growing accumulation of power and influence on the part of evangelical groups, principally in Rio de Janeiro. Indeed, time is far from a negligible factor in terms of the evangelical presence in Brazil and still less in relation to the problems faced by the social groups to which these religious figures belong. As we know, conversion to these churches mainly takes place among subaltern social groups. Individuals from these groups have been simultaneously the witnesses, victims, and agents of the reconfigurations of the margins con-

[margin note: The typical internal other the enemy w/in and @ the same time externalized by its place in the territories]

tinually associated with violence and criminality and with their religious pairs, magic and witchcraft. These reconfigurations form part of the elaboration of the peripheries as exceptional social spaces that are revealed here as inverted images: in the favela, crime and disorder rule supreme, and the evangelicals crave to be the social actors politically and religiously responsible for expelling evil from the community. In the community of believers, this goal has, in their view, already been partially achieved through the power wielded by the local Pentecostal church. The latter conducts and *keeping* encourages the struggle of its followers to keep evil outside its borders by *the other* effectively controlling public space. *othersnalzed.*

In Brazilian society where imagery of disorder is continually associated with its peripheries, the last fifteen years, perhaps longer, has witnessed a process that has heavily shaped the definition of its spaces and boundaries. I refer to the emergence of violence as a social issue in Rio de Janeiro City and as an obvious product of these peripheries, encapsulated in the favela. The designation of some social dwelling spaces as favelas has a long history, associated with various modalities of constructing alterities, including those associated with marginality, the lack of civilization, and poverty. To the latter category, poverty, was added criminality through the identification of their residents with drug trafficking and violence. Over the years, this identification was gradually naturalized, contributing to a growing feeling of insecurity among residents, who are increasingly threatened by violent death in their residential territories (Leite 2007; Machado da Silva 2007; Farias 2008).[5]

I therefore initially look to explore how favela residents are exposed to the state's interpellations as individuals associated with crime and violence and to the interpellations of the drug dealers who control the same territory through armed force. I focus on a situation in which these two forms of interpellation are connected to the transformation in the economy of religious exchanges in this space caused by the evangelical presence. In so doing, I turn to the testimony of a former Candomblé religious specialist who experienced a number of life-threatening situations in which the danger was attributed to a magical causality.

After this account, I turn to the Pentecostal practices among a community of believers where the mode of intervention of the Assembly of God has yet to be rivaled. Predominantly inhabited by families belonging to the only local church, its territory is perceived to possess distinctive religious qualities.[6] In effect, it is perceived as a holy place. Here I explore the meaning of a witchcraft accusation in this locality where the state's interpellations recognize the morally positive difference presented by the community in question to society.

From this blessed village, its residents watch on television the incessant spectacle of evil in the world, reassuring themselves about the special nature of the place where they live.[7] Among this community of believers, diabolical evil, although omnipresent and threatening, is supposedly situated on its margins since the community's territory possesses a sacredness that distinguishes it from other areas, such the cited favela community, whose predominant image associates it with crime and violence. The relations established by the evangelicals with and through these territories are predicated on the perception that the dynamic of the world is structured by the forces of evil. These forces, however, form part of specific clashes and act in different ways on their spaces owing to the intervention of the men of God and of those others under the sway of demons. The Spiritual Battle explains events in this public sphere and reveals the presence of the devil to the eyes of different religious figures, as we shall now see.[8]

Territories, People, and Relations

It is worth stressing from the outset that the contrast between these two communities would be somewhat less striking had their histories not been shaped by the new value attributed to Evangelism in public space. As recent figures in the city's religious economy, the so-called believers (*crentes*) or evangelicals gained public recognition during the same period in which violence became a social issue (Birman and Leite 2000). In fact, new themes appeared in the press and television media during the 1990s: on one hand, scandals provoked by the emergence of the Universal Church of the Kingdom of God (UCKG) and the subsequent media attention given to these new religious actors in public space; and on the other, daily and ever more sensationalist reports on organized crime and its supposed control of increasingly broader sections of the population. A disturbing aspect of social life, increasingly sensationalized by the media, this brutality has provoked constant appeals for the forces of order to combat the evil of violence and its perpetrators. However, although generic, the violence became attributed to a particular region of the city: the state has switched to searching for its highest incidences among the poor and the areas in which they live.

Although the claim that peripheral areas are a haven of negative moral qualities, linked to poverty and criminality, is far from new, it is only fairly recently that this constructed set of factors has been associated with certain religious practices, such as exorcism and combating witchcraft. The demonization pursued by the religious media—whose power took hold in the 1990s—echoes and complements the theme dominating the Rio de

once again the diabolical evil - so terrifying b/c if comes from w/in is moved to a marginal space + thus contained

Both the new religions actors and the authors of violence acting in the same public space - Symbolic of the war between Good + Evil/ God + Devil?

Janeiro mainstream media over the last fifteen years or so. Each in its own way has intensified a negative perception of people living in the peripheral areas of the city (Machado da Silva and Leite 2007).

[margin note: Both the religions + mainstream media.]

Martijn Oosterbaan (2006) provides a particularly cogent argument concerning the intertextuality between Pentecostal discourses on evil and media descriptions of the violence associated with drug trafficking in Rio's favelas. Thus the same imagery of evil, whose absurdity challenges the moral conscience of readers and television viewers, confirms the criminal susceptibility of the lower classes and isolates their world as the most susceptible to immoral acts and witchcraft.[9]

However, the continuity between lay and religious discourses is also relative. Indeed, the possibility of conversion transforms the relation that these supposed criminals have to evil and the deadly fate that society predominantly reserves for them. The evangelicals work ceaselessly to transform this link with diabolical evil into a temporary state that can be overcome. The potential fate of criminals and drug dealers is to become converts whose condition will assure them a new right to life. Hence the incessant work of prayers and exorcism also aims to avoid the abolition of the future of those who participate in this logic of warfare. So while Pentecostal churches in a certain way contribute to demonizing young drug dealers and the residents of these peripheral spaces, they look to save their lives through religious activities, separating them from the terrestrial world that the condition of favela dweller continually threatens to undermine.

Innumerable witnesses in the evangelical churches testify that the devil's ceaseless intention is "to steal, kill, and destroy." From the pulpit, the converts recount their evil deeds before accepting Jesus into their lives. Yet it is from this degraded condition of someone subject to the forces of evil that a new person emerges, an individual saved by the Gospel. The outcome of this play of identities is that there is no one closer to a bandit than a believer.[10] According to the testimonies ritualized in the church services, evangelicals (especially men) are past sinners who had been virtual bandits. A liminal time is therefore involved in the process of forming these men who can nonetheless obtain salvation in the evangelical churches. The path from bandits to believers is not only desirable but today is the clearest future for those living on the urban peripheries who find themselves in constant contact with criminal factions and the forces employed by the state to combat them.

Hence the two communities I examine here are very often defined through these antagonisms. Both reveal the importance of this religious axis, which emphasizes the complete incompatibility between Good and Evil. Indeed, the two cases of witchcraft analyzed below make sense to their protagonists as people who participate in the dynamics of their neighborhoods. They are also informed by the discourses that seek to define them and delimit their behavior and conflicts by containing these within this dualist scheme, particularly developed by Pentecostalism, as well as the lay discourses that stigmatize the peripheral territories inhabited by the poor.

Let us present the protagonists involved in the two cases. While Alice's background is in Candomblé and she interacts with her Afro-Brazilian entities in the context of a "war" between drug gangs in a Rio favela, an area frequently linked to evil and witchcraft, Bruno and Carlos interact with the devil and *macumba* entities on the margins of a public space with an evangelical church at its center.[11] In the favela, "all the cats look gray," as the Brazilian saying goes, when the police attempt to pursue and kill supposed criminals in the middle of a densely populated area. It should be stressed, of course, that the difficulties faced by police forces in identifying and hitting the right targets, and nobody else, when they shoot quadruples as a problem for the favela inhabitants themselves: evading being targeted by police, their aim fed by social stigma, involves "identifying" oneself or being "identified" as moral exceptions. On the contrary, in the community of believers there is no room for anonymity. The pastor testifies about who belongs to the church.

The construction of identity in very visceral circumstances

Alice and the Wink of the Exu

Part of the experience of Alice and other residents of this favela involves living day to day with the Pentecostal discourses that project themselves as an alternative to the secular and violent power wielded by the state and the drug gangs. Caught in the social and political dynamics that traverse the favela, Alice needs to act in recognition of the power of the guns wielded by the gang members, as well as the fact that the latter have proven their own political importance by controlling the territory effectively in the form of a sovereign power.[12] She has also seen her neighbors gradually adopt different life strategies to her own, following their decision to convert and join local Pentecostal churches. These women, aged between forty and fifty, former frequenters of Afro-Brazilian cult houses, seemed to have recognized the emergence of a new local mediatory power, accompanied by the decline experienced by the Umbanda father-of-saint. In contrast to herself, still linked to Candomblé, another older woman—also her neighbor and the owner of a small store—was living testimony to what the Pentecostal churches could offer: she radiated satisfaction and made no attempt to hide her pride in her son, who had become a pastor for the

context of gang violence + control — a contested space of gangs challenging the State for control.

enter a 3rd contender — the pentecostal church.

Universal Church. Meanwhile, Alice's own daughter was at the time going out with the biological son of this father-of-saint in decline, who still provided consultations in his home to a reduced clientele. To Alice's dismay, since she disapproved of her daughter's love affair, the young man was also linked to drug trafficking, and furthermore his brother had been killed the previous year.

At the end of the 1990s, at the height of the attacks by the UCKG on Afro-Brazilian cults, Alice told me why she had abandoned Candomblé after thirty years of devotion to the *orixás*. At the time I was studying the conversion of followers of Afro-Brazilian religions to Pentecostalism and, as a working hypothesis, proposed the importance of a continuity between the practices of the former religions and those of Pentecostalism. Today I believe that by emphasizing the continuities between the two religions, I failed to give sufficient value to the project of breaking with the former that informed the desire to change and that also was a way of working through the transformations in their living conditions (Birman 1996).[13] Thus I return now to Alice's account with this new preoccupation. At the time of our conversation, she must have been around forty and was employed as a cleaner for upper-middle-class households in Rio.

Her biggest worry at the time was the risk faced by her daughter. Among the people whom I knew there, in this small favela, the two women were among the few people who made no attempt to hide their connection to Candomblé and made this religious belonging an eternal topic of conversation: they could talk for hours on end of the beauty of the saint festivals and the pleasure they derived from these.[14]

Let us return to the circumstances surrounding Alice's abandonment of Candomblé. This was a story that she herself connected to a conflict between two gangs vying for control of drug sales points in the favela. Alice provided an emotional account, cast in religious terms, of the fight between the drug gangs and the impact of these events on her own life. Against her will, she found herself partly responsible for killings that occurred between the two gangs and that almost killed her daughter too.

Returning from work one day, she recounted, she found her house had been transformed into a hiding place for the guns held by her daughter's boyfriend. Indignant, she lost her temper and shouted at the youth, expelling him from the house along with his arsenal. However, her daughter continued to see him, and the situation merely worsened, intensifying her fears. At the peak of her anger and indignation over the risk the young man was introducing into her life, Alice one day voiced aloud an appeal—overheard by her curious neighbors—to her Exu (a Candomblé entity who

Alice asked the Exu to remove a drug dealing b/f from her daughter's life

keeps an ambiguous relationship with evil and who could be conceived as a trickster and/or a demon) to intervene. Her request was for the latter to avenge her by causing the youth to disappear from her daughter's life.

Unfortunately, a short time later, the favela was invaded by a rival drug gang and the young man was killed in the shoot-out, dying in the arms of her daughter who herself was lucky to escape injury. Alice heard the shots, ran out into the street, and encountered the killer, gun in hand, who was coming down the hill where she lives, having left the body of his enemy strewn on the ground. As she passed the killer—who, she pointed out, was not from the area—he made a gesture of complicity, winking and letting Alice understand that he was her Exu, the same one to whom she had appealed for revenge and with whom she had a special relationship in Candomblé. As though this were not enough, the youth became the new *dono do morro*, "owner of the hill,"[15] and began a love affair with her daughter, offering her all the wealth that drug trafficking could buy. Alice, aware that the new gang leader was her Exu, embodied in a young drug dealer, did not dare to ask him to leave through fear of him exacting even greater revenge on herself. Finally, it was the turn of the police to invade the favela. The young man tried to flee but was caught in a stream of bullets. His body fell over a precipice, striking an iron railing, which pierced and killed him. She saw him die. In his final moments, he still had enough life force to appear to her for a brief second in the traditional image of her Exu, dressed as Zé Pilintra,[16] assuming the same form in which he appeared to her in the Candomblé festivals.

The drama contained in this narrative made her abandonment of Candomblé both morally and socially inevitable: it would have been virtually impossible to continue in a religion that, aside from never having brought her prosperity (as she emphasized, she had never been rich and had never known a mother-of-saint who was), had thrown her into the middle of a violent factional war that transformed her thoughtless gesture into a bloody tragedy she had never wanted. But not only this. Alice's appeal to the entity is perceived as the cause of the deaths, for which she came to see herself as at least partly responsible—or, perhaps more importantly, as a motive for incrimination by one of the groups taking part in this conflict. The comments of neighbors, for example, could give this spiritual relation another dimension and thus give an even more realistic cast to the image she already possessed as a Candomblé adept.

Now Alice said she was "religionless" because, although rejecting her former relations with the Candomblé saints, she saw no need to join a Pentecostal church. Nonetheless, Alice did think it would be a good idea to at least attend the evangelical church services. She went with her daughter to the Renewed Baptist Church, the Assembly of God, and the Universal Church but had no wish to give up smoking or beer, much less abandon her love affairs. She decided not to convert. But, in a way, she was faced by a demand to transform her person that would be difficult for us to conceive of without taking into account all the elements involved in the situation she described to us.

Her new perception of the Afro-Brazilian religious entities taught her their potential to respond violently in a world marked by irreparable antagonisms, resolved mainly through the use of physical force. Beings who were always prone, like herself, to join forces, take sides, and become involved in the causes of those who protect them were now thought of as agents of an absolute evil that could assume factional forms, and, owing to this identifying trait, they may be persecuted by others in the name of the common good. Moreover, the presence of evil in the favelas could facilitate the incrimination of their residents by the state and wider society. But this fact fails to explain Alice's abandonment of Candomblé. The accusation of being an accomplice becomes more complex insofar it involves conceptions of exchange in the Afro-Brazilian cults and the war waged on them by Pentecostals.

In fact, the accusations of the state and the media concerning the collaborationism of favela residents with drug gangs makes use of various arguments, including the fact that these residents have kinship and affine ties with drug dealers. This fact supposedly leads them to protect the latter against the state's attempts to identify gang members and distinguish them from their networks of relations. Another interpretation, however, shows us that it is the state that incriminates individuals, transforming their affective and kinship relations into relations of complicity with crime. Denouncing supposed criminals to the state's forces is seen as the only real way of showing a lack of complicity, as the mayor of Rio de Janeiro and the secretary of public security have stated a number of times over recent years. Silence, in turn, is demanded from residents by drug dealers as a means of ensuring their noncomplicity with the police. Gossip among neighbors is a key source of information for the drug gangs, allowing them to identify potential informers and sometimes inflict punishment in the form of death or mutilation (Machado Silva and Leite 2007; Cunha 2009).

In other words, an appeal for spiritual intervention within the context of Alice's family relations acquired a public and political dimension related to the drug gang war: as a result, the violence entered her own house and also became Alice's responsibility. Alice did not narrate her story as a change that took place in the way she perceived the world around her but as a change in the real relationship with her Exu, transformed by the violent relations in the favela where she lived. In becoming autonomous, the entity behaved like a Pentecostal devil, destroying the lives of the people closest to her. A person of the family circle, such as the daughter's boyfriend, was the victim of a magical act that targeted him not as a member of a circuit of exchanges with Alice as a mediator but as one of the many faces of a universal evil.[17] Losing her mediating role meant being unable to control the magical attacks and counterattacks that formed her everyday religious experience.

Her Exu, now a devil, therefore acted as the conduit of an absolute evil that took Alice as his accomplice. By becoming autonomous from Alice, he revealed a transcendent nature, that is, submission to a principle that simultaneously transcends and determines the localities in which he acts. The devil, under any circumstance, is a devil: his behavior is defined by being an enemy of God. And it is through the cosmic battle with the divine principles of good since the origin of the world that we can apprehend the malefic nature of his actions. Had his behavior been guided by his ties with Alice, he would have been unlikely to have caused the death of two people close to her. Far from helping her as an entity that participates in her life and lies within her power (albeit relatively), he caused an evil that can only be comprehended through its absolute and universal form, recognizably the same anywhere and under any circumstance. The Exu/devil destroyed the circuit of exchanges in which Alice exerted her power of mediation through her entities in order to meet the demands of her family and friends.[18] As a result, he indirectly convinces those who seek protection from his actions to revoke their local religious roots, particularly those roots in the place where they live, and redefine themselves through ties that transcend the terrestrial world.

The relativity of evil, dominant in the magic of Candomblé and highlighted in academic works on the religion, was therefore unmasked under the severe gaze of the Pentecostals and continually reaffirmed through the stigmatizing identification with the favela promoted by the state. Rather than obtaining a favor from her Exu, in this case, the separation of the boyfriend from her daughter, she received a refutation of the beneficial (or at least ambivalent) nature of Candomblé's magical interventions for herself. The entity himself unexpectedly confirmed the extent to which his action in the present exceeded Alice's control. In conclusion, Alice's experience primarily taught her that she had lost some of her capacities for intervening in the world in which she lives. This experience seems to be readily translatable into Pentecostal religious terms: after all, who if not God can challenge the violence of the countless demons who control life in this world? And, in the case of the community in which she lives, perhaps it would be better, as it is for so many others, for her to consider divine action as the only intervention capable of guaranteeing its residents the possibility of transcending the evil that tirelessly pervades and defines their territory.

The Laughter of the Pomba-Gira[19]

As mentioned earlier, in the territory where Carlos and Bruno live, the pastor has the state's approval to run the community's public services, as well as to ensure social and moral order. However, we would be doing an injustice to the importance of his church were we to imply that this control was simply juridical-political in nature and ignore the religious construction of its territory. What makes the control exerted by this church fascinating is the way in which the political universe is embedded in evangelical conceptions and practices. The forms of controlling its territory, as well as the church's implementation of its authority, submit the secular conceptions—which theoretically, at least, provide the basis for the state's actions—to the principles that make this community a collective especially blessed by God. Up to now, the community's identification as an evangelical territory has been presented as the most important source of legitimacy recognized by the state for exercising power.

However, to comprehend the church's procedures more clearly we need to examine the form in which it conceives divine interventions among its members and over the territory where they live. Since our very first trips to the village, we learned about its foundation myth. We heard the story of an evangelical individual who, returning to the place where he had been born, a small fishing village, begins to preach the Gospel and gradually convert its inhabitants. On converting, the residents became witnesses to a miracle that affected them personally and also redefined the territory as a whole. God intervened by changing the natural conditions of the locality as well as the social, political, and moral order prevailing in what then became His territory. The three generations succeeding this first one—the immediate target of conversion and the eye witness of its miraculous effects—are identified as the beneficiaries of the transformations made by God during this founding moment.

Here I cite the narrative of this reconversion of the territory, as I have previously quoted elsewhere:

> Some geographical features are therefore recognized as signs of this divine election. Close to the entry to the bay, from the fishing boat that transports us, it is possible to see on the coastline an enormous boulder

balanced on top of another. This strange rocky sculpture is frequently mentioned as proof of God's choice. In a fairly unorthodox appropriation of the recognition that *the Indians*, the country's first inhabitants, made of the Catholicity of the *Terra de Santa Cruz*, we find that these testimonies—which, in earlier times, guaranteed the inaugural act of the foundation of Brazil—supplied the community's population with Biblical proof of God's action. Its meaning in the *language of the Indians* refers to a geographical feature whose divine meaning is inscribed in the Gospels: *"I shall found my church on rock and the doors of hell shall not prevail over it." "The rock is Christ,"* says the pastor. (Birman 2006)

In sum, the community is ideally imagined as a territory whose frontiers were established through this primordial rupture, only after which did it truly begin to exist. The rupture with the past, in contrast to most of the stories we know concerning the foundation of Pentecostal churches, was achieved through an overriding territorial principle, which gave rise to an apparent religious isolate, the community of believers, whose foundation seems to have afforded it a specific political status: in this place, the law of men is duplicated by the law of God, a fact recognized by everyone, outsiders and insiders alike. In day-to-day life, the pastor reaffirms and looks to exert (fairly successfully, in fact) his authority over the village as a whole.

However, the pastor's administration of the territory as a whole also provokes a certain discomfort in another group—namely, the "deviants" (*desviados*) from the church who sometimes perceive themselves to be treated with excessive rigor. The category "deviants," frequently used in Pentecostal churches to indicate their lapsed and particularly sinful members, here designates a group whose main defining condition is that of being youths, young men from the Pentecostal families who behave as though they were "in the world," enjoying its pleasures and sins (see Birman 2008; Bakker 2008; Cretton 2007).

In fact, the divine appropriation of this territory has been accompanied by the development of a form of entry into adult life for youths involving what we could call a "ritual exercise of sins." Young men, condemned at the pulpit for partying, drug use, and drinking, are absolved in the conversations among their families and even encouraged by narratives recounted in hushed tones in which the pastor himself is described as a former member of this "brotherhood." In sum, these deviants are attributed a special—if ambivalent—condition of liminality, whose meaning centers on this transition from adolescence to the world of adult men. In enjoying this condition, young men rely on the reluctant approval of their parents. They drink, use drugs, play football, dance, and practice fornication, prompting loud condemnation from the pastors. In sum, they do precisely everything that a certain youth culture encourages them to do, but on the margins of a territory that they themselves consider holy. This connection, particularly interesting here, makes the transition from youth to adulthood a religious deviation, related to a position of liminality in both social and territorial terms.[20]

Far from the church, but not oblivious to its admonitions, the deviants seem to embody an evangelical compass that forces them to locate themselves preferentially on the margins of the village's central places and events. They respectfully accede to the divine appropriation of the territory. Hence deviants, lapsed members, and nonevangelicals—all the degrees of distance from the church and proximity to diabolical evil recognized in the village—form part of a resistance, sometimes deaf, sometimes strident and even guilty, to the limits imposed on them for the evangelical utopia to be realized there.

It was in one of these marginal places and at night that Carlos and Bruno became involved in a form of behavior judged by their peers and the church alike as witchcraft.

It was a rainy day in the village [. . .], and they and their group of friends were in the "Canto Brabo" [. . .] drinking and taking drugs (such as cannabis and cocaine, especially the latter, which is the drug of choice for many youngsters [. . .]) when they decided to roast a chicken. Bruno went to his house and fetched a rooster, came back and handed it to Carlos who immediately wrung its neck and began to pluck it. They took the bird to an abandoned house nearby and tried to make a fire, but the firewood was damp, which ruined their plans. Then Carlos said: "you know what, I'm going to eat it raw." He described what happened:

I began to take a few bites, chewed and chewed and chewed, and swallowed. Then I threw it across to Bruno and he took a few bites too. Our faces became covered in blood, like vampires, when I bit the skin, it stretched and then burst, splattering blood over my face. Then I flung the chicken over my back and we walked through the middle of the village with our bloodied faces, laughing loudly and with the headless chicken bleeding down our backs [. . .] I expelled people from the two bars; I arrived in that bar next to Negão's house and I threw the bird, bleeding everywhere, on top of the bar and asked him to cook it for me; there it splattered blood on other people, covering the whole bar in blood [. . .] I even said I was going to become a *macumbeiro* [*macumba* specialist].[21]

The account provided by the two protagonists of this enactment of a *macumba* ritual initially describes their gestures as the result of practical aims, cooking the chicken to eat. However, it acquires an increasingly provocative meaning: while at first they were messing about and simply wanted to improvise the means to roast a chicken over a fire, their lack of tools and skills meant that they ended up using their own teeth to chew the raw and bloody meat. The bites on the raw chicken apparently provoked a shift in the direction and intentionality of their gestures. With their "faces covered in blood, like vampires," one of them said, borrowing from film imagery of the mythical devourer of human blood, they deliberately looked to startle and strike fear in people. In other words, they turned their gestures imitating diabolical possession into a parody, a carnival act, through which they mocked, ridiculed, and distanced themselves critically from the threats posed by the diabolical evil they themselves were embodying.[22] And indeed, according to them, people reacted to their behavior by translating it—for anyone who had not yet understood its significance—as evidence that the two had "turned into *macumbeiros*." The improvised and clumsy way of killing the chicken reveals the initial absence of any intention to perform a ritual or at least in the form that a *macumba* ritual would assume in the Pentecostal imagination. However, the chance events that enabled their gestures to be redirected made the presence of the devil guiding their actions even more unquestionable for themselves and for those witnessing the scene. Embodied in this way, the devil transforms into a being who laughs uproariously at the church's attempts to confine him to the margins of its territory.

Bruno and Carlos recognize that their gestures appear like those the pastors identify as actions of a diabolical entity without ever having this subjective experience as members of Candomblé. There are no divergences in interpretation, therefore. In fact, the religious experiences of the protagonists of these two cases is very different. The two young deviants were accused of being possessed by a devil identified by Pastor Pedro from the community. The latter concluded that the author of the *macumba* performed there was a Pomba-Gira—in other words, a female entity identified as the spirit of a prostitute. Although these manifestations were likened to diabolical practices, they differed, at least in degree, from a "presentification" of the devil in the village's central square, during the day and in front of the church. Most people from this age group, I would point out, did not challenge the church so openly as Carlos and Bruno did by bringing the devil "in person" to a public space, parodying/performing a scene of witchcraft.

Becoming an adult implies making moral choices that allow the person to abandon diabolical practices after experimenting with them. This, at least, is the the religious aim found in that community of believers. What parents crave for their children, therefore, is the recognition of the centrality of the church values in the constitution of their selves. Consequently, the fate of the deviants depends on what they will make of the family inheritance they carry, whose relative importance in the local hierarchies helps to establish certain expectations for the young men concerning their future. Thought to be slightly crazy, frequently drunk, and a habitual drug user, Bruno's behavior exacerbated his marginality and brought him perilously close to the limits of criminality. Although he still believes in his future salvation, he proves hesitant when it comes to the advantages offered by the path of redemption. The latter involves much more significant problems for himself than for many of his companions, who are more clearly linked to the families favored by the church's hierarchy. Carlos, for his part, also carries a heavy burden in terms of family inheritance. Neither of their fathers—fishing workers, known for their difficulties with drink— had ever enjoyed a good standing, despite being heirs of the evangelical tradition through family ties, and for a long time had been considered as lapsed members by the church. It was through their mothers that the two young men preserved, despite everything, some ties with the church, however slight, and through their fathers that they seemed to share a certain scepticism concerning the promised redemption. After the scene involving the Pomba-Gira, one of the youths returned to the church's fold, stopped drinking, and got married. The other, on the contrary, intensified his identification with deviancy and its margins beyond what we could call a ritually controlled liminality. Despite his increasing stigmatization, Bruno continues to display confrontational and mocking behavior, which marks his distance from the church. Even so, this behavior has not so far led to his association with criminality—something that would probably occur very quickly in other social margins.

As anticipated, the pastor is guided in his leadership of the village by evangelical criteria, which include permanent guidelines for the different services offered by the state that look to intensify the boundaries of the community with the forces emanating from the Holy Spirit. Jurisdiction over the deviants is the most apparent, since this contrasts with the state's tendency toward criminalization, implemented elsewhere by its police forces. The police station, also located on the beach, indicates that this liminal space is also permanently observed by the police. However, these forces of order seem to pay little real attention to the transactions that occur there. Contradicting my own expectations, a certain distancing and even degree of avoidance prevails when it comes to identifying and pursuing the trafficking of drugs in the village and criminalizing the drug users. The relative freedom enjoyed by the latter there, although always accompanied by the threats of eternal damnation, contrasts strongly with what happens in other neighborhoods in which the police take violent action against drug sellers and users. The association of the deviance with criminality on the margins of the village is conscientiously avoided by the church for those who belong to the community and whose foreseen future is to join the church, at some point, perhaps not too distant, when they will fully share the evangelical heritage that blessed their territory.

The avoidance of reducing deviant individuals to the status of criminals first derives from the possibility of conversion, which anticipates their full incorporation into the community of believers. Second, in this specific case, the belonging to a holy place in which the state recognizes its own configuration and control by evangelical values makes sin a more clearly temporary part of existence. Within its sanctified space, we can suggest, the evangelical community sees the return of the deviants to the church as an anticipation of God's victory over those who would seek to destroy it from its margins and alleyways. As one young man looking to return to the church explained, he did not want to miss the day of ecstasy when his church rose to the sky, that is, the day, perhaps imminent, of the Final Judgment.

The somewhat distracted monitoring of the youths by the police seems to be based on a respect of the local authorities but also on sharing the evangelical view that attempts to persuade outsiders of the positivity and effectiveness of divine agency in defining their territory and the community's moral unity. Under the community's control, young people are rarely interpellated by the state through its abstractly determined rules. The relation with the latter involves the mediation of the pastor and the values defined by his church.

I said that sectors of the state help maintain public order within the evangelical community through behavior that expresses an affinity with the church's criteria for governing the village. Were this not the case, most of the employees of the state would have not been appointed by the church. Although not isolated, the evangelical community is protected in part from social fragmentation and the presence of other institutions and churches by the protective net surrounding the community, constructing it as a kind of Pentecostal enclave. This takes the form of more or less covertly barring the presence of other religious and secular groups in the locality. The church's filter is part of the lines of force that traverse the municipality's political dynamics. The police, when called upon, know which suspects to choose. Street cleaners recognize the political importance of keeping the square where the church and pastor's house are located clean, while being aware of the places where rubbish can be freely left to accumulate. The supply of electricity to the village also accompanied the definition of the territory, respecting the religious borders and conferring on them social and legal legitimacy through administrative decrees that ensured better living conditions for those residents included in the evangelical community. Hence the state's presence in the village complies with the values and demands of the local religious elite, controlling the flux of services and the exchange relations with supralocal institutions. It would not be unreasonable to say that the state became "Pentecostalized" in the village and, in this way, by corroborating the church's orientations, it looks to set the limits for those living there.

Final Notes

Evangelical efforts to "Pentecostalize" the sectors of the state with which evangelicals relate have not been entirely innocuous. The drama faced by Alice can also be seen in this light. Conversion to a Pentecostal church quickly appeared to her as a means of transcending her moral failings and her imbrication in local conflicts through the identificatory interpellations imposed by the state. Her response to these multiple questions was not conversion. Only the latter would have allowed a permanent form of purification and an effective rupture with local devils. However, many like Alice cultivate a relative distance from the trenches of the spiritual battle, following the ambivalent path of partial adherence to the evangelical word. Alice recognized the precariousness of her magical resources in those circumstances without adopting, as an outcome of this realization, the spiritual battle as a guide to her existence. The resigned coexistence with diabolical evil therefore presents itself as one possible form of marginal resistance to the state's suspicion and to the community imperatives proposed by evangelicals.

witchcraft as a form of resistance

The Pentecostal actor in the favela appears as an other positively differentiated from the contaminated moral environment of the place where he or she lives. Evangelical religious affiliation consequently alters the forms through which the Pentecostal individual participates in the circuits of exchange among those occupying the margins. Distant from *macumba*, they offer conversion to those who find themselves on the margins and, as we can read in the account below and as propagated by the media, is said to assure even drug dealers protection from the Afro-Brazilian entities. They even raise the possibility of altering the malign nature of the community in the future:

> The strong Evangelical presence in Chatô is not only visible in the small churches that sprout up in the little streets, or in the men and women with their bibles under their arms, but also, unexpectedly, in a monument erected by the drug dealers in a highly visible area of the favela. The bible sculpted in stone and protected under a glass dome represents a homage from the *movement* to the faith of their relatives and friends.[23] "Deep, deep down, their desire too is to find Jesus," one of the missionaries of the Youths with a Mission (Jocum) explained to us. Many attribute the drop in violence in Chatô to a "quasi-conversion" of the dealers, an explanation that also reveals the strong prejudice faced by Afro-Brazilian religions: "at least they don't practice *macumba* any longer, they don't need to kill to mollify the saints," one of the interviewees commented. (Chinelli, Freire-Medeiros, and Medeiros 2005, 137)[24]

The social, physical, and symbolic death of the person held under the sway of the devil that the drug gangs encapsulate is contrasted, in this article, to the redemption provided by the church, whose effects can be felt even before conversion. After drug dealers had commissioned a sculpture of a bible, people spoke of their "quasi-conversion." For one pastor from the favela in question, these were clear signs that the church had succeeded in reducing barbarity. And in this way the pastor described himself as a mediator between the peripheries and those from the "other side" of the city. It is not for nothing that evangelicals claim to be the main architects of a future moral reconfiguration of these marginal spaces.[25]

The accusation of witchcraft in both cases is associated with the Pentecostal universe and its relation with territories/communities. More precisely, I have examined how certain enunciations involving witchcraft "affected" the protagonists of these histories.[26] I looked to broaden our comprehension of these situations by showing how the force of the claims of witchcraft is also associated with processes of demonization related to the criminalization of certain social figures and territories located on the margins.[27] I suggested that the identifications promoted by the state favor Pentecostal universalism and its calls for transcendence and the uprooting from local religious traditions. As a result, I have pointed out the religious and political mutation occurring within these territories where the evangelical message grows along with its political goal, which identifies evangelicals as probably the people responsible for the future moral reconfiguration of these territories. I also highlight, as a result of these situations, the participation, resistance, and discomfort of my protagonists as objects and subjects of magic and witchcraft. Although they are convinced and concerned by the accusing and redemptive word of Pentecostalism, I describe, through their attitudes, a mitigated response to these political-religious imperatives, a relative distancing that engenders a precarious, resistant, and frequently provisional adherence to the social and moral order offered to them.

Notes to Chapter Eleven

Translated from Portuguese by David Rodgers.

1. I conducted various periods of fieldwork between 1993 and 1997 in a small favela, an enclave situated in the wealthy zone of Rio de Janeiro City, where I accompanied a group of people recently converted to Pentecostalism. The collaboration of Patricia Guimarães was fundamental to this work. I began my research on the community of believers described in this article in 2004: this project lasted until 2008 and involved the intense participation of students, whom I thank, and resulted in four monographs and a master's dissertation (Bakker 2008; Cretton 2007; Lopes 2009; Mendonça 2009). This fieldwork also involved the participation of Eduardo Pereira and more recently Angélica Ferrarez and Helena Guilayn. My thanks also to Roger Sansi for his comments on the first version of this text, which was sent to him as a draft for the colloquium Sorcery and Politics in the Black Atlantic: From the Colonial World to Globalization, which was held in London, in 2007, and which I was unfortunately unable to attend. I also thank Márcia Leite and Marc Piault for careful readings. I presented the paper at the CEAf (Centre d'Études Africaines) Seminar coordinated by Michel Agier and at UFJF, at the invitation of Marcelo Camurça. The critical comments received on these occasions proved extremely helpful when it came to finishing this article.

2. Also see Noiriel (2005, 2007) and the Foucauldian notion of biopolitics vis-à-vis processes of identification and identity and their relation to the state.

3. I refer to these margins as the "periphery," frequently associated with places containing those yet to be civilized. Veena Das and Deborah Poole (2004), who elaborated this notion, also expound on the idea that the state, far from being absent from the margins, is a fundamental actor in the configuration of these areas and is itself being shaped by local dynamics. They therefore argue forcefully against the idea that there is a lack of the state on the margins. This idea of a lack has indeed allowed authors to ignore the extent to which the state participates in the political and social configurations of the peripheries.

4. For a rich discussion of the concept of culture and its essentialist tendencies in Brazil, as well as its socially discriminatory developments, see Andreas Hofbauer (2006) and Jean-François Veran (2003). For a critical commentary concerning the use of the notion of "community" in relation to favelas, see note 5, where I explain Lícia Valladares's argument. See also Duarte (1992) and Leite (2000, 2007) on the relations between citizenship and community and Birman (2008) for a discussion on the uses of the category of community related to favelas.

5. Lícia Valladares (2005) has rightly called attention to the essentialist form in which social scientists construct favelas. In these territorial, cultural, and class units, the researchers found it easy to search for the form in which poor people behave in relation to sexuality, religion, politics, and so on. A wide range of analyses describe favela residents with social, cultural, and moral attributes that are supposedly homogenous and derived from the shared condition of residents. As Valladares critically points out, "In the favela, the poor are at home. Insofar as they form a city within a city, the illegal city within the legal city, the residents demarcate their territory, a de facto enclave where the identificatory mark is omnipresent. Perceived in this way, the favela is imputed with its own economy, internal laws and private codes, developed in spaces left to their own luck and abandoned by public authorities" (Valladares 2005, 151). Although we need to discard the perception criticized by Valladares for its essentialism and for the abusive totalization that it thereby constructed, we cannot, however, ignore the extent to which these totalizing images are necessarily taken into account by the inhabitants of these places in the strategies that they build for their lives and in the power relations that inescapably concern them.

6. I presume that most families have at least one member in the church. Furthermore, I believe that this local demographic criterion, whose religious premises I discuss later, allows the church to claim that the majority of people from this village are evangelical.

7. Cf. Birman (2006, 2008) for the local conception of the community of believers and its relation to the territory. For a discussion of the space within the village, see Cretton (2007), and on the perception of religious figures concerning the presence of God and the devil, see Bakker (2008).

8. Cf. Mariz (1999) for a discussion and bibliographic review of the "Spiritual Battle." André Bakker (2008) provides an excellent ethnographic description of the reading evangelicals make of the lay media. From an evangelical viewpoint, the television news reports with their litany of crimes and violence prove the validity of the bible verses on a daily basis and above all the prophecies of the Apocalypse.

9. "Witchcraft" is the term used by Edir Macedo in his description of the procedures supposedly employed by Afro-Brazilian cults. First published in 1996, *Orixás, caboclos e guias, deuses ou demônios?* is the most well-known work by Bishop Macedo, leader of the UCKG. At the time of its release, the UCKG's spiritual battle against the diabolical manifestations of Afro-Brazilians and Catholic idolatry had already provoked much debate and controversy, although these failed to hinder the church's growth and the expansion of its doctrine. We can recall the relations established in this text between the practices of the Candomblé *terreiros* (ritual spaces) and criminal activities:

> a father-of-saint told me how on one occasion he cast a spell for a young man to go mad. He entered a cemetery at midnight and, after opening a grave in which someone had been buried just five hours earlier, removed the corpse (that of a young man in his early twenties), cut off the head and replaced it with another made of wax, engraved with the name of his enemy [...] Is there any way a sect that pursues such practices can be considered religious? We see stories like this being published almost daily in our newspapers and, given that our society is unable to take any measures against this, we are obliged, in the name of Jesus, to raise our voices! An ex-mother-of-saint also confided to me that she had performed rites in a *terreiro* in Recife, where they brought newborn children to be sacrificed in

cemeteries or at crossroads. In 1979 we had a case in which the police discovered a farm where the orishas [divinities], *caboclos* [indigenous spirits] and *guias* [spiritual guides] requested something similar. (Macedo 2000, 108)

10. In every corner of the city there's a favela,
    In every corner of the favela there's a drug dealer
    And every dealer has a mother who's a believer
    Who prays for her son in despair
    Tired of crying, fighting, suffering
    She believes one day he will repent
    And recall everything she taught him,
    Return to his roots or to whatever is left
    Of a poor life, I know,
    Not much can be expected.
    But a mother's love and affection are always there.
    What life is this?
    People always asked.
    What God is this?
    Who seems to do nothing.
    It's true little changed between now and then
    But love and faith in God will never be lacking.
    A difficult life, yes,
    Far too unfair
    Going through life in search of peace. (DJ Alpiste, cited by Oosterbaan 2006, 6)

11. While the term "Candomblé" is positively valued by its practitioners, the term *macumba* has a pejorative association, its practices being frequently associated with malefic rituals.

12. During this period, the drug gangs effectively controlled the borders of the small favela but did not intervene openly in the free transit of inhabitants and outsiders. This control gradually increased with the growth in drug trafficking and the war that took hold in the city.

13. We should note that by transforming Afro-Brazilian entities and spirits into devils, Pentecostalism demands that converts make a complete break with the former, uprooting themselves from them, rather than maintaining them as part of their locally constructed identities. The Pentecostal transcendence of evil (cf. Robbins 2008) enables the coexistence with the latter to be conceived through another relation with time: no longer the time in which religious practices are rooted in the person and places through the cultivation of a tradition, guaranteed by the circularity of religious exchanges, but a time whose evolution depends on this rupture with a sinful past. For evangelicals, the control of evil requires a rupture with life "in the world," and those individuals who desire salvation will always have a provisional sense indicating its gradual elimination. This other relation with time cannot be separated from what Appadurai describes as a movement of constructing identities that does not take belonging to a place as a condition for its realization (cf. Birman 2006, 2008).

14. Here I have drawn on my own direct experience with Alice and on an interview conducted by Patricia Guimarães.

15. Many of the favelas in Rio de Janeiro are built on the surrounding hillsides, meaning that *morro*, "hill," functions as a synonym for favela.

16. "Zé Pilintra" is the name of an entity typically portrayed as a trickster, a figure that developed in the 1950s as an emblem of the popular classes, inhabitants of Rio's favelas: a samba lover, an enemy of work and capable of surviving through small con tricks.

17. For an analysis on the importance of the circuit of exchanges among religious figures and their clienteles in the constitution of cult houses and their leaders, see the classic text by Peter Fry (1982). See also Baptista (2007). Joel Robbins (2008) calls attention to a common trait of Pentecostalism that contrasts with "traditional" cults: as a religion that separates and distantiates the transcendental and the mundane in a radical form, Pentecostalism enables individuals to recognize their own lack of control and power over their conditions of existence. This interpretation seems to fit perfectly with the experience described in Alice's account. I would merely observe that, in the latter case, the transcendent dimension that is foregrounded is that of evil. Alice did not experience divine grace but the impersonal and malefic power of the devil.

18. Kelly Hayes (2004) provides an excellent ethnographic analysis of the social and family resources possessed by a mother-of-saint in Rio de Janeiro through her entities. The author highlights the importance of the agency attributed to the entities and their forms of participating in the circuits of exchange of their owner. On this point, also see the pioneering analysis by Véronique Boyer (1993) on the ties between the women and their invisible entities.

19. Pomba-Gira is the name of a female Exu.

20. The category of deviants applies only to men. Sinful events usually occur with the participation of outside women, such as the occasional tourist, or, more frequently, among men. In the context under study, the young women of the village avoid taking part in these events. Even when women move away from the church, the division of gender roles prevents them from exercising a "floating" sexuality, characterized by free circulation in space.

21. The account cited here is included in the research report by Eduardo Pereira, a research assistant for this project in 2006.

22. Here I am referring, of course, to carnivalization as a disruptive and inventive action, as described by Bakhtin (1987).

23. "Movement" is the name given to themselves by some dealers who consider their activities to possess a political sense.

24. Generally speaking, the literature suggests that Pentecostal missionary action is directed toward the conversion of individuals rather than territories. However, we can see here in relation to the favela and to the case of the community of believers that the discourse of conversion possesses strong territorial dimensions: "expel the demons" acquires a sense of conquest and purification in relation to a world marked by barbarity. The work of Philippe Gonzales (2008, 50) provides a valuable description of the potential of evangelical action. As he writes,

> Evangelization is an incursion into enemy territory and an overturning of the order reining there. The Evangelicals are conscious of working at the intersection between two worlds, their action is designed to free those captured by the demon and to introduce them to the divine reality [...] Missionary action appears therefore as a raid into enemy terrain and aims to install a new spiritual division of the territory.

25. Cristina Vital da Cunha (2009) draws attention to the fact that in the "war" fought by the police against the traffickers and bandits, invasions of the favela territories were frequently accompanied by the destruction of the objects of Afro-Brazilian cults (*despachos*). Here I recall the work of Yvonne Maggie (this volume) and also her text (1992) on the "Museu da Polícia" in which the belief in witchcraft acquires a positive value through the participation of the police.

26. I use the verb "affect" in the sense proposed by Favret-Saada (1977, 2009), in other words, without opposing and separating the emotional experience of the actors from their social and symbolic relations—much the opposite: I consider affectations as essential to comprehending the meanings of witchcraft. Favret-Saada (2009, 146) claims a point of view that distances her from anthropological works that remain bound "to cultural productions of understanding."

27. Here it is interesting to note the approach opened up by a number of works by removing witchcraft from the spaces allocated to it by the Great Divide: it is always associated with popular groups, preferably from the south, and absent from intellectual elites and the societies of the north (Favret-Saada 2009; Pels 2003; Geschiere 2003).

12

Witchcraft and Modernity: Perspectives from Africa and Beyond

PETER GESCHIERE

THE END OF the last century brought for anthropology a quite abrupt renaissance of witchcraft/sorcery studies—in itself quite surprising at the end of a century so strongly preoccupied with things modern. Indeed, this renaissance was deeply marked by modernity. After several decades of relative neglect, the old anthropological topic of witchcraft reemerged quite strongly, but now in a new dress: most of the new publications linked it more or less explicitly to modern changes.[1] Of course, both terms, "witchcraft" and "modernity," are highly problematic, although for different reasons. "Witchcraft" (like "sorcery," "magic," *sorcellerie*, etc.) is a precarious translation—especially because of the pejorative implications of this Western notion—of African terms that often have much broader implications and might, therefore, be better translated by a more neutral term like "occult force" or even "special kind of energy." However, these Western terms have been so generally appropriated by the African public that is has become impossible to ignore or even avoid them. The term "modernity" is also of a disconcerting fluidity. In this text I use it—like other authors writing on its concatenation with "witchcraft"—in the sense of an ideal or even a myth that is never fully realized, recurring elements of which are the autonomy of the individual, a scientific outlook (that supposedly makes the world ever more transparent), the spread of new technology, and mass consumption of industrial products.[2]

Some colleagues—especially those who are critical of this new tendency—discern even a new paradigm in this linking of "witchcraft" and "modernity." Harri Englund and James Leach (2000), for instance, warned that modernity is becoming a "metanarrative" that tends to "organize" the fieldwork of anthropologists, and even more their ethnography; thus, it would risk blocking "the production of anthropological knowledge." In their view, even though the anthropological version of this metanarrative on modernity heavily emphasizes its multiple character and the different cultural ways in which it is appropriated, it is nonetheless inevitable that anthropologists using this popular notion take at least some sort of basic core for granted, that is common to all these different appropriations. Thus, all these references to modernity or to processes of commodification—for example, in the study of novel transformations of witchcraft beliefs or in new religious movements (like Pentecostalism)—would engender a prejudiced anthropology that restricts the anthropological eye and sins against the very principles of what anthropology used to be.

Blair Rutherford (1999, 89) equally criticizes "an emergent anthropological analytic that situates African witchcraft within modernity, global capitalism and state formation." For him, however, this analytic is not really new: it continues "earlier anthropological functional exegesis" by reducing witchcraft to modernity—just as anthropologists of earlier generations related it to social control. Rutherford's main criticism is that this allows the anthropologists concerned to neglect "the genealogy of current representations of African witchcraft [. . .] in anthropology" and more specifically their own engagement in "the politics of witchcraft" (1999, 91-2). He is certainly right that more reflection is needed on the reasons for this sudden renewal of anthropological interest in witchcraft and on the wider impact of our writings—for instance, of our adoption of precisely this notion. Throughout Africa, it is rapidly becoming a panacea concept of considerable power, because of its kaleidoscopic character; and anthropological writings seem to reinforce this tendency rather than defuse it. Yet, for this field of study in particular, there is a risk that anthropological self-reflexivity leads to an overestimation of the anthropologist's role. Insisting, like Rutherford (1999, 92), that anthropologists should "explicitly engage in the politics of witchcraft" strikes me as overly ambitious.[3] During my fieldwork in Cameroon, my spokesmen considered me, at most, as a very clumsy player in this tricky field. Indeed, this was the preeminent domain for which they were sure of my complete ignorance, so that at least here it was clear that they had to teach me (and not the other way round). Indeed, I felt more or less that they drew me into this secret domain: I wanted to study politics, but they insisted on talking *djambe*—a term they invariably translated by *sorcellerie*. My informants repeated time and again that they knew that the *mintang* (the whites) think these things do not exist but that this only proves how "innocent" they are. So, if I as an outsider tried to understand how things worked in their society, I should shed at least some of my clumsy ignorance of this hidden side of power. With such a division of roles, the anthropologist himself may worry, like Rutherford, about his "engagement in witchcraft politics," but the people around him may have other things on their minds.

Welcome as Rutherford's plea may be that also in this treacherous field more anthropological self-reflexivity is required, this should not imply that the interest in the link between witchcraft and modernity is mainly the product of the anthropological imagination and of motivations particular to anthropology—such as the inclination to fit such representations onto the Procrustes' bed of Western epistemology and rationality. His article seems to neglect somewhat that in many parts of present-day Africa, there is a general consternation about the supposed proliferation of witchcraft, notably in the more modern sectors of society: in the cities, in relation to new forms of enrichment, in politics, at the university, or in the hospital. Interest in the modernity of witchcraft is not just a novel twist of the anthropological tradition. It imposes itself in often quite dramatic and also unpleasant ways in the field. It is difficult to affirm that there is, indeed, an increase of witchcraft, but it is quite clear that witchcraft is ever more out into the open.[4] In the first decades after independence, it was still bad taste to speak too openly about the witches and their dealings: this meant primitivizing Africa and denying its rapid progress on the road to modernization. But during the last two decades this occult discourse has invaded the public domain: it now dominates not only in the rumors of *radio trottoir* but also in the official media (radio, TV, the *faits divers* in the newspapers). The *nganga* (traditional healers) are no longer trying to keep a low profile; on the contrary, they advertise their therapies and their "clinics" with flashy notices, boasting their expertise in "modern" forms of magic (like the Rosecrucian lore or secret knowledge from the Orient). Indeed, witchcraft discourse seems to offer an obvious language, both for the rich and for the poor, for trying to make sense of the modern changes—and notably the shocking new forms of wealth and inequality. Like witchcraft, these changes are both fascinating (since they open up new horizons) and deplorable (since so few people acquire access to these tempting new opportunities). Yet, the question remains as to why this link between witchcraft and modernity seems to be so utterly persuasive to so many people. There is, indeed, some urgency in arriving at a closer understanding of this strange convergence of witchcraft and the modern.

In the field of African studies, the most radical criticism—all the more so since it remains implicit—of this effort to understand the proliferation of witchcraft rumors by linking them to modernity comes from outside anthropology—from two French political scientists, Patrick Chabal and

Jean-Pascal Daloz, in their book *Africa Works* (1999). These authors refer several times to my 1997 book on witchcraft and politics, but they do so in a chapter entitled "The *Retraditionalisation* of Society" (italics mine); there is some contradiction here since the title of my book is *The Modernity of Witchcraft*. Their use of this quite audacious notion of retraditionalization seems to reflect their general inclination, at least in this book, to go against what they see as the current tide of political correctness in African studies and therefore not to mince their words. However, on closer inspection they seem to see this trend toward a retraditionalization of society somewhat paradoxically as part and parcel of a form of modernity specific to Africa with its blending of traditional (or pseudotraditional?) and modern elements. The dynamics of witchcraft representations is, to them, a good example that it is impossible to maintain any radical dichotomy between "traditional" and "modern." Indeed, they consequently put these two terms in quotation marks, which makes it all the more striking that they do maintain it.[5] To Chabal and Daloz, therefore, the resilience of witchcraft seems to be characteristic of an African modernity. Of course, this last notion evokes, again, a wide array of questions: Is there then a specific African modernity? Next to a Latin American, an Asian, or a European one, and so on? I hope to return to these questions below. But it will be clear that the Atlantic view of witchcraft/sorcery developed in this collection suggests a different perspective that surpasses the view of specific continental trajectories. This might be of special interest in trying to understand the quite enigmatic convergence of witchcraft and modernity. The nomadic quality of ideas on the occult and the ease with which they cross geographic boundaries—so strongly emphasized in the introduction to this volume—reflect in unexpected ways the increasing mobility that many see as the hallmark of modernity (Appadurai 1996).

An Example: The Emergence of a New Witchcraft of Wealth

An example may help to clarify and concretize the broader implications of such convergences. In many regions of West Africa—especially along the coast, but more and more in the interior as well—powerful rumors circulate about the secret sources of novel forms of wealth that are both tantalizing and shocking since they introduce new and glaring inequalities. For Cameroon, a series of regional studies are available that can throw some light on variable patterns in the emergence of such rumors on this new witchcraft of wealth. Their core is everywhere more or less the same: they refer to the emergence of a new type of witches who no longer cannibalize their victims—as in older forms of witchcraft—but rather transform them into some sort of zombies who have to work for them. These people are supposed to be so rich precisely because they exploit their zombies' labor. However, this core idea is subject to quite different regional elaborations.[6]

In the Cameroonian context, two places are of special importance in these rumors. First of all Douala, the main port through which the European trade has penetrated the country since the sixteenth century and now Cameroon's metropolis. People often say that Douala is also the place from which this new form of witchcraft originated. And second, Mount Kupe, sixty miles from the coast, which has a sinister magical reputation throughout the country. It is there that the witches would put their victims to work on their invisible plantations.

Among the Douala, this form of witchcraft is called *ekong*. According to Eric de Rosny—a French Jesuit priest, who had himself initiated as a *nganga* (traditional healer) and who published a series of seminal texts on *ekong*—[7]it is still highly feared in the city. The basic scenario of *ekong* is vividly summarized by René Bureau, another missionary/anthropologist who worked for a long time in this city:

> A person who is interested in *ekong* goes to visit an *ekoneur* (French for "*ekong* owner"—a commonly used neologism), who puts him to sleep by hypnosis. In his dreams, this person will see a land where money flows and many laborers work for him. An estate owner will offer him his plantations on condition that he offers the life of, for instance, his mother in return. His first reaction will be to refuse. When he wakes up, the *ekoneur* will say to him: "Now you have seen, now you know what you have to do." His client will ask for some time to think about it. Some day he will make up his mind. (Bureau 1962, 142).[8]

De Rosny (1981, 93) gives an equally vivid picture of the other side—the anxiety of the potential victims: "[. . .] when someone dreams he is taken away, his hands tied, towards the river or the Ocean while he cannot see the face of his capturers, he knows that he has to see a *nganga* (witch doctor) as soon as possible." *Ekoneurs* are supposed to steal their victims' bodies from the grave and then sell them to one of their customers. In their magical pursuits they use a huge snake, the *nyungu*, which is linked to the rainbow and brings riches.

One can imagine why in these areas an expression like "I'll sell you" has a particularly ominous ring. Indeed, de Rosny's informants made a direct link between this idea of selling someone and the old slave trade.[9] The same association can be recognized in de Rosny's dream picture of someone being taken away "to the Ocean," without recognizing his capturers. Actually, the Douala and other people in the area still tend to relate *ekong* to the Europeans. This is what de Rosny found out to his distress when he visited an old *nganga* (healer) and a chief in a village near Douala and offered them both a bottle of whisky. When he wanted to leave, he found to his surprise that the road was blocked by the village youth who abused him and refused to let him pass. Apparently, both the chief and the *nganga* were suspected to have the *ekong*. The rumor that a white stranger had come to offer them presents was enough to resurrect old fears of people being sold to the whites (de Rosny 1981, 93).[10]

De Rosny's spokesmen made a clear distinction between the *ekong*, "where one kills and sells someone," and older forms of witchcraft (in Douala *lemba* or *ewusu*), where the witches eat their victims. The *ekong* is considered to be something new, and special to an urban setting. Nonetheless, the Douala must have known the *ekong* before the colonial conquest (1884). In earlier days, the *ekong* was an association of chiefs, notables, and traders: it represented "the well-to-do classes" (de Rosny 1981, 92). But nowadays the *ekong* has been "democratized": it is believed to be in everybody's reach and therefore people are even more afraid of it. De Rosny

"modernity"

(1981, 92) connects this change with the spread of wage labor and the expansion of the money economy. The power to buy and sell is no longer a prerogative of a few family heads and notables. However, this has not made the economy more transparent. The dramatic fluctuations of cash-crop prices and the uncertainties of the labor market have become crucial to the survival of ever more people and seem to be utterly uncontrollable and unpredictable. One of the attractions of the *ekong* belief is—still according to de Rosny—that is has integrated the mysteries of the market. It continues to be so generally accepted because it can offer an explanation for the growing inequalities of wealth and poverty.

Although Douala is often mentioned as the place of origin of the *ekong*, its center is now clearly located on Mount Kupe. This is a densely wooded mountain in the heart of the land of the Bakossi who speak of *ekom* to indicate a similar, new form of witchcraft. S. N. Ejedepang-Koge describes this *ekom* as an association of witches who frequent Mount Kupe in order to get riches. The Bakossi also believe that one can buy the *ekom* from someone who possesses it already and that one has to sell a close relative for this. Only then can one go to Mount Kupe. There, the initiated will find "mysterious, closed bundles" that contain riches but also all sorts of misfortune (illness or even death). In the night, the *ekom* people secretly go up the mountain to steal a bundle, but they should on no account open it until they are safely back. If one discovers misfortune in one's bundle one

night flights to far away places

must immediately throw it into the river. But one can be lucky and find riches. People call this the "market of sorcery" (Ejedepang-Koge 1971, 200, and 1975).

The missionaries of Basel who, in the 1890s, were among the first Europeans to reach this area, noted already that Mount Kupe had a strong magical reputation throughout the area. And they observed also that this reputation had quite special overtones among the Bakossi. Initially, they had great trouble in reaching the mountain, since their carriers from the coast were so afraid of it that they blandly refused to go on. The Bakossi from their side did everything to stop the Europeans from climbing the mountain. Apparently, they feared that the whites would appropriate the riches hidden there. In 1893, the missionary Fr. Authenrieth wrote, "Just as the mountain appears dangerous and ruinous to the coastal tribes, so it is a promise of good luck to the Bakossi people" (Balz 1984, 327–8).

In the 1970s, Heinrich Balz found that people in certain parts of Bakossiland believed that Mount Kupe's riches were exhausted and that it was no longer of any use to go there. But he found also that among other Bakossi groups, the belief in these riches was still very much alive, having integrated all sorts of modern elements related to the colonial plantation economy. Alobwede d'Epié indicates that the Bakossi even integrated the postcolonial manna of development into the *ekom*. He notes that during the secret meetings on Mount Kupe, "development projects of great significance are believed to be highly contested for among the different racial or tribal spirits, and the race or tribe whose spirits win, wins the project." But here again the segmentary logic of Bakossi society asserts itself:

for example, a fight breaks out among the spirits of the tribe that won the project so as to determine the clan in which the project would be located. Another fight breaks out among the spirits of the victorious clan to determine the village in which the project would be finally situated. (Alobwede d'Epié 1982, 80)

Ejedepang-Koge (1971, 202) describes the *ekom* in more detail:

This invisible town on Kupe is something like a labor camp. First of all the ancestral spirits need people who should work to keep the fortunes flowing in such a way that they can be distributed during the *ekom* meetings. Secondly the great men have invisible estates there and they need people to cultivate them. The source of this labor supply is widespread: from all the area surrounding the mountain, from Victoria, Bakweri area, from Douala etc.

Ejedepang-Koge says furthermore about these invisible laborers that they are enslaved people but that they are "very contented" (sic); many of them are recruited from among the victims of "ekong witches" in the south. Apparently, the fear of being sold and put to work on Mount Kupe, so widespread among the coastal people, has its reverse in a kind of wishful dreaming among the Bakossi, who believe they are entitled to profit from the magical riches of their mountain. Heinrich Balz (1984, 331) speaks of a "capitalist or ruling-class dream." Maybe one should rather speak of an absentee landlord's dream. When the cultivation of cocoa spread in this area, during the 1920s and 1930s, the Bakossi tried to profit in a particular way from the new possibilities for enrichment: many farmed out their land to "strangers," mostly Bamileke from the present-day West Province, who descended from their highlands and who were willing to pay a substantial rent—often one-third of the harvest or even more—to the landlord. In the following decades it seemed possible for the Bakossi to get rich without much effort, profiting from other people's labor. The Bakossi conceptions around Mount Kupe seem to reflect the memory of those happy days, which, unfortunately, are over.[11] No wonder that to them the *ekom* is certainly not unequivocally evil: if someone is believed to have enriched himself through *ekom*, this is—according to Balz (1984, 331)—"not criticized, but seen as just good luck." There is indeed a clear contrast here with the general fear or even panic about *ekong* in the coastal areas.[12]

The variations become even more marked if one compares them with developments in the Grassfields of the present-day West and Northwest Provinces, respectively, among the Bamileke and the Bamenda. This area is of special interest since it is from here that, after independence, a new bourgeoisie of entrepreneurs emerged who are generally supposed to dominate the national economy of present-day Cameroon. Similar notions on the new witchcraft of wealth, here mostly referred to as *famla* or *kupe*, spread somewhat later in this area, where they acquired particularly strong capitalist overtones. They are often associated with notions of debt and with the rotating credit associations, the famous *njangi*, which in this area gained particular momentum and are often quoted as one of the secrets of Bamileke and Bamenda economic dynamism.

Nowadays, people quote examples of *njangi* of big businessmen where billions of Central African Francs are accumulated. So much money is circulating, particularly in the Bamileke *njangi*, that this would endanger the cash flow through the official banks.[13] But these *njangi* are supposed to have a more sinister side as well. People tell horror stories about how, through them, one can be recruited into a *famla* coven without knowing it: a man goes to town and accepts a beer from some strangers; suddenly he realizes that he is involved with a *famla-njangi*, but by then it is already too late: he has contracted a debt that he can only pay off by selling a close relative.

In the last decades of the last century, *famla* became a major issue of debate in present-day Cameroon, precisely because of its supposed link with the success of the Bamileke—and to a lesser degree Bamenda—businessmen, but unfortunately it has been studied very little in a more systematic way.[14] It is clear that, in these societies as well, the "witchcraft of the rich" is considered to be a new and highly shocking phenomenon. Here also *famla* or *kupe* rumors can create true outbursts of panic. Patrick Mbunwe-Samba (1996), for instance, cites several cases from villages in the Grassfields in which such rumors triggered a true avalanche of accusations. It is striking, however, that in other contexts the fact of being associated with *famla* does not seem to have serious consequences. Jean-Pierre Warnier (1993) remarks that many of the big Bamileke entrepreneurs are the object of strong *famla* rumors; but he adds that these rumors hardly seem to affect their position. Young Bamileke often complain that the *famla njangi* have become so strong that it would be futile to try and attack them.[15] The only way to escape them would be to migrate. To many, *famla* seems to have become a normal aspect of modern entrepreneurship.

A series of case studies from this area, presented by Mbunwe-Samba (1996) and Cyprian Fisiy (Fisiy and Geschiere 1991), highlight a recurrent pattern. People react sharply against *famla* when it is supposed to be active in the village. Then the *fon* (chief) will mobilize the associations of his court to chase suspected *famla* witches from the village. However, when a successful entrepreneur returns to the village and dedicates his new wealth to the *fon*—by offering him an important present or buying a title at his court—he is accepted. In several of these cases this even concerned persons who only a few years earlier had been chased out of the village. In Fisiy's words, the chief still has the power to "whitewash" the suspected wealth of the new rich and the occult powers behind it. He can still act as a crystallization point for reintegrating his successful "sons" abroad into the structures of the chieftaincy. The *fon* is still credited with the moral authority to neutralize the dangerous powers of the new rich and thus ally fears about the proliferation of new witchcraft threats.

The broader institutional setting in this area is very different from that of the more segmentary societies along the coast and in the forest zone of southern and eastern Cameroon. The Grassfields societies have a strong hierarchical tradition: the *fon* was and is the center of social life in all respects. Around his court are organized a number of more or less secret associations, the most important one being a kind of police society, often called *kwifoyn*. These associations are based on a complex system of graded titles controlled, again, by the *fon*. In his historical studies, Warnier (1985) emphasizes the importance of long-distance trade and the accumulation of wealth abroad for people's status in these societies as well as in the precolonial period. However, then as well, individual success in trade was only acceptable if it was backed by the authority of the *fon*. Indeed, the strict control of the *fon* over outside relations and wealth was the very basis of his power. This model proved to be highly resilient in colonial times. The present-day role of the chiefs and their associations in containing *famla* rumors and in reintegrating the new urban elites into the local structures continues this tradition.

This central position of the chiefs goes together with another interesting difference with the more segmentary societies along the coast and in the forest: the strong tendency in the Grassfields to compartmentalize the witchcraft discourse. Many elements in the discourse on the occult are the same as along the coast and in the forest: witchcraft is supposed to live in someone's belly; those who possess it can fly away at night to meet their fellow conspirators at some sort of witches' Sabbath; there they will betray their own relatives, delivering them up to their fellow witches to be devoured. However, in the Grassfields societies there seems to be a conscious effort to overcome the ambiguity and the circularity of this discourse and to try and institutionalize clear-cut distinctions—notably between acceptable and illegitimate uses of the occult forces. As is to be expected, the *fon* plays a crucial role in this. Just as in the segmentary societies to the south, all authorities are closely associated, in one way or another, with these occult forces. However, in the Grassfields, there is a heavy emphasis on all sorts of institutional boundaries between the chief and the evil expression of occult power. In principle, it is the chief who decides whether these powers are used in an acceptable or unacceptable way. If someone is suspected of having access to sources of occult power without the blessing of the *fon*, this is automatically seen as asocial and therefore marked as witchcraft. And the *kwifoyn*, the chief's secret police association, is supposed to deal with this in its own, secret ways. However, the pursuit of wealth by a subject who has the blessing of the chief can never be witchcraft. On the contrary, this is supposed to strengthen the chief and, therefore, the community as a whole.[16] To put it in simpler terms, in the last instance it is the chief who decides who is a witch and who is not. He has the moral authority to reveal someone's true identity.

Yet, as is only to be expected when witchcraft is at stake, this last conclusion has to be nuanced. It is, for instance, a moot point whether the Grass-

[handwritten margin note: appropriation of European models or imposition by the author in attempt to understand Cameroon traditions?]

fields chiefs will retain enough moral authority to exercise this kind of control in the future as well. The eagerness with which so many chiefs try to share in the wealth of their successful subjects—by creating all sorts of pseudotraditional titles at their courts that the *nouveaux-riches* can buy, but also by privatizing and selling their customary land rights—makes people wonder whether the chief still controls the new elite or whether the roles are reversed (cf. Fisiy 1992). Warnier (1993) characterizes the Bamileke chieftaincy as a "shell" that is emptied and refilled by the new elites. Goheen (1996, 145 and 161) sketches a highly evocative image expressing the doubts of the Nso people about the collaboration of their chiefs with the new elites. The people wonder whether these nouveaux riches with their newly bought titles will be "the chief's new leopards," accompanying him at night, like the notables of former days, when the chief, transformed as a lion, rides the country in order to protect it against evil. Or will they prove to be "sorcerers of the night" who corrupt his court from the inside.[17]

Old and New Aspects: Surprising Convergences

In the Grassfields, as in the coastal zone, people insist on the novelty of these horrendous witchcraft threats and their differences with older forms. Yet it is clear that, at least in certain respects, these representations build on old elements. It is striking, moreover, that precisely these continuities allow for a quite surprising intertwinement with the growing impact of the market. In many respects, the traditional witchcraft discourse does not constitute the opposite of capitalist logic—on the contrary, it can be grafted upon it in unexpected ways.

A clear continuity is the enduring role of kinship as central to witchcraft representations and practices. For instance, even in Douala, among people who have already lived for generations in the city, the *ekong*—like older forms of witchcraft—is closely linked to kinship.[18] As said, one of *ekong*'s more shocking aspects is that one can only get it by what people call "selling" a close relative. And the therapies of the *nganga* against this novel witchcraft—so movingly described by de Rosny—can only work if the family members want to collaborate, even if they are living far away. If they refuse to join the ritual, the *nganga* has to drop the case, since he will be powerless. Even this new witchcraft of wealth is always supposed to come "from within"—that is, from within the family. This continuing emphasis on the family seems to be the opposite of the modern order, which is dominated by the market. However, the core phrase of the *ekong* discourse, the notion that you have to *sell* your own relative, already shows how easily kinship and market can blend.

[margin, handwritten] seems to a discourse of the market overwhelming the family

This is even clearer for the notion of debt that played such a central role in the description above of a *famla-njangi*: the young man coming to town, hungry and thirsty; accepting food and a beer from a stranger; and realizing too late that he has been recruited for a *famla* credit association, incurring a debt that can only be redeemed by the sale of a relative. In itself, this emphasis on incurring a debt is certainly not novel in witchcraft discourse—it is a familiar motif in other contexts as well. For instance, people will often say when somebody dies that he (or she) had been a powerful witch who had refused to offer a relative for redeeming the debts incurred vis-à-vis his or her accomplices; thus, the dead "witch" is seen as some sort of martyr, sacrificing himself so as not to make his relatives the victims of his terrible debt. But even if the notion of debt is not foreign to witchcraft discourse, it does acquire new aspects when linked with *famla* and the new consumption goods—that is, with the new market economy in general. Clearly such elements—like, for instance, the basic idea in *famla/ ekong* of a hidden control over the labor force of others—fit in very well with capitalist logic.[19]

a Marxist approach? →

More generally, this applies to an aspect that notions of the new witchcraft of wealth share with older representations of the occult: their tricky ambiguity. Whatever term one uses—*ekong*, *famla*, or *kupe*—basic to these representations is the close link with the highly coveted consumption goods, newly introduced by the market and rapidly becoming the very symbols of what people see as "modern" life: refrigerators, TV sets, sumptuous villas, and most of all cars (the omnipresent Mercedes, but lately rather the Pajero). Yet, as said, people's perceptions of these new goods are highly ambivalent: their provenance makes them highly suspect, but at the same time they are enchanting, in the full sense of the word. The same moral ambiguity is central to popular conceptions of the new witchcraft of wealth: as said, *ekong* in Douala is seen now as a horrendous force, but it used to be the appanage of well-to-do groups; for the Bakossi, *ekom* is a more or less accepted way to try to get rich; and in the Grassfields, *famla* may be seen as highly amoral, yet it is at the same time conceived of as an almost normal aspect of modern forms of entrepreneurship. It is this basic ambiguity that facilitates, again, a convergence between witchcraft and market talk: the latter is, of course, equally perceived as morally ambivalent (and certainly not only in Africa).

It is this very ambiguity that can also highlight the dangers of a notion like retraditionalization, as quoted above from Chabal and Daloz (see note 5). The problem is that such a notion risks denying that the images sketched above express a determined effort by people to participate in the modern changes and even to control them; or, as it is so well formulated by Bogumil

Jewsiewicki, "[T]he strenuous work accomplished by men and women [...]" who are among the most excluded of our world of globalization, to re-think the world in order to figure in it as actors and not as passive victims" (Jewsiewicki 2001, 639).

New witchcraft imaginaries—like the one of the witchcraft of wealth—do not just express some sort of longing for a supposedly traditional past. On the contrary, their very ambiguity, expressing both horror and fascination with the new opportunities, highlights people's efforts to cope with the modern changes. With such a perception, it becomes all the more urgent to understand why witchcraft discourse has such an elastic capacity for capturing novel elements introduced from outside: why is it such an obvious discourse for many people in order to cope with the modern changes?

The elements discussed above—the emphasis in witchcraft discourse on debt, hidden control over the labor force, the "selling" of kin, and more generally the elastic ambiguity of these notions—can point out certain convergences with idioms of the market and capitalist relations. Elsewhere I tried to develop a more general explanation for such convergence by focusing on the centrality of ideas of flux and closure in both types of discourses (Geschiere 1997; Ciekawy and Geschiere 1998). Indeed, there are quite striking (and even worrying) parallels here. People tend to see witchcraft as forcing a treacherous breach in the closure of the local community. The basic instinct of the witch—whether he has the *ekong* or an older type of witchcraft—is to betray his own parents and deliver them to his outside accomplices. This is why witchcraft can be characterized as the dark side or even the reversal of kinship. Basic to the kinship order is a tendency toward a closure of the local community. Of course, the obligation for exogamy creates openings, but people strive to control that in all sorts of ways. Witchcraft, in contrast, opens up breaches that are much more radical because they are secret and therefore impossible to ascertain, let alone control. Witchcraft is, thus, supposed to drain the life forces of the community toward a hostile outside. Yet, as is only to be expected, there is a basic ambiguity here. Witchcraft may create a treacherous opening; it is at the same time crucial as some sort of protection to anybody trying his or her luck in the dangerous outside world. In the olden days, young men leaving the safe environment of home in order to prove their worth—whether it was in war or in trade (or in both)—had to be protected by all sorts of charms and "armoring."[20] The same still applies to anybody who wants to venture into the world outside that is not only dangerous but also full of opportunities and promises.

These basic notions may help to conceive why witchcraft discourse lends itself so well to make sense of the modern changes. After all, the world market, with its chaotic effects at the local level, has similar effects. It imposes an opening, often forcefully, that seems to drain the life force from the local community—think of all the coercive recruitment of labor during both colonial and postcolonial times—but it simultaneously opens up new horizons for self-promotion and individual ambition. In its open-endedness that is both frightening and fascinating, it is similar to the image of an equally unbounded witchcraft world. Indeed, witchcraft discourse has a surprising capacity to link the local realities of family and home to the global changes that make themselves felt ever more directly at the local level. After all, witchcraft is intrinsically related to the local kinship order; yet it can equally integrate the open-ended horizons imposed by the world market. This special capacity to relate—or even articulate—what in the jargon of modern social science is termed the "micro" and the "macro" might be the secret of its continuing resilience.

Linking witchcraft to modernity is, therefore, not just a new academic caprice. This conceptual link can help to understand why the witchcraft discourse impregnates and conditions the ways in which people try to cope with the baffling modern changes. It can help also to elucidate the modern dynamics of this discourse itself. To give just a quick example, until the 1990s, Mount Kupe was generally seen as the final destination of the *ekong* victims; as said, they were supposed to be put to work there on invisible plantations. But more recently people characterize it rather as a relay station from which these zombies would be sold off to distant places throughout the world. Witchcraft is a discourse of flux that transgresses all borders. This is why it articulates itself so easily with processes of globalization, whether recent or from an earlier period.[21]

Toward an Epistemological Pluralism?

Some of the authors quoted above suggest that the new trend toward relating witchcraft to modernity may tend toward an epistemological renewal.[22] This might be an overly ambitious attempt to shape it into a new paradigm. Still, understanding the dynamics of witchcraft discourse and its continuous hold over people's minds, despite all changes, might imply a reconsideration of current approaches in some respects.

A first problem is that the delicate issue of witchcraft's "reality" becomes more difficult to skirt. If it is no longer possible to treat it as a traditional relict that will disappear with modernization, the anthropologist may have more difficulties in confronting the questions with which people will pursue him in the field: does he believe that witchcraft exists? Or is he like the other whites who categorically deny its truth? Clearly, a flat denial of their reality is not very helpful if one wants to understand why these representations have such a hold over people. In his beautiful book on Indian shamans in the Amazonian corner of Colombia, Michael Taussig (1987) suggests that one can only understand the power of the *pintas* ("images") evoked by these healers if one is prepared to go along with them. And how can one experience such an exuberant production of meaning if one denies their very reality? However, this raises other problematic questions: if one accepts "going along"—and there are many recent examples of anthropologists who have had themselves initiated into the secret world of *nganga* and other "healers"—does this not also mean that monstrous accusations against old women or horrible punishments imposed on child witches have to be taken seriously?

Luckily reality has become an ever more elastic notion in academic discourse. Even our colleagues from the natural sciences are no longer so sure that there is just one Truth. The experienced anthropologist will, therefore, know how to deal with these kinds of thorny questions: witchcraft is a discourse, and as such it has its own reality; the question is rather to understand how words and images acquire such power (cf. Favret-Saada 1977). However, such academic answers have their limits, notably in the field when the anthropologist is confronted with the terrible consequences of these representations. Insisting that, as an anthropologist, one just studies "discursive practices" may become somewhat futile when the power of these words have very violent effects (lynching of supposed witches, their condemnation by state courts, etc.). Rather than declaring the whole reality question a nonissue, it might be better to admit that this is a dilemma difficult to solve, not only for people directly involved but also for academics.

A related issue is the abandoning, more or less implicitly, of the search for unequivocal definitions and strict classifications in recent anthropological writings on witchcraft. The examples above may have already indicated that, if one wants to understand the resilience of these representations and the ease with which they integrate modern changes, it is vital to do full justice to their ambivalences and fluidity—as said, it is precisely its kaleidoscopic character that seems to be the secret of the dynamics of witchcraft discourse. In retrospect, it is quite striking with how much self-assurance anthropologists of earlier generations—notably those of the structural-functionalist persuasion—imposed radical oppositions while studying the mysteries of magic and witchcraft: black versus white magic, witchcraft versus sorcery, and so on. Such classificatory ardor stems, of course, from the very principles of the scientific approach. A researcher must, first of all, put some order into his or her data—that is, classify them—all the more so if the field is as confusing as the domain of the occult. It is also striking that, preoccupied as they were with issues of social control, these anthropologists gave their classifications a highly moral tenor. A primary concern seemed to be to distinguish "eu-functional" aspects from "dys-functional" ones.

Yet, it is precisely the moral ambiguity of witchcraft discourse—and its sliding tenor, which undermines each and every distinction or classification—that reinforces its dynamic potential. Nearly everywhere in Africa, the occult forces are seen as a primordial evil. But since they exist, it becomes indispensable to be informed about this secret world, in one way or another. Moreover, another general principle is that these forces can be canalized and used for constructive purposes. The *nganga* is the prototype of this ambiguity. *Nganga* can only heal because they have developed the witchcraft in their belly with the special help of a "professor." They are, therefore, highly ambivalent figures, able to heal and protect but also to attack and kill. Often, the occult forces in which witches excel—as the source of all evil—are also supposed to be indispensable for any accumulation of power and wealth. As said, this is precisely why this discourse lends itself so well to interpreting the modern changes and the shocking inequalities they bring.

Such ambiguities and sliding qualities tend to disappear in the unequivocal classifications imposed by earlier anthropologists.[23] This may be one of the reasons why, for some time, anthropology seemed to show a certain reluctance to confront the spectacular expansion of these representations into the more modern sectors of postcolonial societies.[24] It seems, therefore, no accident that the revival of witchcraft studies in the 1990s was especially carried by anthropologists affected by the postmodern variant of the discipline. In this approach, the anthropological reality is viewed as no more than a provisional outcome of negotiations between the researcher and his informants. This automatically implies that any classification—whether by the anthropologist or by the informant—is relativized and subject to constant reinterpretations.[25] Apparently, a certain relaxing of the scientific principle of univocality was necessary for anthropologists to cope with the conceptual slidings and ambivalences that are so central to the modern dynamics of witchcraft. Witchcraft as a field of study is, indeed, a domain for which Bogumil Jewsiewicki's evocation of the researcher being in some sort of schizophrenic situation applies very well (Jewsiewicki 2001). This author, in his exploration of what the challenges to social sciences for the new century will be, shows himself to be especially worried about the claim to exclusivity of what he calls *le regard scholastique* ("the scientific view")—all the more worrying because of its obvious limitations.[26] For him the main challenge to the social sciences is now to work out some sort of epistemological pluralism that allows scope for other ways of knowing. Indeed, it seems that *le regard scholastique* of earlier anthropologists and their preference for nonequivocal classifications and definitions did away with the very thing that requires explanation: the reversals and ambiguities that are precisely the strength of witchcraft discourses. Does this mean that taking witchcraft seriously as a preeminently subversive and blurring discourse obliges us to sin against the very principles of scientific knowledge?[27] Such questions are part of a broader *problématique*. If the central issue is, indeed, to understand how words can acquire so much power, in witchcraft but also in other fields, their very ambivalence might be an important element in the reply. And how does this fit in with the celebration of univocality in the canons of science? My dogged efforts to understand what was going on in Maka village "palavers" (meetings) during my fieldwork in East-Cameroon Province in the 1970s might serve as a telling example here. Among the Maka, as in other segmentary societies, such village palavers are highly animated or even dramatic happenings. My problem was especially to understand how the old *lessje kaande* (literally, "speaker in the council") succeeded not only in calming the audience but also in arriving at some sort of a solution that was generally accepted. I was especially frustrated because, most often, I could not find a clear line in their speeches. Indeed, it seemed that people returned with quite different interpretations of what the elders had "really" said in the council.

This was, therefore, a good example of "words acquiring power"; the rhetorical performances of the elderly notables in the din of the palaver, where everybody seemed to speak at once, were often quite impressive. But how this worked out exactly—how they succeeded in bringing things to some sort of closing—remained quite unclear, at least to me. However, during a very complex palaver (the noise and all the confusion gave me a severe headache), a young university student who had returned for his holidays suddenly accused the witnesses that they were trying to confuse the palaver and that they should rather stick to the affair at hand. This was exactly what I wanted to say. This palaver concerned an affair that was in itself already very difficult to follow, and the witnesses seemed to talk about anything that came to their minds. However, the most prestigious notable cut him short and told him that he did not understand anything of what a palaver was about. "Didn't he know that a palaver proceeds like the women when they go fishing in the pool? They stamp and trample in the pond and make a lot of noise in order to chase the fish from their holes." The idea was clear: a palaver should never be univocal; a certain confusion was necessary so that all problems would come out in the open; only then could the notables intervene and try to reconcile the people involved.

Indeed, ambivalence and polyinterpretability seemed to be central to the rhetorical powers of this notable and his colleagues. After my return to the Netherlands, sitting in on long, long university meetings, I could not help thinking that, compared with these Maka notables, the words of my colleagues were conspicuously lacking in power, precisely because Western standards require people to stick to the topic and to be as univocal as possible. Does this mean that if one wants to understand how witchcraft words acquire so much power, the academic principle of clarity is an obstacle rather than an asset? The limits of the *regard académique* that inspire Jewsiewicki to make a plea for a more pluralist epistemology are in any case quite manifest in the study of witchcraft.

Similar complications emerge around the other pole in this article's title, the notion of modernity. Is it helpful to speak—like Patrick Chabal and Jean-Pascal Daloz (1999), quoted above, do—of an "African modernity" that would be characterized inter alia by a continuing presence of witchcraft in the more modern sectors of society? Such a notion, just like their term retraditionalization, may encourage precisely the kind of misunderstandings that the authors are trying to avoid. To speak of an African modernity all too easily suggests a contrast with a Western form of modernity. But this very suggestion is quite dangerous, especially if witchcraft is at stake. It seems quite urgent, on the contrary, to emphasize that in this respect Africa is not so exceptional as is currently taken for granted. Several recent anthropological studies try to show that modernity Western style is deeply marked by its own forms of enchantment that, even if they are not exactly the same as witchcraft representations, do as effectively disturb the dream of modernization as a continuous progress toward ever more transparency.[28] The broader interest of a reading of modernity starting from Africa is precisely that it can help to bring out the enchanted character—in highly variable forms—of modernity as such. Distinguishing an African variant from a Western (or even an Asian?) one risks blocking a more profound understanding of modernity's dream that derives its power precisely from its multiple and paradoxical character.

The Atlantic Perspective

The issues raised by linking witchcraft to modernity surpass, therefore, the field of African studies. This link offers, on the one hand, a strategic departing point for conceiving the complexity of modernity as such:

its enchantment under the guise of an apparent disenchantment and the continuing role of the secret that remains essential to any form of power, disturbing time and again the dream of an ever-increasing transparency (see Pels 2003). On the other hand, these unexpected convergences with modernity can help to further historicize witchcraft.[29] An Atlantic perspective is of special interest for this since—as highlighted in nearly all preceding contributions—it highlights how directly transatlantic mobility affected the emergence of new (modern?) perceptions of witchcraft. But the present collection of papers also raises more specific starting points for further research.

Earlier in our discussions, the old distinction by Evans-Pritchard between witchcraft and sorcery played a role, especially since it was recently revived by Bruce Kapferer (2002, 13), who relates it to Mary Douglas's distinction between group and grid—witchcraft is associated with the community, while the sorcerer would bring in outside techniques for individualistic pursuits. Yet in the preceding contributions to this book, this distinction, even in its new and more sophisticated version, remains highly precarious. Another distinction emerges more forcefully from several texts—especially the ones by Sansi, Souza, Palmié, and Maggie—the one between witchcraft and religion; this might also be more relevant in the globalizing context of the black Atlantic.[30] Many Africanists will feel some jealousy when they read how at the other side of the Atlantic—Brazil, Cuba, and also Haiti—beliefs and practices that used to be qualified as witchcraft could develop into religion and become an inherent element of national pride.

This may be linked to another difference, the fact especially highlighted by Maggie and Palmié that in Latin America and the Caribbean the colonial or early modern state tended to pursue witches—apparently taking their occult powers very seriously—while in Africa, colonial rulers, at least the French, British, and Belgians,[31] set out to challenge the reality of such beliefs, intervening against healers for defamation and disturbance of the peace rather than against witches.[32] A straightforward denial of the reality of occult powers in the name of modernity is hardly conducive to their emancipation as religion or national symbol. Of course, the contrast is not complete. After independence (for most African countries around 1960), there were increasing signs that the new African elites tended to take the occult a lot more seriously. As the people in the village in Cameroon's East Province where I came to live in 1971 used to tell me, "You whites do not believe in witchcraft. This is why your laws protect the witches. But now we have Africans ruling us and they know witchcraft is real. Soon they will change the law and then all witches will be in jail."

Yet these were also the times during which modernization ideology still had full sway—when the "young states of Africa" hoped "to do in decades what the West did in centuries," as the *évolué* of our village used to tell me. In this view, witchcraft had to be ignored, as a relegate of the past that, supposedly, would go away with electric light. However, already in the 1980s, the state courts in the region started to convict accused witches rather than healers. The expertise of the latter for "smelling out" witches was now fully recognized by the judges, who accepted them as key witnesses. Clearly, the courts now took witchcraft very seriously. But this coincided with the rapid rise of Pentecostalism in this part of Africa. Like on the other side of the Atlantic, Pentecostalists, despite all internal disagreement, do recognize the reality of the occult powers; yet they see it as the work of the devil and will certainly not celebrate it as part of the national heritage, let alone as an object of national pride.

as in the prior article

Of course, such contrasts have to be nuanced. In some regions along the West African coast—Benin, Togo, part of Ghana—*vodun* was accepted openly by at least some as a religion, despite official disapproval. Another and most intriguing example comes from Ghana, where the local Afrikania Mission intends to propagate "traditional religion." Strongly supported since the 1980s by Jerry Rawlings during his presidency—he hoped it would become the official religion for Ghana, balancing Western influence—it ran into difficult times by the rapid Pentecostalization of the country in the 1990s. In her challenging analysis of the struggle between the two groups, Marleen de Witte (2008) sketches Afrikania as beleaguered by increasingly aggressive Pentecostalist groups who do not let pass any opportunity to denounce it in the media as inspired by the devil and witchcraft (see also Meyer 1999). This tug-of-war between local religion and increasingly aggressive Pentecostalists will be familiar to many colleagues working on the other side of the Atlantic, certainly to those in Brazil. Clearly then there are all sorts of unexpected parallels, despite overall contrasts.

The changing balance between what is seen as witchcraft and what is seen as religion over time and the wide array of factors that influence such shifting contrasts on both sides of the Atlantic—differences in state formation and market, but probably also different meanings of kinship and alternative forms of social bonding—might offer a promising starting point for further comparative research. Such comparisons might, moreover, have a direct social relevance. One of the reasons why I cannot suppress some jealousy when reading about the gradual recognition of local imaginaries as religion and as a crucial element of the national culture in at least some settings on the other side is that over the last decades witchcraft on the African side seems to have run out of hand, as hardly ever before. Of course, the popular complaints about a proliferation of new forms of witchcraft, against which older sanctions would no longer be of any avail, are as old as the written (or oral) sources that we have. Yet especially over the last decades, popular violence against witches—sometimes supported by the forces of order, sometimes only condoned—is taking on very stark forms: a multiplication of so-called child witches living on the streets in many cities in Africa (see Pereira, this volume), the ever more frequent and violent occasion of popular lynching of witches, and a frantic search for the most far-fetched and cruel protections that seem to lead straight into witchcraft itself.

It is, of course, dangerous to make contrasts here with what is going on on the other side.[33] Yet, after working so long on witchcraft in Africa (and still not knowing what it is), I am always struck that in Bahia—as far as I know, reputed all over Brazil as a hotbed of occult power—people talk so much about witchcraft, while there seems to be so little of the self-help justice and popular violence that increasingly mark everyday life in at least some parts of Africa. In Brazil, sectors of the political elite and the black social movements tend to celebrate Candomblé as a religion, or even more so as Afro-Brazilian culture, and this seems to help in hiding its more dangerous aspects like practices associated with witchcraft. However, in this context as well, the balance between witchcraft and religion seems to be highly precarious and constantly shifting. In the last two decades, in Brazil, there has been a revival of the sorcery discourse with Pentecostal accusations against Candomblé temples that involve several cases of violence as well (see Birman and Maggie, this volume). One might talk of a complex and tense dialectic between a "top-bottom" process of valorization (as when Candomblé is projected as religion) and an inverse movement "down-up" of demonization led by Pentecostalism. Still, Candomblé's uneven career as "truly" a religion has highlighted strikingly different ways of dealing with popular fears about a supposed proliferation of occult dangers.

The contrast with African examples is certainly not radical, yet it is sufficiently striking to suggest further study. Precisely because on both sides of the Atlantic popular ideas about witchcraft seem to feed on a template of similar ideas, it is important to follow their different trajectories in time and space. The shifting ways in which people oppose witchcraft and religion—by now almost universal notions—might be a good entry point for this.

Notes to Chapter Twelve

This text is a translation and a partial rewrite of an earlier French version entitled "Sorcellerie et Modernité: Retour sur une étrange complicité" (Bernault and Tonda 2000). Many thanks to the editors of that issue and of the present one, and also to Jens Anderson, Adam Ashforth, Jean-François Bayart, Patrick Chabal, Jean and John Comaroff, Jan Kees van Donge, James Ferguson, Mariane Ferme, Lisa Malkki, Achille Mbembe, Birgit Meyer, Peter Pels, and Janet Roitman for their helpful comments on various versions.

1. See, for instance, the collection edited by Jean and John Comaroff (1993); for an overview of witchcraft studies in the 1990s, see Ciekawy and Geschiere (1998) and Rutherford (1999); see also Ciekawy and Bond (2001), Moore and Sanders (2001), and Ranger (2007).

2. See also "Introduction" in Geschiere, Meyer, and Pels (2008).

3. Just as I do not consider Johannes Fabian's central role in his own book *Power and Performance* (1990)—mentioned by Rutherford as some sort of example—as the strongest element of this book. However, compare for a more sophisticated reflection on the role of an anthropologist doing research on witchcraft/sorcery West (2007).

4. The secret character of witchcraft—even if it is "a public secret"—makes any form of measurement or quantification quite precarious. Cf. the old anthropological debate on whether witchcraft had been increased or rather decreased by the colonial "pacification" (see, for instance, Douglas 1970).

5. Precisely because terms like "traditional" and "modern" are so central to popular explanations of the crisis in Africa—the kind of explanations Chabal and Daloz want to take their distance from—it seems they are playing with fire by still making such ample use of these notions in their book. Readers may ignore the quotation marks and feel comforted in their familiar ways of looking at Africa and its present-day problems.

6. For a more detailed treatment of this theme, see Peter Geschiere (2001a, and also 1997, notably chapter 5). See also Edwin Ardener's pioneering 1970 article on similar representations among the Bakweri of southwest Cameroon.

7. See especially his *Les yeux de ma chèvre, Sur les pas des maîtres de la nuit en pays douala* (1981) and *L'Afrique des guérisons* (1993).

8. Eric de Rosny (oral communication) doubts that hypnosis plays a role since this practice is not very current among the Douala. But to him also, the notion that one must sell a parent to have access to the riches of the *ekong* is the basic pattern in these representations.

9. The February 2006 issue of *Social Anthropology* (14, 1) with articles by Argenti, Röschenthaler, Warnier, and Palmié documents in detail the travel of local ideas on secret societies and occult forces from the Grassfields in Cameroon, through the coastal forest area, across the Atlantic, all the way to Cuba in the context of slave trading—a striking example of what insights an Atlantic perspective on the occult and its transformations can yield.

10. In these regions, the expression *la sorcellerie des Blancs* has therefore a much less positive ring than in other areas of Cameroon. For instance, the Maka, in Cameroon's East Province (where I did my main fieldwork) rather oppose the *sorcellerie des Blancs*

to the *sorcellerie des Noirs* (the former is supposed to serve "to construct things," the latter, "to kill"—a quite blunt, not to say racist, conceptual dichotomy). According to Pool (1994), the Mbum at the limits of the northwestern Grassfields (near the Nigerian border) make a similar contrast. In the regions touched by the *ekong*, little remains of the positive association of whites and witchcraft.

11. Levin (1980, 229) paints a fascinating picture of a kind of "whisky galore" among the Bakossi during the spread of cocoa cultivation:

> The period most vividly remembered is the postwar period of high cocoa prices and nothing to spend money on. People recollect buying cases of smuggled Spanish gin and brandy and consuming it in long drinking bouts. Shouting and singing echoed through the cocoa farms throughout the night; pits were dug to bury the empty bottles. No farmer had to work. For one-third of the crop, a share-cropper would tend the farm . . .

He adds that after 1960, the dream was over. New ways to invest money (especially in schooling, since people became aware of the potential value of school certificates) made that people wanted to keep it , rather than spending it on drink. In addition, they began to realize that by renting their land to strangers, they risked losing their control over it (see also Ejedepang-Koge 1971). In the postcolonial era, the Bakossi have been involved in a rather desperate struggle to keep their lands in the face of an ever stronger encroachment by Bamileke immigrants especially. Heinrich Balz (1984) explains the Bakossi readiness to have strangers work on their lands by the fact that in this area slavery had only just disappeared when the spread of cocoa began. The images around Mount Kupe and the *ekom* seem, therefore, to correspond to this practice of exploiting other people's labor, first as slaves and later as sharecroppers.

12. Although, one must remember de Rosny's remark (1981, 92) that, in precolonial times, *ekong* among the Douala used to be associated with respected traders and notables and did not yet have "the odious character it has acquired nowadays." Apparently, the interpretations of these images can also vary strongly over time.

13. In the 1980s, the bankruptcy and subsequent closure of several banks were generally attributed to the large-scale withdrawal of cash from the official circuits by the *njangi*. See on the role of the *njangi* in the rise of the entrepreneurs from West and Northwest Provinces: Warnier (1993) and Warnier and Miaffo (1993). Characteristically, Warnier (1993, 198) remarks that, among the Bamileke, *famla* is sometimes described as "a *njangi* of the rich." See also Rowlands (1993).

14. Warnier (1993), Warnier and Miaffo (1993), and Pradelles de Latour (1991) all mention *famla* but only briefly. Patrick Mbunwe-Samba, who produced the longest text on *famla*, has an original explanation for why it is so little studied: "The word *famla* has gained such a mystical force that no one will dare write or talk about it lest he/she dies" (Mbunwe-Samba 1996, 75).

15. The *famla* can therefore be viewed as a hidden script in the epos of "le dynamisme bamileke" (cf. Dongmo 1981). It is clear that the massive migrations of Bamileke to other parts of the country have played a crucial role in the economic ascent of this group. But young men often tend to associate these migrations with *famla* and with the new rich who reinvest the money, accumulated in the diaspora, in the home country; for a boy, the only solution to evade this pressure would be to migrate in his turn.

16. See Miriam Goheen's recent study on the Nso (the largest chiefdom of Northwest Province) for a detailed treatment of the complex relation between the *fon* and *sem* (occult power—in some contexts equated with witchcraft, but never so in relation to the *fon*). See especially her nuanced analysis of the role of such ideas in the precarious pact of the *fon* with the new elites (Goheen 1996).

17. See also an interesting text by Basile Ndjio (1995) on a recent series of performances of the *ngru*, a Bamileke purification ritual. Apparently this old ritual was suddenly revived in 1994 in several rural chieftaincies in the West Province and also in the Bamileke quarter in the city of Douala. Ndjio interprets the renewed staging of the ritual as a somewhat desperate attempt by the chiefs to restore their authority that was severely undermined by their close collaboration with the regime. Typically, the chiefs seemed to have organized this ritual with strong support of the "external elites" (the nouveaux riches in the city) and the administrative authorities. Equally typical is the role of the *nganga* (healers) as a kind of broker between these groups. A year later, Ndjio returned to these places and found that, although the chiefs and some notables were still satisfied with having staged the ritual, people in general were more skeptical. Many talked about it as a swindle that served only to enrich the chiefs and the *nganga* and to strengthen their links with the external elites. See also Ndjio (this volume).

18. Lately there has been considerable speculation in Cameroon—and elsewhere in Africa—about new forms of witchcraft that surpass the borders of kinship (cf. for instance, Basile Ndjio on the "magic money" by which *feymen*, Cameroon's notorious global swindlers, succeed in capturing their victims far outside the circles of their own kinship—Ndjio 2006 and in this volume). However, even Ndjio's more detailed case studies suggest that also for such novel forms there is still the tendency to look at least for allies "from within" who would have betrayed a relative to outsiders.

19. See also the article by Jean and John Comaroff (1999b) on the mounting fear of "zombification" in South Africa; the Comaroffs link this fear to people's worries about the increasing influx of labor from other parts of Africa.

20. In francophone Africa, people often speak of *blinder* (my Maka informants, for instance, always used this French term as an equivalent of the local notion of *bwima*).

21. On "globalization" as a "dialectic of flow and closure," see Meyer and Geschiere (1999).

22. See, for instance, Bernault and Tonda (2000).

23. However, it is not only anthropologists of earlier generations who try to impose rigid classifications. In a recent contribution, the French political scientist Comi Toulabor (1999) criticizes me severely for neglecting the terminological distinction many African languages make between "witch" and "magician" (the first unequivocally evil, the second, in Toulabor's characterization, capable of using his/her special powers in a more positive way). In my experience, such distinctions are certainly emphasized at a normative level, but they are always highly precarious and circumstantial when applied in everyday practice. Does Toulabor not tend to take these terminological distinctions too much as definitive? One can raise similar questions in relation to Ranger's recent insistence on a radical separation of "religion" and "witchcraft" (Ranger 2006, 2007; see also note 30 below).

24. See Geschiere (1997, 215–25), notably the afterword, "The Meanderings of Anthropological Discourse on Witchcraft."

25. Cf. Jeanne Fravret-Saada (1980), who advanced such interpretations already in the 1970s (the French original of her book is from 1977)—that is, considerably earlier than the publications of the postmodern gurus of North American anthropology (Tyler, Rabinow, Clifford, and others). It might be characteristic that Favret-Saada arrived at such a relativization of the anthropological reality—she notably insisted on the role of the researcher and the ways he or she is implicated by the informants in their constructions of reality—in a study executed "at home" (in France).

26. Jewsiewicki's text (2001) was originally written as a comment on the well-known Gulbenkian report (by Wallerstein and others) on the same theme.

27. For a more detailed discussion of the dangers of such an oversystematization in the study of witchcraft and the epistemological problems involved, see Geschiere (2001b). Jean-François Bayart shows with an avalanche of well-chosen examples that a broader epistemological problem is at stake here; cf. his characterization of *l'imaginaire* as "the very principle of ambivalence" (Bayart, 1996, 16).

28. See, for instance, Jean Comaroff's 1997 article, comparing recent panics in the West over child abuse and satanism—in her view integral parts of modernity in the West—to witchcraft in Africa. Cf. also Jean and John Comaroff (1999b) and Geschiere (2003). Cf. also the emphasis in the collection *Magic and Modernity* edited by Birgit Meyer and Peter Pels (2003) that modernity produces its own magic.

29. See Rosalind Shaw's challenging interpretation of how witchcraft was not just the expression of traumas of the transatlantic slave trade in Sierra Leone but also played a crucial role in producing its articulation with local inequalities (Shaw 2002).

30. This same distinction was central in a recent polemic among Africanists, which in a somewhat different sense might be relevant to our discussions about an Atlantic perspective. In a seminal text, quoted above, Terence Ranger (2007) notably attacked Steven Ellis and Gerrie Ter Haar's earlier book *Words of Power: Religious Thought and Political Practice in Africa* (2004) for confusing the distinction between religion and witchcraft (see also Ter Haar and Ellis 2009; Meyer 2009). Indeed, in their 2004 book Ellis and Ter Haar proclaimed a kind of general ban on the use of the word witchcraft since in their view the loose use of this notion by academics (notably anthropologists) served to encourage popular fears about an unstoppable proliferation of occult aggression throughout Africa. For these authors, all these phenomena could best be discussed under the heading of religion (or spiritual power). Ranger's critique was that people do make a clear contrast between the two, so we have to take such distinctions seriously. Elsewhere (Geschiere in preparation) I tried to show that such distinctions are crucial but that that they are also constantly shifting and continuously subjected to reinterpretations. It is too easy to equate the one with evil and the other with good (as Ranger tends to do in this short article). The constantly shifting debates in society about whether a certain force is witchcraft or religion rather seem to reflect people's search for clarity in all the ambivalent manifestations of evil and good. Such a point of view, focusing on how conceptual boundaries between witchcraft and religion are constantly shifting, might also be useful for following different trajectories in people's interpretations of spiritual force on both sides of the Atlantic.

31. Portuguese colonial rule in Africa may have been some sort of an exception in this regard.

32. Of course there were many nuances in this respect as Fields (1985) and Pels (2003) have shown: there are examples of colonial civil servants who tried to use

the knowledge of local healers in order to reach compromises in difficult cases. Yet the official line of the state courts was to refuse dealing with accusations of occult aggression unless there was hard evidence of physical violence (see Geschiere 1997).

33. Many thanks to Luis Nicolau Parés for his inspiring comments, especially on this last section.

Bibliography

Abimbola, Wande. 1977. *Ifá: An Exposition of Ifá Literary Corpus*. Ibadan: Oxford University Press.

Ajayi, J. F. A. 1974. The Aftermath of the Fall of Oyo. In *History of West Africa*, ed. J. F. Ade Ajayi and Michael Crowder. London: Longman.

Almeida, Ronaldo. 2009. *A Igreja Universal e seus demônios*. São Paulo: Terceiro Nome.

Alobwede d'Epié, Charles. 1982. *The Language of Traditional Medicine—A Study in the Power of Language*. PhD diss., University of Yaounde.

Amin, Shahid. 1995. *Event, Metaphor, Memory: Chauri, Chaura, 1922-1992*. Berkeley: University of California Press.

Andrade, Mário de. 1983. *Música de Feitiçaria no Brasil*. São Paulo: Livraria Martins.

Anonymous. 1968. La sociedad secreta abakua. *Militante Comunista*, August.

Antunes, Eleonora Haddad. 2002. Raça de gigantes: a higiene mental e a imigração no Brasil. In *Psiquiatria, loucura e arte: fragmentos de história brasileira*, ed. Eleonora Haddad Antunes, Lucia Helena Siqueira Barbosa, and Lygia Maria de França Pereira, 83-102. São Paulo: Editora USP.

Appadurai, Arjun. 1996. *Modernity at Large, Cultural Dimensions of Globalization*. Minneapolis: University of Minnesota Press.

Apter, Andrew. 1993. Atinga Revisited: Yoruba Witchcraft and the Cocoa Economy, 1950-1951. In *Modernity and Its Malcontents: Ritual and Power in Postcolonial Africa*, ed. Jean Comaroff and John Comaroff, 111-28. Chicago: University of Chicago Press.

Arata, Steven D. 1990. The Occidental Tourist: Dracula and the Anxiety of Reverse Colonialism. *Victorian Studies* 4 (33): 621-45.

Araujo, Maria da Graça. 1932. Os delírios episódicos no hospital de alienados. *Arquivos da Assistência a Psicopatas de Pernambuco* 2 (1):234-37.

Ardener, Edwin. 1970. Witchcraft, Economics and the Continuity of Belief. In *Witchcraft Accusations and Confessions*, ed. Mary Douglas, 141–60. London: Tavistock.

Argüelles Mederos, Aníbal, and Ileana Hodge Limonta. 1991. *Los llamados cultos sincréticos y el espiritismo*. La Habana: Editorial Academía.

Argyriadis, Kali. 1999. *La religion à la Havane*. Paris: Editions des Archives Contemporaines.

———. 2005. Religión de indígenas, religión de científicos: construcción de la cubanidad y santería. *Desacatos* 17: 85–106.

———. 2008. Speculators and Santuristas: The Development of Afro-Cuban Cultural Tourism and the Accusation of Religious Commercialism. *Tourist Studies* 8:249–65.

Argyriadis, Kali, and Stefania Capone. 2004. Cubanía et santería: Les enjeux politiques de la transnationalisation religieuse (La Havana-Miami). *Civilisations* 51:81–138.

Ariès, Philippe. 1973. *L'enfant et la vie familiale sous l'Ancien Regime*. Paris: Seuil.

Ashforth, Adam. 1998. Reflections on Spiritual Insecurity in a Modern African City (Soweto). *African Studies Review* 43 (3): 39–68.

———. 2005. *Witchcraft, Violence, and Democracy in South Africa*. Chicago/London: University of Chicago Press.

Auslander, Mark. 1993. "Open Your Wombs!" The Symbolic Politics of Modern Ngoni Witchfinding. In *Modernity and Its Malcontents: Ritual and Power in Postcolonial Africa*, ed. Jean and John Comaroff, 167–92. Chicago: University of Chicago Press.

Austen, Ralph. 1993. The Moral Economy of Witchcraft: An Essay in Comparative History. In *Modernity and Its Malcontents: Ritual and Power in Postcolonial Africa*, ed. Jean and John Comaroff, 89–110. Chicago: University of Chicago Press.

Ayorinde, Christine. 2004. *Afro-Cuban Religiosity, Revolution, and National Identity*. Gainesville: University of Florida Press.

Azzi, Riolando. 1979. *História da Igreja no Brasil*. 2d ed. Petrópolis: Vozes.

Balandier, Georges. 1963. *Sociologie actuelle de l'Afrique noire*. Paris: PUF.

Balz, Heinrich. 1984. *Where the Faith Has to Live, Studies in Bakossi Society and Religion*. Basel: Basler Mission.

Baptista, José Renato. 2007. Os Deuses vendem quando dão: os sentidos do dinheiro nas relações de troca no candomblé. *Mana* 13 (1): 7–40.

Bakker, André. 2008. Deus, o diabo e a televisão: mídia moderna de massa e Pentecostalismo em uma comunidade evangélica. MA thesis, Universidade Estadual do Rio de Janeiro.

Bakhtin, Mikhail. 1987. *A cultura popular na Idade Média e no Renascimento*.

O contexto de François Rabelais. São Paulo/Brasília: Editora Hucitec/Editora da UNB.

Barbot, Jean. 1992 [1688-1732]. *Barbot on Guinea: The Writings of Jean Barbot on West Africa 1678-1712*, ed. Paul Hair, Adam Jones, and Robin Law. 2 Vols. London: Hakluyt Society.

Barnes, Sandra T., and Paula Girshick Ben-Amos. 1997. Ogun, the Empire Builder. In *Africa's Ogun: Old World and New*, ed. Sandra T. Barnes, 39-64. Bloomington: Indiana University Press.

Barreto, Tobias. 1990. *Crítica de religião*. Rio de Janeiro: Editora Record.

Barros, João de. 1553. *Décadas da Ásia*. Lisboa.

Bastide, Roger. 1971 [1960]. *As religiões africanas no Brasil*. São Paulo: Pioneira/EDUSP.

———. 1973. *Estudos Afro-Brasileiros*. São Paulo: Editora Perspectiva.

———. 1978 [1960]. *The African religions of Brazil*. Baltimore: Johns Hopkins University Press.

———. 2001 [1958]. *O Candomblé da Bahia: rito nagô*. São Paulo: Companhia das Letras.

Bayart, Jean-François. 1993. *The State in Africa: The Politics of the Belly*. London: Longman.

———. 1996. *L'illusion identitaire*. Paris: Fayard. (English translation, 2002. *The Illusion of Cultural Identity*. London: Hurst).

Bayart, Jean-François, Peter Geschiere, and Francis Nyamnjoh. 2001. Autochtonie, démocracie et citoyenneté en Afrique. *Critique Internationale* 10:177-94.

Beinart, William. 1982. *The Political Economy of Pondoland, 1860-1930*. Cambridge: Cambridge University Press.

Bernault, Florence, and Joseph Tonda. 2000. Dynamiques de l'invisible en Afrique. *Politique Africaine* 79:5-17, special issue on *Pouvoirs Sorciers*, ed. F. Bernault and J. Tonda.

Bethencourt, Francisco. 1987. *O Imaginário da magia: feiticieiros, saludadores e nigromantes no século XVI*: Lisboa: Projeto Universidade Aberta.

Birman, Patrícia. 1996. Cultos de possessão e Pentecostalismo no Brasil: passagens. *Religião e Sociedade* 17 (1-2): 90-109.

———. 2006. O Espírito Santo, a mídia e o território dos crentes. *Ciências Sociais e Religião* 8 (8): 41-62.

———. 2008. Favela é comunidade? In: *Vidas sob o cerco: violência e rotina nas favelas do Rio de Janeiro*, ed. Luiz Antônio Machado da Silva, 99-114. Rio de Janeiro: Nova Fronteira/FAPERJ.

Birman, Patrícia, and Márcia Pereira Leite. 2000. Whatever Happened to What Used to Be the Largest Catholic Country in the World? *Daedalus, Journal of the American Academy of Arts and Sciences* 129 (2): 239-70.

Bloch, Marc. 1941. *Apologie pour l'Histoire, ou métier d'historien*. Paris: Armand Colin.

Bluteau, Rafael. 1713. *Vocabulario portuguez e latino*. Coimbra.

Borges, J. C. Cavalcanti, and Dinice C. Lima. 1932. Investigações sobre as religiões no Recife: o "espiritismo." *Arquivos da Assistência a Psicopatas de Pernambuco* 2, 1.

Bosman, Willem. 1705. *A New and Accurate Description of the Coast of Guine*. London: James Knapton.

Boyer, Véronique. 1993. *Femmes et cultes de possession au Brésil. Les compagnons invisibles*. Paris: L'Harmattan.

Brain, Robert. 1970. Child-witches. In *Witchcraft, Confessions and Accusations*, ed. M. Douglas, 161–79. London: Tavistock Publications.

Brasio, Antonio. 1952. *Monumenta missionaria africana—Africa occidental (1471–1482)*. Lisboa: Agencia Geral do Ultramar.

Bronfman, Alejandra. 2004. *Measures of Equality: Social Science, Citizenship and Race in Cuba, 1902–1940*. Chapel Hill: University of North Carolina Press.

Brooks, George E. 2003. *Eurafricans in Western Africa: Commerce, Social Status, Gender, and Religious Observance from the Sixteenth to the Eighteenth Century*. Athens, OH: Ohio University Press.

Brosses, Charles de. 1988 [1760]. *Du culte des dieux fétiches ou parallèle de l'ancienne religion de l'Egypte avec la religion actuelle de Nigritie*. Paris: Fayard.

Brown, Diana. 1986. *Umbanda Religion and Politics in Urban Brazil*. Ann Arbor: UMI Research Press.

Bureau, René. 1962. Ethno-sociologie religieuse des Douala et apparentés. *Recherches et Études Camerounaises* 7/8 (Yaounde).

Cabrera, Lydia. 1954. *El Monte Igbo. Finda. Ewe Orisha. Vititi Nfinda*. La Habana: Ediciones C. R.

Calainho, Daniela Buono. 2000. Metrópole das mandingas: religiosidade negra e Inquisição portuguesa no Antigo Regime. PhD diss., Universidade Federal Fluminense. Niterói.

———. 2004. Africanos penitenciados pela Inquisição portuguesa. *Revista Lusófona de Ciência das Religiões* 3(5): 47–63.

Camargo, Cândido Procópio. 1961. *Kardecismo e umbanda: uma interpretação sociológica*. São Paulo: Pioneira.

Campello, José. 1938. Xangôs. *Folha da Manhã*, January 27.

Carneiro, Edison. 1948. *Candomblés da Bahia*. Salvador: Museu do Estado.

Cascudo, Luís da Câmara. 1972. *Dicionário do folclore brasileiro*. Brasília: INL.

Castañeda, Mireya. 2003. 8° congreso mundial tradición y cultura orisha: intensos debates académicos sobre aspectos culturales y religiosos. *Granma Internacional*, July 23.

Castellanos, Israel. 1916. *La brujería y el ñáñiguismo en Cuba desde el punto de vista medico-legal*. La Habana: Lloredo y Companía.

Castillo, Lisa Earl, and Luis Nicolau Parés. 2007. Marcelina da Silva e seu mundo: novos dados para uma historiografia do candomblé ketu. *Afro-Ásia* 36:111–51.

Castro, Yeda Pessoa de. 2001. *Falares africanos na Bahia—um vocabulário afro-brasileiro*. Rio de Janeiro: Academia Brasileira de Letras/TopBooks.

Cavalcanti, Pedro. 1933. Investigações sobre as religiões no Recife: uma seita panteísta. *Arquivos da Assistência a Psicopatas de Pernambuco* 3 (1): 58–68.

———. 1934a. *Contribuição ao estudo do estado mental dos médiuns*. Recife: Faculdade de Medicina do Recife.

———. 1934b. Contribuição ao estudo do estado mental dos médiuns. *Arquivos da Assistência a Psicopatas de Pernambuco* 5 (2) :135–44.

———. 1935. As seitas africanas do Recife. In *Estudos Afro-Brasileiros: Trabalhos apresentados ao 1° Congresso Afro-Brasileiro realizado no Recife em 1934*, ed. Gilberto Freyre, 243–57. Rio de Janeiro: Ariel.

CCF/Christian Children Fund. 2003a. Diagnóstico realizado no município de Mbanza Congo. Luanda: CCF.

———. 2003b. Relatório do Seminário de formação de formadores comunitários. Primeira fase—Desenvolvimento da Criança. Mbanza Congo/Luanda: CCF.

———. 2003c. Relatório do Seminário de formação de formadores comunitários. Segunda fase—Desenvolvimento da Criança e Impacto da Guerra. Mbanza Congo: CCF.

———. 2004. Relatório do Workshop "Crianças com necessidades especiais de proteção". Mbanza/Congo: CCF, INAC and associated NGOs.

Chabal, Patrick, and Jean-Pascal Daloz. 1999. *Africa Works*. Oxford: Currey.

Chalhoub, Sidney. 2003. *Machado de Assis historiador*. São Paulo: Companhia das Letras.

Chávez Álvarez, Ernesto. 1991. *El crímen de la niña Cecilia*. La Habana: Editorial Ciencias Sociales.

Chinelli, Filipina, Bianca Freire-Medeiros and Lidia Medeiros. 2005. Reflexões sobre a percepção de direitos e formas alternativas de acesso à justiça com base em um estudo de caso em uma favela do Rio de Janeiro. *Interseções* 7:131–46.

Ciekawy, Diane. 1992. Witchcraft Eradication as Political Process in Kilifi District Kenya. PhD diss., Columbia University.

———. 1998. Witchcraft and Statecraft: Five Technologies of Power in Colonial and Postcolonial Coastal Kenya. *Africa Studies Review* 41 (3): 119-42.

Ciekawy, Diane M., and George Clement Bond, eds. 2001. *Witchcraft Dialogues, Anthropological and Philosophical Exchanges.* Athens: Ohio University Press.

Ciekawy, Diane M., and Peter Geschiere. 1998. Introduction. *African Studies Review* 41(3): 11-14, special issue on *Containing Witchcraft*, ed. D. Ciekawy and P. Geschiere.

Claridge, G. Cyril. 1922. *Wild Bush Tribes of Tropical Africa.* London: Seeley, Service & Co.

Clark, Stuart. 1984. The Scientific Status of Demonology. In *Occult and Scientific Mentalities in the Renaissance*, ed. Brian Vickers, 352-74. Cambridge: Cambridge University Press.

Cobain, Ian, and Vikram Dodd. 2005. How Media Whipped up a Racist Witch-Hunt. Despite the Lurid Headlines, Police Dismiss Claims of Child Sacrifice. *The Guardian*, June 25. media.guardian.co.uk/site/story/0,14173,1514334,00.html.

Comaroff, Jean. 1997. Consuming Passions: Child Abuse, Fetishism and the "New World Order." *Culture* 17: 7-19.

Comaroff, Jean, and John Comaroff, eds. 1993. *Modernity and Its Malcontents: Ritual and Power in Postcolonial Africa.* Chicago: University of Chicago Press.

———. 1999a. Occult Economies and the Violence of Abstraction: Notes from the South African Postcolony. *American Ethnologist* 3 (26): 279-301.

———. 1999b. Alien-Nation: Zombies, Immigrants and Millennial Capitalism. *Bulletin du Codesria* 3/4:17-29.

———, eds. 2001. *Millennial Capitalism and the Culture of Neoliberalism.* Durham and London: Duke University Press.

Corrêa, Mariza. 1998. *As ilusões da liberdade: A escola Nina Rodrigues e a antropologia no Brasil.* Bragança Paulista: Editora da Universidade São Francisco.

Crais, Clifton. 1998. Of Men, Magic, and the Law: Popular Justice and the Political Imagination in South Africa. *Journal of Social History* 32 (1): 49-72.

———. 2002. *The Politics of Evil: Magic, State Power, and the Political Imagination in South Africa.* Cambridge: Cambridge University Press.

Crawford, J. R. 1967. *Witchcraft and Sorcery in Rhodesia.* London: International African Institute/ Oxford University Press.

Cretton, Vicente. 2007. Território sagrado: a geografia das relações sociais em uma comunidade evangélica. Monograph (mimeo). CIS, Universidade Estadual do Rio de Janeiro.

Cunha, Cristina Vital da. 2009. Evangélicos em ação nas favelas cariocas: um estudo sócio-antropológico sobre redes de proteção, tráfico de drogas e religião no Complexo de Acari. PhD diss., Universidade do Estado do Rio de Janeiro.

Da Costa, Emilia Viotti. 1994. *Crowns of Glory, Tears of Blood: The Demerara Slave Rebellion of 1823*. Nork/Oxford: Oxford University Press.

Dantas, Beatriz Góis. 1984. De feiticeiro a comunista: acusações sobre o Candomblé. *Dédalo* 23:97-116.

———. 1988. *Vovó nagô e papai branco: usos e abusos da África no Brasil*. Rio de Janeiro: Graal.

DaMatta, Roberto. 1981. The Ethic of Umbanda and the Spirit of Messianism: Reflections on the Brazilian Model. In *Authoritarian Capitalisms*, ed. Thomas Brueneu and Philippe Faucher, 239-65. Boulder: Westview Press.

———. 1985. *A casa e a rua*. Rio de Janeiro: Editora Brasiliense.

Das, Veena, and Deborah Poole. 2004. Introduction: State and Its Margins: Comparative Ethnographies. In *Anthropology in the Margins of the State*, ed. Veena Das and Deborah Poole, 3-33. Oxford, Santa Fe: James Currey/School of American Research Press.

Davies, Owen. 1999. *Witchcraft, Magic and Culture, 1736–1951*. Manchester: Manchester University Press.

De Boeck, Filip. 2000. Le "Deuxième Monde" et les "Enfants-sorciers." *Politique Africaine. Le dossier enfants, jeunes et politique* 80:32-57.

———. 2004. On Being Shege in Kinshasa: Children, the Occult, and the Street. In *Reinventing Order in the Congo. How People Respond to State Failure in Kinshasa*, ed. Theodore Trefon, 155-73. London/New York: Zed Books.

———. 2005. The Divine Seed: Children, Gift and Witchcraft in Democratic Republic of Congo. In *Makers and Breakers: Children and Youth in Postcolonial Africa*, ed. F. De Boeck and A. Honwana, 188-214. Oxford: James Currey.

De Boeck, Filip, and Alcinda Honwana. 2000. Faire et défaire la société: enfants, jeunes et politique en Afrique: introduction au thème. *Politique Africaine. Le dossier enfants, jeunes et politique* 80:5-11.

———. 2005. Introduction: Children and Youth in Africa: Agency, Identity and Place. In *Makers and Breakers: Children and Youth in Postcolonial Africa*, ed. F. De Boeck and A. Honwana, 1-18. Oxford: James Currey.

Dongmo, Jean-Louis. 1981. *Le dynamisme bamiléké*. Yaounde: CEPER.

Douglas, Mary. 1970. Introduction: Thirty Years after Witchcraft, Oracles and Magic. In *Witchcraft: Confessions and Accusations*, ed. Mary Douglas, xiii-xxxviii. London: Tavistock.

Duarte, Luiz Fernando. 1992. Légalité et citoyenneté dans le Brésil contemporain: la question du particularisme des quartiers populaires à partir de l'observation anthropologique d'une experience d'aide légale et d'education civique. *Cahiers du Brésil Contemporain* 17:53-64.

Durham, Deborah. 2000. Youth and the Social Imagination in Africa. *Anthropological Quarterly* 73 (3): 113-20.

Egerton, Douglas R. 1993. *Gabriel's Rebellion: The Virginia Slave Conspiracies of 1800 and 1802*. University of North Carolina Press: Chapel Hill & London.

Ejedepang-Koge, S. N. 1971. *The Tradition of a People: Bakossi*. A Historico-Socio-Anthropological Study of one of Cameroon's Bantu Peoples. Yaounde (mimeo).

———. 1975. *Tradition and Change in Peasant Activities*. Yaounde: Ministry of National Education, Department of Private Education.

Ellis, Stephen, and Gerrie Ter Haar. 2004. *Words of Power: Religious Thought and Political Practice in Africa*. London: Hurst.

Englund, Harri, and James Leach. 2000. Ethnography and the Meta-Narratives of Modernity. *Current Anthropology* 41, 2: 225-48.

Evans, Ivan Thomas. 1997. *Bureaucracy and Race: Native Administration in South Africa*. Berkeley: University of California Press.

Evans-Pritchard, Edward E. 1937. *Witchcraft, Oracles and Magic among the Azande*. Oxford: Oxford University Press.

Fabian, Johannes. 1983. *Time and the Other*. New York: Columbia University Press.

———. 1990. *Power and Performance*. Madison: University of Wisconsin Press.

Farias, Juliana. 2008. Da asfixia: reflexões sobre a atuação do tráfico de drogas nas favelas cariocas. In *Vidas sob o cerco: violência e rotina nas favelas do Rio de Janeiro*, ed. Luiz Antônio Machado da Silva, 173-90. Rio de Janeiro: FAPERJ.

Favret-Saada, Jeanne. 1977. *Les Mots, la mort, les sorts. La sorcellerie dans le Bocage*. Paris : Ed. Gallimard. (English translation: 1980. *Deadly Words, Witchcraft in the Bocage*. Cambridge: Cambridge University Press).

———. 2009. *Désorceler*. Paris : Éditions de l'Olivier.

Fernandes, Gonçalves. 1937. *Xangôs do Nordeste: investigações sobre os cultos negro-fetichistas do Recife*. Rio de Janeiro: Civilização Brasileira.

———. 1938. *O folclore mágico do Nordeste: Usos, costumes, crenças e ofícios mágicos das populações nordestinas*. Rio de Janeiro: Civilização Brasileira.

———. 1941. *O sincretismo religioso no Brasil: Seitas, cultas, cerimônias e prá-ticas religiosas e mágico-curativas entre as populações brasileiras.* Curitiba: Editora Guaíra.

Fick, Carolyn. 1990. *The Making of Haiti: The Saint Domingue Revolution from Below.* Knoxville: University of Tennessee Press.

Fields, Karen E. 1982. Political Contingencies of Witchcraft in Colonial Cen-tral Africa: Culture and the State in Marxist Theory. *Revue Canadienne des Études Africaines/Canadian Journal of African Studies* 16:567–93.

———. 1985. *Revival and Rebellion in Colonial Central Africa.* Princeton: Princeton University Press.

Fisiy, Cyprian F. 1990. *Palm Tree Justice in the Bertoua Court of Appeal: Witch-craft Cases.* Leiden: African Studies Centre.

———. 1992. *Power and Privilege in the Administration of Law: Land Law Re-forms and Social Differentiation in Cameroon.* Leiden: Afrikastudiecentrum.

———. 1998. Containing Occult Practices: Witchcraft Trials in Cameroon. *African Studies Review* 41 (3): 143–64.

Fisiy, Cyprian F., and Peter Geschiere. 1990. Judges and Witches, or How Is the State to Deal with Witchcraft? Examples from Southeastern Camer-oon. *Cahiers d'Etudes Africaines* 118:135–56.

———. 1991. Sorcery, Witchcraft and Accumulation: Regional Variations in South and West Cameroun. *Critique of Anthropology* 11 (3): 251–78.

———. 1996. Witchcraft, Violence and Identity: Different Trajectories in Postcolonial Cameroon. In *Postcolonial Identities,* ed. Richard Webner and Terence Ranger, 193–221. London and New Jersey: Zed Books Ltd.

Florence, Afonso Bandeira. 1989. Nem escravos, nem libertos: os 'africanos livres' na Bahia. *Cadernos do CEAS* 121:58–69.

———. 2002. Entre o cativeiro e a emancipação: a liberdade dos africanos livres no Brasil (1818–1864). MA thesis, Universidade Federal da Bahia.

Fogui, Jean-Pierre. 1990. *L'intégration politique au Cameroun: une analyse centre-périphérie.* Paris: LGDJ.

Freyre, Gilberto. 1933. *Casa grande e senzala. Formação da família brasileira sob o regime de economia patriarcal.* Rio de Janeiro: Livraria José Olympio Editora.

———. 1936. Pae Adão. *Diário de Pernambuco,* April 28:3.

Friedman, Kajsa Ekholm, and Biluka Nsakala N'Senga. 2002. *Estudo sobre as crianças em situação de risco nas províncias de Zaire, Uíge e Luanda.* Relatório Preliminar (mimeo). Luanda.

Frigerio, Alejandro. 2004. Re-Africanization in Secondary Religious Dias-poras: Constructing a World Religion. *Civilisations* 51:39–60.

Fry, Peter. 1982. *Para inglês ver. Identidade e política na cultura brasileira.* Rio de Janeiro: Zahar Editores.

————. 1998. As religiões africanas fora da África o caso do Brasil. *Povos e culturas* 6: 439–471.

————. 2000. O Espírito Santo contra o feitiço e os espíritos revoltados: "civilização" e "tradição" em Moçambique. *Mana* 6 (2): 65–95.

Geertz, Clifford. 1996. *Los usos de la diversidad*. Barcelona/Buenos Aires/ México: Ediciones Paidós/ I.C.E. Universidad Autónoma de Barcelona.

————. 2001. *Nova luz sobre a antropologia*. Rio de Janeiro: Jorge Zahar Editor.

Genovese, Eugene. 1974. *Roll, Jordan, Roll: The World the Slaves Made*. New York: Pantheon Books.

————. 1979. *From Rebellion to Revolution: Afro-American Slave Revolts in the Making of the Modern World*. Baton Rouge: Louisiana State University Press.

Geschiere, Peter. 1994. Domesticating Personal Violence: Witchcraft, Courts and Confessions in Cameroon. *Africa* 3 (64): 32–42.

————. 1995. *Sorcellerie et politique en Afrique: La viande des autres*. Paris: Karthala.

————. 1996. Sorcellerie et politique: les piège du rapport élite-village. *Politique Afrique* 63:82–96.

————. 1997. *The Modernity of Witchcraft: Politics and the Occult in Postcolonial Africa*. Charlottesville: University of Virginia Press.

————. 2001a. Witchcraft and New Forms of Wealth: Regional Variations in South and West Cameroon. In *Powers of Good and Evil—Social Transformation and Popular Belief*, ed. P. Clough and J. P. Mitchell, 43–77. Oxford: Berghahn.

————. 2001b. Regard académique, sorcellerie et schizophrénie (commentaire). *Annales—Histoire, Sciences Sociales* 56 (3): 643–49.

————. 2003. On Witch-Doctors and Spin-Doctors: The Role of "Experts" in African and American Politics. In *Magic and Modernity. Interfaces of Revelation and Concealment*, ed. Birgit Meyer and Peter Pels, 159–82. Stanford: Stanford University Press.

Geschiere, Peter, and Basile Ndjio. 2003. Democratization and the Uncertain Renaissance of Chieftaincy: Varying Trajectories in Cameroon. Paper presented at the conference on *Chieftaincy in Africa: Culture, Governance and Development* organized by University of Cambridge/University of Legon, Accra, January 6–10.

Geschiere, Peter, and Francis Nyamnjoh. 1998. Witchcraft as an Issue in the "Politics of Belonging": Democratization and Urban Migrants' Involvement with the Home Village. *African Studies Review* 41 (3): 69–91.

Geschiere, Peter, Birgit Meyer, and Peter Pels, eds. 2008. *Readings in Modernity in Africa*. Oxford/Bloomington: Currey/Indiana University Press.

Gell, Alfred. 1988. Technology and Magic. *Anthropology Today* 4 (2): 6-9.

———. 1992. The Technology of Enchantment and the Enchantment of Technology. In *Anthropology, Art, and Aesthetics*, ed. J. Coote and A. Shelton, 40-66. Oxford: Oxford Unversity Press.

Ginzburg, Carlo. 1966. *I benandanti*. Torino: Einaudi.

Giumbelli, Emerson. 1997a. *O Cuidado dos Mortos: uma História da Condenação e Legitimação do Espiritismo*. Rio de Janeiro: Arquivo Nacional.

———. 1997b. Heresia, doença, crime ou religião: O Espiritismo no discurso de médicos e cientistas sociais. *Revista de Antropologia* 40 (2): 31-82.

Glover, David. 1996. *Vampires, Mummies, and Liberals: Bram Stoker and the Politics of Popular Fiction*. Durham, NC: Duke University Press.

Goheen, Miriam. 1996. *Men Own the Fields, Women Own the Crops: Gender and Power in the Cameroonian Highlands*. Madison: University of Wisconsin Press.

Gonzales, Philippe. 2008. Lutter contre l'emprise démoniaque. Les politiques du combat spirituel evangélique. *Terrain* 50: 44-61.

Gluckman, Max. 1963. *Order and Rebellion in Tribal Africa*. Glencoe: Free Press.

Graden, Dale. 2006. *From Slavery to Freedom in Brazil. Bahia, 1835-1900*. Albuquerque: University of New México Press.

Graeber, David. 2005. Fetishism as Social Creativity or Fetishes Are Gods in the Process of Construction. *Anthropological Theory* 5 (4): 407-38.

Guanche, Jesús. 1983. *Procesos etnoculturales de Cuba*. La Habana: Editorial Letras Cubanas.

Guha, Ranajit. 1983. *Elementary Aspects of Peasant Insurgency in Colonial India*. Delhi: Oxford Press.

Hagedorn, Katherine J. 2001. *Divine Utterances: The Performance of fro-Cuban Santería*. Washington: Smithsonian Institution Press.

Harding, Rachel. 2000. *A Refuge in Thunder. Candomblé and Alternative Spaces of Blackness*. Bloomington: Indiana University Press.

Hayes, Kelly. 2004. *Magic at the Margins: Macumba in Rio de Janeiro. An Ethnographic Analysis of a Religious Life*. PhD diss., University of Chicago.

Hearn, Adrian. 2004. Afro-Cuban Religions and Social Welfare: Consequences of Commercial Development in Havana. *Human Organization* 63:78-87.

Hegel, Friederich. 1956 [1837]. *The Philosophy of History*. New York: Dover.

Helg, Aline. 1995. *Our Rightful Share: The Afro-Cuban Struggle for Equality, 1886-1912*. Chapel Hill: University of North Carolina Press.

———. 1996. Políticas raciales en Cuba después de la independencia: Represión de la cultura negra y mito de igualdad racial. *América Negra* 11:63-79.

Henningsen, Gustav. 1990. "The Ladies from Outside"—an Archaic Pattern of the Witches' Sabbath. In *Early Modern European Witchcraft—Centers and Peripheries*, ed. Bengt Ankarloo and Gustav Henningsen, 191-215. Oxford: Clarendon Press.

Herskovits, Melville. 1966. *The New World Negro*. Bloomington and Indianapolis: Indiana University Press.

Hofbauer, Andreas. 2006. *Uma história do branqueamento ou o negro em questão*. São Paulo: FAPESP/Editora UNESP.

Holbraad, Martin. 2004. Religious "Speculation": The Rise of Ifá Cults and Consumption in Post-Soviet Cuba. *Journal of Latin American Studies* 36:643-63.

Hutzler, Celina Ribeiro. 1987. Ulysses Pernambucano: psiquiatria social. *Ciência e Trópico* 15 (1): 23-40.

Israel, Paolo. 2009. The War of Lions: Witch-Hunts, Occult Idioms and Post-Socialism in Northern Mozambique. *Journal of Southern African Studies* 35:155-74.

James Figarola, Joel. 2006. *Cuba: la gran nganga*. Santiago de Cuba: Ediciones Caserón.

Jewsiewicki, Bogumil. 2001. Pour un pluralisme épistémologique en sciences sociales. *Annales—Histoire, Sciences Sociales* 56 (3): 625-41.

Johnson, Paul Christopher. 2002. *Secrets, Gossip, and the Gods. The Transformation of Brazilian Candomblé*. Oxford: Oxford University Press.

Joseph, Richard. 1977. *Radical Nationalism in Cameroon. Social Origins of the UPC Rebellion*. Oxford: Oxford University Press.

Kapferer, Bruce, ed. 2002. Introduction: Outside All Reason—Magic, Sorcery and Epistemology in Anthropology. In *Beyond Rationalism. Rethinking Magic, Witchcraft, and Sorcery*, ed. Bruce Kapferer, 1-30. Oxford: Berghahn Books.

Keane, Webb. 2007. *Christian Moderns: Freedom and Fetish in the Mission Encounter*. Berkeley: University of California Press.

Kidder, D. P., and J. C. Fletcher. 1857. *Brazil and the Brazilians. Portrayed in Historical and Descriptive Sketches*. Philadelphia: Childs & Peterson.

Kiernan, James, ed. 2006. *The Power of the Occult in Modern Africa: Continuity and Innovation in the Renewal of African Cosmologies*. Berlin: Lit Verlag.

Kirsch, Thomas, and Bertram Turner, eds. *Permutations of Order: Religion and Law as Contested Sovereignties*. Aldershot: Ashgate, 2008.

Koselleck, Reinhardt. 1985. *Futures Past: On the Semantic of Historical Time*. Cambridge: MIT Press.

La Fontaine, Jean S. 1998. *Speak of the Devil: Tales of Satanic Child Abuse in Contemporary England*. Cambridge: Cambridge University Press.

Lapassade, George and Marco Aurélio Luz. 1972. *O segredo da macumba*. Rio de Janeiro: Paz e Terra.

Latour, Bruno. 1993. *We Have Never Been Modern*. Cambridge: Harvard University Press.

———. 2001. *L'espoir de Pandore*. Paris: Éditions de la Découverte.

Leite, Márcia Pereira. 2000. Entre individualismo e solidariedade: dilemas da política e da cidadania no Rio de Janeiro. *Revista Brasileira de Ciências Sociais* 15 (44): 73–90.

———. 2007. *Para além da metáfora da guerra: violência, cidadania, religião e ação coletiva no Rio de Janeiro*. São Paulo/Brasília: Attar Editorial/CNPq-Pronex-MCT.

Levin, Michael D. 1980. Export Crops and Peasantization: The Bakossi of Cameroon. In *Peasants in Africa: Historical and Contemporary Perspectives*, ed. M. Klein, 221–43. London: SAGE.

Levine, Robert M. 1975. The First Afro-Brazilian Congress: Opportunities for the Study of Race in the Brazilian Northeast. *Race* 15 (2): 185–92.

Lima, Diana. 2007. Trabalho, mudança de vida e prosperidade entre fiéis da Igreja Universal do Reino de Deus. *Religião & Sociedade* 27:132–55.

Lima, Vivaldo da Costa. 2003 [1977]. *A família de santo nos candomblés jejes-nagôs da Bahia: um estudo de relações intragrupais*. Salvador: Corrupio.

Lopes, Juarez Brandão. 1971. *Desenvolvimento e mudança social: formação da sociedade urbano-industrial no Brasil*. São Paulo: Editora Nacional.

Lopes, Natânia. 2009. Uma comunidade que não é deste mundo. Monograph (mimeo). CIS, Universidade Estadual do Rio de Janeiro.

López Valdés, Rafael. 1985. *Componentes africanos en el etnos Cubano*. La Habana: Editorial Ciencias Sociales.

Luz, Marco Aurélio. 1995. *Agada: dinâmica da civilização africana-brasileira*. Salvador: Editora da UFBA.

Mabeko Tali, Jean-Michel. 1995. La "chasse aux Zairois" à Luanda. *Politique Africaine* 57:71–84.

Macedo, Bispo Edir. 2000 [1996]. *Orixás, caboclos e guias, deuses ou demônios?* Rio de Janeiro: Universal.

MacGaffey, Wyatt. 1970a. *Custom and Government in the Lower Congo*. California: University of California Press.

———. 1970b. The Religious Commissions of Bakongo. *Man* 5 (1): 27–38.

———. 1983. *Modern Kongo Prophets: Religion in a Plural Society*. Indiana: Indiana University Press.

———. 1986. *Religion and Society in Africa: The Bakongo of Lower Zaire*. Chicago: University of Chicago Press.

Machado, Maria Helena P. T. 1987. *Crime e escravidão: trabalho, luta, resistência nas lavouras paulistas, 1830–1888* . São Paulo: Brasiliense.

————. 1994. *O plano e o pânico: os movimentos sociais na década da abolicāo*. Rio de Janeiro: Editora UFRJ; Sao Paulo: EDUSP.

Machado da Silva, Luiz Antonio. 2007. Rompendo o cerceamento da palavra: a voz dos favelados em busca de reconhecimento. Research report. Rio de Janeiro: FAPERJ.

Machado da Silva, Luiz Antonio, and Márcia Pereira Leite. 2007. Violência, crime e polícia: o que os favelados dizem quando falam desses temas? *Revista Sociedade e Estado* 22 (3): 545-91.

Magalhães, Agamenon. 1939. *Relatório apresentado ao Exmo. Snr. Presidente da República*. Recife: Estado de Pernambuco.

Maggie, Yvonne. 1975. *Guerra de orixá: um estudo de ritual e conflito*. Rio de Janeiro: Zahar.

————. 1992. *Medo do feitiço: relações entre magia e poder no Brasil*. Rio de Janeiro: Arquivo Nacional.

————. 2001. Fetiche, feitiço, magia e religião. In *Fazendo Antropologia no Brasil*, ed. Neidi Esterci, Peter Fry, Mirian Goldenberg, 57-91. Rio de Janeiro: DP&A Editora.

Mariz, Cecília. 1999. A teologia da Batalha Espiritual: uma revisão da bibliografia. *Revista Brasileira de Informação Bibliográfica em Ciências Sociais* 47 (1): 33-48.

Marques, Xavier. 1975 [1897]. *O feiticeiro*. São Paulo: GRD.

Martínez Echazábal, Lourdes. 1998. *Mestizaje* and the Discourse of National/Cultural Identity in Latin America, 1845-1959. *Latin American Research Review* 25:21-42.

Martínez Furé, Rogelio. 1979. *Diálogos imaginários*. La Habana: Editorial Arte y Literatura.

Marwick, Max. 1964. Witchcraft as a Social Strain-Gauge. *Australian Journal of Science* 26:263-68.

————. 1967. The Sociology of Sorcery in a Central African Tribe. In *Magic, Witchcraft and Curing*, ed. J. Middleton, 101-26. Austin: University of Texas Press.

Matory, J. Lorand. 1994. *Sex and the Empire That Is No More: Gender and the Politics of Metaphor in Oyo Yoruba Religion*. Minneapolis: University of Minnesota Press.

————. 2005. *Black Atlantic Religion: Tradition, Transnationalism, and Matriarchy in the Afro-Brazilian Candomblé*. Princeton: Princeton University Press.

Mbeki, Govan. 1984. *South Africa: The Peasant's Revolt*. London: International Defence and Aid Fund for Southern Africa.

Mbunwe-Samba, Patrick. 1996. *Witchcraft, Magic and Divination: A Personal Testimony*. Bamenda/Leiden: Afrikastudiecentrum.

Mendonça, Mariana. 2009. O paraíso abençoado. Turismo e religião em uma comunidade evangélica. Monograph (mimeo). CIS, Universidade Estadual do Rio de Janeiro.

Menéndez, Lázara. 1999. *Translating the Devil: Religion and Modernity among Ewe in Ghana*. Trenton: Africa World Press.

———. 2002. *Rodar el coco: proceso de cambio en la santería*. La Habana: Editorial Ciencias Sociales.

———. 2009. Response to Ter Haar and Ellis. *Africa* 79 (3): 413-16.

Meyer, Birgit, and Peter Geschiere, eds. 1999. *Globalization and Identity: Dialectics of Flow and Closure*. Oxford: Blackwell.

Meyer, Birgit and Peter Pels, eds. 2003. *Magic and Modernity: Interfaces of Revelation and Concealment*. Stanford: Stanford University Press.

Middleton, John. 1961. *Lugbara Religion: Ritual and Authority among an East African People*. London: Oxford University Press.

Middleton, J., & Winter, E.H., eds. 1963 *Witchcraft and Sorcery in East Africa*. London, Routledge & Kegan Paul.

Miller, Joseph. 1978. *Way of Death: Merchant Capitalism and the Angolan Slave Trade, 1730-1830*. Madison: Wisconsin University Press.

Minnaar, A. 1992. *To Leave in Fear: Witchburning and Medicine Murder in Venda*. Pretoria: HSRC.

———. 1997. Witch Purging in the Northern Province of South Africa: a Victim Profile and an Assessment of Initiatives to Deal with Witchcraft. Paper presented to the Nineteenth International Symposium on Victimology. Amsterdam, August 25-29.

Mintz, Sidney, and Richard Price. 1992 [1976]. *The Birth of African-American Culture: An Anthropological Perspective*. Boston: Beacon Press.

Molina, Javier Aguilar. 2005. *The Invention of Child Witches in Democratic Republic of Congo: Social Cleansing, Religious Commerce and the Difficulties of Being a Parent in a Urban Culture*. London: Save the Children UK.

Monga, Celestin. 1998. *Anthropology of Anger. The Civil Society and Democracy in Africa*. Boulda, CO: Lynne Rienner Publishers.

Montero, Paula, ed. 2007. *Deus na aldeia: missionários, índios e mediação cultural*. São Paulo: Globo.

Moore, Henrietta and Todd Sanders, eds. 2001. *Magical Interpretations, Material Realities: Modernity, Witchcraft and the Occult in Postcolonial Africa*. Londres: Routledge.

Moret, Erica. 2008. Afro-Cuban Religion, Ethnobotany and Healthcare in the Context of Global Political and Economic Change. *Bulletin of Latin American Research* 27:333-50.

Mott, Luiz. 1986. Acotundá: raízes setecentistas do sincretismo religioso afro-brasileiro. *Anais do Museu Paulista*, nova série, 31:124-47.

———. 1988a. A vida mística e erótica do escravo José Francisco Pereira 1705–1736. *Tempo Brasileiro* 92/93:85–104.

———. 1988b. *Escravidão, homossexualidade e demonologia.* São Paulo: Ícone.

———. 1993. *Rosa Egipcíaca: uma santa africana no Brasil.* Rio de Janeiro: Bertrand.

———. 1994. O calundu angola de Luzia Pinta: Sabará, 1739. *Revista do Instituto de Artes e Cultura* 1:73–82.

———. 1997. Cotidiano e vivência religiosa: entre capela e o calundu. In *História da vida privada no Brasil: cotidiano e vida privada na América portuguesa.* São Paulo: Companhia das Letras.

———. 2006. Transgressão na calada da noite. Um sabá de feiticeiras e demônios no Piauí colonial. *Textos de História—Revista da Pós-Graduação em História da UnB* 14, 1/2:57–84.

Mouiche, Ibrahim. 2005. *Autorités traditionnelles et démocratisation au Cameroun: entre centralité de l'Etat et logiques du terroir.* Munster: Lit Verlag.

Mudimbe, Valentin Y. 1994. *The Idea of Africa.* Bloomington: Indiana University Press.

Navarro, Desiderio. 1998 [1978]. El folklor y unos cuantos peligros. In *Estudios afrocubanos: selección de lecturas I,* ed. Lázara Menéndez, 295–326. La Habana: Editorial Felix Varela.

Ndedi Penda, P. 1992. *Le pouvoir aux deux visages: la terreur et la prospérité.* Douala: Publications Galaxi.

Ndjio, Basile. 1995. Sorcellerie, pouvoir et accumulation en pays Bamileke: cas du Gru. Yaounde. Mimeo.

———. 2005. Popular Deconstruction of the Postcolonial Public Sphere. *Africa* 75 (3): 265–94.

———. 2006. *Feymania*: New Wealth, Magic Money and Power in Contemporary Cameroon. PhD diss., University of Amsterdam.

———. 2008. Millennial Democracy and Spectral Reality in Postcolonial Africa. *African Journal of International Affairs* 11 (2): 115–56.

———. 2009. *Mokoagne Moni*: Sorcery, Magic Money and New Forms of Wealth in Contemporary Cameroon. In *Religion of Fools? Superstition in Historical and Comparative Perspective,* ed. Alan Knight and Steve Smith, 271–89. Oxford: Oxford University Press.

Niehaus, Isaac A. 1998. The ANC's Dilemma: The Symbolic Politics of Three Witch-Hunts in the South African Lowveld, 1990–1995. *African Studies Review* 41 (3): 93–118.

———. 2001. *Witchcraft, Power and Politics: Exploring the Occult in the South African Lowveld.* London: Pluto Press.

Nkatazo, Lebo. 2006. Zimbabwe Outlaws Practise of Witchcraft. *News*

Zimbabwe, 24 April. http://www.wwrn.org/article.php?idd=21276&se
c=39&con=62.

Nogueira, André. 2004. Da trama: práticas mágicas/feitiçaria como espe-
lho das relações sociais—Minas Gerais, século XVIII. *Mneme, Revista Virtual de Humanidades* 11 (5): 1-16. http://www.seol.com.br/mneme.

Noiriel, Gérard. 2005. *État, nation, immigration. Vers une histoire du pouvoir*.
Paris: Gallimard.

————, ed. 2007. *L'identification. Génèse d'un travail d'État*. Paris: Belin.

Oats, Stephen B. *The Fires of Jubilee: Nat Turner's Fierce Rebellion*. New York:
Harper & Row, 1990.

Olivier, Bert. The Need for a College of Ideas. *Thought Leader*, May 12, 2008,
http://www.thoughtleader.co.za/bertolivier/2008/05/12/the-need-
for-a-college-of-ideas/.

Oosterbaan, Martijn. 2006. Divine Mediations: Pentecostalism, Politics
and Mass Media in a Favela in Rio de Janeiro. PhD diss., University of
Amsterdam.

Ortiz, Fernando. 1921. Los cabildos afrocubanos. *Revista Bimestre Cubana*
16:5-39.

————. 1973 [1906]. *Los negros brujos*. Miami: Ediciones Universal.

————. 1940. *Contrapunteo cubano del tabaco y el azúcar*. La Habana:
J. Montero.

Ortiz, Renato. 1991. *A morte branca do feiticeiro negro: umbanda e sociedade
brasileira*. São Paulo: Brasiliense.

Palmié, Stephan. 1996. Which Center, Whose Margin? Notes Towards an
Archaeology of U.S. Supreme Court Case 91-948, 1993. In *Inside and
Outside the Law*, ed. Olivia Harris, 184-209. London: Routledge.

————. 1998. Fernando Ortiz and the Cooking of History. *Iberoameri-
kanisches Archiv* 24:353-73.

————. 2002. *Wizards and Scientists: Explorations in Afro-Cuban Modernity
and Tradition*. Durham: Duke University Press.

————. 2005. The Cultural Work of Yoruba Globalization. In *Christianity
and Social Change in Africa*, ed. Toyin Falola, 43-83. Durham: Carolina
Academic Press.

————. 2006. Thinking with Ngangas: Reflections on Embodiment and
the Limits of 'Objectively Necessary Appearances.' *Comparative Studies
in Society and History* 48:852-86.

Pantoja, Selma. 2004. Inquisição, degredo e mestiçagem em Angola no século XVIII. *Revista Lusófona de Ciência das Religiões* 3(5-6): 117-36.

Parés, Luis Nicolau. 2006. *A formação do candomblé: história e ritual da nação jeje na Bahia*. Campinas: UNICAMP.

———. 2010. Memories of Slavery in Religious Ritual: Comparing Benin Vodun and Bahian Candomblé. In *Activating the Past: Latin América in the Black Atlantic*, ed. Andrew Apter and Robin Derby. Cambridge: Cambridge Scholars Press.

Pedroso, Luis Alberto. 2002. Las exposiciones de "cultos afrocubanos" y la necesidad de su reconceptualización. *Catauro* 3:126–41.

Peel, J. D. Y. 1997. A Comparative Analysis of Ogun in Precolonial Yorubaland. In *Africa's Ogun: Old World and New*, ed. Sandra T. Barnes, 263–89. Bloomington: Indiana University Press.

Pels, Peter. 1998. The Magic of Africa: Reflections on a Western Commonplace. *African Studies Review* 41 (3): 193–209.

———. 2003. Introduction: Magic and Modernity. In *Magic and Modernity. Interfaces of Revelation and Concealment*, ed. Birgit Meyer and Peter Pels, 1–38. Stanford: Stanford University Press.

Pereira, Luena. 1999. *Os regressados na cidade de Luanda: um estudo sobre identidade étnica e nacional em Angola*. MA thesis, Universidade São Paulo.

———. 2004. *Os Bakongo de Angola: religião, política e parentesco num bairro de Luanda*. PhD diss., Universidade São Paulo.

Pereira, Nuno Marques. 1939. *Compêndio narrativo do Peregrino da América*. 6th ed. Rio de Janeiro: Publicação da Academia Brasileira.

Perez, Helena, and Casimira Benge. 2006. *O Impacto das acusações de feitiçaria contra crianças em Angola: uma análise na perspectiva da proteção dos direitos humanos*. Luanda: INAC/UNICEF.

Pernambucano, Ulysses. 1932. Assistência a psicopatas em Pernambuco: idéias e realizações. *Arquivos da Assistência a Psicopatas de Pernambuco* 2 (1): 3–57.

Pichardo, Ernesto, and K. B. Forbes. 2006. *Blasfemia: An Investigative Report on Fidel Castro's Intelligence Gathering Religious Front Group*. Washington, DC: Concejo de Latinos Unidos.

Pietz, Willam. 1985. The Problem of the Fetish. I. *Res, Anthropology and Æsthetics* 9: 5–17.

———. 1987. The Problem of the Fetish. II. The Origin of the Fetish. *Res, Anthropology and Æsthetics* 13:23–45.

———. 1988. The Problem of the Fetish. IIIa. Bosman's Guinea and the Enlightenment Theory of Fetichism. *Res, Anthropology and Æsthetics* 16:106–23.

Pool, Robert. 1994. *Dialogue and the Interpretation of Illness—Conversations in a Cameroonian Village*. Oxford: Berg.

Povinelli, Elizabeth. 2002. *The Cunning of Recognition*. Durham: Duke University Press.

Pradelles de Latour, C. H. 1991. *Ethnopsychanalyse en pays bamiléké*. Paris: EPEL.

Prandi, Reginaldo. 1991. *Os candomblés de São Paulo*. São Paulo: Hucitec.

Price, Richard. 2003. O milagre da crioulização: retrospectiv. *Estudos Afro-Asiáticos* 25 (3): 308-419.

Purchas, Samuel. 1605. *Hakluytus Posthumus or Purchas: His Pilgrimages in Twenty Volumes. Volume VI*. Glasgow: James MacLehose and Sons.

Putnam, Lara. Forthcoming. Rites of Power and Rumors of Race: The Circulation of Supernatural Knowledge and Sacrifice Tales in the Greater Caribbean, 1890-1940. In *Obeah and Other Powers: The Politics of Caribbean Religion and Healing*, ed. Diane Paton and Maarit Forde. Durham: Duke University Press.

Querino, Manuel. 1955. *A raça africana e seus costumes*. Salvador: Livraria Progresso Editora.

Queiroz, Martha Rosa Figueira. 1999. Religiões afro-brasileiras no Recife: intelectuais, policiais e repressão. MA thesis, Universidade Federal de Pernambuco.

Raboteau, Albert J. 1978. *Slave Religion: The "Invisible Institution" in the Antebellum South*. New York: Oxford University Press.

Rafael, Ulisses Neves. 2004. *Xangô rezado baixo: um estudo da perseguição aos terreiros em 1912*. PhD diss., Programa de Pós-Graduação em Sociologia e Antropologia, IFCS/UFRJ.

Ramos, Arthur. 1931. O Problema psicológico do curandeirismo. *Brasil-Médico* 42: 978-80.

———. 1934. *O Negro brasileiro: etnografia religiosa e psicanálise*. Rio de Janeiro, Ed. Civilização Brasileira.

Ranger, Terence. 2006. African Religion, Witchcraft and the Liberation War in Zimbabwe. In *Studies in Witchcraft, Magic and War and Peace in Africa*, ed. B. Nicolini, 351-79. New York: Edwin Mellen Press.

———. 2007. Scotland Yard in the Bush: Medicine Murders, Child Witches and the Construction of the Occult: A Literature Review. *Africa* 77 (2): 272-84.

Redding, Sean. 2006. *Sorcery and Sovereignty: Taxation, Power and Rebellion in South Africa, 1880-1963*. Athens, Ohio: Ohio University Press.

Rediker, M., and P. Linebaugh. 2001. *The Many-Headed Hydra: Sailors, Slaves, Commoners, and the Hidden History of the Revolutionary Atlantic*. London: Verso.

Reis, João José. 1988. Magia jeje na Bahia: a invasão do calundu de Pasto de Cachoeira, 1785. *Revista Brasileira de História* 8, 16: 57-81.

———. 1989. Nas malhas do poder escravista: a invasão do candomblé do Accú. In *Negociação e conflito: a resistência negra no Brasil escravista*, ed. João José Reis and Eduardo Silva, 32–61. São Paulo: Companhia das Letras.

———. 1993. *Slave Rebellion in Brazil: The Muslim Uprising of 1835 in Bahia*. Baltimore: Johns Hopkins University Press.

———. 2001. Candomblé in Nineteenth-Century Bahia: Priests, Followers, Clients. In *Rethinking the African Diáspora*, ed. Kristin Mann and Edna G. Bay, 116–34. London: Frank Cass.

———. 2008. *Domingos Sodré, um sacerdote africano: escravidão, liberdade e candomblé na Bahia do século XIX*. São Paulo: Companhia das Letras.

Ribeiro, Leonídio and Murilo de Campos. 1931. *O espiritismo no Brasil, contribuição ao seu estudo clínico e médico-legal*. São Paulo: Editora Nacional.

Ribeiro, René. 1956. Possessão—problema de etno-psicologia. *Boletim do Instituto Joaquim Nabuco de Pesquisas Sociais* 5:6–44.

———. 1978 [1952]. *Cultos afro-brasileiros do Recife: um estudo de ajustamento social*. Recife: Instituto Joaquim Nabuco de Pesquisas Sociais.

Ribeiro, René, and Eulina Lins. 1935. Quatro anos de atividade do Serviço de Higiene Mental. *Arquivos da Assistência a Psicopatas de Pernambuco* 5 (1/2): 71–7.

Rio, João do. 2006 [1904]. *As religiões do Rio*. Rio de Janeiro: Editora José Olympio.

Roa del Rey, Annet, and Yalexy Castañeda Mache. 2002. El revivamiento religioso en Cuba. *Temas* 31:93–100.

Robbins, Joel. 2008. Sobre a alteridade e o sagrado em uma época de globalização. O "trans" em "transnacional" é o mesmo "trans" de "transcendente"? *Mana* 14 (1): 119–39.

Rodrigues, Raimundo Nina. 1935 [1896, 1900]. *O animismo fetichista dos negros baianos*. Rio de Janeiro: Civilização Brasileira.

———. 2004 [1906]. *Os Africanos no Brasil*. Brasília: Editora Universidade de Brasília.

Román, Reinaldo. 2007. *Governing Spirits: Religion, Miracles, and Spectacles in Cuba and Puerto Rico, 1898–1956*. Chapel Hill: University of North Carolina Press.

Roper, Lyndal. 2000. "Evil Imaginings and Fantasies": Child-Witches and the End of the Witch Craze. *Past and Present* 167:107–39.

Rosny, Eric de. 1981. *Les yeux de ma chèvre—Sur les pas des maîtres de la nuit en pays douala*. Paris: Plon.

———. 1993. *L'Afrique des guérisons*. Paris: Karthala.

Routon, Kenneth. 2006. The Cuban "Ministry of Orula" or the Transnational Politics of Prophecy. *Anthropology News* December: 6–7.

———. 2008. Conjuring the Past: Slavery and the Historical Imagination in Cuba. *American Ethnologist* 35:634–49.

Rowlands, Michael. 1993. Economic Dynamism and Cultural Stereotyping in the Bamenda Grassfields. In *Les itinéraires d'accumulation au Cameroun*, ed. Peter Geschiere and Piet Konings, 71–99. Paris: Karthala.

Rowlands, Michael, and Jean-Pierre Warnier. 1988. Sorcery, Power and the Modern State in Cameroon. *Man*, New Series 23 (1): 118–32.

Rush, James. 1990. *Opium to Java: Revenue Farming and Chinese Enterprise in Colonial Indonesia, 1860–1910*. Ithaca, NY: Cornell University Press.

Rutherford, Blair. 1999. To Find an African Witch: Anthropology, Modernity and Witch-finding in North-West Zambia. *Critique of Anthropology* 19 (1): 89–109.

Ryle, John. 1998. Miracles of the People: How a French Ethnologist Became a Magician in Brazil. *Times Literary Supplement*, July 31.

Sá, Vera Borges de. 2001. *Religião e poder: introdução à história do espiritismo em Pernambuco*. PhD diss., Universidade Federal de Pernambuco.

Sanders, Todd. 2008. Buses in Bongoland: Seductive Analytics and the Occult. *Anthropological Theory* 8:107–32.

Sansi, Roger. 2003. *Fetishes, Commodities, Images, Art Works. Afro-Brazilian Art and Culture in Bahia*, PhD diss., University of Chicago.

———. 2005. Catholic Saints, African Gods, Black Masks and White Heads: Tracing the History of some Religious Festivals in Bahia. *Journal of Portuguese Studies* 21 (1): 182–200.

Schatzberg Michael G. 2000. La sorcellerie comme mode de causalité politique. *Politique Africaine. Le dossier povouirs sorciers* 79: 33–47.

Scheper-Hughes, Nancy, 1995. Who's the Killer? Popular Justice in a South African Squatter Camp. *Social Justice* 22 (3): 143–64.

———. 1996. Theft of Life: The Globalization of Organ Stealing Rumors. *Anthropology Today* 12 (2): 3–5.

Schmitt, Jean Claude. 1976. Religion populaire' et culture folklorique'. *Annales: Economies, Societes, Civilisations* 31 (5): 941–53.

Scott, James. 1985. *The Weapon of the Weak: Everyday Forms of Peasant Resistance*. New Haven and London: Yale University Press.

———. 1990. *Domination and the Arts of Resistance. Hidden Transcripts*. New Haven and London: Yale University Press.

Shaw, Rosalind. 1997. The Production of Witchcraft/Witchcraft as Production: Memory, Modernity, and the Slave Trade in Sierra Leone. *American Ethnologist* 24 (4): 856–76.

———. 2002. *Memories of the Slave Trade: Ritual and the Historical Imagination in Sierra Leone*. Chicago: University of Chicago Press.

Silveira, Renato da. 2006. *O candomblé da Barroquinha: processo de constituição do primeiro terreiro baiano de Keto*. Salvador: Maianga.

Skidmore, Thomas E. 1993. *Black into White: Race and Nationality in Brazilian Thought*. Durham: Duke University Press.

Smith, James Howard. 2008. *Bewitching Development: Witchcraft and the Reinvention of Development in Neoliberal Kenya*. Chicago: University of Chicago Press.

Soares, Cecília Moreira. 1992. Resistência negra e religião: a repressão ao candomblé de Paramerim, 1853. *Estudos Afro-Asiáticos* 23:133-42.

Southall, Roger. 1982. *South Africa's Transkei: The Political Economy of an "Independent" Bantustan*. London: Heinemann.

Souza, Laura de Mello e. 1986. *O diabo e a terra de Santa Cruz*. São Paulo: Companhia das Letras (English edition. 2003. *The Devil and the Land of the Holy Cross*. Translated by Diane Grossklaus Witty. Austin: University of Texas Press).

———. 1991-92. Witchcraft and Magic Practices in Colonial Brazil—1580-1770. *Acta Ethnografica Hungarica* 34:243-56.

———. 1993. *Inferno Atlântico—demonologia e colonização*. São Paulo: Companhia das Letras.

———. 2002. Revisitando o calundu. In *Ensaios sobre a intolerância—Inquisição, Marranismo e Anti-semitismo*, ed. Lina Gorenstein and Maria Luiza Tucci Carneiro, 293-317. São Paulo: Humanitas.

Sterling, Stuckey. 1988. *Nationalist Theory and the Foundations of Black America*. Oxoford: Oxford University Press.

Stewart, Charles, ed. 2007. *Creolization: History and Ethnography*, Walnut Creek, CA: Left Coast Press.

Stobart, Eleanor. 2006. *Child Abuse Linked to Accusations of "Possession" and "Witchcraft."* Research Report n. 750. UK: Departament for Education and Skills. http://www.dfes.gov.uk/research/data/uploadfiles/RR750 .pdf.

Styers, Randall. 2004. *Making Magic: Religion, Magic, and Science in the Modern World*. New York: Oxford University Press.

Sweet, James H. 2003. *Recreating Africa. Culture, Kinship, and Religion in the African-Portuguese World, 1441-1770*. Chapel Hill: University of North Carolina Press.

Takougang, J., and M. Krieger. 1998. *African State and Society in the 1990s: Cameroon Political Crossroads*. Oxford: Westview Press.

Tardits, Claude. 1960. *Les Bamileke de l'Ouest-Cameroun*. Paris: Editions Berget-Levrault.

Taussig, Michael. 1980. *The Devil and Commodity Fetishism in South America*. Chapel Hill: University of North Carolina Press.

———. 1987. *Shamanism, Colonialism, and the Wild Man: A Study in Terror and Healing*. Chicago: University of Chicago Press.

————. 2003. Viscerality, Faith, and Skepticism: Another Theory of Magic. In *Magic and Modernity: Interfaces of Revelation and Concealment*, ed. Birgit Meyer and Peter Pels, 272-306. Stanford: Stanford University Press.

Ter Haar, Gerrie and Stephen Ellis. 2009. The Occult Does Not Exist: A Response to Terence Ranger. *Africa* 73 (3): 399-413.

Terreblanche, Sampie. 2002. *A History of Inequality in South Africa, 1652-2002*. Durban University of Natal Press.

Thomas, Keith. 1991. *Religião e o declínio da magia*. São Paulo: Companhia das Letras.

Tilly, Charles, 2003. *The Politics of Collective Violence*. Cambridge: Cambridge University Press.

Toulabor, Comi M. 1999. Sacrifices humains et politique: quelques examples contemporains en Afrique. In *Trajectoires de libération en Afrique contemporaine*, ed. P. Konings, W. van Binsbergen, and G. Hesseling, 207-223. Paris: Karthala.

Trouillot, Michel-Rolf. 1991. Anthropology and the Savage Slot: The Poetics and Politics of Otherness. In *Recapturing Anthropology*, ed. Richard Fox, 17-44. Santa Fe: SAR Press.

————. 1998. Culture on the Edges: Creolization in the Plantation Context. *Plantation Society in the Americas* 5:8-18.

Turner, Victor. 1954. *Schism and Continuity in an African Society: A Study of Ndembu Village Life*. Manchester: Manchester University Press.

Vainfas, Ronaldo. 1995. *A heresia dos índios*. São Paulo: Companhia das Letras.

Valladares, Lícia. 2005. *A invenção da favela: do mito de origem a favela.com*. Rio de Janeiro: FGV Editora.

Veran, Jean-François. 2003. *L'esclavage em héritage (Brésil)*. Paris: Karthala.

Verger, Pierre. 1981. *Orixás, os deuses iorubás na África e no Novo Mundo*. Salvador: Corrupio.

————. 1985. *Fluxo e refluxo do tráfico de escravos entre o golfo de Benin e a Bahia de Todos os Santos*. Salvador: Corrupio.

Warnier, Jean Pierre. 1985, *Echanges, développement et hiérarchies dans le Bamenda précolonial (Cameroun)*. Stuttgart: Steiner.

————. 1993. *L'esprit d'entreprise au Cameroun*. Paris: Karthala.

Warnier, Jean Pierre, and Dieudonné Miaffo. 1993. Accumulation et ethos de la notabilité chez les Bamiléké. In *Les itinéraires d'accumulation au Cameroun*, ed. Peter Geschiere and Piet Konings, 33-71. Paris: Karthala.

Warwick, Max. 1965. *Sorcery in Its Social Setting: A Study of Rhodesian Cewa*. Manchester: Manchester University Press.

West, Harry G. 2005. *Kupilikula: Governance and the Invisible Realm in Mozambique*. Chicago: University of Chicago Press.

———. 2007. *Ethnographic Sorcery*. Chicago: University of Chicago Press.

White, Louise. 2000. *Speaking with Vampires: Rumor and History in Colonial Africa*. Berkeley: University of California Press.

Witte, Marleen de. 2008. *Spirit Media: Charismatics, Traditionalists and Mediation Practices in Ghana*. PhD diss., University of Amsterdam.

Whiteford, Andrew, and M. McGrath. 1994. *Distribution of Income in South Africa*. Pretoria: Human Sciences Research Council.

Whiteford, Andrew, and Dirk Van Seventer. 1999. *Winners and Losers: A Report on South Africa's Changing Income Distribution in the 1990s*. Pretoria: Wharton Econometric Forecasting Associates.

Wilson, Monica Hunter. 1951. Witch Beliefs and Social Structure. *The American Journal of Sociology* 56, 4: 307–313.

———. 1961 [1936]. *Reaction to Conquest: Effects of Contact with Europeans on the Pondo of South Africa*. 2d ed. London: Oxford University Press for the International African Institute.

Wirtz, Kristina. 2004. Santería in Cuban National Consciousness: A Religious Case of the Doble Moral. *Journal of Latin American Anthropology* 9:409–38.

Wood, Felicity, and Michael Lewis. 2007. *The Extraordinary Khotso: Millionaire Medicine Man from Lusikisiki*. Auckland Park, SA: Jacana Press.

Xavier, Regina. 2003. Dos males e suas curas: práticas médicas na Campinas oitocentista. In *artes e ofícios de curar no Brasil: capítulos de história social*, ed. Sidney Chaloub, Vera Regina Beltrão Marques, Gabriela dos Reis Sampaio and Carlos Roberto Galvão Sobrinho, 331–54. Campinas: Editora Unicamp.

Journals and Magazines

O Jornal da Bahia
O Alabama (Bahia)
Cameroon Tribune
Tribuna da Bahia
Diário da Bahia
Diário da Tarde (Pernambuco)
Diário de Pernambuco
Folha da Manhã (Pernambuco)
Diário do Estado/Diário Oficial
Boletim de Higiene Mental (Pernambuco)

Fronteiras (Pernambuco)
Revista Realidade (Rio de Janeiro)
News Zimbabwe
Evening Standard
The Guardian
BBC News

Archives

APEBa (Arquivo Publico do Estado da Bahia, Salvador, Brazil)
ANTT (Arquivo Nacional da Torre do Tombo, Lisbon, Portugal).
CA (Cape Archives, Cape Town, South Africa)

Contributors

PATRICIA BIRMAN received her PhD from Federal University of Rio de Janeiro in 1988 and is professor of anthropology at the State University of Rio de Janeiro. She has worked on Afro-Brazilian religions and Pentecostalism in Brazil. Her recent publications include the edited volume *Religião e espaço público* (Attar Editorial, 2003) and the articles "Conversion and Participation: Pentecostalism and Political Change in Brazil," in *Conversion of a Continent: Religious Identity and Change in Latin America*, edited by Edward Clearly, Henri Gooren, and Timothy Steigenga (Rutgers University Press, 2007); and "Future at the Mirror: Media, Evangelicals and Politics in Rio de Janeiro," in *Religion, Media and the Public Sphere*, edited by Birgit Meyer and Annelies Moors (Indiana University Press, 2006).

KATHERINE FIDLER received her PhD from Emory University in 2010 and is assistant professor of history at the Loyola University New Orleans. Her research interests are in African history (especially Southern Africa), comparative imperial history, decolonization and independence, state formation and political culture, history and anthropology, transnational history, theories of resistance and revolution, and the history of human rights. She has conducted research in Southern Africa, Rwanda, and the eastern Democratic Republic of Congo. She is a contributing author for a collection of essays on the Pondoland Revolt in South Africa edited by Thembela Kepe and Lungisile Ntsebeza. She is currently working on a project on rural insurgency and the history of trauma in the Eastern Cape of South Africa.

PETER GESCHIERE is professor of African anthropology at the University of Amsterdam (formerly Leiden University), fellow of the Royal Netherlands Academy of Sciences, and board member of the Prince Claus Fund. He did fieldwork in different parts of West Africa, but mainly in Cameroon, on topics like the local effects of state formation, citizenship and belonging, and the dynamics of local cultures in interaction with broader processes of change. His main publications are *The Modernity of Witchcraft, Politics and the Occult in Postcolonial Africa* (University of Virginia Press, 1997; 3d edition, 2005); with Birgit Meyer, *Globalization and Identity, Dialectics of Flow and Closure* (Blackwell, 1999); and *Perils of Belonging—Autochthony, Citizenship and Exclusion in Africa and Europe* (University of Chicago Press, 2009).

YVONNE MAGGIE received her PhD in social anthropology from the Federal University of Rio de Janeiro in 1988 and is a chaired professor at the Cultural Anthropology Department of the Institute of Philosophy and Social Sciences of the Federal University of Rio de Janeiro. She has been director of the Institute of Philosophy and Social Sciences of the Federal University of Rio de Janeiro, as well as director of the university press of the same institution. She has been awarded three prizes: the *Premio Arquivo Nacional*, the *Premio Érico Vannucci Mendes* SBPC/CNPq, and the *Comenda Nacional da Ordem do Mérito Científico do Governo do Brasil*. Among her publications, the most important ones are *Guerra de orixá: um estudo de ritual e conflito* (Zahar, 1977), *Medo do feitiço: relações entre magia e poder no Brasil* (Arquivo Nacional, 1992), *Raça como retórica* with Claudia Barcelo Rezende (Civilização Brasileira, 2002), and *Divisões perigosas* with Peter Fry, Simone Monteiro, Ricardo Ventura Santos, Marcos Chor Maio (Civilização Brasileira, 2007). She currently coordinates a research project named *Culturas de gestão e a educação no Rio de Janeiro*.

BASILE NDJIO received his PhD in social and cultural anthropology from the University of Amsterdam, 2006, teaches social and political anthropology at the University of Douala in Cameroon, and has been a visiting lecturer or a research fellow in several universities in Europe and the United States. He has written on topics as varied as popular culture, the democratization process in Africa, civil society and the state, autochthony and the politics of belonging, and new forms of wealth and power in postcolonial Africa. His most recent works include "Intimate Strangers: Neighborhood, Autochthony and the Politics of Belonging," in *Crisis and Creativity: Exploring the Wealth of the African Neighbourhood*, edited by P. Konings and D. Foecken (Brill, 2006); "Douala: Inventing Life in an African Necropolis," in *Cities in Contemporary Africa*, edited by M. Martin and G. Myers (Palgrave/Macmillan, 2006); "Millennial Democracy and Spectral Reality in Postcolonial Africa," in the *African Journal of International Affairs* (volume 11, 2008); and "Shanghai Beauties and African Desires: Migration,

Trade and Chinese Prostitution in Cameroon," in the *European Journal of Development Research* (volume 21, 2009).

STEPHAN PALMIÉ received his PhD from the University of Munich in 1989 and a Habilitation from the University of Munich in 1999 and is associate professor of anthropology at the University of Chicago. He conducts ethnographic and historical research on Afro-Caribbean cultures, with an emphasis on Afro-Cuban religious formations and their relations to the history and cultures of a wider Atlantic world. His other interests include practices of historical representation and knowledge production, systems of slavery and unfree labor, constructions of race and ethnicity, conceptions of embodiment and moral personhood, medical anthropology, and the anthropology of food and cuisine. His works include the edited volumes *Slave Cultures and the Cultures of Slavery* (University of Tennessee Press, 1996) and *Africas of the Americas: Beyond the Search for Origins in the Study of Afro-Atlantic Religions* (Brill 2008) and the monograph *Wizards and Scientists: Explorations in Afro-Cuban Modernity and Tradition* (Duke University Press, 2002).

LUIS NICOLAU PARÉS received his PhD from the School of Oriental and African Studies, University of London, in 1997 and is professor of anthropology at the Federal University of Bahia. With ethnographic fieldwork in Bahia, Maranhão, and the Republic of Benin, his interests include the history and anthropology of West African and Afro-Brazilian religions and their cultural transformations in the Atlantic context. He is the author of *A formação do candomblé: história e ritual da nação jeje na Bahia* (Editora Unicamp, 2006) and is a past editor of the journal *Afro-Ásia*.

LUENA NUNES PEREIRA received her PhD in social anthropology from the University of São Paulo in 2005 and is currently a tenured professor at the Rural Federal University of Rio de Janeiro. Her main research interests include studies of the relations between ethnic and national identities and, more recently, religious identity in Angola. These issues are addressed via fieldwork in Luanda among the Bakongo community, one of the main ethnic groups in Angola and the Congos. Her latest research project is entitled "Igrejas, parentesco e feitiçaria: um estudo sobre Crianças-Feiticeiras em Angola."

JOÃO JOSÉ REIS received his PhD from the University of Minnesota in 1983 and is professor of history at the Federal University of Bahia in Brazil. He has worked extensively on slavery and rebellions in nineteenth-century Bahia. He is author of *Slave Rebellion in Brazil: The Muslim Uprising of 1835 in Bahia* (Johns Hopkins University Press, 1994) and *Death Is a Festival: Funeral Rites and Rebellion in Nineteenth-Century Brazil* (University of North Carolina Press, 2003), which is a winner of the Clarence H. Harring Prize of the AHA 1996.

ROGER SANSI received his PhD in anthropology from the University of Chicago in 2003 and is a lecturer in anthropology at the Goldsmith College of the University of London. He has conducted research on art, religion, and Afro-Brazilian culture in Salvador, Bahia. Currently he is studying the problem of the *feitiço* in the lusophone Atlantic. His recent publications include *Fetishes and Monuments: Afro-Brazilian Art and Culture in the 20th Century* (Berghahn Books, 2007) and the edited volume *Cultures of the Lusophone Black Atlantic* (Palgrave, 2007).

LAURA DE MELLO E SOUZA received her PhD in social history from the University of São Paulo in 1986 and is currently a chaired professor in modern history at the University of São Paulo. Her research interests include culture and society in colonial Brazil, magic, and popular religion in Portuguese America (1500s to 1700s), as compared with Spanish America. She is the author of *O diabo e a terra de Santa Cruz: feitiçaria e religiosidade popular no Brasil colonial* (Companhia das Letras, 1986); *Inferno Atlântico— demonologia e colonização: séculos XVI-XVIII* (Companhia das Letras, 1993); editor of *Discurso histórico e político sobre a sublevação que nas Minas houve no ano de 1720* (Fundação João Pinheiro, 1994); and coordinator of the *História da vida privada no Brasil.- Vol. I. Cotidiano e vida privada na América Portuguesa* (Companhia das Letras, 1997).

DANIEL STONE received his PhD in Portuguese and Brazilian Studies from King's College London in 2008 and has conducted research in Recife, Brazil, on the study of Afro-Brazilian religion by intellectual elites during the 1930s. His doctoral thesis looked at the relationships between these intellectuals and members of the religious groups they were studying, as well as examining concepts of sorcery, mental health, and culture during this period.

Index

Abimbola, Wande, 139

Abreu, Custódia, 51

Abreu, Joana Pereira de, 50–51

accusations, sorcery/witchcraft, 2–4, 12–13, 16, 19, 68, 76, 80, 91n4, 96, 98, 111–12, 121, 149, 150–52, 159, 165, 166, 168, 169, 174–75, 177, 183, 184, 198, 201, 203, 209–11, 247; Azande political system and, 157; against *macumbeiros*, 149, 155–56, 162n6, 222; mutual, 68, 157; Pentecostal, 194–95, 197, 202, 226, 253. *See also* child witch accusations; Rio de Janeiro; *specific topics*

accuser and accused, ambiguity between, 22

Adão, Pai, 108–9, 112, 118n61, 119n69, 120n74

Adechina (Remigio Herrera), 142

adolescents. *See* child witch accusations; Rio de Janeiro

Africa, 26–28; as "other," 19; sorcery and, 19. *See also specific topics*

African National Congress (ANC), 78, 82, 90, 91, 166, 178, 182, 184

Africanness of witchcraft, 37

Afro-Brazilian Congress, 110, 113, 119n67

Afro-Brazilian cults, 35, 45, 109–10, 112, 146, 157, 209, 215, 217, 228n9, 231n25

Afro-Brazilian devils, 210

Afro-Brazilian practices, 17, 36, 44, 46, 115n7. *See also* Brazil; Candomblé houses

Afro-Brazilian religion(s), 15, 46, 56, 95–97, 99, 102, 107–13, 114n1, 114n7, 115n13, 116n26, 145, 147–53, 157, 160–61, 215, 226. *See also* Brazil; Candomblé; Macumba; Xangô

Afro-Brazilian rites, 47, 161n1, 162n6

Afro-Brazilian spirits/entities, 160, 214, 217, 225, 229n13

Aguirre, Mirta, 144n11

alterity/othering, 8–9, 78, 170, 211. *See also* otherness; subalternity/subaltern; witch-others

Álvarez, Chávez, 127

ambiguity, 3, 4, 8–10, 242, 244–45; forms of, 22; between secrecy and skepticism, 7, 21–22; suspicion and, 206–7. *See also under* moral; sorcery; witchcraft discourse

Amin, Shahid, 78

amulets, 8, 22–23, 55, 69

Andrade, Mário de, 41

Angola. *See* Bakongo; child witch accusations

Angola, Antonio, 52–53, 64

Angola nation, 46

Angolan National Child Institute (INAC), 196, 197, 199

animism, 36

animismo fetichista dos negros baianos, O (Rodrigues), 115, 147–48

anthropologists, 3, 6, 13, 148, 165, 234, 246–49; engaging in the politics of witchcraft, 234–35. *See also* Brazil

antisorcery. *See* witch-hunts

apartheid. *See* Pondoland; South Africa

Argüelles Mederos, Aníbal, 136, 138

Arnold Janssen Centre of Luanda, 188, 197–203

Asociación Cultural Yorubá, 140–42

atabaques, 154

Atlantic, denial of its existence as a space of culture, 5

de Witte, Marleen, 252

debt redeemed through selling a relative, 243–45

democracy: "appeased," 177; vs. demonocracy, 167–72, 180, 185n5; liberal, 165, 167, 168, 170, 182 (*see also* neoliberalism). *See also* Cameroon

democratization: political, 190, 238 (*see also* Brazil; Cameroon); of witchcraft, 204

"demoncrats," 168, 181; defined, 185n5

demonocracy vs. democracy, 167–72, 180, 185n5

demons, 51, 220n24. *See also* Pentecostal exorcism and curing rituals

d'Epié, Alobwede, 239

"deviants," 130, 175, 220–24, 230n20

devil, 21, 30, 51–52, 62, 222; Exu as, 154, 160, 218; Exu contrasted with the, 160–61; presence in the Brazilian imaginary, 41. *See also feitiçaria*

devil pacts, 122

devil worship, 213

diabo e a terra de Santa Cruz, O (Souza), 14, 41–43, 46

Díaz, Zoila, 126

discourse: definitions and meanings, 18n7. *See also* sorcery discourse; witchcraft discourse

disenchantment, 3, 49, 172, 182, 251

divination, 42, 48, 55, 58, 59, 70, 142, 144n14

diviners, 58, 64, 67, 68, 70, 78–79, 85, 119n69

do Rio, João (Paulo Barreto), 34, 148, 149, 157

Dossu, Francisco, 68–69

Douala, 167, 238, 243, 244, 256n17; as ethnic group, 237, 238, 254n8, 255n12

doubt, 2, 7, 11, 21, 160, 179

Douglas, Mary, 121, 123, 251

drug dealers, 17, 210, 211, 213, 216, 217, 224–26, 229n10; as Afro-Brazilian devils, 226; "quasi-conversion," 226

drug gangs, 214–17, 226, 229n12

drug trafficking, 211, 213

drug use, 221

drugging people, 65

economic inequality, 166, 182, 235. *See also* power inequalities; social inequality; wealth

Ejedepang-Koge, S. N., 238, 239–40

ekom, 238–40, 244

ekong, 237, 238, 240, 243–46, 254n8, 255n10, 255n12

elders, 82, 185nn9–10, 192–93, 249; accused of by witches, 175

enchantment, 2, 30, 121, 250–51; techniques of, 7

Englund, Harri, 233–34

"enlightened spirits," 147–48, 160

Enlightenment, 5, 31–33, 49, 146, 158

enslavement, 16, 33, 135, 172, 180–81, 183, 240. *See also* slavery; zombification and enslavement

Europe-Africa dialectic, 5–6, 9, 19, 21, 26, 28, 30, 33, 36–37

European tradition and sorcery, 3, 41

evangelical action, potential of, 17, 230n24

evangelicals, 161, 211–13, 219, 221, 223–26. *See also* Pentecostalism

Evans-Pritchard, Edward E., 3, 6–7, 10, 23, 31, 79, 121–22, 143n3, 146, 156–58, 251

evil, 213; occult forces as, 248; Pentecostal transcendence of, 209, 229n13; as relative vs. absolute, 218; sorcery and, 9, 79, 161; witchcraft and, 79, 161. *See also* devil; Exu; magic; Pondoland

"evil forces," 167, 169, 172, 173, 175, 180, 181, 212, 213

exorcism, 62, 220n24. *See also* Pentecostal exorcism and curing rituals

Exu, 154–56, 160–61, 230n19; Alice and the wink of the, 214–19; Seu Sete da Lira and, 154–56

"false spiritualism." *See* spiritualism, "false" or "low"

families: tension between paternal and maternal, 193. *See also* child witch accusations; relatives

famla, 176, 185n12, 240–42, 244, 255nn13–15

famla-njangi, 241, 244. See also *njangi*

favelas, 17, 209–11, 213–18, 225–26, 227n4, 228n5, 229n10, 229n15

Federation of Afro-Brazilian Cults, 110

feitiçaria (sorcery/witchcraft), 14, 22–27, 110; discourse of, 21, 24–26, 37; vs. *fetichismo*, 35; meanings and etymology of the term, 19, 21, 191; slavery and, 24, 68–69. *See also mandinga*; sorcery; witchcraft

feiticeiro(a), 25, 27, 69, 71, 115n12, 115n16, 150-51, 161n3, 162n4
feitiço (*fetisso*, spell/hex/charm/witch power), 14, 19-23, 30, 31, 37, 38n4, 53, 70-72, 162n4, 188, 191, 198, 200; children acquiring, 190; vs. fetish, 26, 27, 33; meanings and etymology of the term, 8, 19, 21, 33
Fernandes, Gonçalves, 108-9, 113, 116n26
Ferrão, João de Argolo, 67-68
fetish (*fetiche*), 26, 28, 37, 148; Africa and, 20-21, 30-31, 33, 35; discourse of, 20, 21; vs. *feitiço*, 26, 27, 33; history of the term, 14, 19-21, 29, 33; personalization, 26; Protestantism and, 32
fetishism (*fetichismo*), 26, 28-33, 35, 39n12, 129; Africa and, 20-21, 35, 37; and capitalism, 4, 19, 20, 32; discourse of, 5, 6, 20, 21, 35-36, 184; as general theory of creativity, 20; history of the term, 14, 19-21, 32, 34-37; and religion, 8, 32-33, 36; and sorcery, 19, 28; and the trap of history, 35-37; triumph of modernity over, 20
"fetishist animism," 13, 99
Fetishistic Animism of Bahian Blacks, The (Rodrigues), 115, 147-48
"fetishistic suggestions," 105
"fetish-men," 27
fires. *See* burning
Fisiy, Cyprian F., 169, 175, 241
fons (chiefs/customary rulers), 171, 173-75, 177, 241-42, 256n16
Fontaine, Jean, 3
foreigner as powerful sorcerer, 25, 122, 204
freedom. *See* slave resistance
Freemasonry, 34
Fry, Peter, 158, 230n17

Gell, Alfred, 10-11
Geschiere, Peter, 4-5, 9, 17, 19, 77, 122, 122, 146, 165, 175-76
Ghana, 252
Giumbelli, Emerson, 97, 98, 101, 113, 116n23, 116n27, 120n73
global capitalism, 122, 140, 142, 234
global capitalist sorcery, 125
globalization, 4, 19, 54, 121, 121, 191, 245, 245, 246, 246, 256n21
Gonzales, Philippe, 230n24
Gracinda, 66

Grassfields, 173, 176, 177, 240-43, 254n9
gru ordeal (*ngru*), 16, 166, 181, 183, 256n17; and the political invention of witches, 172-78, 185nn8-10, 186n12
Guanche, Jesús, 136, 137
Guerra de orixá: um estudo de ritual e conflito (Maggie), 18n14, 149, 156
Guha, Ranajit, 78
Guinea, 23, 29, 33; fetish worship in, 30-31. *See also mandinga*

Harding, Rachel, 24, 56-57, 66, 70
healers, traditional, 44, 58, 61, 64, 68, 153, 156, 167, 188, 190, 193, 197-200, 202, 235, 237-38, 247, 251-52, 256, 258n32. *See also* child witch accusations; *curandieros*; *nganga*
herbalists, 79, 85-87. *See also* medicine men
herbs, 46, 48, 64, 65, 67, 69, 70, 85
Herrera, Remigio (*Adechina*), 142
Herskovits, Melville, 113
Hodge Limonta, Ileana, 136, 138
hypnosis, 100, 101, 150, 237, 254n8
hysteria, 100, 165

Ifá, 59, 142, 144n11
impundulu (lightning bird), 86
individualism, 3, 179, 180
Inferno Atlântico—deomonlogia e colonização (Souza), 44
initiation process, 65-67
Inquisition, Holy, 23-25, 46, 47, 49, 50, 52, 53; records, 13, 22, 41, 44, 45
Instituto Nacional da Criança (INAC). *See* Angolan National Child Institute
intermediate spaces, 5
internationalism, 125, 140, 142
"invention" of sorcerers and witches, 172, 177, 183, 184
Israel, Paolo, 123

James Figarola, Joel, 139
Jeje, 55, 63, 68
Jewsiewicki, Bogumil, 244-45, 248-50, 257n26
João I, King, 21, 38n4
Jojo, Gaulibso, 83

Kapferer, Bruce, 7, 8, 10, 23, 251
Kardec, Allan, 114n2

Kardecist spiritualism, 114n2, 115n7. *See also* spiritualism

kindoki (occult power), 191. See also *feitiço*

kingship, 28

kinship, 9, 203, 205–7, 217, 243, 245, 246, 252, 256n18; and churches in the redefinition of witchcraft, 16, 191–95; and the market, 243–45; reversal of, 245; ritual, 161

kraals (huts), burning, 76, 85–87, 89

kundu, 191

kupe, 240, 241, 244

Kupe, Mount, 237–40, 246, 255n11

lançados, 23, 29. See also *tangomago*

Lapassade, Georges, 149, 156

lavagem, 34, 39n11

Leach, James, 233–34

liberal democracy, 165, 167, 168, 170, 182. *See also* Cameroon; democracy; neoliberalism

liberalization: economic, 204, 208n13; political, 167–70, 178

lightning, 86, 90

liras, 154–55

Lombroso, Cesare, 130, 147

Lopes, Ivo, 48

Los negros brujos, 131

Luis de Lima, 23

Luso-American magical practices, 42, 44

Luso-Brazilian sorcery, 49. *See also* Brazil

Lusophone Atlantic world, 14, 21–23, 26, 28, 69, 184, 185n6; Black Atlantic and the, 12–14, 17, 18n15

Luz, Marco Aurélio, 149, 156

Macacos, 52

Macedo, Edir, 228n9

macumba, 6, 105, 156, 214, 221–22, 225–26; as Afro-Brazilian religious institution, 145, 162n6; meanings and connotations of the term, 162n6, 229n11. *See also* Seu Sete da Lira

macumbeiros, 162n6, 221; accusations against, 149, 155–56, 162n6, 222

mães-de-santo (mother of the saint), 160, 161n1

Magalhães, Agamemnon, 109–10, 119n70

Magalhães, Antonio Carlos, 159–60

Maggie, Yvonne, 12, 16, 18n14, 34, 96, 98, 98–99, 111–12, 111–12, 231n25, 251

magic, 1, 29–31, 36, 43, 77–79, 81–82, 90–91, 96–99, 105–6, 111–12, 143n1, 145–47, 153, 160, 211, 218, 227, 233, 247; low, 106–7, 121; and modernity, 3–4, 16, 18n12, 19, 77, 79, 90, 124, 257n28; money, 181, 183, 186n16, 256n18; vs. sorcery, 6–8, 10–11, 18n10; as a symbolic technique, 10–11; used for good vs. evil, 34, 79, 85, 149–51, 156; in Western social thought, 122–23. *See also* Obeah

magical practices, 22, 34, 42–49, 53, 56, 107, 121

magicians vs. witches, 256n23

Maka, 249–50, 254

Mandinga, 23, 28, 42

mandinga, 6, 20, 21, 23–26, 30, 37, 38n1; *bolsas de mandinga*, 8, 23–26, 38n2, 42, 49. See also *feitiçaria*; pouches

Manuel (enslaved cult head), 64

Manuel de Piedade, 23

market economy, 191, 203, 243–45. *See also* capitalism; neoliberalism

Marques, Xavier, 34, 35

Martínez Furé, Rogelio, 137, 139

Matanzima (chief), 82, 85–86, 88

Mbanza Kongo, 196–98, 206

Mbunwe-Samba, Patrick, 241, 255n14

media, 91, 139, 167, 208n6, 235, 252; Brazilian, 17, 210, 212–13, 217, 225, 228n8

mediation, 193, 202–3, 218, 224. *See also* Arnold Janssen Centre of Luanda; power mediation

medicine men, 79, 87, 102, 108, 149–50. *See also* herbalists

mediums, 53–56, 97, 100, 101, 105, 153–54, 156; licensing, 103; "manifestations" of, 104; psychiatric evaluation of, 103, 104, 110, 117n35; research on, 104, 107

Medo do feitiço: relações entre magia e poder no Brasil (Maggie), 34, 149, 153, 156, 158

Mende, 28. *See also* Mandinga

Mental Hygiene Service (SHM), 15, 95–98; Afro-Brazilian religion and, 107–11; the charlatan and the sorcerer, 111–13; legal and medical approaches to magic and spiritualism, 98–102; spiritualism and, 102–7

mental illness: spirit possession and, 100, 101, 108, 109. *See also* Mental Hygiene Service

Mina, Maria, 69
missionaries, 29, 38n5, 50, 52, 53, 191, 226,
237, 239; Congo and, 29, 193. *See also
under* Pentecostalism
modernity, 21, 112, 122, 233, 250; Africa and,
112, 140, 234, 236; African, 250; Afro-
Cuban religious, 125, 140-42; capitalist,
123, 143n5; Congo and, 91; denial of the
reality of occult powers in the name of,
251; fetishism and, 20, 21; increasing
mobility as hallmark of, 236; indigenous
Caribbean, 142; malcontents of, 122, 172;
metanarrative on, 233-34; nature of, 32,
122; primitivism and, 112; scientific, 125,
141-42; socialist, 140, 141; sorcery and,
2-5, 19, 20, 27, 36, 77; vs. tradition, 21, 91,
163n12; Western form of, 250; of witchcraft, 39n17, 77, 184, 235; witchcraft and,
19, 77, 122, 125, 145-47, 191, 233-36, 246,
250-51; without sorcery, belief in a, 36.
See also Cameroon
Modernity and Its Malcontents (Comaroff and
Comaroff), 122
Modernity of Witchcraft, The (Geschiere),
122, 236
Molina, Victor, 126
money. *See* economic inequality; magic;
wealth
Montané, Luis, 134, 135
moral ambiguity, 9, 99, 154-55, 158, 161,
244, 248
moral artifacts, 15, 124-25
moral control, sorcery accusations as instrument of, 3, 8, 241-43, 248
moral discourses, 17, 88, 131, 166, 169, 172,
177, 212-13
moral economies, 27, 121, 123
moral economy of witchcraft, 150, 171-72
moral evolution, 130
moral order, 219, 227
moral reconfiguration, 226
moral relativism. *See* relativism
morality, Christian, 9, 56, 224-25
Mott, Luiz, 13, 46-47, 56
Muller, Leonard Eugene, 89
Museo de Antropologia, 135
*Museo de la Cátedra de Medicina Legal de la
Universidad*, 141, 142
mutilation of bodies, 75, 76, 86, 87, 89, 132, 217

Nagô, 45, 55, 60, 97
Nagô (nation), 59, 67, 71
nation: and the Congo Movement, 15, 76, 78,
84, 88-91; Cuban, 127, 135, 139, 142; socialist, 137, 140
national culture, 13, 129, 136, 252
National Deliberative Council of Umbanda-
CONDU (*Conselho Nacional Deliberativo
de Umbanda*), 153
national elites, 12
National Front for the Liberation of Angola
(FNLA), 204
national identity, 15, 149
national independence, 127-28
national pride, 251-52
nationalism, 15, 76, 88, 91, 92n6; Western, 78
Nationalist Party of South Africa, 81, 83
nation-state, 78, 88, 91
Ndjio, Basile, 16, 17, 146, 256nn17-18
neoliberalism, 123-25, 141, 167, 168, 184, 191
nganga (witch doctor/traditional healer),
135, 139, 142, 235, 237, 238, 243, 247, 248,
256n17
"niña Cecilia" case, 131
"niña Luisa" case, 127
"niña Zoila" case, 127-29
"niño Cornelio" case, 131
njangi, 240, 255n13. See also *famla-njangi*
Noberto (Xangô priest), 105-6
nocturnal flight, 8, 42, 43
nongovernmental organizations (NGOs). *See
under* child witch accusations
nouveaux-riches (new rich), 178, 181, 186n12,
186n16, 243, 255n15, 256n17
Nso, 243, 256n16
nzambi (God), 29

Obeah, 6, 56, 144n9
objectification, 8-9, 26, 27, 130
occult, 18n10, 77, 91n5, 123, 124, 143n5, 145,
180-81, 236, 244, 248
occult discourse, 172, 183, 235, 242
occult economies, 16, 123, 125, 165, 183, 191
occult epistemology, 168
occult forces, 12, 77, 106, 186n16, 189, 191,
233, 242, 248, 254n9
occult power, 175, 190-91, 201, 203, 241-42,
251-53, 256n16
occult practices, 121

occult violence/aggression, 168–69, 172, 174, 177, 179, 182–84, 257n30, 258n32
occult weapons, 142, 175–76
occultation, 21–22, 123–25
occultism, 165, 166, 168, 169, 179, 184, 186n16
ogã, 148, 162n5
Ogun, 59, 73n7
Oliveira, Isabel Maria de, 43
Oliveira, Manoel Inácio de, 66–67
Oosterbaan, Martijn, 213
opposants (political opponents), 175, 181
Orisala (Oxalá), 63, 163n13
orisha/orixá, 47, 59, 142, 144n13, 148, 149, 158, 160, 163n13, 215, 229n9; Congress (in Cuba), 139–42
Ortiz, Fernando, 129–33
otherness, 126, 129, 135, 187. *See also* alterity/othering
Ouidah, 23, 29, 31
outsider: as powerful sorcerer, 25. *See also* otherness

pais de terreiro, 39n12, 118n56
pais-de-santo (father of the saint), 70, 107, 118n54, 118n61, 119n72, 145, 156, 159, 161n1
Palmié, Stephan, 2, 15, 251, 254n9
Pan-African Congress (PAC), 78, 90
Pedroso, Luis Alberto, 142
Pels, Peter, 9, 10, 21, 35–36, 257n32
Pentecostal Africans, 2, 252
Pentecostal churches, 213, 220; antisorcery discourse, 36; Bakongo, 195; Brazilian, 1, 208n9; children accused of witchcraft and, 16, 190, 193–95, 197, 199–202; Congo and, 204–5; dualism and, 214; emergence and expansion of, 13, 192, 203–5, 207n5, 220, 252; leaders, 194; power, 211; state and, 17, 225, 226
Pentecostal discourses, 213, 214
Pentecostal exorcism and curing rituals, 1, 2, 16, 197, 199, 208n6
Pentecostal transcendence of evil, 209, 229n13, 229n17
Pentecostalism, 13, 136, 210, 225–27, 234, 252; Afro-Brazilian religions and, 17, 215, 217, 222, 229n13; Brazilian, 1, 36; Candomblé and, 214–18, 252–53; family system and, 193–94; missionary action, 230n24; neo-

Pentecostalism, 160–61; witchcraft and, 194, 195, 209, 226
Pereira, Nuno Marques, 47
Pernambucano, Ulysses, 95, 97, 102–4, 109, 110, 119n70
Philippines, 132
Piauí, 50–53
Pichardo, Ernesto, 141, 144n15
Pietz, William, 20–21, 26
Pinta, Luzia, 46–48
Pinto, Cipriano José, 60
Pinto, Oscar Moreira, 104
police, 85, 89, 149–52, 182, 197, 199, 216, 217, 223–25, 242; Candomblé and, 56–69, 99, 229n9; slaves and, 56–69; spiritualism and, 97, 102–3, 107, 109, 110; of witchcraft/the occult, 169, 234–35. *See also* Rio de Janeiro, laughter of the Pomba-Gira
police persecution, 12–13, 34, 119n67, 159, 162n5, 214, 231n25
police raids, 63, 65, 105–6, 126, 129, 134
political opponents (*opposants*), 175, 181
politics: of collective violence, 182; parallelism between witchcraft and, 159; witchcraft as taking the place of, 159–60
Pondo Revolt. *See* Pondoland
Pondoland, South Africa, 90–91; emergency years, 89–90; hardships of 20th century, 80–83; outbreak of insurgency and "smelling out" evil, 84–89; sorcery and witchcraft in, 79–80
Ponte, Count of, 60–61
Poole, Deborah, 227n3
Portuguese colonial society, 25. *See also* Brazil; *feitiçaria*; *feitiço*; fetishism; lusophone
Portuguese Inquisition. *See* Inquisition
possession cults, 43, 49, 55, 64, 107, 156. *See also* spirit possession
postcolonial Africa, 3, 10, 16, 169, 172
postcolonial countries and societies, 5, 12, 248. *See also specific countries*
postcolonial elites, 5, 9, 37, 177, 184, 185n6
postcolonial modernity, 125
postcolonial power, 169–70, 172, 175
postcolonial state, 168, 169, 171, 175–77, 184, 185n10, 203
postcoloniality/postcolonialism, 6, 10, 170, 183, 185n6, 203, 239
pouches, 24–26, 29, 42. See also *mandinga*